THE

White Witch of Ardwick

THE
White Witch of Ardwick

Liz Roberts

Disclaimer

Although the author has made every effort to ensure that the information in this book was correct at press time, the author does not assume and hereby disclaim any liability to any party for any loss, damage, or disruption caused by errors or omissions, whether such errors or omissions result from negligence, accident, or any other cause.

© Elizabeth Mary Roberts, 2017

Published by Liz Roberts

All rights reserved. No part of this book may be reproduced, adapted, stored in a retrieval system or transmitted by any means, electronic, mechanical, photocopying, or otherwise without the prior written permission of the author.

The rights of Liz Roberts to be identified as the author of this work have been asserted in accordance with the Copyright, Designs and Patents Act 1988.

A CIP catalogue record for this book is available from the British Library.

ISBN 978-0-9955674-0-5

Book layout and cover design by Clare Brayshaw

Cover image of Manchester Central Library © Atosan | Dreamstime.com

Prepared and printed by:

York Publishing Services Ltd
64 Hallfield Road
Layerthorpe
York YO31 7ZQ

Tel: 01904 431213

Website: www.yps-publishing.co.uk

Dedicated to my grandchildren;
Joely Roberts & Anna Jackson

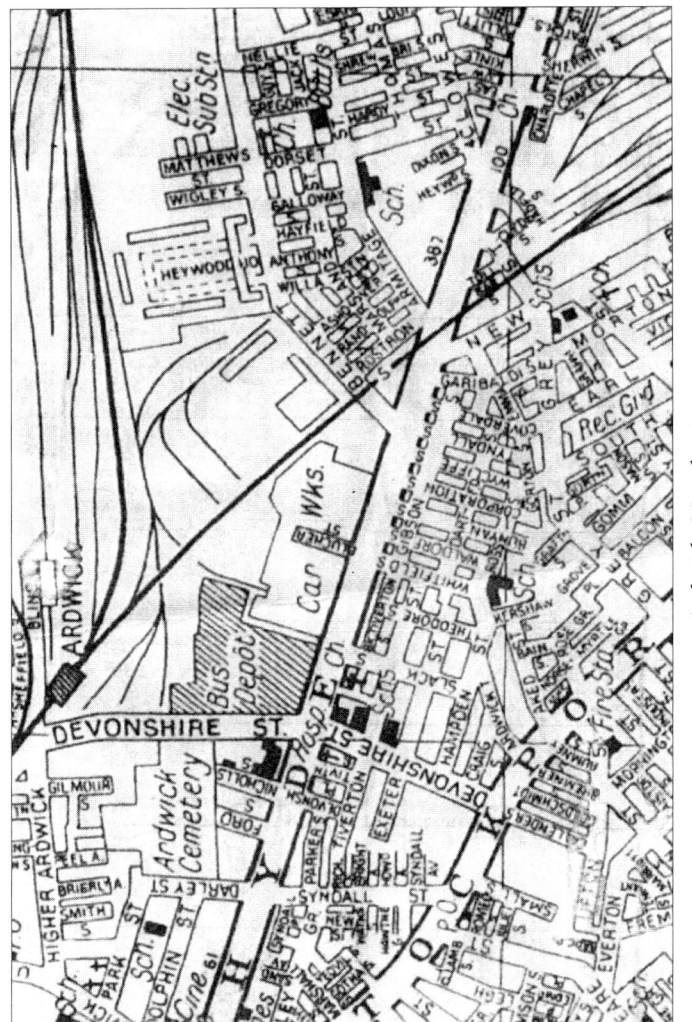

Ardwick, Manchester

Chapter 1

As I felt myself slowly moving down the birth canal, past memories floated over my head like fluffy clouds sailing across an evening sky. It seemed as if each small cloud was translucent and as I peered closely, my third eye could see a picture – as if it were the cover of a book. The book's spine was tightly bound but it was beckoning me to turn back the pages and explore the tales it had to offer. I reached out to grasp a picture but as I did, it simply disintegrated. Again, I placed my tiny dimpled hand on another passing cloud and this time it was strange. It broke up and a million little pieces floated away.

I stretched out a somewhat miniscule arm, again and again. Failing repeatedly, the pictures got higher and drifted away as if to tease. Gradually, they faded into the stars. Suddenly, a still, small voice whispered "don't clutch". I frowned in confusion. It continued, urging me not to grab but to simply ask to read the memories. "The stories, for they are yours – do with them what you will but if you are wise, you will read, analyse and digest each and every page". I, now, knew that I had to use the knowledge and wisdom displayed in front of me to write yet another book. For this is what I had chosen to do. I had to take the tests and tasks that

I set myself and pass them. For all things are a circle, there is no beginning and no end. Round and round through each lifetime, you begin to understand your soul has fulfilled its purpose. Being good or bad as it is my choice ….so I went forth and began.

I sent out a single thought, a request to read a single book. As I watched lone clouds fall ever so elegantly from the heavens. As it hovered over me, it almost told me "It's here, it's yours – take it".

I took the small, nameless book with no title. Its cover simply displayed an embossed wreath – puzzling as it held no meaning to me. As I flicked through the worn pages, I realised that they were torn and few in number. No words could be seen. Then, the same soft voice whispered "Read it backwards and you should learn"

The last page was adorned with a single illustration. Displaying a young girl wearing a gown of very pale blue with long, flowing sleeves edged with a silver thread. A gold chain and charm hung from her swan- like neck. In the distance was a harp and flute playing their mournful music? Large crystal chandeliers flickered in a bizarre fashion as its candles dimmed and burned away. Many people stood silently looking down as the ladies in their long silk ball gowns were weeping whilst the men appeared horrified and pale. They were looking at the raven haired girl lying on the seemingly cold floor. A small window, creating an opening in the stone wall, rattled and creaked as the wind gathered and blew out the remaining candles.

An eerie silence pervaded the scene. The men, dressed in their tunics and breeches, gasped as some ladies swooned. As the girl's blue dress turned crimson-red, I could see her life being drained from her. A silver-headed dagger carved with some form of Irish family crest protruded from just below her rib cage. Her blue, vacant eyes were fixed looking at a large wooden door. Her pink lips parted as if to utter the name of her assassin, yet no words came forth and she breathed her last.

The surreal moment suddenly came back to me – when I hovered over my lifeless body and watched the black hair become mottled and damp with the dark red blood.

I dropped the book. I saw his blond hair dripping with sweat. His sweaty brow mixed with tears covered his ashen face. For he had a jealous heart; and the horror of his wicked deed had finally come home to him.

The second book in my view was bound in a type of parchment – a single red ribbon running through the centre of its pages. I looked at the last page. It was blank. I turned to the centre where the ribbon acted as a marker. There was no date or time, just a picture of a stocky dark haired man. I felt that he was in his middle thirties yet he looked much older. His face was weathered and pockmarked, almost like leather. The man had been a common sailor – no fancy seafaring uniform, just an old baggy set of worn-out clothes. Underneath his beard he had a tattoo shaped like an anchor. His dark and beady eyes matched his hard and unflinching face. Instantly, alarm and fear tore into my soul as I realised, just like the girl, he too was another representation of myself.

At approximately 6 am on the 20th April, 1943, I reluctantly came onto this mortal plane.

As a general and psychiatric trained nurse spanning a 30 year career, I have witnessed death and suffering on a daily basis but despite this, there were plenty of good and fun times. Having convinced myself that I am of sound mind, I will endeavour to do my best to document these events in chronological order. In doing this hopefully a pattern will emerge shedding some light and understanding on a subject which defies any logical explanation. As a professor once said to me, "Liz, you can only take logic so far, then leave it and trust your own faculties.

I am now in the winter season of my life. The days are cold and the nights draw in. I will now settle myself on my old rocking chair beside the coal fire and put pen to paper in an attempt to document these events which have puzzled and astonished me for decades? I am hardly equipped or experienced enough to write a book. All I have is an old typewriter, which frequently misspells, surely serving to lengthen rather than hasten the completion of these true stories. Nevertheless, I will not let this hinder me for "time and tide wait for no man".

Chapter 2

I was born in the 40's as an only child of elderly working class parents. My father was of Irish descent and worked as a postman in the days when letters were delivered on foot and carried in large Hessian mail bags made by prison inmates. These bags were so tough and strong that after my father's postal life was over, he used them to make peg rugs which adorned our rented terraced house and were a great source of delight to our pet dog, Bimbo. Many hours were spent pulling out the coloured pieces of cloth until all that was left was the Hessian.

Lily, my mother, was Welsh. She appeared to me to be permanently out of place living in this Lancashire mill town where factory chimneys constantly puffed out great clouds of thick, black smoke. The mill workers, in their shawls and clogs, could be seen in the early mornings scurrying towards the dark and foreboding mills. Their footsteps, like the horses pulling their laden carts on the empty cobbled roads, still echo in my mind, clip, clop, clip, clop.

"Early to bed, early to rise, makes a man healthy, wealthy and wise"

With this little ditty ringing in my ears, I was sent off to bed. Little did my parents know that I had already hidden scraps of bread, cheese and sometimes a piece of an egg or bacon rind. After I had reassured myself that all was quiet downstairs, out of the bed I would get and place the scraps on the bedroom floor. Shortly after I whispered "Minnie, Minnie", little scratching sounds would emanate from behind a large wardrobe, followed by tiny squeaks. Out she would come scuttling along the cracked oilcloth towards my bed: the fattest Mouse you have ever seen! Minnie was not faddy: she would eat the Bacon first (if there was any) and then the rest of the food. Neither did she appear to be afraid of the lady in the long skirt and frilly high necked blouse, with her dark hair scraped back revealing a thin, pale face. I never did tell my parents about the lady who would stand at the bottom of my bed occasionally smile and then simply disappear. For even at the tender age of four, I knew a thing or two about mouse traps.

Downstairs in the parlour (our visitors room) were a number of family photographs. The one on the chimney breast fascinated me even as a four year child. It was of a lady dressed in fashionable Victorian clothes with a large cameo brooch pinned to her breast. She was, I was told my maternal grandmother who had died some twenty years previously in the house next door, now occupied by my Aunt Cissy and Uncle Fred. Her name was Sarah Fleetwood.

One year later

"One, two, buckle my shoe. Three, four, knock on the door. Five, six, pick-up sticks. Seven, eight, don't be late." This is how we would learn to count.

Always a difficult and disorganised child, I detested the discipline and routine that school life brought. However, there are benefits to be had in all situations, mainly more freedom to roam around out of school hours. One day, with my two friends Doris and Roy, I set off down the flagged streets gaily skipping past the street vendors selling their meat pies and roasted chestnuts at three pence a bag. We stopped at the dairy to stroke Molly, the milkman's horse that always had her beautiful, golden mane plaited with great care and adorned with brightly coloured ribbons. As we reached the main road, the 213 trolley bus passed by followed by wagons, horses and carts weaving their way towards Manchester City Centre. We raced across the road towards Ardwick Green Park and climbed over the rubble towards the sycamore and chestnut trees which had been spared during the bombings of World War II. Their branches stretched forlornly towards the heavens. We gathered the conkers, tying them to pieces of string and began to play. Shortly, as five year olds do, we began to squabble. I gathered my conkers up putting them into my pockets and singing "One, two, buckle my shoe, three, four, knock at the door".

I headed for home jumping over the mangled, iron railings which surrounded the park and onto the pavement where rainwater had gushed over the kerb and onto the road. With shoes and socks wet and muddy, I skipped onto the road. About half way across I heard a female voice call out "Beth, Beth". As I looked around I was unable to see anyone other than a large wagon which was hurtling towards me! I ran as fast as my little legs would carry me, landing in a heap at the side of the kerb surrounded by conkers. Two ladies, who were strangers to me, rushed forward dropping their shopping bags to pick me up and dust me down. By this time a small crowd had gathered and one man was remonstrating with the wagon driver who had climbed down from his cab and stood mopping his brow with a large, white handkerchief repeatedly saying "I am sorry, I did not see her, she's only little" (I was about three stone wet through)

To this day I do not know who called my name and possibly saved my life but I often ask myself if it was the dark haired lady who used to stand at the bottom of the bed and whose photograph was on the parlour wall, Sarah Fleetwood, my grandmother?

Two years later

The back to back terraced houses with their little entries and ginnels led like a rabbit warren onto what we called "the concrete". This area housed a dozen or so more dwellings along with a disused air raid shelter. Most "Ardwick" people preferred to take shelter from the falling bombs under their huge wooden kitchen tables until the all clear sirens were sounded.

These houses were surrounded on three sides by a high brick wall which we would frequently climb, taking bets on who would be brave enough to drop down onto the other side and into the cemetery. Now broken and covered in lichen and moss, the graves and vaults served as a great home to many forms of wildlife. Squirrels jumped from tree to tree and voles and mice made their homes in cracked and broken urns that had once stood proudly on the gravestones. The gravestones dated back as far as the 1600's and some names and dates could still be deciphered. Once I had learnt to read, I would spend many a happy hour trying to imagine what these people had been like and how they had lived their lives. I still remember a little rhyme on a young girl's grave which went like this:

"Do not chew gum; do not chew wax, for it has brought me to my grave at last"

One particular sunny August afternoon, my mother had taken to her "sick bed". I suspected food poisoning as cooking was never her forte. This meant that Uncle Fred from next door was in charge of me which was great. He would just sit at the kitchen window overlooking the back yard smoking his Woodbines and studying the horse racing in the Daily Dispatch. I was frequently sent to the back gate of the illegal bookies to place bets of a shilling or half-crown for both my father and him in return for three pence which I would duly spend on liquorice and bulls eyes (big, round sweets which changed colour once sucked). He often picked the winner whilst I was swatting flies with a rolled-up newspaper which, incidentally, was not the Daily Dispatch (I knew better than that!) but an old Evening Chronicle which hung from a piece of string on the back of the toilet door located at the end of the backyard. These flies were then gently placed on Fred and Ginger's webs, two large spiders who appreciated what a delightful child I was.

Chapter 3

Suddenly, out of nowhere, I heard a male voice call out "Are you there, Mrs Powell?". This was repeated a number of times and then, silence. Uncle Fred, with a cigarette behind his ear, came out into the yard closely followed by my mother (Mrs Powell) who looked like she had seen a ghost. (Best described as a pale shade of green) By the time they arrived, I had already opened the yard gate and was looking up the ginnel. I saw a man about fifty yards away walking towards me. The man wore a dark grey coat and reddish cravat. I ran towards him and as I got closer, he turned round the corner and out of sight into the "concrete". Ignoring my mother's calls, I ran onto the "concrete' but there was nobody there so I assumed that he had quickly gone into one of the houses. By this time, Uncle Fred had arrived and grabbing my hand, took me home. After what I can only describe as an inquisition from my mother, questioning who I had seen, how tall he was and whether he was thin or fat. It became very clear to me that neither my mother nor uncle had seen the man. Uncle Fred never forgot about the incident until the day he died and always maintained that it was something he could never explain. On the other hand, many years after my mother died, I was to find a "skeleton in her cupboard" as related to me by my cousin Kathleen.

Before she married my father in the 1930's, at the age of thirty two, my mother had worked for Lever Brothers (a large glass bottle manufacturer) as a private secretary. Being very attractive and a competent shorthand typist, she had gained many promotions and was eventually put in charge of the accounts department. As her story goes, she and an accountant stole a large amount of money over a period of several months. Although, she was never formally charged, she lost her job and was unable to find further employment. (I wonder why!). The accountant, on the other hand, was formally charged with fraud and bailed by the courts. Whilst awaiting trial, he committed suicide by throwing himself under a train at one of London's underground tube stations. This, I believe, was the man that I saw, for in hindsight, my mother had been incredibly afraid and constantly badgered me about his description and manner i.e. "did he appear angry??". I did not know but I do know this and if I am correct, how after twenty years of being "dead", did he know her married name. Her maiden name was Fleetwood. I believe that after her demise, she would have to face him and the consequences of her actions. What a book that would be!

July, the following year

Almost every summer, my Aunt Bunny (my mother's sister) would give us two large, white five pound notes which were sewn into the lining of my mother's coat for safe keeping. We would then set out to catch the train from Victoria Station, our destination being Blackpool. This, of course, was a great thrill for me. The excitement, the pleasure, the laughing clown and not forgetting the Big Dipper and ghost train filled me with delight. Having received lots of pennies and halfpennies from my father, I was eager to fill the slot machines and get three matching symbols in order to win the sixpence or shilling prize.

It was usually mid-afternoon when we arrived at the boarding house. We would unpack our shabby, brown suitcases and head off to the beach. Aunt Bunny would buy a bucket and spade which I usually took ages to choose and a bunch of paper-flags to put on top of my sandcastles.

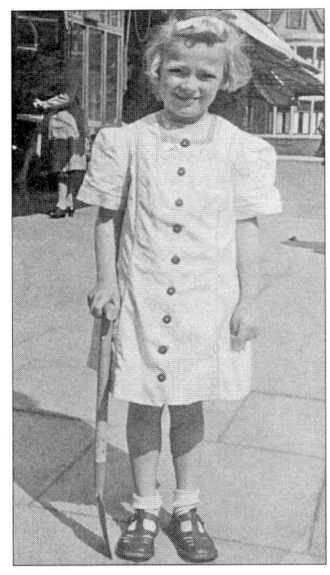

Me with my sand shovel

Aunt Bunny was a large woman with thin, steel coloured hair and had great difficulty getting in and out of the deck chairs without my mother's aid. I found this extremely amusing for my mother was a tiny, little woman with hair that resembled a horse's mane in texture. Having had a three

Aunt Bunnie

penny ride on the donkeys, I would find my spot and build castles whilst listening to the cries of the gulls and the sound of the waves as they washed up on the shore leaving cockle shells and seaweed to decorate my castle. It was as if the waves were beckoning me to remember my past life as a man who had sailed them centuries ago.

We arrived, having spent a pleasant journey watching the world go by, seeing sheep and cattle in green fields and pastures which delighted me. The only ones I had ever seen in Ardwick were hung up in a butchers shop. The boarding house was near the North Pier and I gaily ran up the "donkey brown steps", rang the bell and waited. We were greeted by a pleasant, smiling lady who ushered us into the lobby. Suddenly, a great sense of fear and danger seized me. It was as if the whole house was dark and evil. I screamed and ran outside, almost falling down the steps and into the street. I was followed by three, bewildered adults who spent the next few hours trying to persuade me to go back into the house. I was bribed with ice-cream and candy floss but all to no avail. Nothing would induce me to go back into that house. I can still remember my father's face when we arrived back home having caught the last train back. A few weeks later, the front page of the Evening Chronicle had a major headline "Girl's skeleton found buried in cellar. Couple accused of murder". It just happened to be the exact same boarding house which I had refused to stay in Blackpool.

In late November of the same year, my father gave me two shillings and six pence to buy my mother a birthday present. I set off on my bicycle to the Methodist church fete. There were a number of stalls selling homemade jam, mince pies and Christmas cakes. I bought four chocolate mice from the sweet stall, ate the lot and feeling slightly sick, turned to the task in hand. I trotted past the Christmas stall with its' brightly, coloured crepe paper and string, only to turn around as if some presence was drawing me back. It was then that I saw some charming, framed calendars costing one shilling and six pence each. I could get four more mice and a calendar. I chose one with a floral design as its centrepiece. Suddenly, something happened, I know not what, but a still, small voice in my head said "put it down and buy that one". I put it back and intuitively, picked up a small, glass framed calendar adorned with a tiny, thatched cottage and a proverb printed in italics at the bottom of the picture.

On December, 11th, my father and I gave my mother her presents. She picked up the small, brown parcel and untied the strings. She took one look and suddenly, burst into tears as we stared agog waiting for an explanation for her behaviour. She stared at me tearfully saying that "this proverb had answered my prayers". No more was ever said but that calendar remained on her bedroom mantelpiece until the day she died.

A few days later, Aunty Cissie, my mother's oldest sibling from next door, set off with us to the Hulme Theatre, taking me to see Jack and the Beanstalk. Aunt Cissie had never married. Her fiancé, Arthur Metcalfe, had been killed in World War I, however, that wasn't to say that she did not have a number of gentlemen friends. She was small and dainty like my mother, with lovely brown eyes and a small mole that accentuated her cheek bones. As we alighted from the trolley bus, we could see the theatre in the distance which stood tall and proud amongst the rubble of bombed sites that had once been streets of terraced houses; their inhabitants, long since re-housed or dead, as we crossed the road towards the theatre.

I could see lots of daffodils amongst the wet grass and broken bricks, their bright, yellow heads swaying in the wind. I let go of Aunt Cissie's hand, pointed towards the daffodils and asked if I could pick some of them. "Daffodils, what! In December" was their startled response as I pointed to an old mill which had lost its' roof and gable end. I was promptly dragged back by my mother who shouted at me for neither of them could see the flowers, it was dusk when we left the theatre and I forlornly looked towards the mill to see the flowers, however, they had sadly disappeared.

By this time, I was beginning to understand that I, for some reason, could see and hear things which other people could not. I would spend many a happy hour looking at the faces of people and animals either in the coals of the fire or in the mirror above the mantelpiece. I would stand on a chair and my mother would always make me get down so I would wait until she went down to the cellar to do the washing or other task. She performed the washing using a dolly tub and mangle and afterwards, hanging the clothes on a line in the backyard to dry.

After the daffodil incident, Aunt Bunnie, a paediatric nursing sister at Booth Hall Hospital, was duly consulted about my "mental state". I did not take kindly to this. As far as I was concerned I was far more rational than her. After all, I did not whinge or moan about everything such as taking saccharine in my tea because I was diabetic and then, promptly eat a huge slice of my mother's homemade cake whilst darning a sock with a bodkin on a wooden mushroom, followed that down with tinned pears and condensed milk.

Her diagnosis was I reckon that I was a highly strung child as that was what my mother would say to relatives and friends to explain my bizarre behaviour.

Chapter 4

In 1951, I was eight years old and attended Ardwick Municipal School. My favourite teacher was a Mr Teasdale who taught maths and drama. He was definitely a no-nonsense teacher and the boys would get a clip round the ear for misbehaving whilst all he had to do with the girls was to raise his voice. The effect was the same- total silence-. I never remember him shouting at me even though my maths was abysmal. I like to think that it was because I loved his drama classes and would sit thrilled and enraptured when he sat and sang "Bye, Bye Blackbird". I still recall the first few lines "make my bed and light the light, I will arrive late tonight".

Now Mr Teasdale, it was said, was a variety performer prior to World War II. He had a song and dance routine which he performed all over the country. I can still vaguely recall his very short, wavy, black hair and swarthy skin. He would frequently take off his jacket and neatly, place it on a chair before playing the piano. Sadly, I have no school photographs of him but I still remember that unlike my father and Uncle Fred, he did not wear braces to hold up his trousers, but a belt. He always wore a very white shirt without a tie. The open-necked shirt revealed a very hairy

His brow was frequently covered in beads of sweat he would mop with his handkerchief.

The school register ran in alphabetical order so Powell was way down the list. When on the first lesson, Mr Teasdale arrived at my name and said "Beth Powell, that is not what you were christened. I shall call you "Elizabeth". Now everybody called me Beth because I was nicknamed after Beth in the book "Little Women". I tried to explain to him but he wasn't having it. . It took a while to get used to it but for some reason or other, I was very proud of my new name and when I told my mother, she just frowned.

The following year in which the education system changed, boys and girls were separated. Under 11's went to Ross Place School and because of the distance, mothers had to take and collect their children.

On one particular day after school, my mother and I had reached the traffic lights at the junction of Hyde Road and Devonshire Street. There was a bus depot at one side of the road and standing next to it was a memorial with the names of all the soldiers who had been killed in the last two wars. Facing this were the gates of my old school. As we stood waiting for the lights to change to green, we heard a male voice call out "Elizabeth, Elizabeth". I said "that is Mr Teasdale" as we both turned round towards the school gates and the voice but there was nobody there. No more was thought about this incident until a few days later. There was an entry in the Obituary section of the Evening Chronicle which read "Mr Teasdale, teacher, died in hospital following an accident". My mother questioned me on numerous occasions about the voice calling my name, was I sure that it was Mr Teasdale. Yes! I responded as I recognised his voice and besides, nobody else ever called me Elizabeth. I neatly cut out the article documenting his death and kept it. Sadly, it is now lost and I cannot remember how old he was or any other details.

Of course then the rumours started which said that he had killed himself because he was facing a prison sentence for homosexuality. Being inquisitive I asked what this meant but never got a satisfactory answer from my mother. As I got older, I fully understood what it meant. I believe the law regarding homosexuality was repealed in 1967.

Shortly after that incident, I would wake up in a cold sweat having dreamt on a number of occasions that I was being tied to a post and burnt, apparently for crimes of witchcraft. There was a large crowd dressed in long, coarse clothing. A young man was being restrained by a group of people who I knew was trying to rescue me. But of course, he could not manage to do so. In the vivid dream, men with thick, flaming sticks dipped in tar, lit the straw and wood underneath me and then, the flames engulfed me. I screamed and screamed but then I must have fainted and felt no more. Weeks later, I would wake in a cold sweat feeling at my neck and face. The repetitive dream was extremely vivid as I could see and feel the orange, red flames engulf my body.

In the crowd, the women had their heads covered with peculiar looking caps. I was, barely, a seventeen year old girl together with two other people, one of whom was called an old hag and witch. She had taught me the rudiments of herbal healing and witchcraft. In the dream, the crowd was cheering and I was screaming. My last, living memory was of a young, fair haired man, being held back by the crowds as he attempted to rescue me. Suddenly, the pain was gone as if

I was floating above my charred remains; Looking towards the young man who was kneeling on the ground with tears streaming uncontrollably down his cheeks. I stepped forward to comfort and reassure him that I was fine and that I understood why he could not save me. However, I got no response as he continued to lie on the ground all alone as the crowd began to disperse.

As I got older, I began to understand that the dream was again one of my past lives. I am convinced that I was in Scotland as the memory is so vivid with the red hair and the accents. I was later to discover that witches were hanged in England and burnt in Scotland. I researched in the library and looked at many pictures depicting modes of dress etc. I would roughly date this incident to be between 1448 to 1600 in Scotland where Pope Innocent V111 had issued his papal bull "SummisDesiderantes" (5th December, 1484) and hundreds of folk were burnt at the stake for crimes of witchcraft. This Act was repealed in 1763.

To this day, I have a tremendous fear of fire and have instructed my two daughters that they must not cremate me when I die. I have written that I wish to be buried in a local environmentally friendly cemetery in a coffin made of cardboard, no headstone, just a small tree or bush to be planted in my mound of earth. One never knows, perhaps I will come back and visit myself.

Chapter 5

In 1954, my mother and I set sail to the Isle of Man to visit my Uncle Arthur whose wife, Cissie, had recently died of a stroke. He was the oldest of my mother's surviving brothers; A tall, thin man, most unlike the rest of the family who were petite with soft features and full mouths. He had a hookish nose, thin lips that constantly puffed on a pipe. His glass eye, acquired during World War I, fascinated me for it roamed about his eye socket often swivelled up revealing just a piece of white pot. Unfortunately, I would stare at it and wondered where the iris had disappeared to. My reasoning was that it had gone into his brain and was the likely cause of his grumpy disposition. He was a rich accountant who had left England some years previously due supposedly, to a tax evasion scandal. (Criminal genes must run in the family).

I was awe struck by his home which was a large, detached house called "Bracken", set in its own grounds on Ramsey Road, Laxey. On the other side of the narrow road was a brook which ran through a wooded area. Its water, which I would cup in my hands and drink, bubbled over small rocks and tiny pebbles. I can recall sitting on a large boulder, eating a banana whilst listening to the sound of a cuckoo. Suddenly, I caught something in the corner of my eye, just above my head. The only description I can give is of four, little, hairless, naked green people hovering around a very big tree. I blinked and blinked again, I just could not believe my eyes as everything else appeared normal. The sunlight weaved its way through the tree branches and the leaves waved slightly in the breeze. Even the cuckoo continues to sing whilst the little people bobbed up and down and then, suddenly, they were gone. I dropped my half-eaten banana and then, I slipped whilst crossing the brook in my haste to tell my mother what I had seen. Arriving back at Bracken in squelching pumps, I told her what I had seen – four little green pixies -. In hindsight, this was a gross mistake, as it did little in my mother's eyes to reinforce her daughter's sanity.

The following week, we went to see Uncle Arthur's wife's grave which was a mound of damp earth laden with dead flowers and a withered wreath; – 'To my Beloved Wife' As I stood there, I remarked to my mother that the lady in the ground was the one that told her that she would not rear me as I was too delicate. My mother just stared open-mouthed at me and responded "how do you know that, you were only 18 months at the time?". She made you cry: I replied, adding that it was her that was dead now and not me. My attention was diverted by a cat with no tail. I had never seen a Manx cat before so I set off to have a better look at it.

We sailed for home, two weeks later. The sea was extremely rough with waves sweeping over the ships' decks whilst the helpful sailors with their buckets were swilling the passengers vomit over the side. The rain lashed down and I spent my time sheltering under some tarpaulin watching this scene whilst my mother had disappeared along with many other passengers into the toilets.

In the following year, my mother developed a brain tumour and was hospitalised for many months in Manchester Royal Infirmary. So it left just my dad, Bimbo and me at home. Bimbo had overcome his passion for trashing the rag rugs preferring, instead, to just sleep on them. I became very independent as I did not see much of my father who was either visiting my mother or doing his early morning postal round and then working late into the evening to sort the mail. When not at school, I spent my time roller skating, swimming and taking Bimbo for long walks.

During this period, an educational school visit was arranged to go to the Round House Museum in Ancoats. We set off, clambered onto the school bus with Miss Wells, our teacher in charge. There were about twenty of us, all girls on our best behaviour, as we filed through the thick, oak doors, two by two just like Noah's Ark. The main room was dark and dingy and had a damp and musty smell. Miss Wells blew her whistle and we all gathered round to see more wooden artefacts which were quite boring but unlike the now cream dress, once white, in the display case which grabbed my attention. It was so tiny that it was difficult to imagine how anyone could have worn it as we filed along a narrow corridor with dirty, high windows almost touching the ceiling. I had just reached the end of the corridor, when I was hit with an overwhelming sense of fear. It was like a prison and I knew that I had to get out of there quickly. I managed to do this by asking Miss Wells if I could go to the toilet. 'Don't be long, dear" she said, and as soon as I was out of sight, I ran to make my escape into the street. I sat on the surrounding wall and almost immediately, felt fine. Puzzled as to what was wrong with me, I started to think and it came to me that it was the same feeling that I had about the boarding house in Blackpool where the girl had been murdered. As I write this now more than fifty years later, the hairs still stand up on the back of my head.

After a couple of restless night's sleep, I decided to investigate that building for I was convinced that there was a body somewhere. I took myself off to the local library and found out that it had been used during the reign of Charles 1 in the battle between the Roundheads and the Cavaliers. That really did not answer my question about the body and eventually, I forgot about it.

About fifteen years ago, I was listening to the radio and pricked up my ears when the Roundhouse was mentioned. Evidently, it had just been demolished due to the fact that it was too expensive to maintain and added to what I already knew about the history of the Roundheads and Cavaliers. Apparently, a number of secret passages had been discovered, presumably used as escape routes for priests. In one of these tunnels, a number of human remains were found who had obviously met with untimely deaths.

Chapter 6

In 1959, I was sixteen years old and my mother who had survived the brain tumour was far from well. Things tended to get a bit out of control at home which was probably not helped by my wilful and rebellious disposition. There had been no further unexplained incidents and it was said by the family that "I must have grown out of it'. I had failed my 11+ exams, but surprise, surprise: had passed my 13+ having spent the last twelve months of my schooling attending Loburn College. I studied shorthand and typing which I detested as I found it boring and repetitive. I guess that I was supposed to follow in my mother's steps. In retrospect. I do not think that I was very much like any of them except for my small build which is a Fleetwood gene as my father was nearly six foot and well built.

My closest friend was Dorothy Smith (honestly) and she was about twelve months older than me with two younger sisters and two brothers. She, like me, worked in Manchester also. I worked for the M/C Envelope Company and she was a junior tailoress. This was brilliant as I earned £3 per week whilst Dot earned £2.75. We both gave our mothers half our salary, leaving us very little to spend on ourselves. We would buy materials from the market and make our own clothes.

Of course, Dot was in charge of this and we actually made some very attractive clothes, saving money in the process. We managed to go to Butlins Holiday Camp, Pwilheli in Wales with the proceeds. We arrived one Saturday in July and as typical, teenage girls, we were more interested in boys than anything else. We paraded in our swimsuits by the pool during the day and in the evenings, we got 'dolled up'. We met amongst others, two boys named Bill and Lawrence who came from Blackburn. Bill, the joiner, latched on to me whilst Dot went out with Loll as we called him.

I think it was a Wednesday night, when the boys escorted us to our chalets and left about 1am. Anybody who had visited Butlins during that era would know that the chalets are very basic. They consist of two beds on either side of the room which was about 12ft long and 8ft wide with a wardrobe, curtain and sink. The room was illuminated by the lamps outside. Laughing and giggling, we got undressed and got into our separate beds. We must have continued our conversation for about twenty minutes when, suddenly, I saw Dot standing at the bottom of her bed dressed in a night gown. "What are you doing there?"I said.; "What happened to your pyjamas?"I uttered. "Are you daft? I am in bed"she replied. I then took a closer look and could make out the outline of Dot in her bed. I, then, knew that I had not grown out of it after all. The girl with the dark, long hair like Dot remained standing at the end of her bed. 'It's not you 'I said: Dot looked and screamed as she dived under the covers. Being a brave soul, or so I thought, I started to get out of bed, however, my courage failed as I froze when she disappeared through the wall.

The following day after a somewhat very restless night, we went very early to the administration block and told our story. We requested, at Dot's insistence, another chalet immediately. Well, it was the usual response and we got nowhere. They obviously thought that we were totally insane and categorically stated that there were no vacancies. So we told Bill and Loll our story. They humoured us by swapping chalets with them. Needless to say, nothing happened in either chalet and we continued to have a great holiday. I am sure that the boys thought that we had imagined the whole episode. We said our farewells on the Saturday with promises of keeping in touch.

A few days later during my lunch break, I went to visit the main library in Manchester City Centre. Standing outside under the large pillars that formed part of its entrance to this magnificent stone-faced building, I was suddenly seized with what only can be described as a sense of great sadness. I just wanted to cry and then it hit me. It was the very building that Mr Teasdale had thrown himself off all those years ago and now, I felt his presence around me.

An hour later, I hurriedly left the building, obviously late for work, but my instinct had been right: Butlins Holiday Camp had been built on the site where WAFFs' had been housed in World War II. It had been bombed during the Blitz and many had died and been injured. An air raid shelter had been damaged causing the concrete blocks to cave in and crush them. I, now, know why the people of Ardwick preferred to shelter under their large, stout kitchen tables.

Chapter 7

There were big changes afoot in Ardwick as all the rented, terraced houses, including our house, had been condemned. We were all to be moved to a modern, housing estate in Hattersley. We would have bathrooms with running hot water and indoor toilets. We were told that even some of the family homes would have their own gardens. Anyway, for the time being, life continued as normal. Dot and I continued with our full, social schedule with Saturday nights at the Plaza and Sundays at the Ritz. We did not hear from Loll and Bill until the latter end of August when Bill knocked on our front door. He had acquired lodgings and work with Mac Alpines, a large, building construction company.

I got engaged to Bill when I was seventeen years old and we married in September, 1961. We moved to Denton, having bought a two bedroom bungalow with all mod. cons. plus a garden front and back. Life was good and everything seemed to fall into place. There were no further paranormal incidents until one night when I awoke knowing that there was a large spider above our bed. I was afraid that it would crawl into my mouth whilst I was sleeping. So with great difficulty, I woke up Bill to remove the offending spider. He was not best pleased and announced that I was quite mad, for it was 'pitch black' according to him and how could I possibly see anything? At my insistence, he turned on the light and low and behold, there was a big spider

He then diligently removed the spider, opened the window and placed it on the sill. He asked me as to how I knew it was walking up the bedroom wall. "I heard it", I said. With that, he just looked at me and said that I was odd; nobody can hear a spider walk. I must admit that I had to agree and we spent the next thirty minutes, as we were both fully awake now, discussing my 'odd behaviour'. Bill carried on saying that on the occasions that I went to Bingo that I usually would win. I told him that it was just luck and that luck was a figment of our imagination: but still powerful nonetheless. Not satisfied with my answer, he went on to point out the time when he arranged to go out with the lads on Friday night and I had told him not to go. I had a funny feeling about it. He said that it made him afraid so he stayed home whilst Dot and I went to the pictures. Early the next morning, we were informed that his three friends had been involved in a car accident whereby John was on the critical list. Fortunately, he survived but had to spend many weeks in the hospital.

In 1963, we were expecting our first child and we were both very thrilled at this unplanned event. I was just 21 years old when Patsy, as we called her, was born in 1964. She was 7.5 lbs. with a mop of wavy, red hair.

Bill was working on a high rise building in Manchester City Centre and left for work as I was giving Patsy her 6am feed. I remember that day very clearly, it was a beautiful, sunny August morning so I did not return to bed. I was pottering about the bungalow and doing 'this and that'.

I was preparing the 10am feed in the kitchen when suddenly, I was overcome with a great sense of doom and sadness and Patsy started screaming just at the same time. It took nearly an hour to get her to take less than 5 ounces of milk. I became more and more agitated as her screaming continued. I just knew that something bad had happened. I tried to rationalise my thoughts (a big mistake) as I just became more and more worried so I decided to contact Bill's place of work as I was convinced that he had an accident. I did not think that it could be anyone else as he was the only one working in a dangerous area. I put Patsy in the pram and headed for the phone box at the corner of Ruby Street. There was a lady making a call so I waited and waited as she put more money in. I looked at my wrist watch and it was now 11.30 am, Patsy had stopped crying and I was feeling less anxious and the sun was shining.

Bill would think that I was completely mad if I contact his company to see if he is alright so I pushed the pram back home and tried to busy myself to stave off the anxious feelings. I prepared the evening meal, something very easy as I, like my mother, was not a good cook.

Around 6.30 pm, I heard the key in the door and Bill arrived home safe and sound.

I put the overdone pork chops on the table but the accompanying egg and chips looked fine. Patsy was in her cot by now and Bill goes over to say hello. I began my tale about how I felt this morning and Bill raises his brow with that familiar look on his face indicating that he is convinced that I am barking mad. I had just made a pot of tea when the doorbell rang. Bill answered it to find my mother in floods of tears on the doorstep. As she sits in the chair, she looks so vulnerable and tiny. She takes her glasses off to wipe her tears again as she informs us that she had found my Dad dead in bed this morning at 10am. Bill just looked at me for it was now obvious to both of us that this was what I was sensing this morning. I believe that my Dad came to say 'Goodbye'. His spirit had travelled from Ardwick to Denton and then on to wherever we all go.

There was an inquest for although he was a diabetic and had been for many years, it was not expected that at the age of 66 years for him to die of Congestive Cardiac Failure. I was glad that he went quickly in his sleep for since his retirement, he had never been an early riser. I guess he was making up for the 5am rises when he was doing the early rounds for the post office.

Chapter 8

In October 1965, I had another baby daughter whom we named Julie. What little hair she had at birth was jet black and so unlike her sister's curly red hair. Even today, they are as different as chalk and cheese. When Julie was about five months old, my mother died from a fractured skull, having apparently stumbled and fell headlong down the stairs.

It was at my mother's funeral that Cousin Kathleen, twenty-three years my senior and the daughter of Uncle Arthur with the roaming glass eye, told the story that I have already related about the embezzlement and the man who committed suicide by jumping under a train. Unfortunately, she could not remember his name or any details that would have enabled us to confirm this story.

Aunt Cissie and Uncle Fred moved to a little bungalow near Bolton. Other people moved to Wythenshawe and Hattersley as the terraced houses were bulldozed down row by row. Whole communities were destroyed and Higher Ardwick resembled a bomb site. The mills were blown up and people watched as their tall chimneys shuddered and fell to the ground. All that was left standing was a pub and the Methodist Church where I had bought my mother's calendar. I have racked my brains but I cannot remember, no matter how hard I try, as to what was written that affected my mother so much.

Forty years on, when I drive past the place where I spent my childhood, the church is now some kind of warehouse and nothing has been built to replace the rows of terraced houses. Only patches of grassland littered with empty bottles and cans are to be seen now. So much for redevelopment! The railway arches still stand with their tiled, old walls covered in lichen and smelling of damp. Of course, the station is closed now and Blind Lane where I used to play as a child and watch the steam trains hurtling by, wondering who the people were and where they were travelling to, is now the only familiar site to be seen. Some of the railway stables still stand and I remember feeding these horses with bread and carrots, stolen from my mother's food safe, as we called it then. It was a large wooden box with a number of shelves with the front being covered with a fine mesh wire so that the air could circulate whilst protecting it from flies and rodents. Would you believe that statistically today, there are more cases of food poisoning than they were in those bygone days?

Ardwick Green Park still stands next to the spot where St. Gregory's School was, just opposite the old dairy with its huge steel containers that were filled with large blocks of ice to keep the milk fresh. Sadly, it is another type of warehouse today. Gone are the children in their cotton white socks and the boys in their short trousers playing hop-scotch, skipping or playing marbles, being closely observed by the cats that used to sit high above on the old stone bedroom window-sills. I remember so well for they were purring whilst washing their paws and faces and eying up the sparrows and pigeons. Of course, these birds were well aware of their intended enemies and would perch on top of the high wooden poles that secured the lines for the 213 trolley bus which ran from Platt Fields to Ancoats. We all knew the guards who issued the two penny tickets for they would hang on to the brass pole with their brown leather shoulder bags, rattling with coins in an effort to catch individuals like myself who would hop on and off the bus to get a free ride. There is another pile of litter where Mrs Winter's corner shop stood with its' bulls-eyes and liquorice sticks displayed in tiny glass paned windows, nowadays the sweets are wrapped and contained in mounds of plastic which one has to fight with in order to eat them. We call this progress but I wonder if that is so, or have I not taken off my rose coloured spectacles.

For now, I am just so glad to return home to my cat 'Cindy', my Belgian Shepherd Dog named 'Bess' and 'Rocky' my German Shepherd whom I got from a 'Dogs Home' many years ago. My cottage is 400 years old and resembles a rabbit warren with steps hither and thither. Its thick stone walls keeps us warm in the winter and the dogs have a whale of a time in the huge garden which backs –on to moorland.

Well, I must cast my mind back to the task in hand and settle down in my old rocking chair. I put coal on the fire and pour a glass of wine as I continue my story.

I had no further unexplained experiences until 1972, when I commenced general nurse training at Stepping Hill Hospital, Stockport. Prior to this, I had rekindled an old relationship with a man named 'Harry' that was twenty-two years older than me and as we were both now married, we tended, shall we say, to keep our relationship under wraps.

We met purely by chance at a nightclub in Stockport when I was out celebrating my birthday. Oddly enough, our birthdays were three days apart. He was a self-made, wealthy man who unfortunately, had no children. After the War, when he came out of the Air Force where he worked as an engineer, he built a successful fire/ central heating business.

He always maintained that when he died, the 'Vultures' as he put it, would be after his money. In a way, he reminded me of Mr. Teasdale, as he was of a similar height and build with a swarthy complexion due to his Jewish ancestry. He always referred to me as 'Elizabeth', refusing to call me 'Liz' like everybody else.

In July 1972, I was allocated as part of my nurse training to a male medical ward known as 3B. At around 8pm on the 21st, the longest day of the year, I was asked, being the most junior nurse, to make up an admission bed for a patient being transferred from the 'Infirmary'. No name was available and the only information being that he had suffered a severe cerebral vascular accident or commonly called a 'Stroke'.

I remember that longest day of the year, forty years on, as one of the worst days of my life. For it was Harry, completely unconscious, with tubes and catheters protruding from almost every orifice of his body. To this day, I do not know how I maintained my composure, but possibly due to the arrival of his wife shortly after his admission and also to a number of doctors and senior nurses surrounding his bed. I just hid in the sluice room, surrounded by urinals and bedpans, until the night staff arrived and we changed shifts. Over the next three months, he hovered between life and death and I spent as much time as appropriately possible at his bedside. I think Sister Medena and the nursing staff were well aware of the situation. He would follow me with his eyes and I was asked on a number of occasions if I knew him or did he know me from somewhere. In early September, I completed my allocation to that ward with a fortnight's holiday before commencing my surgical ward placement.

Bill, my husband, and I had previously arranged to take the girls to 'Butlins' holiday camp which was actually the same camp where Bill and I first met all those years ago... I can always remember that it rained and rained, so much so that one afternoon, I stayed in the chalet with the excuse of 'washing my hair'. While Bill took the girls out somewhere, I felt terrible; for what could I do there with no one to talk to and nowhere to cry. I was looking out the window at the pouring rain when suddenly, I saw Harry walk towards me.

I ran to the chalet door, opened it and was ready to welcome him with open arms. He wore his old familiar smile and his grey eyes sparkled. As he reached the window almost to the open door, he simply disintegrated. I then knew that at fifty-two years old, he was gone or was he? For I had surely seen him!

Life for us was never the same again and Bill and I slowly drifted apart.

Chapter 9

I had now completed 18 months of training and had passed my Intermediate Examination. In the days that I trained, we worked mainly on the various wards, gaining clinical experience and developing good nurse/patient relationships which were invaluable to professional nursing care. Unfortunately, nurse training today, is based in colleges leaving little time to practise the practical side of nursing. As the old saying goes 'You are only as good as Nellie'.

Towards Christmas 1973, I was working on an acute surgical ward where the pace was fairly rapid as we had theatre cases almost on a daily basis. This involved mainly pre- and post-operative procedures. On one particular morning, I was preparing a patient for theatre when I noticed that the middle-aged chap in the next bed had an early morning female visitor. This was fairly unusual as visitors were not allowed during the morning routine as the workload was heavy… She appeared to be much younger than him so I assumed that the blond –haired, pretty girl must be his daughter.

After lunch as I was administering medication, I asked if this visitor was his daughter. He explained that he had not had a visitor this morning and that I may have been mistaken. Now knowing that he was fully orientated, I was feeling a little confused especially when he added that he did not have a daughter. So I jokingly said that 'You must be her sugar daddy then' as I had seen this pretty girl next to his bed that very morning. He stared at me with the colour draining from his already pale face and I thought to myself 'What on earth have I said'. At this stage, I was also a shade paler and stared at him. 'Describe her', he said and so I duly did in great detail as I was only feet away from where she was sitting next to his bed. After what seemed an eternal length of time, he began to relate the story of a young woman who he was very much in love with, who was killed in a tragic car accident. By this time, he was very emotional so I drew the curtains round his bed for privacy...'Did she fit my description' I asked and he nodded his head so I explained that I had tendency to see deceased people. He pleaded that if I see her again, to please tell him. I nodded my head but I never did see her again despite my vigilance. Later, when I ever passed by his bed, he would give me a special smile which always warmed 'the cockles of my heart'. Sadly, he died a few weeks later, but I was sure that she would be there waiting for him.

The second incident happened months later whilst I was working on a male unit dealing with lung and heart conditions along with other inoperable diseases such as cancer etc...

Now I was a 3rd year student nurse and was almost ready to take my qualifying exam. As such, I was involved in ward round discussions with consultants and junior doctors etc. On one such occasion, we were discussing a Quaker gentleman who had been diagnosed with inoperable stomach cancer. This man whom I shall call Fred was constantly asking doctors and nurses if he was going to die and nobody would tell him the truth. We would evade his questions as much as possible to avoid telling him. The consultant felt that like many other seriously ill patients that they were justifiably seeking reassurance that they would recover. Fred was very persistent, his reasons being that he needed to know if he had to put his house in order and make a will. Nothing really constructive came from our debate with the consultant regarding whether we should tell him or not as there were so many varying opinions. Eventually the consultant in his wisdom decided that he would make the decision after his fortnight holidays. This was of little use to the nursing staff that would have to deal with him on a daily basis. The general opinion was that Fred would probably be dead by the time of his return from his holidays. Consequently, the staff who felt that Fred should be told decided that whichever one he asked again that they would tell him the truth.

I went home and spent a very fretful night like many other of my colleagues, wondering how I should approach this very difficult task and what words would I choose. I had a little knowledge about the Quaker Religion for my grandmother, Sarah Fleetwood, was a Quaker, according to my mother. Apparently, the family had reverted back to the Methodist Religion though I had never seen them attend church except for weddings and funerals so not much could be relied upon regarding that information. I realised that I was clutching at straws, but nevertheless, felt that it would be me that he would ask first.

So I prepared a little speech of how to tell him that he was going to die. The very next day as I finished the early morning bedpan round, Fred beckoned me over to his bed and asked for a urine bottle. I can remember it to this day so as I approached the bed, Fred asked 'Am I dying?'

So I took a deep breath and opened my mouth only to hear a male voice coming from my vocal chords, uttering the exact opposite of what I had planned to say. In fact, this same voice briefly stated that he was not dying and would be well very soon. My lips continued to move, but it was definitely not me speaking.

I cannot describe the expression on his face. It was one of total shock with his mouth wide opened as he stared at me. The urine went spraying over the covers as he dropped the urine bottle. Shock, no doubt! This all happened in a matter of seconds and probably less than a minute and then my voice returned back to normal. I tried to compose myself and told him that I would change his bed linen. I dashed off to the Sluice Room and in total shock, lit a cigarette to calm my frazzled nerves. I spoke out loud to check if my normal voice was definitely back and was greatly relieved when it was so. My legs were still like jelly as I returned to re-make his bed armed with clean linen.

Unsurprisingly, he never uttered a word and just stared rather vacantly towards me. From that moment on, believe it or not, Fred started to recover. By the time of the consultant's return from leave, he was able to perform his basic needs unassisted and was nimbly walking round the ward. Nobody could understand what had happened and I certainly was not going to breathe a word (would you?) but needless to say, we were all very pleased. Fred and I never broached the subject again but I believe that somehow, Fred recognised that voice. About four weeks later, he was discharged home, fully fit.

Chapter 10

In 1975, I qualified as a State Registered Nurse and moved to Stockport Infirmary working three nights per week. My contract was such that I could be moved to any ward, consequently, I gained experience in many areas ranging from young babies, orthopaedics, ear, nose & throat, casualty and theatre work.

About three weeks into my job at the Infirmary, I went alone to the Rest Room at the very top of the building to have a break whilst the ward I was working on was quiet. To reach it, after one had left the lift on the second floor and climb the wooden stairs past the children's ward, you then ascend some more steps to this small room with its large window where the road lamps as well as the town hall lights streamed in, lighting up the entire room.

As I entered, the town hall clock struck 3a.m. I was thinking that I would have one hour to rest as I walked towards my favourite armchair which was beside the window next to the radiator. I noticed that a nurse had got there before me and was fast asleep with her cap askew and her shoeless feet propped up on a small stool. I crept by the side of her in order not to wake her up and got myself another chair and began to settle myself down. I briefly glanced over to her just to make sure that I had not disturbed her and suddenly noticed that she was no longer there. 'Where on earth could she be' I thought as I looked around this small room with its four or five chairs. I even looked out the window, wondering for a second or two if she had jumped out for some reason or other as there was no way that she would have got up and walked past me. The town hall clock read 3.15 a.m. and then I realised that, despite her solid appearance with her red and navy cape wrapped snugly around her, she was indeed dead. I could not settle and returned to the Accident & Emergency Department at 3.30a.m., to relate my story.

Not caring whether my colleagues thought if I was raving mad, I did just that and related my story only to be told to speak to the Nursing Officer who had just left the Unit and returned to her office. She was a small, plump, jolly middle-aged woman with her brown eyes fixed on me as I told her my tale. 'So you have seen her as well, describe her to me' she responded. I recalled her thick, dark hair and her glasses on the end of her nose. She went on to tell me that this 'Ghost' was the ward sister of Skye's, the children's ward, and that she had been killed on the A6 road just outside the hospital as she went home one morning.

About five or six months later, due to staff sickness, I went to take charge of a female orthopaedic ward. There were two nursing auxiliaries, Irene and Rachel, and myself on the night shift. As we sat around a small table in the centre of the ward, all was quiet with twenty patients fast asleep, when I spotted what appeared to be a female patient in her dressing gown. She was heading towards the fire exit.

I jumped up and grabbed the lamp on the table and said 'Look, she is out of bed'. Rachel followed me as I headed in the direction of the fire exit only to find nobody there. I asked Rachel if she had seen her but she shook her head saying that there couldn't be anybody as they all have broken bones and on traction and cannot walk. Just then, Irene headed towards the area which became icy cold within a six foot radius and we found that we could step in and out of this coldness.

Suddenly, the bed pan washing machine in the sluice room started up which frightened the life out of us as our nerves were already a bit frazzled. Slowly, holding on to each other, we went to investigate. As we opened the door of the sluice, we noticed that everything was normal except for the bed pan washer which was girdling and grinding. But nobody had pushed the large steel handle in order to operate it. It eventually stopped but there was not a single pan in it.

The Infirmary, which is now sadly no longer in existence, was an old Victorian building and full of nooks and crannies. Consequently over the years, there were many 'Ghost Stories' circulating amongst the staff. Irene told us that it had been said that when a bed pan washer started up on its own, that some patient would die. Needless to say, armed with our torches, we checked twenty separate pulses. Luckily, all were alive and fast asleep.

The two of them went into the kitchen to make a pot of tea and I sat back at the table. Back they came with a plate of biscuits, three mugs and an old metal teapot. As we sat munching our biscuits, one of them asked 'Liz, can you read tea-leaves? I raised my eyebrows and said 'No! I have never done it'. Funnily enough, I was told by my mother that my grandmother used to do it and tell people's fortune. I continued to tell them about my Great Grandmother, Sarah Blackmoor, who lived in Shrewsbury in the 1800's, was called a 'witch'. She was a 'white witch' who made potions and medicines from plants and herbs.

'Go on, Liz, have a go' they said so we duly twirled our empty cups upside down to let the leaves settle. I picked up Rachel's cup and whilst staring intently at the bottom, I could see a long dark tunnel. 'Oh! I am off to London with my husband' she said. Irene added that there were a lot of train tunnels to London but as I had never been there, I could not say.

Next, I took up Irene's cup and could see bits of pictures, a man and a dog but not a lot else which she seemed to understand. It was now almost 5.30a.m. so we began our ward round. This involved various procedures including medication, toileting and blood pressure readings. When I handed over to the day shift, I recalled the nights' events and they too confirmed that a patient would die, going on to hazard a guess as to which one would be next. I must add that this was done in a kindly manner, for nurses become almost immune to death as otherwise we could never do our job. Somebody added that perhaps the lady was coming for whoever it was. Food for thought! over the next week, I would pop in to see if anybody had died but nobody had. I dismissed the whole night's event from my mind.

A couple of nights later, I woke up with a start as I had been dreaming of past lives, the sailor and the girl who had been murdered. But the clearest picture in full colour was of this old lady who stumbled and fell crashing her head on the hearth of a huge, stone fireplace narrowly missing the burning coals. Now was this me? Who lived in a little, corner cottage with its upper floor resembling a very large shelf? In the corner of this tiny room were wooden ladders which she climbed to get to her straw bed. On the wattled ceiling hung plants and herbs and a large cauldron stood in the corner, next to a cluttered table. On the fire, a black, iron kettle bubbled away and there was a large sea shell which rattled about as the kettle boiled. As I hovered over my body, my life flashed before my eyes. My three daughters who had now children of their own and my husband who had gone to fight in The Indian Uprising, never returned. I had waited for him over the years and watched as the wounded and limbless soldiers returned from this war in their tattered, blue uniforms and some with wooden crutches under their arms. Their hair and beards matted and very filthy, many had patches over their eyes which were the lucky ones to return to their family and friends.

Now I ask myself, are these memories or just a dream or perhaps has something triggered in my mind as I was recently talking about my great grandmother, Sarah Blackmoor. After all, as a qualified nurse, I had been taught that children under the age of 3 years could not remember as their brains were not developed enough. I consoled myself with the fact that this may have all been rubbish for after all; nobody had died on the ward despite the many rumours and speculations.

Two days later when I had recommenced night duty, Irene came to see me on my ward. Her news shook me to the very core for whilst I was off, Rachel had died from a possible thrombosis caused by taking the contraceptive pill. She was just 38 years old and never got to visit London with her husband who was now naturally, utterly devastated. Despite many requests, I never read the tea leaves again whilst I worked at the Infirmary. Even today when I see tunnels, I understand what it means.

Chapter 11

The death of Rachel affected us all as she was a very loyal and experienced member of staff.

I think the last straw that broke the camel's back, as they say, was when a young lad was admitted overnight to the casualty department and immediately taken to the operating theatre. They were attempting to remove the crushed crash helmet that was embedded in his skull. Just as the surgeon was removing the helmet, the young lad had a cardiac arrest.

'The Red Devil' as we called it, i.e. the resuscitation machine was rushed into theatre and the 'Crash Team' began to resuscitate him. He was brought back from death and against all odds, made a remarkable recovery in the orthopaedic ward.

A few weeks later, I went to see him as the stories circulating amongst the staff suggested that he remembered everything which occurred whilst in theatre. As I walked on to the ward, I immediately recognised him despite one leg in traction, a fractured skull and a plastered right arm. I hesitantly explained to him that I was there at the time and was interested to hear his recall of events as I was intrigued by such matters.

'Yes, I know! I recognise you with the ginger hair', he said and went on to talk about the doctor who was present named 'Malik', the one that is always in the pub at the top of the road. I did not respond to this remark but secretly thought that he was right. He went on to say what he had seen and it was an accurate blow by blow account of the incident. He was correct in everything he said claiming that everyone was rushing around from his position, hovering above us near the ceiling.

'What do you think' he said. I nodded my head saying 'you are dead right, lad' No pun intended. 'I am never having another motorbike again if I get better' he said. My smiling response was that he would be fine as it was not his time to die. We bid our farewells and I thanked him for telling his story.

Chapter 12

I thought a great deal about what he told me and to me, it made sense that one does not die but in fact goes somewhere else; But where to?

The old lady who died when she struck her head on the fireplace – was she actually me? Were the memories of the children who called her a witch when she passed them in her long, dark clothing, walking up the stony and often muddy path that led towards the village?; as she was well known for her medicines and potions with which she treated those who asked.

The young girl that was burnt at the stake – was that also me? Is that why I am so afraid of fire and would not stand the thought of being cremated when I die or is it that we return many, many times.

I, myself, remember the Five Books in the clouds meaning five previous lives. The fifth life is the one I find most interesting and I will recall it here to support the evidence that I accidently obtained years later, proving beyond doubt that we do, indeed, come back.

For my part, it is a completely unfinished business by putting wrongs to right and paying back what is owed whether good or bad. I also know that to do this, we meet the same people that we met in previous lives in order to complete what our spirit requires us to do. The spirit to me is the core essence of our personality and the soul is the examination of one's conscience. I must add that this is not entirely clear because my spirit frequently has different ideas when the past and present lives collide.

Are the daughters that I have now the same ones who threw out my belongings and tools that I used to heal people way back in the 1800's? Who knows? It is said that if one dies of an injury that in the next life, they will bear a birth mark in the exact same area. Oddly enough, I have a strawberry birthmark at the back of my head just above the neck.

I have little evidence, just a gut feeling, regarding these past lives that they did exist and so did I. In these times although the dates and countries are vague, it is possible that we all reincarnate and experience numerous lives. The reason that I vividly remember three out of the five lives is probably because the deaths were so traumatic. I guess the other two deaths were due to natural causes.

This then brings me to the fifth life in which a young woman is walking along a harbour as dusk is falling. There are a number of wooden ships with their carved figureheads anchored. I am ambling along and suddenly, grabbed from behind by a couple of rough-looking men. I am being dragged by these men, kicking and screaming for help towards the stony shore. I am roughly handled up a gangplank and then onto a small boat. Then as one of the men start rowing, I notice that it heads for the ocean. I seize my chance and jump overboard in an attempt to escape but am grabbed from the water and hauled back into the small boat. They are angry and threatening me causing me to fear for my life.

About a mile from shore, we reach a large ship with its cloth sails full mast which can be seen in the setting sun. I am hauled on board by a number of smelly sailors, taken below deck and locked in a large cupboard. Released hours later, only to find it is pitch black and can only see the stars as the ship pitches and rolls in the middle of the sea.

Petrified and again in fear for my life as the sailors are now leering at me and I know that it would be only a matter of time before they would abuse and rape me. Survival is a very strong instinct and after much contemplation, I decided that the only way to survive was to become somebody's mistress. Not the captain, I thought as I had noticed that one man in particular seemed a very strong character and the crew jumped to his commands. So I set my cap at him. Not a very difficult task seeing that I was the only female on this God-forsaken ship sailing to some unknown country. Hopefully, I would escape when this ship docked.

Chapter 13

I continued working at the Infirmary noting in particular the numerous people who attempted to take their own lives. I wondered if they were aware that they at some point return to Earth. Sadly, the doctors and nurses, myself included, had little sympathy or understanding of mental anguish that they were experiencing. We were much more orientated to the accident victims, at least those that survived. Many poor individuals came to us in body bags, some even decapitated. It was not unusual to see severed limbs, burns, fractures, heart attacks and strokes and the odd gunshot wound.

So in late 1977, I became a student again studying psychiatric nursing at Cheadle Royal Hospital. By this time, my marriage was completely doomed. Bill went working in the oil rigs in Saudi Arabia and the girls and I moved to a small cottage in Haughton Green.

We obtained this cottage in the oddest of ways. Patsy, my oldest, had picked up a leaflet in the street about it and brought it home as she knew that we needed somewhere to live quickly. So I borrowed some money off my solicitor and claimed a grant as it had rain pouring in from an unstable roof. The little two-bed roomed cottage next door was also empty and in a dilapidated state. Apparently, they were built around 1880.

The rest of this little cul de sac contained a dozen modern semis. The two old cottages were once surrounded by farmland. So, in we moved along with Smokey, our seven year old Golden Labrador whom we had since he was a very small puppy.

Now Smokey was definitely a great character, being very supportive towards me and the girls who were now 12 and 13 years old and attending grammar school. I had no qualms about leaving them in the house when I worked late shifts or night duty. We already had one unwelcome visitor who made a hasty retreat down the street clutching his bottom where the seat of his pants had been ripped by Smokey's strong teeth.

So I commenced my training along with nine other students who apart from Jean and Pat, as we were already qualified general nurses. The three of us became good friends. I cannot really remember now, possibly from too much drink but I read their tea leaves which escalated to a number of private readings; in essence, 'fortune telling'. There were no further ghostly sightings or unexplained experiences until I had nearly finished my training. I was on night duty when the most interesting and fortunate thing happened.

Prior to commencing night duty, I was on days off and doing my shopping at Denton Market. As I was returning home in my little, bright yellow 2CV6, a still, small male voice whispered 'Your brakes are faulty'. This was repeated during the next couple of days every time I got in to the car and I just could not shake it off. 'Was I going mad?' I thought for it reminded me of the memories I had when being born.

I took the car into John, my local mechanic in Denton and told him that I thought the car brakes were faulty. 'Are they spongy, does the car swerve to one side when you use them'? he asked. Feeling a little silly, I said No! Raising a bushy eyebrow and a confused expression, he asked me why I had brought it in. My courage deserted me and I responded by saying' please, just check them for me'. 'OK, it is your money' he said. So I left the car and went shopping.

About an hour later, I returned to the garage. 'I had a look and run it around the block and I believe there is nothing wrong with the brakes' he said confidently. So I drove back home. The girls and I had our evening meal and I set off to work. Noting that the still, small voice was now completely silent, I came to the conclusion that I was probably schizophrenic (hearing voices). It was about forty minutes' drive as the crow flies to Cheadle Royal and it was pouring with rain.

As I was heading towards some crossroads, I started to brake at the 'Halt' sign and nothing happens and the car just continues on through the main road. Not a vehicle in sight as I struggle to stop it for the brakes had failed. The next thing I knew was that I found myself out of the car and above it, watching me struggle. (Talk about jumping out of your body in fright!!!!). I was then back in the car, having mounted a grass verge undamaged and the engine had stopped.

I lit a cigarette and tried to gather my wits. Still no car in sight!! I do not know which scared me the most, was it the complete failure of the brakes or was it the fact that having felt myself all over, no broken bones and I was completely bone dry. So how could I have been out of the car, looking down during the pouring rain? That incident convinced me that I was not mad as the information about the brakes had been correct and this man, whoever or wherever he was, tried to warn me in order to protect me. It was just like the lady I heard as a small child when the wagon was hurtling down towards me. Did the car stall on its' own or did he turn off the engine? After I had gathered my wits, I continued the short distance to the hospital very slowly using the hand brake to stop.

John's face was very solemn when I arrived at the garage at 8.30a.m.; the following morning. I was very tired, having worked all night and I was angry. What if the girls had been in the car? He profusely apologised but still maintained that he himself had checked them and that they were working perfectly. But when he jacked up the car again, the brakes were 'knackered' as he put it.

Chapter 14

I have pondered and puzzled over what has happened and I cannot find a rational explanation. My cigarette and wine intake has spiralled but I console myself on that issue with the fact that both my parents were heavy smokers and also Uncle Arthur with the glass eye and he died in his 80's of old age, I guess. The other five members of my mother's family, all died of cancer, the point being that not one of them ever smoked to my knowledge. Neither did smoking appear to affect my children's birth weight; both well over 7lbs and as regards intelligence, they both passed their 11+ exams. In fact, an acquaintance of mine, Joan, was a very heavy smoker and her baby boy weighed in at over 12lbs, amusingly asking her doctor 'How big would he have been, if I didn't smoke?

When the girls were at school, I would often speak out loud to see if the same, male voice would respond. My favourite question being 'Who are you?' but no response, in fact, nothing out of the normal happened. I just consoled myself with the meagre fact that at least the neighbours would not hear me talking to myself as the cottage next door still stood empty and isolated. None of the neighbours knew why that was, they just said that the couple just 'up and left' and that there had never been a 'For Sale' sign up.

In 1979, I passed my finals and was working as a staff nurse on the private wing of Cheadle Royal Hospital. I had a gentleman friend, named Abraham who was also in the medical profession. We got on quite well and the girls appeared to like him. On one particular day, we set off in his car to Blackpool. It was a nice sunny day and everything appeared normal until about half way through the trip. Suddenly, that same male voice which only I can hear says 'The front wheel is loose, get out of the car'. Startled, I responded by telling Abraham to pull up at the garage which I could see just a short distance ahead. Needless to say, there was a confused response from him as to why. 'Just do it' I said, adding that the front wheel was loose.

We drove into the garage and the mechanic jacked up the car. Moments later, he said that this wheel is extremely dangerous and in a few more miles, it would have come off entirely! We never did get to Blackpool that day. My explanation to Abraham being that I heard the wheel rattling (psychiatric nurses do not readily admit to hearing voices). 'Impossible' he said in broken English but wisely, did not pursue the subject.

Shortly after that incident, Smokey, our dog who had been going blind, died. The girls and I were grief-stricken and vowed that we would never have any more dogs as it was too upsetting.

About six months later, I was at home alone doing some household chores when in the middle of washing the dishes, that same male voice said 'Go and get a dog'. I looked around the kitchen but there was nobody there. I realised that it is not through my ears that I hear it but just pops into my head. 'No! ; said I 'who are you?—No response, but as soon as I had time to consult with the girls, I headed to Manchester Dogs Home. There were dozens of dogs who look forlornly at you and I wished that I could take them all home. I had no idea what kind of dog I wanted but after walking around, I found myself drawn to one particular kennel in which was housed an elderly German Shepard. Now I reasoned that to get this dog would be a little stupid due to its age so I moved along only to be drawn back to the same one. It reminded me of the time I was drawn to that calendar for my mother's birthday so many years ago.

Despite the sound advice from the staff saying that the dog was old and would probably need a lot of expensive veterinary fees, I brought this rather thin dog home and managed to lift her into the bath as she smelled something terrible. I guess she wasn't impressed as she let out a few growls which I duly ignored. I then managed to dry her and gave her a hearty meal. The girls were thrilled and Muffin as we named her due to her coat which resembled burnt bread in colour. She appeared to be very happy.

A few weeks later, I had two weeks leave from work and as we could not afford to go on holiday, I decided to decorate the cottage. I also wanted to take Muffin to explore when I had time. I had heard about Denton Woods and decided that it would be nice to go there when it was not raining. So we set off and Muffin never left my side but as we entered the woods, she trotted off towards a river as she loved water other than being bathed. She jumped in and swam towards the opposite bank and got out despite my calls and just sat there. Having found a wooden bridge, I was making my way across when I saw an elderly man stood next to her. Suddenly, he just disappeared and Muffin stood up and came towards me. I knew that he had been her previous owner and had died. Consequently, Muffin ended up in the dogs' home. My feelings were that he could not settle and that is why I had to give her a home so that he could peacefully move on to wherever it is that we go.

We continued our walk until we came across a row of delightful, old mill cottages. I immediately fell in love with them and just wanted to live there. Funnily enough, down towards the end of the row, there was a 'For Sale' sign. I had a good look and made a spontaneous decision to contact the agents. I discovered that it was priced at £17, 000 which was way out of my league. I could probably get about £12,000. Oh Well! It was a nice dream while it lasted.

A few days later, Muffin was out in the communal back and I heard a big racket outside and wondered what she was up to. So I hurried out of the kitchen door to find half a dozen dustbins knocked over. Muffin had somehow managed to knock through next doors rotten, wooden kitchen door and was busily chasing a rat. I squeezed through the door with its hinges hanging off and was not surprised that there were rats as it was in a terrible state. I thought that I could hear her running around upstairs so hoping that the floorboards would not cave in after all I was only 9 stone, I still made my way, gingerly, upstairs to find Muffin puffing and panting however the rat had escaped. Thinking that I would have to do something about the state of this property next door to me, I duly had a good nosey round amongst the broken furniture, empty bottles and cans to find numerous bills and unpaid demand notices. They were mainly from the Allied Irish Bank whom I thought must own the property. We went back home after securing the door to the best of my ability which wasn't very good and picked up the dustbins. It was time for the girls to return home from school so I made dinner. As we were eating, I related to them about Muffin's escapade next door and vowed that I would phone that Irish Bank first thing in the morning and complain about the state of their property.

At 9.30 the following morning, armed with cigarettes and coffee, I made the call as I knew this would be a long drawn out scenario. Eventually, I find a sympathetic manager in the complaints department who assured me that he would look into the matter and contact me. 'Yeah right! Unlikely, I thought, but he did. The upshot of it was that they were not really interested in the cottage, adding that the mortgagees had 'up and left'. I guess I engaged mouth before brain saying 'Sell it to me'.

After a few weeks of negotiations, I borrowed more money from Mr Davies, my solicitor who was also dealing with my complicated divorce. It entailed an 'F' Classification on the bungalow so even though I had a buyer, she had not been able to move in. My solicitor had got nowhere with Bill's legal team, the reason being that they said that he was working in Saudi Arabia. The only way round it was for me to default on the mortgage in order to get it repossessed which the Building Society duly did as they were aware of the legal situation. Unfortunately, the proceeds were frozen and I had to wait for the funds to be released.

So now here I was in even more debt and the proud owner of a dilapidated cottage that only rats would live in instead of a lovely mill cottage in the heart of Denton Woods. So I asked the 'Voice' to help me, adding that he had done so many times before. 'Please, please' I said and let me live in the 'Ivy Cottage', as Muffin and I now would take regular walks down to see them. Sadly, the empty No. 18 had now been sold.

A few days after my request to the 'Voice' he responded by telling me to return my books to the library. Now I always had to pay a few pence for overdue fees so I could not understand this. However, I did as requested, tied Muffin outside and went into the library. A few minutes later, Christina spotted me. She was a friend who I knew when I was living at the bungalow. To cut a long story short, through Christina, I acquired a builder who got me a grant which really was a favour as I was 'a friend of a friend'.

I can still remember his face on seeing the state of the place. 'It is a bit dilapidated '; he said but will sort it out. About three months later, I put both cottages on the market and asked 'Harry' (the name I, now gave the' Voice') to find me another Ivy cottage for sale. This he did and within 3 or 4 months, I had sold both cottages in David Street without ever having to put the buyers 'on hold'. No.11, Ivy Cottages came on the market as Muffin and I had kept an eagle eye on them by going for walks down in the woods on every available occasion.

Chapter 15

In September 1980, with 2 weeks off from work, we moved into the cottage. It was a beautiful time of the year as the trees were turning into a golden hue. There were owls and wood pigeons; not to mention the goat and geese at No 20, the last cottage. The girls shared the large bedroom which overlooked the front where the garden ended just short of the river which weaved its way as far as the eye could see. I had the back bedroom which overlooked a very narrow ginnel from where the ground rose steeply, obliterating the view of the village. The staircase was stone and led directly into the kitchen which was pine with all reproduction units. At the end of the kitchen, there was another stone step leading into the living room which had a low beamed ceiling just like the rest of the cottage. I especially liked the old chimney breast in which was fitted a 'living flame' gas fire.

The only drawback was the fact that there was no door in the low narrow casing. I guess it was because it was built around 1850 when people were much smaller and one would have to have it made to measure. Thinking as I hung the green velvet curtains which exactly matched the carpets which the last tenants kindly left there, that a barn door would be quite nice.

Unfortunately, the front of the house which was rendered had been painted a ghastly yellow; so I had to 'let my fingers do the walking' through the local reporter. Luckily, I had someone coming in the afternoon to paint it white. I had hardly seen the garden as I had been so busy making the cottage our home so with time to spare, Muffin and I made 'the cock stride' across the narrow potholed track which ran the length of the cottages. It ended in a style where the goat and the geese lived and on into the woods and the now dilapidated mill.

As we went down the stone steps into the garden which was hedged with pink, rambling roses, I noted that the cottage gardens varied in size due to the river bank which flowed directly at the back of them. It was lovely so I sat on the steps to admire the view. Suddenly, I heard 'Elizabeth, Elizabeth'! Muffin also heard this pleasant, male voice call my name as she responded by running up the steps to the front door. I followed, thinking it must be the decorator but there was nobody there and then I thought—nobody ever calls me Elizabeth, it is always Liz and anyway how would the decorator know my Christian name? Shortly after that, the painter arrived and the incident was forgotten. By the end of the day and thankfully no rain, my yellow walls were now a brilliant white. He also said that he could find a joiner to make the barn door for the living room.

Two days later, armed with a pair of shears, I headed to prune the roses. After about half an hour, as I was putting the prickly branches in a heap at the bottom of the garden, I heard the same, male voice calling out 'Elizabeth, Elizabeth'! about three or four times. I ran back up the steps but nobody was there so I headed back down the garden, thinking maybe someone is playing a joke on me. Muffin and I explored the area and we scrambled over the fence and went a short distance into the woods. All we saw were a couple of squirrels up a tree. Well, it could not be them, I thought, so I made a mental note to ask Gladys who lived next door at No.10; if anybody called Elizabeth lived in these cottages.

I saw Gladys a few days later and invited her in for coffee. I reiterated what had happened on the two occasions whilst I was in the garden; adding that although I had been in several times since these incidents, nothing else had happened. Now, Gladys knew everybody for she had lived there for well over twenty years. Being a stay-at-home housewife, married to her second husband, Ken, they appeared very wealthy and Ken was a mason at 'Peace Lodge'. Her response was that nobody of that name lived in the cottages so we concluded that someone must have had visitors with that name.

It was now drawing towards the end of September and I was back at Cheadle Royal, working my usual shifts. Julie had a new boyfriend called Stephen, who was working as an apprentice engineer at the G.P.O… So frequently, when I arrived home from a late shift, the girls were out as Patsy, spent a lot of time with her college friends.

I arrived home one particular evening to find the lounge in complete disarray. The cushions from the settee and the rocking chair were scattered on the floor and my new, lovely, green velvet curtains were in a heap on the window sill with the curtain pole hanging down. Muffin was looking very sheepish as it was obviously her doing. It was odd as it seemed that she had been chasing something. I wondered if a cat or a mouse was in the house but found nothing. Anyway, I managed to fix the curtain rail and luckily, the curtains were still in one piece but I was puzzled as it was so unlike Muffin to behave in this way.

My bespoke, wooden, barn door with its' old fashioned, black, metal latch was now in place. I had stained and varnished it to match the beams. I placed a small coffee table and a candle lamp on the side of the door which opened into the kitchen.

As I sat on the settee later that night, I noted that the leather, rocking chair which I still have to this day, was rocking as if somebody was sitting on it. Then, as quickly as it stopped, I heard footsteps on the stairs. I ran into the kitchen and then up the stairs but nobody was there. I thought that it must be Gladys or Ken, next door but I had never noticed it before. Afterwards, I kept a furtive eye on the rocking chair but it remained still.

I did not mention the incident to the girls but not long after that, both Patsy and Julie were saying that they, too, were hearing footsteps on the staircase. In a way, that reassured me as for I knew that it was not just my imagination.

I heard the footsteps on a number of occasions but, suddenly one morning, I heard a man cough upstairs in one of the rooms. I ran up very quickly, only to find nobody there.

Christmas had now come and gone and Easter was upon us. I was working but the girls were home on holidays. I think it was Easter Monday when I arrived home from the early shift, to find our Julie, Gladys and Stephen in the living room. The story they told me went as follows; Stephen had to come around to take Julie out but having changed their minds, they decided to stay in on their own (When the cats away, the mice do play). So 'Groomey', Julie's nickname for him, walked up to the village to get some cigarettes. Now whilst, he was out, Julie went to the bathroom to brush her teeth when she suddenly, heard Groomey call her by her nickname which he used for her i.e. Cooie (Don't ask me why as I haven't a clue).She responded by going into the main bedroom but there was nobody there. Again, she heard 'Cooie, Cooie, Cooie' but quickly, realised that there would not have been enough time for him to get to the village and back.

Gladys now takes over the story. There was a frantic knock on her door, only to find Julie clutching a toothbrush, her face as white as the toothpaste around her mouth. She reiterated what happened and said that Julie refused to return to the house until Groomey returned from the village. Muffin, at this stage, wonders into Gladys' house as she normally sits on our little tiled porch, her favourite spot, waiting for one of us to return home.

Groomey, his face agog, is still clutching the Bulmer's Cider bottle when I come in. (I was sick of telling them not to drink or smoke). Julie is now 15 yrs. old and Groomi, a couple of years older. Obviously, having now seen the evidence, my words were falling on deaf ears; exactly what I did with my mother, too.

Gladys puts the kettle on, I don't like cider, and I went upstairs to change out of my uniform. Low and behold, the beds were in disarray and pillows all over the floor.' Muffin, again' I thought as I cast my mind back to the incident with the velvet curtains.

Despite the autumn almost being upon us, there had been no further incidents. I am almost convinced that there is a man around the house as I get a strong feeling of his presence. 'Is it the owner of the still, small voice'? I ask myself, but no response when I ask or could it have been somebody who lived in the cottage. Many souls had possibly died here in the last hundred years or so but according to Gladys, all the people that she has known over the last 20 years had sold up and moved on.

Chapter 16

My ex-husband, Bill, returned from Saudi Arabia and was not 'a happy bunny' to find out that I was claiming all the proceeds from the bungalow, in lieu of maintenance for the girls as I had never received a penny from him for their upbringing. In fact, he was so angry that he caused a scene on the ward at Cheadle Royal Hospital. I had no choice but to get a 'Restraining Order' so that he was not to come anywhere near us. However, this did not seem to be working as Gladys had seen a man answering his description, loitering around the cottages. Now, Bill, in his early forties was tall with dark hair and fairly good-looking, did not easily 'blend into the wallpaper' and besides, I had already shown Gladys a photograph of him in happier times.

By now, we had lived in the cottage for almost two years and small items started to go missing. They would turn up later in different places. I accused the girls when I could not find my wristwatch which I was convinced I had left in the bathroom, only to find it the next day on the small coffee table in the lounge. Julie accused me of taking her cigarettes which I did not do and then they turn up in the middle of the welsh dresser. We could not have missed them during our search of the whole house.

'This man is a comedian', I thought to myself but I was really getting fed-up with his antics and whilst hoovering I gave him a piece of my mind i.e. 'This is my cottage, please leave things alone and do something useful instead'. I had finished my cleaning and was sitting on the settee when the latch rattles on the door. I watch it move up and down as if somebody is trying to come in from the kitchen. Just as quickly, it stops. Now, one seeks to find logical explanations so I explained it to myself that it was the way the door had been hung and possibly the air coming down the chimney.

About four days later, my favourite hair slide which was bought when we went to France for a week's holiday, went missing. It turns up the next morning right in the middle of a leather cushion on the settee and could not have missed it the previous night. Patsy pointed out that I must be dementing which did not go down too well. Julie, on the other hand, was more understanding due to the fact that she had experienced some of these incidents. However, she now moves from room to room turning the lights on constantly, which is great for my electricity bill.

One day, I happened to be in the bathroom whilst Patsy was in the bedroom next to it. The house had been divided up many moons ago so the walls were very thin. As I was sitting on the loo with my knickers around my knees, I noticed the basket waste bin, at the side of the door, started to slowly move across the bathroom floor and stopped at my feet. I was gob-smacked and shouted for Patsy who was convinced that I was quite mad at this stage. Despite numerous attempts at stamping and walking across my bedroom floor in an effort to make the bin move in the bathroom, we were unable to do so. Needless to say, every time I went' to spend a penny', I watched that bin like a hawk but it never did it again.

I was, now, utterly convinced that this guy was playing jokes. But I have to trust my own faculties and ignore Patsy' opinions. I asked myself if this is all connected with the man who called mine and Julie's names. I did think that it maybe Harry whom I saw at Butlins Camp after he died as he was the only person that would come back to me.

One evening, about a week later, there was a knock at the front door. I opened the door into the small, quarry tiled porch only to find Bill drunk and aggressive. 'Oh Shit!!!' I thought as I tried to slam the door shut but there was no chance as he had firmly wedged his foot in the doorway. Suddenly, I was nearly knocked off my feet by the variegated ivy potted plant which I had neutered in order to keep 'evil spirits' out of the house (one cannot be too careful) which came crashing down as Muffin, my, now, six stone German shepherd grabbed Bill by his thigh. Shocked and horrified, Bill began to flee with Muffin in hot pursuit. Gladys is highly amused as she is out front chatting to Frank, the quiet widower, who lived next door to me at No. 12.

The last memory that I have of Bill, apart from The County Court case, was of him legging it passed the cottages, hotly pursued by Muffin who was on anti-arthritic tablets for her back legs. Obviously, these were very effective as she managed to bite him again for I could see his bare bottom with the seat of his pants hanging down as he rounded the corner of the cottages and fled up Meadow Lane. Later, Muffin trotted back to a hero's welcome, what a good dog and a lot better than any 'Injunction'.

Christina, whom I met at the library and had kept in contact with, informed me (as news travels fast) that Bill had ended up at Tameside Casualty Department which for me was the icing on the cake.

Chapter 17

A couple of months had passed since the litter bin incident and my County Court case was imminent. Bill claimed that he had given money to Patsy for maintenance which of course, was untrue. Apparently, Patsy had gone to see him in his new house which he bought with his money from Saudi Arabia. There was a ghastly argument with the girls closing ranks and have never spoken to their father from that day on. Fortunately, the Court accepted my version of events and awarded all proceeds from the bungalow to me and the girls.

About one month later, the girls woke me up as Patsy said that she had been awakened by somebody calling her name. Being half asleep, she thought it was Julie but suddenly realised that it was a male voice. She had jumped out of bed to look out the window only to find nobody there. She woke Julie up and they both heard 'Patsy, Patsy'. I put on my slippers on and together with Muffin who was very happy to go 'walkies' at 3 o clock in the morning, set off all round the cottages to investigate. Nobody was there so we returned home and put the kettle on. I lit a cigarette and just turned around to find the girls staring, speechless, at the wall of the stairs where little, round, white lights, about 2 or 3 inches in diameter, were bobbing up and down as they ascended the staircase. They headed towards the girl's bedroom and then simply disappeared. I later learned that these were 'spirit orbs'.

Nobody went back to sleep except for Muffin, curled up on the kitchen floor, who was now tired after her nights' adventure. Patsy is now 'singing a very different tune' as she cannot offer an explanation. I reiterated my feelings that there was a 'ghost' of a man who was trying to attract our attention and I was going to find out who he is.

The following Sunday morning, I got up to put the kettle on and put some bread under the grill. Suddenly, to my astonishment, one of the silver trims that surrounded the four electric plates on the cooker, rises up and hovers about four inches in the air. Just as quickly, it drops back into place. I stared at the four rings but nothing else happened except that my toast was now on fire. I spent the next five minutes trying to scrape it off in the kitchen sink and wondering what was happening or was I going mad. I rejected the latter and said aloud 'Who are you and what do you want?' No response.

We had now got a stray cat named 'Tillie'. Needless to say, Muffin was not impressed but 'when push came to shove', the little, black and white cat stood her ground and clouted Muffin on the nose. I guess Muffin decided that retreat was the better part of valour. This was not as easy as chasing my six foot ex-husband. They become best friends eventually and as the evenings get colder, they lie side by side in front of the gas fire, stretching their paws towards the meter cupboard at the side of the brick fireplace.

Chapter 18

It was October and Julie's birthday was fast approaching. No doubt that she would be following in her sister's footsteps and go to college. Nothing eventful had happened other than, Muffin had taught herself to open the fridge when we were out (clever dog) and had scoffed everything except the eggs. I am guessing that she did not share the food with Tillie so we now had to wedge a kitchen chair against the handle before going out.

There was a decided chill in the air when I returned from work one evening. The girls were out so I could look forward to a peaceful night watching TV. The gas fire was full on as the animals stretched out next to the hearth. I brewed up, lit a cigarette and pulled the settee up nearer to the fire, stretching out to watch a film.

About ten minutes later, the barn door latch rattles and the door opens. The little coffee table tumbles over as if someone had knocked into it. At this point, I hear the key in the front door; Julie and Groomie walk into the lounge. So much for my quiet night! They sit down on the settee as I close the barn door. Just as I was opening my mouth to tell them what had happened, the barn door opens again. Their faces were 'a picture' and completely silent; until I said very loudly that 'I have had enough of this and he, jolly well, should have the good manners to show his face so we can know who he is'. A discussion followed and all of us agreed that these things could not happen on their own accord.

The following morning when the girls had left, I decided to attack this bizarre situation full on. So without more 'ado', I looked out the window to make sure nobody would see me talking to myself. I reiterated in no uncertain terms what I thought of him and that he should show his face. Nothing happened so I took Muffin for a walk before I commenced the late shift.

The following Saturday morning, as usual, I got up, placed some bread under the grill, made a brew and then I heard footsteps coming down the stairs. Thinking it was one of the girls, I shouted out if they would like some toast but no answer. I then guessed it was him so I darted into the living room to see what I thought was cigarette smoke rising above the settee. It was as if he was invisible, sat down having a smoke. I ran upstairs to see if Julie was having a cigarette, only to find both girls fast asleep. Back down the stairs, I went and into the lounge. The smoke was still there so this time, I shout and ball at him. Suddenly, more smoke as my toast went on fire, only this time it was beyond salvaging so I threw it in the sink with a tantrum.

Suddenly, I realised that he had gone as I could not sense his presence. 'That will have sorted him', I thought as I bet he did not know what a temper I had. Surprisingly, the girls slept through the entire episode and only Muffin and Tillie were looking with puzzled expressions.

It was now, January 1983 and strangely enough, I was beginning to miss his antics as the house had returned to normality. Of course, that was until the end of February, when I returned home from a late shift at the hospital. The girls were out and I was delighted at the prospect of a long soak in the bath in peace and quiet. It had been a horrendous day at work and everybody, including myself, and all the staff had completely gone daft.

I pampered myself in the bath, came down and pulled up the settee to the fire and put my coffee and cigs. on the floor beside me. I turned on the TV and settled on the sofa to watch a war film. Suddenly, for some reason, I glanced at the chimney breast and there as 'plain as daylight' was a man's' face with black, wavy hair. I guess he was in his early forties and good looking as he constantly smiled as his face slid down the chimney breast and disappeared into the meter cupboard.

Chimney and Fireplace

With my mouth wide-open, I looked for logic, thinking perhaps, it was a reflection off the TV but the faces in the film were Japanese. I sat glued to the sofa and then it dawned on me that I had asked him to show his face. This is exactly what he had done! Obviously, he could communicate with me but who was he? He was not 'my Harry'. I did not move from the sofa, the face had gone and everything appeared normal. So, I ask myself if somehow I imagined the whole episode. I ruled this out as surely, I would have seen who I thought was Harry who had died. I dashed next door to Gladys but they were out so I came back home as it was pouring with rain and pondered my next move.

I got the vodka bottle and together mixed with orange juice, downed quite a few stiff drinks. Gladys and Ken's car draws up and I rush out to meet them. 'Whatever, is the matter, 'Gladys enquires as I jabber on and on about the 'face'. 'You are drunk, Liz,' pipes in Ken which I agreed but was not drunk when I saw the face. Gladys kindly comes back with me to the house and I reiterate what had happened.

'What does he look like?' she says and I describe him as best I could. She thought about it and then says that this man could be Elsie Hyde's husband. Apparently, they had lived in my house about 20 years ago and he died at a young age. She added that Elsie was still alive and perhaps I should go and see her as she would still have some photographs of her husband. So we decided to visit her after Gladys phoned her and explained the reason for the visit.

The following morning, I went to work with a terrible hangover and decided during the course of the day that psychiatric nurses do not see faces sliding down chimney breasts unless they were schizophrenic. I came to the conclusion that the girls were right and I had imagined the whole episode.

This, of course, did not stop me staring at the chimney breast, every time I sat down to watch TV. Consequently, I lost track of all the programmes until it eventually faded to the back of my mind, many weeks later. The house appeared to have returned to normal as there were no footsteps on the stairs, no coughing and no rattling of the latch on the barn door. Needless to say, I kept 'an eye' on my mental state and I was still my normal self.

Even though, I did not recognise the man's face, I just had a funny feeling that I did know him. I racked my brain but nobody came to mind as I had nursed so many people who had died, I just could not remember all their faces.

Chapter 19

About three months later, when the girls were out, I was sprawled out on the couch watching a film on TV. I was thankful for the peace and quiet as Muffin and Tillie lay snoring by the fire. As I went to pick up my cigarettes, I was shocked and horrified to find that I appear to have three arms. Believe it or believe it not, a dark and weightless slightly hairy forearm lay across my lap.

Dog ends scattered on the carpet as I dropped everything. I began to rise in utter disbelief from the couch, only to see the profile of a perfectly formed man with dark hair, wearing a short-sleeved, white shirt and black trousers which were held in place by a buckled, black belt. I stared, mesmerised, as he turned his face towards me and smiled as if to acknowledge me. I recognised him as the same face I had seen on the chimney breast three months previously. He proceeded to walk the breadth of my lounge and I noted that he was of medium build and about 5' 8" tall. Just as I was gathering my wits, he slowly walked through the wall between the window and the meter cupboard and disappeared.

I ran out of the house and banged on Gladys's door, frantically. As she opened it, I dashed in with Muffin in hot pursuit at my heels and blurted out what had happened.

After a stiff brandy, I calmed down and both Gladys and myself agreed that it could not have been a hallucination as he was perfectly solid and normal looking. In fact if I had introduced him to someone, they would only think that his mode of dress was a touch, old fashioned and besides, it took him almost a minute to walk across the lounge.

'So who was he and what did he want with me'? Sadly on reflection, I only wished that I had the wits to speak to him but to no avail. A few days later, Gladys and I went to visit Elsie to have a look at her deceased, husband's photos. She appeared quite disappointed when I told her that this was not the man I had seen. So I was back at square one in my endeavour to discover his identity and needed a plan of action.

When I was a few days old, I was baptised Church of England in St. Marys Hospital due to the fact that I was 'failing to thrive' according to my mother. No further explanation was given and to date, I have been unable to find any information as the hospital was bombed during the 'War' thus destroying many medical/maternity records. I have never, like my father, had any religious convictions. My mother, however, was brought up in the Methodist religion and continued to practise it to a large extent. Consequently, I was forced to go to the Methodist Church and attend Sunday school where they spent their time teaching, us children, the merits of goodness and Jesus. However, the preacher was taken to court for letting two dogs starve to death. After that, no matter what my mother said, I flatly refused to enter the church again. Uncle Fred, from next door, would come to the rescue and almost every Sunday, he would take me to the pictures; saying to my mother 'Lily, stop trying to control that child as it will not work'.

With this in mind, I tentatively visited a Spiritualist church, sat through a service and then, asked for some more information about life after death and briefly, reiterated my story. From there, I contacted the Spiritualist National Union and spoke to a gentleman about my story. He listened attentively and proceeded to ask me a series of questions;

Q: Do you have any teenagers in the home? ------ *Yes*

Q: How many and are any of them girls? ------ *Yes, two of them*

Q: Is there any running water near where you live? --- Yes, a river at the bottom of the garden.

Momentarily, there was silence and then, he went on to say that 'you are clairvoyant' and possibly, a medium. He continued on to explain that it was someone who could capture vibrations, radiations or frequencies which does not involve the five senses.

Suddenly, everything fell into place so I was not mad but just a bit different. I went on to tell him that I felt 'Harry as I call him, puts thoughts in my head', recalling the incidents with the cars which probably saved me from serious injury. I also told him about the time I was sitting my first, nursing exams. Due to raising two children and having a house to run, I had great difficulty in finding time to study for them and only really did a few hours for a couple of nights before the exam date. In those days, they were written papers with outside examiners and basically, any subject could come up. I was drawn to half a dozen medical /surgical diagnoses and nursing procedures. Low and behold. They were all on the exam paper so I passed.

I said that I really owed this stroke of good fortune to who I believe is 'Harry. 'Yes' he said and then went on to explain that for whatever reason, he has 'attached himself' to me; adding 'that like attracts like'. Because of the teenagers and the river at the bottom of the garden, they give energy called 'ectoplasm' and consequently, he is able to show himself or 'materialise'.

A date was set-up for a séance and three people came to my house; two females and a man called 'Harry'. Attempts were made to contact 'my Harry' but he did not accept the invitation. However, they did pick up 'an imprint' of a woman called Elizabeth who they said, lived in the house many years ago. They asked me if I had ever seen her but I had not. 'What is an imprint'? I asked and apparently, it is a mark or a stamp which we leave in place; just like a photograph. She, herself, was not in the house so we were unable to communicate with her.

It was then suggested that I find a method of contacting Harry, other than asking for a verbal response. Apparently, the method I was using would take a great deal of energy and it was obvious to them from what I was saying that I was having difficulty in distinguishing my thoughts from his thoughts but in time, it would rectify itself. Harry no.2 suggested that I ask my Harry to alter the time on my clock which was on the wall facing the window.

Now, this wooden, five day, chiming, pendulum clock had me arrested so I set off laughing as I recalled this incident. I had bought the clock in China and I was attempting to cross the border back into Hong Kong where I had been visiting Jean, (my friend from the time of our psychiatric training days at Cheadle Royal). The clock which was wrapped in cardboard and newspaper began to tick and suddenly, all hell broke loose as the Chinese guards thought it was a bomb. Tick, tock, tick, tock, it went as the guards came closer. I, now, believe that this was one of Harry's little jokes. The guards eventually released me after an hour of incarceration so tired and bedraggled, I arrived back at Jean's house, tightly, clutching my clock.

The following evening, I asked Harry to alter the time on my 'China Clock' and knowing that thoughts are living things, I let my request go off into the 'Ether', had a bath and went to bed, reading a few pages of my Agatha Christie thriller beforehand. I was always a sound sleeper and I recall once when the neighbours were banging on my door as there had been an accident and they needed my assistance. It was to no avail and I slept through their knocking.

The next thing, I remember, is the alarm clock going off at 6am the following morning. Now, I am not a morning person but I did get up, had a coffee and a cigarette before taking Muffin for a quick walk. We headed off down to the end of the cottage and over the style, where Bob, the goat lives. I am convinced that he doesn't like us as he paws the ground and puts his head down. Anyway, Bob must have been having 'a lie in 'as he is nowhere to be seen. Within twenty minutes, we are back at the house and I cannot resist looking at the clock. Low and behold, Harry has done it; the clock reads 5.45, one hour slow.

I rush upstairs to put my uniform on and as I fasten my wrist watch, I notice it reads 6am. Now, I am confused so I check the alarm clock by my bed and it is at 7am. Back down the stairs, I go and check the cooker clock; it is 6am so I turn on the radio to get the right time. Suddenly, 'the penny drops', Harry had altered my alarm clock. The bugger! I thought, had got me up one hour too early. I just had to laugh as nobody would ever believe this.

Chapter 20

I contacted Harry no.2 and when I told him about the incident, I got the distinct impression that he did not believe me. He suggested that I contact a Mr Lee Hadfield who belonged to the Spiritualist National Union (S.N.U.). Now, Lee, as I shall call him, was a retired optician who turned out to be very knowledgeable in his chosen field of life after death. His advice was that I should join his development class in order to practise my psychic skills, stating that there were a number of written courses which I could obtain from the S.N.U. These would give me, initially, a basic understanding of this subject and more advanced at a later stage. To date, I have done many theoretical examinations in this field.

At first, I found his development class confusing and difficult but along with his other pupils who had various depths and skills in their ability to communicate with 'the dead', I soon grasped the art of this type of communication. It was a couple of weeks later after starting the development class which was held at Lee's large, detached house just outside of Hyde's town centre that I got a call from Harry no. 2 in the morning. I was having a coffee with Gladys who, by now, was having weekly updates on what was happening.

In fact, most of Ivy Cottages inhabitants were interested in the current situation.

I picked up the phone to hear Harry's voice at least one octave higher than normal, accusing me of altering his clocks. I did not know what he was shouting about but eventually I gathered that all the three clocks in his house had gone 'haywire'. 'Calm down', I said as I glanced at Gladys who could also hear the accusation. 'It will be your electrics' I said. 'No, no, two of them are battery operated' he fired back. Apparently, the other clock was a wind up type and none of them would stay at the correct time. He went on to say that it was my entire fault that I was a witch and he was having nothing more to do with me. He slammed down the phone. 'Oh, dear' Gladys sighed and I proceeded to fill her in on the details she had missed during my conversation.

Suddenly, the latch on the barn door begins to rattle and the door slowly opens. Gladys gulps and spills her coffee as I say 'It's only Harry'. It was then that I understood that he was letting me know that he was back, having been to Harry's no. 2 flat in order to alter his clocks. Evidently, he was not impressed that Harry no. 2 had not believed me. 'Brilliant' I said to Gladys as I got up to get a cloth to mop up the coffee. 'Just wait until I go to the next development class and tell Lee' I said which were now being held twice weekly. Gladys then said 'I hope he doesn't come to my house, Ken will not be happy about that'! Ken already thought that we are both quite mad in believing in this stuff. After Gladys left, I had a thought. Neither my Harry nor I take kindly to unbelievers so perhaps we could alter Ken's wrist watch but not a word to Gladys. It would be interesting to see what happens, I smiled to myself.

A few days later, Gladys comes around with her curlers still in her hair and suggests putting the kettle on to have a brew. She sits as far away from the barn door as possible and begins her story whilst intermittently, casting an eye towards the door. 'Ken's watch has stopped', she uttered as I tried to keep my face straight and not break out with roars of laughter. Apparently, she went to get his gold watch from the bedroom wall safe as he was going to a lodge meeting that evening. 'Liz, what have you done?' she said but as quick as a flash, I said it was not me but Harry. 'Shall I ask him to repair it' I said but Gladys shook her head saying that she had already taken it to the village for repair, adding that' it serves him right as he was always saying that you were barmy, Liz'. The conversation then turned to their New Year's Day Party and would I be able to come?

So, on New Year's Day Eve, 1983, I arrived at Glad's party around 9.45pm as I had worked a late shift. Silvia and Derek from No. 9 were there together with Doreen, Gladys sister and her husband plus half a dozen other guests whom I did not know. Needless to say, they were all a little worse for wear and I would have some catching up to do. It did not take me very long as after scoffing a few sausage rolls and trifle, washed down with a good few glasses of red wine, I was happily getting merry.

Gladys had obviously told them 'the Harry story' and Ken managed to see the funny side of his wrist watch incident and so, a debate followed on whether it was a coincidence or not. So with great confidence, possibly due to the wine and gin & tonics, I tell them that it was Harry who did it because he was not dead! Now one of their friends, a rather cocky, arrogant man, said 'I tell you what, Liz, ask Harry to break my watch' and with this, he took off his watch and waved it about. Now, I can be as cocky as the next person and not one to shy away from a challenge so I said 'Give it to me' I held it and asked Harry to break it permanently and as I handed it back, I pointed out that it might take a week or so but you can let Gladys or Ken know when it happens.

A few days later, Gladys receives a phone call from his wife. Apparently, 'the cocky' man and his wife were out shopping when he noticed that his wrist watch was gone. Evidently, it was quite an expensive watch so they retraced their steps, only to spot the watch lying in the middle of the road. Just as the man steps off the kerb to retrieve it, a car comes along and runs the watch over. It was very much squashed and beyond repair. Now I, not being the most Christian of individuals, was absolutely delighted with Harry's antics. It was shortly afterwards that I began to think that if he could do this, perhaps he could do something more constructive such as a new car for me.

My little, yellow 2C V6 was sadly, the worst for wear as the rain leaked in when the wind blew in a certain direction amongst many other faults. Then, to top it all, it rolled with the handbrake on, into Dr Ford's, a consultant psychiatrist, Bentley. He was not best pleased but luckily, there was no damage to his bumper. I really should remember to park it in first gear, in future.

Chapter 21

One day, I tripped over the dog's ball and dropped the typewriter. So 'I have to let my fingers do the walking' only to find that nobody in the 20th Century sells or repairs typewriters. I had tried a friend's computer in the past but I had difficulty co-ordinating the mouse and besides, the cat would walk all over it and the mouse would end up on the floor (no pun intended). So I headed off to the charity shops but I was out of luck. I said to Harry that if he wished me to continue writing my SNU exams, then he was going to have to find me a typewriter.' Bottom Mossley' pops into my head so I set off with Muffin in the car as I would be taking her for a run later, and parked at the computer repair shop. In I go, clutching my useless typewriter which I planted it on the counter and asked the lady if she could fix it? I did not mention the fact that Harry had instructed me to come here. The lady peered over her glasses, frowned and said 'Sorry, No!' Now whether it was my crestfallen face, had Harry let me down or the fact that something had jogged her memory but she suddenly said 'wait a minute'. After many murmurings and shuffling about at the back of the shop, she returned armed with a shiny, green case which she carried by its black handle. You can have this 'she said as I got my purse out ready to pay. 'No charge' she added quickly, insisting that though it had hardly been used and that they were using it as a foot stool anyway. Me of little faith!

Patsy was now studying Law at Liverpool University at this stage and Julie was taking A' levels as she was following in her mother's footsteps and wanted to be a nurse. I had an argument with Julie one day over money as usual. She wanted to borrow £5 for Patsy's birthday present which I flatly refused as I would be a very, rich woman if they had paid me back all the money they had borrowed over the years. I told her that she should have saved some of her spending money and with that; she stormed out of the house. I retaliated by shouting after her that she should ask Harry as that would soon shut her up!

Finally, peace and quiet descended on me and the animals, however, it was very short lived. After half an hour, I heard the key in the door and thought 'Here we go again' I was pleasantly surprised as she had a broad smile on her face as she was waving a £5 note in the air. 'Where is that from?' I asked suspiciously. 'Harry got it for me; I found it on the ground at the top of Meadow Lane', she responded gleefully. 'Pull the other one, it has got bells on it' I replied. She was adamant that she had found it and on closer inspection, it was rather wet and woebegone. Suddenly, the door rattles and the lights go on and off again. 'OK, I believe you, Julie' I said as I mentally gave Harry a gentle nudge about getting me another car.

Chapter 22

I invited my friend, Christina, round one evening and together with Gladys, was hoping that they would help me track down who Harry was? Christina was not in the house for more than ten minutes when the door starts rattling (his favourite pastime) and the meter cupboard door at the side of the fireplace flies open (that's a new trick) .. Now, she is totally different to me as she is immaculate, works in an office and is definitely 'a lady'. Her son, Ian and my Patsy were often fighting each other as best friends do when they are kids but now that they have grown up, they went their separate ways.

Now, the door slightly opens and I say in my own reassuring way which I had often used with patients, 'Christina, don't worry, it is just Harry and he will not harm you'. I am afraid my reassuring voice lost its touch as she screamed out 'Bloody hell, I am out of here'. I have never seen anyone move as quickly as she took off in those stilettos, leaving her handbag on the floor and fled through the door at great speed. I chased after her, clutching her handbag and managed to reach her as she was driving away. With another few expletives, she grabbed the handbag and was gone. To be fair to her, she did phone later that evening and said she would help me and Gladys but we would have to come to her house. Due to staff sickness, I would be doing overtime that night so Gladys and I would go to Christina's the following evening after I had some sleep.

In the early hours of that morning, my acute ward was very, very quiet; unlike the ward next door as my auxiliary nurses had to go in response to the panic button thus leaving me alone. This gave me time to visit Peter, our hypomanic guy in the seclusion room. He had been placed there since early morning to protect himself and other patients. He was driving everyone crazy earlier with his hyperactivity, pressure of speech and word salad (jumbled up words which make no sense). I always had a soft spot for Peter as when he was well, he was a very enlightened vicar. So I trotted off to the seclusion room, armed with my ciggies and two cups of coffee, his favourite beverage. We chatted but not for very long as he was not making any sense. Just as I was ready to leave, a voice in my head says 'Don't lock Peter in'; I had enough faith to know that there must be a reason though I did not know it at the time.

As I walked back to the nursing station and then the treatment room, I am suddenly confronted by a bespectacled, 50 year old psychotic/ psychopathic male patient. He was extremely hostile and verbally abusive and by his body language it was very obvious that he fully intended harming me. I reckoned that he was well aware that I was the only nurse on the ward and he was becoming more and more threatening as he knew I was yards away from the nearest panic button.

'OH Shit' I said as he runs and grabs me. The next moment, I see arms and a leg flying everywhere (not mine) as Peter grabbed hold of him in an arm lock .It was an easy task for Peter to floor him, being 6ft 3 and built like the side of a barn door. The 'weedy looking' psychopath skidded across the highly polished, wooden floor (it was the private wing after all) and only halted when he hit the wall. I hit the panic button and looking at Peter, hurriedly said 'Go back to your room quick'. This he did and I only managed to lock his door before an army of staff came bursting into the ward. Our psychopathic friend is still on the floor at this stage and shouting and screaming that Peter had attacked him. They all looked at me but 'Peter is locked up in the seclusion room, how could he? 'I said. Thank you, Harry and God bless Peter, I said to myself as I would have been in big trouble for breaking the rules regardless of Peter's intent.

After that eventful night, I had a few hours' sleep and set off with Gladys, who was armed with pen and paper like Miss Maple, to see Christina. Gladys was keen to draw up a list and allocate tasks just like a detective sleuth. As I drove past 63 Ruby Street where I used to live, I noticed that sadly, all the bright, pink, rambling roses had all disappeared. They were now replaced with a wooden fence. Christina lived at the end bungalow, on the opposite side of the street which backed on to old clay mine where Smokey and the children used to play. My girls always said that the Labrador brought them up. 'Oh, what a terrible mother I must have been; just wait until they have their own kids and hopefully, all will be forgiven'.

The clay mine was now a building site as more bungalows were been built there. I wouldn't buy one there for fear of subsidence which is now a massive lake mud and water. The old, iron rail tracks were rusted and broken and the old carriages were filled with clay.

Christina had seen us arrive and opened the door. She was immaculate as usual with her coiffured, blond hair. She was one of those people like Gladys whose umbrella never turned inside out or their legs never got splashed with muddy rain water. 'Gosh, what a scruff, I was!'

She apologised for her previous un-ladylike behaviour and this, obviously, gets Gladys' full sympathy. They both then carry on about Harry's antics, so much so that I had to bring them to the task in hand. 'Three heads are better than one', I said and we must write everything down so that we do not duplicate tasks. Gladys was to be the mole and ask around the local community, to see if anyone had information about the cottages.

I had already phoned Reece Davies, my solicitor, who told me that the deeds went back over one hundred years. He then asked me why I wanted to know; so I told him. There was 'a sickly silence' so much so that I thought he had put down the phone but he hadn't. I think he was trying to find another way of saying 'you are just mad, Liz'. However, he gathered his wits very quickly which made me think that it would be a good idea to put him on a retainer in case I ever got into trouble with the Law. 'One never knows, you know!' He continued on to inform me that prior to the mid 1950's, my cottage was owned by Cheetham Estate Agents; so it would be Christina's job to check with the Cheetham Records (fortunately, they were still in existence). I had got the easiest task of tracing the people who had owned the cottage in the past and attempting to ascertain if anything sinister had happened whilst they lived there.

I had not yet heard from Christina but Gladys had a lead which was the only one as I had come up with nothing. Only three families had lived at No. 11 other than Elsie Hyde so I managed to trace two of them and they all said that the cottage was perfectly normal.

Chapter 23

So, Gladys decided to invite our one and only lead round for afternoon tea. 'It will be better at your house as we don't want Harry to put him off before hearing his tale! I said. It was 2 o'clock and the best china tea set was neatly placed on the table. She had baked a beautiful sponge cake; bless her, as the only cake I ever made was out of a packet 'Mary Baker' which was so hard that Bill said he would break his teeth on it. So, I gave it to the birds and they seemed less impressed also leaving large chunks of it on the ground. I had never made one after that and had decided that shop bought was the best.

When I inquired what he was like, Gladys said he was old but definitely 'the full shilling' compared to the other poor souls she had asked. Apparently according to Gladys they were 'half way round the hat rack' and this led me to wonder what her assessment of me would have been if she did not know me? Would I be 'sixpence short of a shilling' in her eyes? Perhaps I was anyway!

We were both on tender hooks to see if he would come as this was our only chance so far. Promptly, at 2 o'clock, the doorbells rang and in walked a middle aged, 60's, tall and erect man who was definitely a gentleman. Gladys fussed over him as he settled himself on the couch. She asked if he would like Indian or China tea and some of her homemade cakes. We all got comfortable, lighting our cigarettes as George produced his pipe. He takes centre stage as one would say and started his tale. Way back in 1932, there was a man called Harry Saunders who lived with his family in the end cottage (where the goat is).'Another piece of cake'? Gladys says as she tops up his cup and he nods his head, obviously enjoying all the attention with a wicked, twinkle in his eye.

He went on to say that this Harry (what a coincidence, another Harry?) was very friendly with a woman called Elizabeth (another coincidence; I don't think so!) who lived in one of the middle cottages; adding that he wasn't sure which one. All he knew was that she had lived next door to the motor bike repair shop which was really a house and it was part of the cottage with an adjoining doorway. Gladys jumped up and says 'it was behind here' pointing to where her cocktail cabinet stood, adorned with sparkling, crystal glasses. She went on to say that Ken and her found it when they first moved in. 'Well, good' said George who was happy to have found the right cottage. 'You see, I as only a young lad and spent a lot of time there having always being interested in motor bikes' George continued. Apparently, Elizabeth was a good looking lass and Harry was always hanging around her, so much so that folks believed that they were lovers.

'Well, in 1933, he and his family upped and moved to Hyde. I remember it well as that was the year that he died. It was all in the local newspapers; he was found in a shed in Hyde with a chisel rammed in his neck but the inquest deemed it as accidental. Apparently, he was making fireworks for his children by putting gun powder in a container which he rammed in with a chisel. The theory being that the chisel and container sparked and ignited as he was possibly having a cigarette. The gun powder exploded, forcing the chisel into his neck. Folks found him gurgling and then he died before any help could be summoned. It was very sad as he was only 38 yrs. old. 'Elizabeth upped and left after that' George said. We were gobsmacked and sat there with our mouths open but I gathered my wits and asked him what this Harry looked like. 'I can't really remember,' said George but if you look in the local papers, I am pretty sure that one carried a photograph.' As he was helped with his jacket by Gladys, he said 'I hope you solve your little mystery. I believe in life after death and maybe he is still hovering around looking for her'.

I went back home, resolving to check with Christina about Elizabeth and my task would be to check the newspapers. Hopefully, there would be a photograph of Harry Saunders and the inquest would clarify how his actions had caused this terrible tragedy. As I went to bed that night, I fell asleep wondering if Elizabeth's imprint was the same Elizabeth which the séance people had spoken about.

My mind was then distracted from Harry as Muffin became ill and required a hysterectomy due to tumours. After making a full recovery, her back legs became useless and we had to put her to sleep. We were all devastated and vowed that we would have no more dogs as it was too upsetting. The only consolation for me was that I believed she would go to her original owner (the man that day that I had seen in the woods) so I asked Harry to see that this happened.

They say that 'bad luck goes in three's'; Abraham has to go to Croydon to study tropical medicine. I am pleased for him but I know that the distance will affect our relationship as when will he have time or the money to make regular trips. Julie has also left the 'nest' and I am also pleased for her. She has decided to take a 'psychiatric nursing course' and will be living in the Nurse's Home at Prestwich Hospital for three years but I am sure she will visit regularly just like Patsy.

So, I am left with just me, Harry and Tillie who forlornly wanders round the cottage looking for Muffin. I tried explaining to her but it is hard for a cat to understand about death or at least, I think so. I think she misses the company when I am at work as she is left on her own some.

Anyway, I have decided to get on with Harry's puzzles and visited the archives of the local rag. I did find, just as George said, an article on Harry Saunders's accident. Luckily for me, there was a photograph of him but I did not think that it was my Harry. Although, there was a resemblance but it was difficult to tell as the photograph was old, 1933, and I did not know how old he was when it was taken. The main problem being that due to the quality of the picture, one could not tell if he was dark or fair as my Harry was quite dark with black hair. So, I tracked down his family who still resided in Hyde but then, I had second thoughts about contacting them due to the 'Elizabeth Story'. They might not be happy as it is bad enough that they lost their father at an early age.

Christina phoned me to tell me that according to Cheetham Tenants Records, an 'Elizabeth' did live there at the time of Harry Saunders's death. Unfortunately, she could not find out how old she was or whether or not, she lived alone. Christina had come up with nothing else as apparently, Elizabeth had upped and left shortly after his death and there was nothing to tell us where she went. So, I have to let Harry know that I was not her. My gut feeling tells me that the photograph is not him but if I am right, well then, who is he?

I had now been out a number of times as a fledgling medium, demonstrating my clairvoyance on the platform at the spiritualist's churches. The next booking was due at Bolton and I was very nervous because Harry might not tell me anything. I was worried that I would be stood on the platform, with all the people looking at me and feel like a real pratt. Lee was very reassuring and said I would be fine but I was edging my bets and had reiterated to Harry that there would be 'big trouble' if he let me down. I also pointed out to him that he was very clever with watches and clocks but my 2.C.V6 was ready for the knacker's yard so 'please, please!!! Could he do something'? I also told him that I had passed three spiritualist exams to date on the subject of life after death and that seeing that I had gone to the trouble of studying 'his domain'; the least he could do was to provide me with descent transport.

I thought 'in for a penny, in for a pound' and added that I wanted a new 2.C.V6 as I thought they were a grand, little car; really cute, using hardly any petrol.

Chapter 24

Well, it was late, about 1 o'clock in the morning, having performed my first demonstration at Bolton, without Lee's moral support. I was really chuffed as it went well and they had booked me for the rest of the year.

The junction to the motorway was closed and being hopeless with following directions, I decided to find another way home. I got to Cheetham Hill and the roads were very quiet. In fact, there was no traffic at all; just a cat dashing across the road and a large, white van about 100 yards in front of me. I thought it was strange at the time that its back window was blacked out. Suddenly, it started to reverse towards me at an alarming rate and I thought 'it is not possible' so I quickly swerved to avoid a collision.

Inevitably, there is an almighty bang as it hits my front passenger side. I had crouched as best I could under the dashboard and as the dust settled, I got up with no apparent injuries. I was confronted by three 'rough–looking fellows' who then started balling and shouting at me. After a moment's hesitation as I was very shaken and scared of them, I suddenly thought that I am not having this and shouted back at them that it was their entire fault.

'What were you doing driving backwards?' I said loudly. A coloured guy who looked to be the oldest, about 40 yrs. old, stepped forward and grinned. 'It's not bloody funny' I said and added a few more expletives. He was in the middle of explaining that they had missed their turn-off and was just backing up a couple of streets but didn't know anyone was behind them. 'That's because your windows are blacked out' I replied as they looked at one another.

Suddenly, I realised that I couldn't see properly out of my left eye. My glasses were still perched at the end of my nose as I shouted 'I am blind in one eye'!! The look of horror on their faces was a sight to see (excuse the pun) as I realised that the lens from my glasses had fallen out. I was so relieved that I started to laugh whilst pointing out what had happened. They obviously all had a sense of humour and grinned even more.

The upshot of this was that they offered to take me home as my car was a write-off. So I got into the van, what else could I do?! (No mobile phones in those days). During the course of the journey whilst I sat in the back of the van, the tattooed man explained that it was not their van (surprise, surprise). Apparently, they had borrowed it from their boss and said that if I did not inform the police, they would make sure that somebody's insurance compensated me. Now, I am not daft but I was in no position, at this point in time, to argue with them. Anyway, the next morning, I went to the insurance broker with their details; fully convinced that I was going to be the loser. However, they were as good as their word and I didn't tell the police. I got a courtesy car and my poor, old, yellow 2C.V6 went to the knackers' yard.

I, then, realised what Harry had done. Let's face it, how many cars go backwards?? . My battered, yellow car was unrecognisable so I played it out and got enough money for a 2 yr. old, blue 2C.V6. Now, I did thank Harry with a little proviso that the experience had been somewhat traumatic and the next time I needed something, maybe he could achieve it in a more reasonable manner. About half an hour later, my 'china' clock, stopped and started up again, whilst chiming on the quarter hour instead of the half hour. Something it never did before! I swear to this day that I heard him laughing.

Chapter 25

As I approached my 42nd birthday, there was just me, Tillie and Harry living in the cottage. I moved into the girl's large bedroom; rearranged it having found a lovely, old fashioned, basket chair in a junk shop. As I dozed off that night, I heard this chair creaking. 'It must be Tillie' I thought as she had decided that she liked the two, new, velvet cushions that adorned it. Suddenly, I felt an arm around me, virtually giving me a big hug. Now, cats, to my knowledge do not do this so on goes the lamp but there was nobody there, not even Tillie. The chair creaks again but no more hugs as I am now fully awake. 'It has got to be Harry' I thought to myself and I am not best pleased as I know I will be pondering on this experience for some time and unable to go back to sleep. So, I acknowledged his presence but no response. The next thing that I remembered was the alarm clock, correct time, oddly enough and then it was off to work.

Following a conversation with a work colleague at the hospital about a man named Eric Bray who happened to be an excellent medium and president of Ashton Spiritualist Church, I decided to pay him a visit. I was living in the vain hope that he would be able to enlighten me on Harry's identity as I was now fairly sure that it was not Harry Saunders, having borrowed a magnifying glass and scrutinising his photo until I was nearly cross-eyed.

So, off I set one evening, in my 'Harry Car' and arrived at Ashton Spiritualist Church just in time for the service. I pushed open the large, oak doors and to my dismay, what was once a church of another denomination now was in a poor state with a chap perched up a wooden ladder doing repairs. I asked the chap if Mr Bray was around to which he answered 'No, he is not here' he said in a faint voice way up high at the top of the ladder. 'He is at home 'he said and on further enquiry, he told me it was 'Chester Square' and proceeded to give me directions. So I set off again but sadly, my sense of direction fails me and I was lost. So I pulled up, lit a cigarette and waited for some passer-by who would know where I was. A few moments later, I spotted three people walking towards my car and as soon as they were abreast of me, I asked directions. 'What number, luv?' said the elder of the three men. '21' I responded to which he answered 'who do you want, Eric Bray?' I was startled by his response as he added that he was, indeed, Eric Bray. So with no more ado, the three rather large men squashed into my tiny car and off we set.

His flat in Chester Square was literally 'a stone's throw away'. I followed him down the hall into the lounge, having already said our goodbyes to the other two people.' How can I help you? Sit down and I will put the kettle on' he said as I plonked myself down into a large, shabby chair. No sooner had I sat down when a rather over-weight golden Labrador, who reminded me of Smokey, made numerous attempts to push me off the chair. Eric returned from the kitchen with a brew and a cigarette in his mouth as he said 'You can't sit there, that is Charlie's chair'. So I took the coffee and rearranged myself on his settee. I began to tell him my story and I was extremely careful not to describe Harry in any way. I rambled on about the voice in the garden and the fact that I thought Groomie might have been playing a joke on me as he would often call in for a brew with telephone communication colleagues, during working hours. I even mentioned the spider on the wall above my bed; adding that I do realise even with the best of ears, one can't possibly hear a spider walking up a wall.

When I stopped for breath, I noticed that he was looking at me like a doting father with a broad grin on his face. 'You're a psychic and a medium, luv. Don't worry because there is a guy who looks after you and he is stood right behind you' he said with a bemused expression. I immediately looked round but nobody was there. I gathered my wits; it's a wonder I had any left and asked Eric to describe him. He managed to describe him to a tee; even down to the slightly wavy hair. I was gobsmacked as I asked who he was. Eric said that when the time was right, I would know who he was.

He, then, asked me to demonstrate at his church and to join in his advanced spiritual development class. We made further arrangements to return to the church when the electrics were repaired. I thanked him for his help as we walked to the front door. 'You are lucky with numbers if you are ever short of cash' he said as we parted. I was still none the wiser who Harry was. I remembered my numerous bingo wins; they always came when I needed money. Maybe Harry is a mathematician? And I made a mental note that when I *needed* some cash, not *wanted* it, as Eric had stressed, I would ask Harry. As I drove home, still missing Muffin who used to sit in the front passenger seat (no seatbelts then), I again said to Harry 'please, please let me see that Muffin is OK'.

A few months later, I cannot remember exactly what time of the year it was, but I had just opened the lounge windows, to get rid of the stale nicotine smell. As I stood there gazing out at my pink rambling roses which were in full bloom, I pondered on the fact that how something so beautiful, was so incredibly painful when inadvertently, one brushed up against them. In fact, I had a row with the dustbin man who claimed that every time they picked up the dustbin to empty it, they 'got scratched to death'. My response, I thought, was maybe a little unsympathetic, but true. I told them in no uncertain terms that my dad had fought in World War I when he was just a lad of 17 and had acquired several injuries including being gassed; so what was their problem with a couple of thorns? They didn't empty the bin for a couple of weeks, so I complained to the Council. They eventually returned to continue with this 'hazardous' task and no more was said.

My thoughts were then interrupted by the sound of the porch door although it was closed. It was making a thudding noise. Thinking that I had left the front door open and the draft was responsible; I opened it only to find inside the porch a large German shepherd dog. It was pushing its rear end against the porch door and then suddenly, the dog just disappeared. It was Muffin who, when she was alive, would put her bum against the door to let us know that she wanted to come back into the house after spending a penny. Well, what can I say, Harry, just wait until I tell Eric Bray whose church I had already served. I thanked Harry and again I asked myself the same question: Who are you and why are you looking after me? Of course, I heard nothing, but I did understand that these sightings and messages usually happened when I was not thinking about him. In other words, they appeared to have emerged when my mind was not thinking about anything in particular. So maybe, it is like Eric says: that I am inadvertently tuning in to a different vibration.

This then reminded me of a story that my mother told me about her mother, not about her grandmother Sarah Blackmoor, the witch, but Sarah Fleetwood who, it was said, whilst making the beds in the morning, heard a knock at the front door. She looked out of the window to see her youngest brother standing under the gas lamp and dressed in full army uniform. She gleefully dashed down to open the door only to find that there was nobody there. Sadly, they received a telegram to say that he was killed in action. So is there some genetic trait that survives in some generations? ; Like red hair or a gap in your front teeth. I must admit that it seemed a Fleetwood trait that my mother or any of her three siblings did not seem to inherit except Uncle Arthur with the roaming glass eye. Apparently he told the story of when he was in the trenches of World War I that the enemy Germans attacked and were coming towards them from all directions. Guns were blazing as the soldiers retreated back over the barbed wire, having sustained many casualties who lay fallen on the ground. Miraculously, there was not one single soldier injured or otherwise that his Manchester Fusiliers had fired upon despite the fact that he and other men in his company had seen them fall.

So I deciphered that it must have been an imprint of a battle previously fought; just the same as Elizabeth who apparently was seen in my cottage when the séance was performed. I have often wondered why I had never seen her or had any inkling that her imprint still remained. Maybe Harry had shooed her away as two is company and three is a crowd.

Chapter 26

A short time after that incident, Patsy who was now in her third year at the University of Liverpool, phoned me as she wanted to borrow some money for her amount of the rented house which she shared with five other students. They also owed, between them, for some utility bills. It was the only time that Patsy ever asked for money and like mothers do, I said O.K.

Now, I hadn't got £440 to spare and it was unfortunately, the middle of the month. Borrowing from the bank was out of the question. So recalling what Eric had told me, gradually a picture began to form of myself camping out at the Barcliff Bingo Hall, in order to win that amount. Thinking that this might be a long shot, I asked Harry, reiterating that this was an emergency.

A couple of afternoons later, I was gathering patient notes for Dr Sayed's Wednesday Ward Round when Bill popped his head through the office door. He was a retired police sergeant whom I had previously nursed due to his alcohol problem. The acute ward was always extremely busy and this day 'took the biscuit'. Jean, my ward clerk, who should have gone home at least an hour ago, was frantically trying to obtain 'Methadone' for our very first heroin addict.

The student nurses were all hovering around, hoping that they could come to the ward round. Two male domestics were busily mopping up copious amounts of water as someone had let a sink overflow. 'It must be a full Moon tonight' I thought to myself wearily. Bill doesn't take no for an answer and is oblivious to all the mayhem round him. He continues to proudly inform me that he has got himself a new job as an agent for 'Littlewoods Pools' and would I please give him 50 pence and choose 10 numbers. Now, anything for a quiet life, so I handed it over and chose the girls and my birth dates, plus Jean's who at this stage was tearing her hair out whilst on the phone trying to explain the urgency for this medication.

The two students looked agog when I asked for their birthdays and I now only needed four more. We then used Bill's and then at last, the pharmacist comes in clutching the controlled drug Methadone so I asked him for his birthday too. 'Christmas Day' he replied. Jean hastily grabbed her coat and set off for home (I was wishing that I could follow her). Two more numbers and Bill will leave me in peace so I make one of the students go and ask the domestics for their birthdays. Bill handed me a copy he had written out, obtained my 50 pence and off he went.

The next moment, in comes Dr Sayed; 'Liz! I haven't eaten all day. I have been too busy so can somebody make me some toast'? He says as if I just needed another task on this day of all days!

His toast was then brought into the ward round on a tray, accompanied by the usual coffee and biscuits. Now this student had obviously chosen her correct vocation as it certainly wasn't cooking. The toast was burnt and smothered in butter; not a good thing for a consultant in his fifties who had a heart bypass and would naturally be concerned about cholesterol levels. So without any more ado, I scraped the toast over the hand basin and handed it to him. He looked at me over his spectacles (a mannerism when he was displeased) so I glared at him as, in my opinion, the toast was definitely a paler shade of brown and the butter had all but disappeared. He ate it silently.

The following Monday, having being on days off at the weekend, I was eagerly told that Bill Selby had been in and that I had 'won the pools'. 'Yeah' I said 'and a pink pig has just flown past the office window'. Bill turned up that evening and excitedly told me I had won £500 so with cash to spare, I treated myself and Bill (no alcohol) but to a pair of shoes, then Patsy had her money.

Now, the strangest thing of all was that Bill had written the pharmacist's birthday on my copy correctly at 25 but on the coupon, it was 26 and that is why I had won so much money. Needless to say, I religiously used those numbers for almost a year but I never won as they say 'another sausage'

I could not wait to tell Eric what had happened so, on the Monday evening, I 'popped up' to see him. He was so different to Lee who was tall and slim, a father of two girls with a number of grandchildren. Eric, being bespectacled and rotund, I guess was younger than Lee who was in his 70's. Again, the difference was so apparent for Lee would have responded to my story in a very scientific way, exploring all avenues. Eric, on the other hand, got out his whiskey and two tumblers and just said 'What did I tell you? Thoughts are living things and your Harry will always look after you'.

Charlie, the fat Labrador (too many Bonios) scratched at the door to come in. Eric got up to let him in as was his habit, removed his toupee and scratching his head, sat down again. 'What about reincarnation; Have you given it any thought?' he said so I told him my feelings on the subject.

As the level of Bells whiskey steadily decreased, Eric went on to tell me about his long-term, male partner who had died a few years ago. As I offered my sympathy, he shook his head and with a beaming smile, replied 'he has gone to the spirit world and after he goes, giving him yet another bonio, I am going too'.

Now, if I had not known any better as he was so cheerful, I would have thought that he meant somewhere like 'Disney World'.

Suddenly, I smelled something burning and as my eyes followed my nose only to find the toupee on fire which he had placed too near the ashtray. I grabbed some water and hastily poured it over the smouldering pile as Eric exclaimed 'Bloody hell, Glory be, what am I to do now'? 'Hairdressers' I replied reassuringly.

Sadly, Eric who was a great character is no longer with us as he collapsed shortly after the death of his beloved Labrador. I still, to this day, do services for Ashton Spiritualist Church, although the venue has changed. The old church was pulled down and we are now in a fabricated, single story building but Eric's photograph takes pride of place upon the wall.

Now Margarita, like me, had been one of Eric's fledgling mediums. She was a little taller than me but younger and was married with a daughter called Julie. She also, I recalled, was an animal lover and owned a Dalmatian and a tiny Yorkshire terrier called Bobby. Now, Bobby was a little scamp as he got the big Dalmatian pregnant Now, how he ever managed it, we will never know but as they say 'where there is a will, there is a way' and ended up with a long-haired, spotted dog which she kept.

Sadly, Margarita, too, is no longer with us, dying in her early 50's of too many cigarettes, like me, I guess. The fact that she was 10 stone overweight did not help but she had a lovely face and gorgeous, long, black hair.

Before she passed, we spent a couple of years working together on the spiritualist circuit. We travelled many miles with me driving and her navigating. Needless to say, we lost our way on many occasions and had to ask Harry's help. Now, no disrespect to him but this was not one of his fortes.

We would share the services between us and actually, began to do quite well. We had both learned a great deal regarding the practical side of clairvoyance from Eric. My funniest memory of her was when she banged on the rostrum to demonstrate her feelings and luckily it was Eric's old church. The whole thing came tumbling down, taking her with it into the arms of the congregation. Luckily, no one needed first aid as I would have been useless. I couldn't stop laughing, especially when Eric with his singed toupee, askew on the top of his head, shouting out 'Don't worry, Margarita, it is the woodworms fault'.

Now to be fair to Margarita, her huge bulk did have its advantages. One day, unable to stand it any longer, she barged into a neighbour's house and literally took a German shepherd dog that was being badly beaten. Guess who she phoned? Yes, me! Now despite having said that I was never having another dog, off I went to her house and took the dog home with me. She was so frightened that she urinated all over the back seat of the car. Not being worried as urine is sterile and it was the summer after all, it soon dried, leaving little or no smell. She was a lovely dog and we became, once she began to trust me, great friends. I named her Tara.

Chapter 27

We often walked with Tillie in tow, minus the lead, talking to the trees and animals who no doubt, thought I was quite mad.

There had been no further 'Harry experiences' until one Friday when I was distributing the weekend leave medication (most patients went home on Fridays and returned on Mondays) leaving us with perhaps only five or six people to nurse on this 17 bedded acute ward. So Trevor, myself and an S.E.N (state enrolled nurse) roughly my age, sat in the office, doing a teaching session with two female students. The office was situated at the front of this acute ward with a glass partition, adjacent to a cubicle thus allowing us an excellent view of the ward area.

About half an hour into our session on 'Schizophrenia', Dr Sayed phoned requesting an emergency bed for an elderly, confused lady who he had visited that morning. Having no empty beds, we shuttled around and decided to use the cubicle as a temporary solution until the patient returned from leave. We put all his belongings into the linen cupboard and Trevor placed his vase of red and white carnations in the office. Now, being a superstitious individual, I said to Trevor 'OH, no! These flowers are red and white, somebody will die'. 'Don't be daft, Liz, these have been here for a couple of days' he replied and went on to say that the few young remaining patients were all physically fit and well. I couldn't argue with this logic, so I let the matter drop.

We had just changed the bed linen when she arrived, shouting and screaming as the ambulance men brought her into the ward. As normal procedure, Trevor phoned the S.H.O (Senior House Officer). Now, after qualifying, these doctors do a six month stint in specialities before being deemed capable to practise as a G.P.

Suddenly, everything went quiet so I looked through the office window and noticed that the lady was completely blue. I dashed into the treatment room whilst shouting for Trevor. I grabbed the oxygen and after administering it, her breathing problems were relieved to some extent. Shortly after this, the S.H.O. Dr Roa arrived.

Now Dr Roa had only been on the Unit for a couple of weeks but I and other staff members were already concerned about his capabilities which I had mentioned to the consultant Dr Sayed. 'Give him a chance, Liz; it is his English that is the problem' was his only response but I was not 'a happy bunny'.

After briefly examining her, his diagnosis was 'confusion due to dementia'. So shall I say that a discussion followed between him and me so I informed him that I was contacting the registrar for a second opinion? I bleeped the registrar who arrived about 15 minutes later. Dr Roa was still hanging about and I began to ponder why he was still an S.H.O. He must have been in his early 40's and about 15 years younger than Dr Sayed. 'What had he been doing all his life? I thought to myself and with that he disappeared off the Unit.

The young registrar arrived and after examining her, picked up the phone and requested a bed on the medical unit whilst telling me that he had told Dr Roa to do 'blood gases'. This test involved placing a solution in a syringe to which the patient's blood is added and then sent to the laboratory to ascertain the level of oxygen etc. in the blood.

The registrar was bleeped by another unit and left the ward just as Dr Roa returned to commence the procedure. I sent a student with him into the cubicle and headed back to the office but something was bothering me. I reached over for my cigarettes and in doing so, somehow managed to knock over the vase of flowers. The water was everywhere and tissues were no use, 'Damn it!' I thought as I headed off for a mop.

I have heard it said that in a time of crisis, the whole situation literally magnifies itself before one's very eyes. As I opened the office door to go to the sluice room for the mop, I saw Dr Roa tapping this large syringe, in order to remove air bubbles (this is something we do before we inject a fluid into a patient). 'Oh, Christ'! I thought. He is going to kill her if he injects that fluid and the student sat there, wouldn't know any better. So, I hastily stopped him in his tracks and luckily the patient was not fully conscious as the words I used, definitely belonged in 'Ardwick'. Needless to say, I reported him through the proper channels and Dr Roa was never seen again. Rumour had it that his qualifications were bogus.

Later, when Trevor and I discussed the incident, I wondered how I had not noticed the flowers earlier in the week. Now, most nurses are superstitious and would have separated them. Was it Harry who pointed them out? and did he try to tell me in the office what was going to happen?

When he failed to get through to me, did he knock over the vase of flowers? As I do not know how I managed to be so clumsy.; If I hadn't being going for the mop, I would never had seen what was about to happen.

I felt that this was Harry's plan as sadly, the lady died in the early hours of the morning on the medical ward. Was my mind stretching things too far? as if his plan had failed, she would have died anyway so no real harm done. There again, he succeeded as hopefully Dr Roa (as he called himself) would never be able to go near a patient again and practise his non-existent skills.

Chapter 28

It was a dull, miserable, Sunday afternoon, in late November when the second incident occurred. As Acting Nursing Officer, I was called in to work to resolve a problem regarding one of the students. Having achieved this, I went onto my own unit to document the incident.

As usual, the desk was a mess with a half dozen patient leave files strewn around. As I placed them on the window sill for Jean to file in the morning, something drew my attention to a certain set of male patient notes. It suddenly hit me and I just knew that he was dead (Harry again). Having had a fretful night's sleep, I promptly arrived at 7.30 in the morning and waited till lunchtime, hoping that I was mistaken. Patients are requested to return from weekend leave by lunch but it was not a hard and fast rule and many returned late in the evening.

Not wishing to make a formal request, I contacted a policeman that I knew and asked him (off the record) to go to the chap's house to see if everything was o.k. A couple of hours later, John, the copper, came onto the ward and relayed his story. Apparently, he knocked on the guy's door but got no response. He was just about to leave when something told him to go round the back. So, up the ginnel he went, to find the backyard gate ajar. He went in and tapped on the kitchen window but no response so he gave it a push. It opened so he called out again but still no answer but everything was neat and tidy. He walked towards the stairs and as he was about to call the chap's name, he looked up and saw a body hanging from the ceiling. He was later identified as our patient and the approximate time of death was Sunday afternoon.

Well, news travelled fast and before I knew it, I was inundated with requests for 'readings'. Sandra, my friend and senior staff nurse, took the bookings from the hospital staff. We raised enough money to take the long-stay patients to Southport which was enjoyed by all concerned.

It was shortly after this that Dr Sayed asked for a 'reading'. Feeling that he might have an ulterior motive, I asked Harry to help me out. Senior consultants are 'a law onto themselves 'and he was, by nature, a difficult man.

About 10 minutes into the 'reading', he looked over the top of his spectacles and said 'Liz, this is all mumbo jumbo' and jokingly asked for his money back. I had expected something of this nature so not to be put off; I told him that he was the only one to complain. From this a discussion ensued on my beliefs in the after-life and Harry. This completely opposed his scientific thinking, consequently, he asked for some evidence to support my views. With great confidence that really I did not feel at the time, I agreed, adding that that just because one cannot see, hear or feel something; this does not mean that it does not exist.

The challenge was this; 'To get Harry to locate a fountain pen which he had lost'. Apparently, it was of great sentimental value, being one of a set of three which had belonged to his now deceased father who had been a G.P in Pakistan.

For the next three or four weekly ward rounds, he would make some scathing remarks about his pen not turning up. Then, just as I returned home from an early shift, there was a knock at the front door and Tara started barking as I pondered who it could be. I soon found out as there was an 'Interflora 'delivery man with a beautiful bunch of flowers.

Guess what?! They were from Dr Sayed and the attached card read 'Thank you for finding my pen'. Apparently, he had gone to Prestwich Hospital to do a psychiatric assessment and when announcing himself in reception, he noticed that the clerk was using a pen identical to the one he had lost. When asked, she said 'don't know who it belongs to, someone must have left it, it has been there for a couple of days'. The only conclusion that he could draw, was that someone must have picked it up from another hospital where he had left it, all those weeks ago and they, themselves, had inadvertently left it at the clerk's desk. However, I had another explanation which I put to him. It is called 'An Apport'.

Apport (from the French verb; apporter – to bring)

These objects first need to be dematerialised in order that bricks and mortar prove no obstacle. Then, using 'ectoplasm', they are rematerialized by the spirit world.

Ectoplasm is excreted from a medium... The word 'ectoplasm' (from the Greek; ecto and plasm---externalised substance) was originated by D. Charles Richet, a French professor of physiology, after witnessing it streaming from mediums on numerous occasions. Baron A. Von SchrenckNotzing, a German physician who specialised in psychiatry, spent thirty five years in research and conducted hundreds of séance experiments. Occasionally, he obtained permission to extract portions of ectoplasm for chemical and microscopic analysis.

His chemical findings showed the following;

Colourless, a slightly cloudy fluid (thread), odourless, traces of cell detritus and sputum, whitish deposit, reacted slightly alkaline.

His microscope results showed the following;

Numerous skin discs, some sputum-like bodies, numerous granulates of the mucous membrane, minute particles of flesh, traces of sulphozyansaurem potash, the dried residue weighed 8.60 gr. per litre, 3 gr, ash.

Idioplasmic by nature, ectoplasm is capable of being moulded to manufacture to the equivalent of the human body.

When I had completed giving this 'scientific information', he was lost for words. 'Well done, Harry' I thought to myself; that took the wind out of his sails.

Chapter 29

Time flies so quickly, winter had turned to spring and the summer of '86 was approaching. We had a new S.H.O. on the ward to replace Dr Roa, His name was Tim Willocks, and a 6'3 chap with bright, red hair. I was impressed; in fact we all were as he was excellent in his approach and understanding of the paranoid mind.

We had only one little catastrophe with an elderly, Polish patient, a heavy smoker, who was involved in the gassing of the Jews during World War II. I had mentioned to Tim, (who like most of us, was a smoker) to buy a box of matches as to be sure, the Polish patient would ask him for a light for his cigarette. Evidently, he decided to ignore my advice. Shortly after that, Tim barges into the office with sputum all over his face and his shirt torn. Our Polish friend, as predicted, had asked him for a light so Tim obligingly took his lighter out of his pocket and flicked it. That was when he was attacked because it was a gas lighter which, to a severely paranoid mind, brought back the horrors of the concentration camp gas chambers. So we made a brew and I gave him a box of matches.

The weeks passed by and Tara and I continued to walk in the woods, dawdling to admire the wonders of nature.

There was even fish in the river and the goat remained very unfriendly with his head down and horns ready for the kill. I did ask Harry to get the goat to like us but without success. So he is either unable to communicate with goats or he finds the whole thing so amusing and is doing his shenanigans; knowing him, I think it must be the latter.1

Harry had now taken to switching my new standard lamp, with its old fashioned shade, depicting a hunting scene way back in the 1800's, on and off to attract my attention. So with this and the china clock, I became very aware of his existence and sense of humour. I suspect that he laughed at me fiddling with the plug and I thinking something was wrong with it. I even swopped it with the one in the hairdryer which was fine but the lamp continued to behave in a bizarre way.

Chris, a work colleague, had been talking to a friend of hers who wanted 'a reading'. I was duly impressed when we arrived as there was a tray of nibbles and a bottle of champagne. (So glad, I was not driving!!!).

We had finished the reading and were on our second bottle of champagne when he tells me that he is a sports journalist and would be much more impressed if I could give him the winner of Saturday's Big Race.

Well, with confidence, fuelled by alcohol, I closed my eyes and asked Harry. No small voice and I thought perhaps he doesn't do horses as well as goats. Then, to my utter surprise, I see two large letters which would signify a name.' The horse or the jockey??' he asks and not having a clue, he pulls the list of runners out of a drawer and by the process of elimination; we find that the initials fit both the jockey and the horse he is riding.

I am so pleased with Harry as he has not let me down and it is the first time, I have seen anything when doing the readings as it has always been the 'still, small voice' or a sense/ a feeling of something, up to now.. My sense of elation lasted the whole of two minutes as he said and I quote 'It has no chance of bloody winning; it's a complete outsider'.

Well, Saturday came round fairly quickly and most of the psychiatric unit was glued to the TV set. Medication had been done for the few remaining patients. Everything else could wait, for most of the unit staff, patients, Tim Willocks, the senior nursing officer and even Father Doyle, the catholic priest, had placed their hard earned cash on my winning horse. This was all down to Chris as she told everyone about 'the reading' but omitted the fact that I was drunk!!! I was mortified when Trevor later explained what had happened so I had to put 'my money where my mouth is' and gave Trevor a fiver and off he pops to 'the bookies'.

'There Off' shouts the commentator with loads of horses, all sizes and colours but I do not know which one is 'Harry's horse'. Trevor pipes up that it is right at the back so I close my eyes as I can't stand the suspense; my name will be mud and I am going to blame Harry!!!; As my 'street cred.' will be in bits.

Just as I wishing for the floor to open up and swallow me, there was an almighty roar and cheering from Ward 20, down the corridor. I open my eyes to see Harry's horse neck and neck as they approach the winning post and I think that I will 'wet myself' with excitement. Harry's horse romps home as the clear winner as they pick me up shoulder high and carry me round the ward like some real hero. All I can say is that 'It's not me, its Harry'!!! Trevor collects all the tickets and sets off to the bookies as Chris phones her 'friend' who apparently, according to her is as sick as a parrot. He had not backed the horse or indeed, as she told me later, had not written anything about it in his sports column.

Later, at home that evening, I began to ponder what actually happened. My first question; how did Harry actually know that this horse would win? Is it that there is no past, present and future as we understand It.? If my theory is correct, then everything must be continuous like a spiral. I likened it to a spider in the centre of its web. It would not be able to see the outer circles. Just because we cannot see something, it does not mean that it does not exist.

We live on the earth but fathoms and fathoms under the ocean, lays a different world full of creatures which could not exist in our atmosphere. Is it that Harry had moved on to a different plane but was still part of the spiral and depending on where we are placed on it? This allows us to have a different view, like standing on the summit of a mountain as opposed to the base of it.

The second question being that Harry and I must be on different dimensions but still able to communicate as I actually could see those initials in my mind's eye. This, then brought me to the same old question; 'Who is he? And for that matter, who am I? There must be some answers somewhere but as usual, no Harry; no answers!

With that, I consoled myself that I could buy a nice leather jacket with my winnings.

A few days later, Fr. Doyle popped onto the ward and a discussion commenced about this very same subject. To my surprise, he informed me that there were indeed, different forms of existence, adding that the Lord said 'my house has many mansions'. I, then, asked him what my connection was to Harry. He responded by saying that 'when the time was right, I would know'. I then told him what I believed about past lives and the feeling of perhaps knowing Harry in a past life.

He went on to explain that there had been a number of studies that appeared to prove my theory. At this point, I wondered if Harry had sent him as a spokesman on his behalf. I was just about to brew up when Tim Willocks came into the office and enquired if I could ask Harry for the winner of the 3 o' clock race on next Saturday?

Instinctively, I knew that this was not on Harry's agenda and told him so. 'I am not doing it again' I said as he proceeded to ask Fr. Doyle if he had placed a bet on that horse which had won. A broad grin crossed the priest's face as he went into the ward to bless the catholic patients.

Chapter 30

I could not believe that it had been so long since I visited Stockport Market. As I wondered around the dozens of quaint stalls, adorned with their gaily coloured canvas tops which stretched almost as far as the eye could see. It was raining 'cats and dogs' and one had to 'duck and dive' to avoid getting tangled up in somebody's umbrella spokes or even worse, getting poked in the eye. I walked up and down the uneven stone flags, crossing from time to time the narrow cobbled roads, searching in vain for a leather jacket. The Town Hall clock struck three as if to remind me of past memories and the unexplained incidents when I worked at the Infirmary. I could not believe that it was nine years since Rachel's sad death.

I needed a ciggy so I stood at the side of the pots and pans stall. I lit up and was still thinking of Rachel, unaware the pots and pans man had decided to prod the canvas top of his stall with a broom in order to stop the sagging with the weight of the rain. I got drenched and even the ciggy had gone out. 'So sorry, I did not see you there' he said as he went on to say what a terrible day it was and not good for business. Most of his pots were now full to the brim with rain water as

I shook my umbrella and myself. 'Not to worry,' I said and enquired if there was a place to buy leather jackets?

I followed his directions, hither and tither, down gunnels and alleyways until I finally found a pet shop and then, right at the corner. There it was; a little shop with a tiny window. I pressed my nose almost to the glass because I could not see due to the condensation. So in I went and there, hanging on a rack, was the most lovely leather coat. Sadly, I could not afford it and was left wishing that I should have put £10 on that horse. I consoled myself with the fact that a jacket is much more practical when driving. I had not delved into my savings as Patsy needed a car and I just spent my winnings on a single-breasted, black, leather jacket. I set off home before the town hall clock struck four, bringing all these memories flooding back.

There had been no change in the weather for almost a week. It was 'bucketing down' as I drove onto the motorway, heading for Liverpool Spiritualist Church. After about ten minutes, I heard it; the still small voice; repeating over and over again saying 'Go home' go home'. 'I cannot' I said as there are people waiting to see me demonstrate my mediumship. The sky grew darker and darker as I drove along and again the voice 'Go home' I was now seriously worried and decided to leave the motorway at the next junction and make my way home from Whitefield.

The following morning, I phoned the booking secretary (most churches did not have landlines and mobiles were a rarity) I have to admit that I told a white lie, apologising profusely, saying it was a puncture. I was thinking that if I told her the real reason for not turning up, she would think I was quite neurotic. I, myself, was actually wondering if maybe it was all in my imagination and had some sort of panic attack. However, her response put paid to that. I was gobsmacked! 'Liz' she said 'we were all worried about you as there was a major pile-up on the motorway. Thank God, you are ok'

I guess I will never know if I would have been involved in that accident but one thing I do know that if Margareta and I had not decided to go our separate ways, I may well have ignored Harry for fear of upsetting her. From that day on, I never ignored him, knowing that I could trust him with my life. Maybe he keeps me from serious harm as he couldn't cope with me if I died as I would surely make a bee-line for him.

The weather finally 'bucked up' as I got 'dolled up' in my new leather jacket as I was going with my new gentleman friend to the Bellevue Car Auction. We were searching for a car for Patsy. He knowingly tells me that one has to have a look at them first and then find one we like. He would check it out that it is in reasonable condition. We would then sit on the wooden benches and wait for our lot to come up. After a couple of bids, the white ford was now mine. (I hope he knows what he is about; me of little faith). I did ask Harry but he was not interested. (Perhaps he was not a car mechanic in a past life). More chance of him being a bookie with a snout in the racing stables.

We got up off the bench to collect the car and somehow or other, I do not know how it happened but I caught the sleeve of my jacket on the metal arm at the end of the bench. I was mortified as there was a four inch ragged tear from the cuff almost to the elbow. My brand new jacket was ruined. To top it all, the new car which my friend was driving, broke down on Hyde Road. There we were, stranded by the roadside with the bonnet up as he was fiddling about with the mechanics. Guess what! There was no petrol in it. I tried very hard not to throw a wobbler as I drove to the nearest garage. I managed to get a can of petrol, pour it into the car and off we set home again.

It is easier said than done as I ploughed through the yellow pages and asked colleagues and friends if they knew where I could go to have my leather jacket repaired. After almost an inquisition, I found a small shop in Manchester City Centre; just down the street opposite The Arndale. So I trotted in there, found out what it would cost i.e. £20 as the man hands me a receipt. 'Give us a bell, luv in a couple of weeks and it should be ready'.

I retraced my steps and stopped dead as there in the middle of his window display; was the most gorgeous, long, black, leather coat. I willed myself away from the shop knowing that I might have 'champagne tastes but beer money'.

A fortnight later, I gave him 'a bell' only to be told that his shop had been burgled and my jacket, along with a number of others which were on a rack in the shop, had been stolen only a couple of days ago.

Well, what could I say? As it was not his fault!!! Now before I could utter a single word in response to this bad news, the very, nice man said 'Come down to the shop and you can choose anything to compensate your losses. As quick as a flash, it dawned on me that Harry was yet again, looking after me. So I took a deep breath and asked 'Is that leather coat, next to the handbags in the window, still there'? 'Yes' he said, adding that they did not touch the window display as there was too much lighting but broke in around the back of the shop. The very next day after an early shift, I went and collected the coat which fit me like a glove.

Chapter 31

During the next few months, my mediumship came on leaps and bounds; so much so that I was seeing single numbers on doors, names and pictures in my 'mind's eye' which would slowly evolve from right to left. This process reminded me of the wooden contraption on Blackpool's North Pier, during the 40's and 50's. To operate them, one put a penny in and wound a wooden handle round and round to see naughty pictures of semi-clad ladies or Lily Langtry, a famous silent movie star. There was also Charlie Chaplin and Laurel and Hardy. The faster one wound the handle whilst peering through the lens, the faster the frames moved from scene to scene, to let the story unfold.

This was in the "old days" when everything was black and white. I soon came to realise that the black and white ones Harry showed me were of the past and the coloured ones were either the present or future. So when I acquired a crystal ball to practise my "seeing" skills at first there was only a cloudy, smoky effect to be seen. However, this quickly changed to colours and then to people or objects and symbols.

A pair of shoes for example would mean a wedding whilst the fish swimming around meant deceit. I also realised that I was not meant to know the person's personal business but they themselves appeared to understand what I was saying. If the pictures were at the left of the crystal ball, then they meant the past events. The centre denoted the present whilst the right indicated the future. Might I add that this looking into the crystal is not, in my opinion, mediumship, but I have a psychic ability that does not make contact to the spirit world; having said that, you cannot have one without the other.

I was still basking in the glory of my enhanced development when things took a more serious note. One evening whilst I was writing the patients' notes, that still, small voice "Harry" said "go downstairs to Ward 20". I put down the pen and paper, shouted to Trevor who was watching TV in the lounge with a number of patients that I was leaving 20A and would return shortly. As I rounded the bottom of the stairs, I noted that the broom cupboard door was slightly ajar. So I went to shut it, but it would not budge. I pulled the door open, kicked the metal mop bucket out of the way and was just about to close it when I saw the body of a young man on the floor. "Oh shit", I thought, bent down towards him; no pulse, pupils pinpointed, so I screamed "fire, fire!" as that always made folks come. It was quite a piercing scream, and extremely loud (folks from Ardwick are good at this). Then I got on my hands and knees and commenced CPR. They all came running; even Trevor heard me and left his beloved football game. The lad quickly recovered as I had done a few thumps on his heart area which did the trick. It was obvious to me that was an accidental heroin overdose.

It was a few weeks after that incident that Harry told me to move house. I had no qualms at following his instructions. The only thing was that he didn't inform me where I was supposed to look for a new house. I waited for a couple of days, but no further information was forthcoming. "Well", I thought, "this takes the biscuit". I had no idea what I was supposed to be doing or where I was going.

I had to have a plan of action and it went as follows. My intention was to drive within a radius of about 20 miles from Ashton Hospital as I did not want to travel too far to work in the bad weather. So early one evening, we set off with Tara sitting proudly in the back seat of my little 2.C.V.6. Off we went to the top of Mossley and towards the hills that I could see in the distance. I had decided to fulfil a childhood dream of living in the country. From then on, I followed my nose slowly driving past any "for sale"signs. Sadly, none of them took my fancy.

By now, it was getting quite dark, but there was a full moon to guide us as we began to climb higher and higher on the narrow, winding lanes. Now, a sense of direction has never been one of my strong points. So it was not long before I realised that I was totally lost. Tara was getting fed up and I thought she wanted to spend a penny. We carried on for another couple of miles but not a road sign in sight. Tara definitely wanted to pee pee at this stage. "I will just go another half a mile, or so", I thought, "And then park up."I decided to go up another steep hill, but unfortunately the car stalled as I was in the wrong gear. "I might as well stop here", I thought, "instead of restarting the engine". We got out onto the road; there was not a vehicle or soul in sight. We walked on the road as there was no pavement that I could see. Everything was very dark as there wasn't any street lighting and I didn't know where we were. After about a hundred yards, I was wishing that I had had the sense to buy a property guide; any normal person would have done this or at least browsed through the local papers. My feet in stiletto heels were killing me as Tara trotted on and on as I limped behind her. At last she stopped and did a turd. She was finally getting on with her business.

As I stood patiently waiting for her to finish, I said to Harry, "this is a cock up"as an owl hooted in the distance and the trees which I could hardly see, began to rustle bringing down their first leaves of autumn. It was then as the wind got up and the rain came down with a rattling sound and a distinct smell of a pig farm. I could just make out the pigsty. I noticed a sign as I got nearer. It was swinging to and fro in the wind saying "for sale". It was then that I realised that it wasn't a pigsty, but an empty house, as there were windows and some steps leading up to the front door. We climbed up the broken stone steps and I nearly broke my neck, but eventually peered through the sullied window. The place looked deserted. Luck was with me as I had a pen and a ciggy packet with which to write down the estate agent's phone number.

Well, as the saying goes, "in for a penny, in for a pound". I sold Ivy Cottages and bought this 400 year old, dilapidated house which had been empty for over two years. When Patsy and Julie came to see it, they were mortified and told me in no uncertain terms that "I'd lost the plot". I did not mention Harry for fear of reinforcing their opinion regarding my mental state. What I said was that this house had great potential. They just gave me funny looks and said "do what you want, Mother, you always do", and with that we went to the pub.

On Friday the 13th of May, 1988, Tara, me and Tilly moved in. The builders had not finished replacing a couple of purlins in the loft space and had managed to put their feet through the bedroom ceiling. Tilly had had enough at this stage and disappeared. I searched high and low, eventually locating her up the chimney. After an hour of coaxing her down, she came down covered in soot. One couldn't see her white bits for days. Tara, on the other hand, was in her element. She was romping around in the large back garden which went up four levels onto the moorland. In fact, one couldn't tell where one ended and the other began. I decided that I had to borrow somebody's goat for I was told that they would eat everything and afterwards I could start afresh.

The next step was to install storage heaters as there was no form of heating except for the two fireplaces. Having accomplished that, I set about the bathroom which housed a plastic bath and a WC.

I was in luck as I managed to buy a small cast iron bath and water cistern at an antiques market in Levenshulme. I was thrilled to bits with my Victorian bath which stood on four tiny legs. Unfortunately the plumber and his mate were not so impressed, having had to carry it up the stairs. "I hope you haven't got any woodworm" was their sarcastic remark as they heaved it into position. I bit my tongue as best I could to be nice to them. The pipes were the wrong way around and the taps were too old to change over for fear of breaking them. . I agreed to allow the hot water tap running cold water and vice versa just to keep the peace I told my visitors that it was a foreign bathroom suite, possibly French.

Well, after two weeks of work, I was absolutely shattered. Ivy Cottages was an absolute doddle compared to this, so I decided to get in some decorators to finish the painting and wallpapering. I managed to find a couple of decorators from the 'local rag', hoping that they were not a couple of 'cowboys'. Anyway, they arrived and gave a quote which was reasonable and they seemed fine. The only thing was that they were afraid of Tara so arrangements were made for me and her to be at work.

It was usually quiet on the ward on Sundays and Tara could stay in Dr Sayed's consulting room which was on Ward 20 A. I piled all the furniture in the centre of the lounge but, sadly, not my 'China Clock' which got broken in the removal. I did not really know if Harry had moved in with us as there had been no sign of him and I was beginning to wonder what he was up to.

Thankfully, Fred Oliver, another consultant psychiatrist, was on call that weekend and had not come round mooching as he did not like me or dogs. So we set off home happily after work. As I retrieved my front door key from its hiding place, I could hear Dough, the farmer who was my neighbour and lived about a quarter of a mile up the road, shout to me.

'You have to ring the decorators as they couldn't do the work because you left the dog in the house' he bellowed. 'No, I haven't, we are just coming home now' I responded. 'No' he said 'Tara was barking and growling; I heard her myself' he went on to say. 'Rubbish!' says I. 'It must have been your collie that you heard' and with that, let the matter drop. I was thinking to myself that they must be all mad round here. (Too much inter-breeding, no doubt!!!)

After I had fed Tara, I rang the decorators only to hear the same story. Further arrangements were then made for a couple of days' time when I would be off work. I was really cross having to heave all the furniture back to its original place.

So a few days later, I was humping the furniture around again as the decorators were due to arrive. They seemed friendly but obviously, they did not believe my story about taking Tara to work with me on that day; so I tried a different tack and asked them if they were psychic?. The one carrying a bucket of water from the kitchen, down the three stone steps into the lounge, replied; 'It is funny you should ask that as when I was first married, about twenty-five years ago, we lived in a little, terraced house near Droylsden'. He then went on to tell me his story. Apparently, he woke up one night, in the early hours of the morning, to the sound of horse's hooves. Puzzled as to why mounted police would be roaming the streets at 3am, he got up and peeped through the curtain. He described seeing an old fashioned, black carriage with its lamps glowing in the dark, being drawn by four horses as it rattled by. 'The lamps flickered and died and so did I' he said as the spectre simply disappeared.

Well, his story certainly gave me 'food for thought'. Perhaps Muffin had moved in with us. In hindsight, I would not know one German Sheppard's bark from another and I guess if I heard it, I would assume it was Tara. So I asked Harry to let me know if it was Muffin guarding the house. (Having said that I was still unsure if Harry had moved with us or was still at Ivy Cottages)

My daughter, Patsy, had finished her Bar School exams, thus making her a fully qualified barrister. She came from London one weekend accompanied by her boyfriend, Phil, who apparently worked with bacteria specimens in order to discover new ways of developing vaccines. We got on very well, partly, I think because we had something in common. I liked him so much that I was persuaded by Patsy to part with my pine bedroom suite as a gift as they had bought a small flat in Golders Green. By the time the weekend was over, I had little but a bed and the basket chair left in the bedroom. Not to worry, I would find something from the second-hand shops that would be more in keeping with my bedroom which had very low ceilings, held up by two, old, oak beams.

The basket chair had started to creek again just like it did in Ivy Cottages so I started to get the feeling that Harry had definitely moved in with us. The only other explanation would be that it was Tillie but there were no dirty paw marks or hairs on the chair's cushion. I was too lazy to get up and turn on the light as you could not see anything to check if it was the cat making the chair creek again and again.

So with this in mind, I asked Harry, very nicely, if he could point me in the right direction for a really old wardrobe and dressing table, explaining that I was persuaded to part with my pine. I also asked him if he thought it would be ok to get a boy dog as Tara was missing her doggie friends from the cottages. I went on to explain to him (though I am sure he knew) that it would be a disaster if she got jealous or aggressive; having said that, she showed little interest in our early morning visitor. A vixen which I named 'Ginger' who was very tame, would come and sit within feet of our backdoor step, awaiting her favourite 'Bonio' biscuits which she gently carried off to wherever she lived. So, I had to call her as well as the dog and cat, whenever there were scraps. ('It is nice to share', I would tell them all).

A couple of nurses (friends of a friend) were due to come for a reading one night so I had set out my stall (as they say!) with fancy, smelling candles and my crystal ball which had been sadly lying in a junk shop. I discovered it when I was mooching around for furniture. I bought it, cleaned and polished it and brought it to my bedroom. It looked really great. Time was passing and they still had not arrived so I was hoping that they had not got lost as people and even Patsy and Phil had difficulty finding the place.

Tara started barking so I guessed they were here so I went to the front door only to find them carrying what appeared to be a dead dog. Apparently, they had found it at the side of the road in Stockport; initially, thinking that it was a large tree stump. 'We think it is 'moribund' (dead)' they said but when I checked its front paw, I could definitely feel a pulse. So, into the parlour we go, away from Tara who was becoming mightily inquisitive at this stage. We settled the dog and started the first reading but only got into it for ten minutes when there was an almighty racket as somehow Tara had got into the parlour (she was not daft) and I, consequently, learned that she could open the doors but never closed them. There she was nudging and licking this bedraggled dog who attempted to struggle on to his wobbly feet; only to fall down again as we watched. I, then, did my 'casualty stuff' but could not detect any broken bones, he just remained semi-conscious.

'What are you going to do with him?' they asked. I was just about to respond and say 'I don't bloody know' when it dawned on me that Harry was here and he had answered my question. Before I looked, I knew this dog would be a male. Sadly, there was not much else in his favour as I didn't specify what type of dog I had wanted. (I am sure that Harry had never heard of the famous 'Crufts Dog Show' as this dog would not be let near the place). To all intents and purposes, he looked like a 'Brindle Staffie' but his wobbly legs were very short and he must have been crossed with a 'sausage dog'.

'I will keep him and call him Woody' I said finally because he looked like a lump of wood with legs and a tail. So thanks to Harry, this story had a very happy ending. Tara loved him to bits and Ginger, the fox, who I guessed knew that he would never be able to catch her on his stumpy, little legs, treated him with complete disdain so much so that after a couple of weeks, Woody totally ignored her.

Chapter 32

It was Christmas, 1988 and the girls were visiting me. They seemed genuinely impressed with what I had achieved with the house. Patsy and Phil had bought me a 'Cuckoo clock' as a thank you for the furniture I gave them. This clock has taken pride of place in my living room and I was glad that it was not battery operated so twice daily, I pulled up the pendulums to get the little bird to pop out every half an hour and 'cuckoo'. This sound reminded me of somebody with whooping cough. When I complained, Phil said 'that is a Swedish cuckoo'. (Pull the other one; it's got bells on). About half way through January, this began to stop for no apparent reason. This brought me to the conclusion that it was Harry's doing as he likely missed the 'china clock' and was now making up for lost time. (No pun intended).

For some time, I had felt a strong presence in my home and Woody would often growl and bark at something. I guessed he was also psychic; just like Muffin so I had to explain to him that 'It is only, Uncle Harry!' but he still, on occasions, continued to chase something around the house.

Back at work, I was very cross as Dr Oliver had reported me to Dr Sayed (his senior) about me bringing the dogs to work. There was a very strong discussion about the therapeutic nature of animals with acute psychiatric patients. To give Tim Willocks, the SHO, his due as he strongly supported my stance on the merits of this but Dr Sayed just glared over his spectacles and said they were unhygienic. Well, that was it and I pointed out in no uncertain terms that one of Fred Oliver's patients had urinated all over my ward floor and that this was something that neither Woody nor Tara would dream of doing. Well, Dr Sayed started laughing and replied 'I will tell Fred what you said'. 'Good' I thought to myself.

Anyway, I kept a low profile for a short time as Tara was not lonely anymore as she had Woody for company. So this brings me to the time, one morning, before going to work that I had to take the dogs out the back gate and onto the moor. It was a short walk towards Salt Lane and then back down by Cunnings Corner; then, past Doughy's barn which housed cows and on to the road.

I was just about to put the key in the door when I heard a dog barking from inside the house. I looked round to reassure myself that Tara was with us, for as sure as eggs are eggs, I could hear the deep bark of a German shepherd dog. Woody, at this stage, started barking and scratching at the door in order to see it off. I looked all around us and walked back down the steps but there was not a soul or dog in sight. Feeling totally confused, I went back up the steps and opened the front door only to find complete silence and even Woody had shut up. It was then on reflection, as I brewed up and got a ciggy, that I recalled what the decorators had told me.

So, I jokingly said to Harry 'This two-bed roomed house is getting a little over-crowded; what with you, a cat and two dogs, not to mention Ginger, the fox. I will shortly need to build an extension so you will have to find me more money'.

Chapter 33

I was now beginning to realise that Harry did not make mistakes. No matter how odd his information and instructions appeared to be; there was always a reason. This did not mean that I had no free will as I could always ignore him if I chose to do so; but as yet, I was not a complete idiot. He had always responded to my requests, albeit, in a humorous or illogical fashion as in the wrist watch and clock scenarios. However, I can only thank him from the bottom of my heart for looking after me.

I was still waiting to find out the reason for the move. Despite my many requests for a script on the awaiting events, I was totally left in the dark. In hindsight, I knew that our path is already written and if I had prior knowledge, I would, most certainly, 'cock it up'.

I continued to pester him for his identity but to no avail. I kept looking into past lives for both of us in the hope of finding the answer. One evening, as I was dozing on the settee, I could see myself as a young woman dressed in long skirts. I was standing at an open shuttered window, watching the crowds of people, dressed in a similar mode as me, shouting and cheering. There were large wooden ships, filled with many sailors, some in uniform, and they were hoisting sails and flags high upon the masts.

I turned towards the man who was my lover and ask if we can go down to the shore and see them off? He shakes his head as he moves towards me and guides me on to the balcony so that we both have a better view of these large vessels with their cannons glinting in the bright sunlight; sailing away into the vast ocean to where the sea meets the sky.

The experience was so real that at the earliest opportunity, I was off to the library to ascertain if my dream corresponded with what I believed was 'The Spanish Armada'.

Now, the librarian was a very nice lady but I knew she was having trouble coping with me as I could not use a computer and was constantly requesting her help. As I entered this little place, she tried to smile but it sort of froze on her face whilst I had a broad grin.

Afterwards, I was convinced that I had revisited one of my past lives as the dates in July 1588, almost corresponded. The only problem was that I did not know if I was Spanish or English as the latter could have been cheering when our guns made a direct hit on the Spanish vessels. I was thinking that the sunny weather would be a dead giveaway but apparently, it was a hot sunny day when the Spanish Fleet was first sited on the coast of Cornwall on the 20th July and the battle commenced on the 21st, the next day. I had no idea how long it took them to sail from Spain.

A few weeks later, when I was in that half state of neither being awake or asleep, I suddenly, found myself flying towards the lounge window. I was descending like a bird, having been to wherever; I know not what or who.

Suddenly, I was wide awake and terrified that I was going to physically hit the window and seriously injure myself. The next minute, I am back on my rocking chair, performing an A&E assessment for any sustained injuries. I was so scared that I asked Harry to supply me with a 'Witches Broom' so that I could sit Tillie, who was almost a black cat, on the front of it whilst we shared some of her nine lives. I had noticed that I got a sort of tingling feeling when Harry was around. It coincided with me either talking about him or doing clairvoyance.

One day, I was completely startled when I heard a single word 'Enora' or 'Adora'. I was not sure so I asked him to repeat it but no luck, he had gone. I spend the rest of the evening, trying to figure out what he means by this. I did not have a clue but I was determined to remember it and imprinted it on my brain. After all, there was not lot there so it should be easy, peasy.

Chapter 34

Christmas had come and gone and the girls were fine. I had never seen so much snow as there was here, since I was a little girl in Ardwick. Icicles hung from the windows, gutters and I had to walk the dogs on the road. It was so deep that Woody got stuck in a snow drift and I had to drag him out. His short legs on his long, sturdy body just couldn't cope and he sank like a stone. He was so different to Tara, who pranced over it like a ballerina but there again; she had much more between her ears than him. Even Tillie couldn't go out so I placed a litter tray in the pantry. Being a hygienic nurse, I went on the logic of the more contact with germs, the more resistance. One only had to look at the 'scruffy' kids of Ardwick and I was one of them; they were healthier than their middle-class counterparts.

During one of these days, I was trudging up Grains Road, with the dogs in tow, as I wanted to go for a short walk before it got dark. Suddenly, Harry said 'Go up there' which really surprised me as I would have taken him to be a more 'fine weather spirit'. Anyway, I took this to mean through the car park at the King's Head and up Salt Lane, past the Golf Course. It did not live up to its name as there was no salt, no nothing, full of potholes and completely untreated.

The snow, at this stage, was now going over the top of my wellies and I said to Harry 'This is daft as there is not a soul in sight and even a 4+4 vehicle would struggle to climb this hill'. Another 100 yards, I would definitely be turning back, I thought to myself.

Suddenly, I notice in the distance, a woman struggling to push a buggy whilst trying to carry a toddler in her arm. I hurried towards her as I could see she was very distressed and the baby looked mightily cold.

The story went as follows; she told me that she was a midwife at Oldham Hospital and having finished work and collected the children from the nursery, was forced to abandon her car on Ribbonden Road due to the snow. She thought that she could make the last couple of miles on foot.

By the time I came across her, she was half way home so it was better to carry on than go back. Apparently, she had two dogs locked in the house and they needed letting out and feeding. Well, it was then that I had a brain wave or rather Harry did. I tied the dogs by their leads to the front of the buggy; effectively creating a dog drawn cart, we then, took it in turns to guide the cart and carry the three year old.

We slowly, plodded the last three quarters of a mile, down to Acres Lane, with me silently, asking Harry 'Please, please, don't let the dogs see a rabbit or hare as they will be off with the buggy and baby in tow'.

Having deposited them safely at home, I declined a coffee as I didn't want a dog fight with her two spaniels. They would not stand a chance and I would definitely have blotted my copybook.

By now, it was almost dark but the sky was crystal clear and the whole landscape was illuminated by the whiteness of the snow. It was relatively easy to follow our tracks from the outlying cottages that I did not even know existed. In fact, the whole scenery reminded me of an old fashioned, Christmas card; where people wore muffs and capes, carrying lanterns whilst singing 'Good King Wenslas'. A couple of weeks later, she left a 'thank you' note and a very large box of chocolates.

About one week after scoffing the chocolates which I managed in a couple of days really, Dr Sayed asked if he could have a word with me. 'Heck, what had I done now' I thought as it was not the dogs, they had not peed anywhere and Dr Oliver was on holiday.

I did know that I had a tendency to bend the rules in order to benefit the staff or patients. These rules or 'Red Tape', being a more apt phrase, were made up by well-meaning bureaucrats and government officials, who never worked 'the shop floor'. They have no understanding of running a busy ward. Their decisions are designed purely to support theories. In essence, they get an idea and use statistics to support it, rather than the other way round. In a nutshell, one can do anything to suit oneself by fudging around words and numbers.

As soon as I could, I popped round to his consulting room which was only a 'stone's throw away', across a small parking area which surrounded a grassed plot. I never walked on this plot as it covered the coffins and bones of the poor souls who died as Ashton Hospital which was originally a 'Work House'.

'Well, here I go' I said to myself as I plopped my bum on the patient's leather chair, facing him on the other side of an oak desk. It was cluttered with umpteen pens and scraps of paper and I didn't reckon much with his filing system.

However, I 'smiled sweetly' as he got his 'confidential face on'. He told me that he was going to buy a nursing home and would like me to run it for him.

Well, you could have knocked me down with a feather, especially when he added that he was willing to pay me more than my current salary. So I lit a ciggy (I needed 'thinking time') as his secretary brought in a tray of coffee and biscuits.

'Milk and sugar' she politely asked; 'No, just black and strong' I replied. His expression rapidly changed when I explained to him that working with 'the elderly' was not my forte which is why I ran two acute admission wards. I really loved the organised chaos and unpredictability of working with this cliental.

'Organised'!!!!! He said; 'you are a maverick, so I take it your answer is 'NO'.

Then for some reason or other, I went on to say that there was nothing for the young and that is why, most of them are a 'revolving door' as they stop taking their medication when they feel well. Afterwards, as the symptoms of psychosis resurface, they self-medicate without much success. I lit another cigarette as I thought to myself 'in for a penny, in for a pound' and added that the 'elderly nursing homes' are two-a-penny so why not for 'the young ones'? Well, I could see by his face that he was interested so I added, without engaging brain before mouth, 'We could be partners'! Well, he looked very surprised, gathered his wits (consultants are not used to being told) and responded by asking me 'Have you got the money?' 'No, but I will find it" I said. He looked very sceptical as he put his hand over the desk and the deal was made. Little did he know that there were three of us in this partnership; a silent partner called 'Harry' who I knew was around as I had that tingling feeling as he was touching the top of my head.

It must have been about eight or nine months later, when we found a suitable property which could be converted to suit our requirements. That was when I realised why I had moved house as the properties in Saddleworth had escalated and it was fast becoming 'Yuppie Country'. What I had bought for 'a song' was now very much sought after, allowing me to re-mortgage and pay my share of the business costs.

By Christmas of 1990, we were up and running. I named it Elphine House but Dr Sayed was not impressed, especially when my probation youngsters called themselves 'The Pixie Possies'. Although initially, I worked around 80 hours a week, I loved every minute of it. Tara and Woody viewed it as a second home. The stories I could relate, would fill another book.

Although I was frequently conscious of Harry's presence, there were no further incidents, other than Sandra who had left the hospital to work with me. She was upstairs sorting out one of the bedrooms for an admission, when she felt somebody touch her on the shoulder. She turned around and there was no one there. She was not at all perturbed when she came back down to tell me 'Your mate, Harry is here'.

Over the years, many of the staff and residents had similar experiences but he never did anything to frighten people. In fact, when these incidents were discussed in our 'Therapeutic Meetings', the residents who had these experiences, were very chuffed with my explanation of 'Harry' who lived in another dimension. I guess it made them feel more at home, being in keeping with their psychotic episodes. As one young lad said 'We are all mad here, even you, Liz'!

The only down side was that my mediumship had to be put on the back burner as there were only so many hours in the day. But now, I could afford to travel which was something I had always wanted to do but could never afford it. So I booked myself on a tour of 'Morocco'. No real reason, just that I fancied it and off I set, leaving Sandra and Dr Sayed at the helm.

Chapter 35

On the second day of my ten day tour, I met Jean, a Canadian nurse, who was also travelling solo so we spent the rest of the holiday in each other's company.

On about the sixth day of this schedule, we were to be up before 'the larks sings'. Now, not being a 'morning person', I scrambled on, as best I could, hung-over from the night before. I was hoping that she had saved me a seat on the coach. I plonked myself next to her just as the guide, a pleasant, little fellow who's English was confusing, announced that we were going to 'Chellah'.

We arrived in the mid-morning heat and some of the party, including Jean, declined to climb a steep hill in order to see some graves. Having already fallen in love with the place and not wanting to miss anything, I trailed behind to the top.

The guide pointed to a large flat stone, one of three, whose Arabic writing was almost invisible due to the passage of time. (Not that I could understand it anyway). He proudly said 'there, lays The Black Sultan'. He went on to say that the grave at the side of the Sultan, houses the bones of his favourite woman, Eddouha.

Suddenly, an adrenaline rush came upon me as I said 'Who?' He realised that he had captured my interest because I was thinking if that was the name/word Harry had told me.? I repeat myself as I know that he has trouble, just like I did with him, understanding what was being said due to my colloquial dialect. He repeats her name, 'Eddouha' and that she was a white, captive woman. I must have gone a funny colour under my tan and then he said the oddest thing 'Is that you'? For once in my life, I was speechless; wondering if the man was psychotic. So I moved away and admired the magnificent views which stretched for miles, incorporating the ocean on the horizon and the tiny villages where perhaps Eddouha once strolled.

As soon as I arrived back at the hotel, I scribbled this information on the back page of a book I was reading by Jonathan Kellerman. When the opportunity arose, I headed to the local library but the information was too vague and I got nowhere. Many years later, however, a friend of mine, Noel, an Irishman, happened to say that he speaks Arabic (I laughed my socks off) I mean where do you find an Irishman who speaks Arabic? There were no limits to Harry's talents!

Noel gave the following information which I was seeking. Apparently, Abou el-Hassan was born in 1297 and because of his mother's religion; he became a Moroccan leader in 1333. He died a miserable death in 1351. Now, whether I outlived him, I don't know as we could not find the date of her death but she was called Shans-ed-Douha (Morning Sun) and she was, indeed, a beautiful, white captive woman. Her original name was unknown. Apparently, to pirate people from foreign shores, was not uncommon in those times. She was not his favourite woman but, in fact, his much cherished wife. (I obviously did myself proud and married the man). I shall ignore Noel's riotous laughter and character defamatory remarks before we got this information as I was thought to be a harlot; another debt which he will have to pay in his next life. (I will get him).

That is why we are both buried side by side. So, are the bones of this girl/woman whom I believe to be myself in a past life, a 'ME'? Did I actually stand at my own grave, wondering what I looked like and who originally, was I? Another question that comes to mind is, 'was Harry, The Black Sultan? Surely, this is too much of a coincidence! That is if one believes in coincidences. I do not... Was that guide,' a genetic throwback, psychic medium' and that is why I followed him up that hill?

After puzzling and pondering, I have come to the conclusion, rightly or wrongly, that this is, in fact, so and that I stood at my own grave where my bones turned to dust. Why did I go to Morocco? I do not know. I guess Harry sent me so that I could ascertain the evidence for myself.

This, then, brings me to the thought 'was Harry, the Black Sultan?' meaning that our two souls and spirits, go way back a long time. Surely, in time, I will find out who he is and what all this was about. One thing that I do know, is that he has great affection for me and I know somewhere in my subconscious, that he was once and perhaps, still is, my soulmate. It is said that we are born many men (past lives, deeds and personalities) but we die a single man. What we are is preordained but what we do is 'choice'.

I could have, from the beginning, chosen to ignore his existence or even, follow the norms of society and seek psychiatric help for my 'mental state'. In this day and age, people who see strange things and hear voices are labelled 'psychotic'; but thousands of years ago, witch doctors and Shamans were the norm. Even today in some cultures, they continue to practise their skills and believe me; I have first class evidence of this from when I visited Africa. One can conjure up various types of entities from the elements i.e. fire, earth, water and air in order to practice juju (magic). These of course are not spiritual beings, like Harry, but the basic principles are the same

In African Juju, it is believed that reincarnation is for a specified period and it only ever occurs when there is unresolved conflict which the departed soul left behind on earth. The phenomena of physical form are similar. The departed consciousness returns to earth to complete unfinished business. (Whilst typing this at 9.55pm, Harry has just stopped the cuckoo clock.) I read an article somewhere months ago written by a professor. His theory being that hearing voices, feeling and seeing things, was a genetic "throwback" still retained by some individuals. This was how mankind communicated by thought, language had not been learned. He gave examples of how it aided our survival. We would instinctively know without using any of our five senses when a wild animal was approaching and quickly get out of its way. Who among us have not experienced the feeling of somebody staring at us only to turn around and find out it is correct. Sadly, due to the lack of use, these skills like wisdom, teeth, appendix and vision are changing: EVOLUTION.

For me, his reasoning makes perfect sense. To put it simply, since I have been a teenager, I have realised that any important decisions that I wish to make, I follow my gut "instinct"rather than using logic. If I use the latter, then it usually turns out badly.

Now are these the words of wisdom, or of a fool? Only time will tell. As my memory turns back the pages, I can see that Harry has instigated the writing of this book. Having gone to a school in Ardwick, where pupils were 40 to a class, I spent some of my time "wagging"it. So much so that the school board man was a frequent visitor to my parents' house. This of course was a mistake as my English and composition skills are extremely limited. I was very lucky to pass my 13+. I know now that this was due to Harry as the little knowledge I had acquired seemed to be written on the exam papers. But one pays for one's sins for when I read back some of what I've written, it hardly makes sense because the grammar is so poor.

My reaction to this was very constructive. I had a temper tantrum and asked Harry to find William Shakespeare or the likes of him from "up there"and get him to help me with this little book. Sometimes I feel sorry for Harry as I must drive him bonkers, but low and behold, who comes to my rescue, but Noel the Irishman, who speaks Arabic. Harry must know that there is more than one way of "skinning a cat".

Our paths had crossed way back when we were both nursing. Harry again! As Noel had done spiritual work on the internet, so we were both likeminded people. But unlike me, he has the patience of a saint. I must add he is not saintly; otherwise we would not get on so well. I must drive him demented with my constant questions regarding history and geography because I was trying to place where I had lived my past lives. At least, Harry is having a breather, but for poor

Noel, it is payback time for something he must have done in a past life. So is there ever such a thing as a mistake? I think not, as I would never have ended aspiring to his capabilities. My daughter says, "Mother, can you please come into the 21st century"as I cannot even coordinate a mouse on a computer.

Chapter 36

Well, I must have gotten the travel bug as Claire, a work friend and I decided to go to Ypres. The idea for the trip actually came from Aunt Cissie, whose fiancé, Arthur Metcalfe, was killed there in the 1914-18 War. I could always remember that she would love to visit his grave but to travel in the 50's and 60's been very expensive.

She was in her eighties when she died in the 60's, long after my Uncle Fred, her brother, who only made it to 66 yrs. of age. I went to try and find him and send her love by proxy. It might have been a bit late in my endeavour as I was betting that she was up there with him now but my Dad was also there so I would get some idea of what they all went through.

Claire and I spent the days in and around the preserved trenches where fierce fighting took place. We stood in awe at the German mineshaft as it was in excess of 30 metres deep and to peer down in the darkness helped us to understand what underground warfare on the Messines Ridge was really like for the British and Germans.

We found Arthur Metcalfe's name, Manchester Regiment, on a beautiful, white stone memorial amongst hundreds of other soldier's names. Each surrounded by red poppies. (Lest We Forget Those Who Gave Their Lives).

The three evenings were spent with stuffing ourselves with food and drink. It was so nice to be waited upon, instead of standing at the kitchen sink and cooker as Claire had two children (boys). As the French wine flowed, we were reminiscing and as women do, we got around to the subject of past loves. I told her about Terry Mc. Donagh, my first love, saying that he was older than me and during his National Service, had seen some terrible things during the fighting over the Suez Canal. I went on to tell her about having a big falling out with him, due to my stubborn pride; something in later years I had regretted.

'Hang on a minute' she suddenly said. 'I nursed a guy at Oldham Hospital with that name and the reason I remembered it was that when working with an auxiliary nurse on night duty, this male patient 'kicked off' and this Terry got out of his bed and sorted him out and saved me from harm'. 'What did he look like?' I asked. 'Not very tall' she said. 'Black curly hair, going grey and he would have been a good looking man, apart from that nasty scar across his cheek' she added.

It was then that I realised Harry was at it again, giving me answers to my questions, in the strangest ways. Now, Terry was indeed a good-looking man; his mother, Eileen, being Italian and his father who died when he was small, being Irish.

I hesitated and took a large gulp of my red wine before telling her that on a couple of occasions recently, he had visited me in a dream. Oddly enough, it was in these dreams that we made our peace... The salient point being that in the dreams, he had that scar which she described but when I knew him, he never had.

So there is no point when I drive through Collyhurst, glancing up Naylor Street, where he and his mother once lived. The passing of time has made the area unrecognisable. The old, dilapidated church where I once hopped off the 213 Trolley, opposite Naylor Street, has now disappeared. Also, along with the picture house and Jazz Club where I once got 'legless' on rum and blackcurrant, trying to cure a common cold. I was so ill that Terry had to take me home to his mothers' until I sobered up. As we come to the crossroads in our lives, I wonder if I had followed the straight path and married Terry, rather than choosing the forked one, with its many twists and turns. Would my destination be the same?

Chapter 37

This then brings me on to 1992 and there had been no further 'Harry 'incidents, other than the usual clock stopping to let me know he was still around.

The elderly mother of the farmer, Doughy, up the lane with the Collie dog had died. I could occasionally see her 'imprint', sitting on the garden wall, where I used to stop with the dogs, to pass the time of day.

Ginger, the fox, continued to come for breakfast, dinner and tea. I told her that she was going to get fat but the look of disdain told me that it was of little consequence so that was 'chapter and verse'.

I was thrilled to bits as Julie was expecting and I was going to be a granny; but the downside was that I was getting well past my sell-by date. I would be 50 in April of that year.

Life had its ups and downs as I had to take Tillie to the vet and have her put to sleep (kidney failure). The dogs and I missed her and the house was not the same any more.

I had now acquired a number of non-paying lodgers and something had to be done. The packets of rice, cornflakes and anything else that their little mouths could get hold of were in shreds. I hadn't realised what a good job Tillie did.

Woody did his best to catch these mice but I just ended up with broken crockery everywhere.

So I acquired a cat from a friend of Claire. She was a gorgeous, all white with blue eyes. Contrary to the myth that all white cats are deaf, her hearing was quite acute and within a matter of days, my unwanted guests had been evicted. I christened her 'Honey', in contrast with her nature, as Woody got a deep scratch across his face.

So now, he pretended that he could not see, by gazing into space every time she brushed past him, purring loudly. She also had a go at Ginger, the fox but she met her match there. I guess they came to some sort of agreement as when Ginger visited us for her daily rations; Honey would sit on the flat roof of the extension, just above the back door and growl loudly. Tara, on the other hand, took it all in her stride and ignored it all.

Chapter 38

I went to Egypt with Ali (Dr Sayed) to celebrate my 50th birthday. We stayed at a posh hotel in the centre of Cairo (he was paying). We were half way through our week's holiday, having visited the Valley of the Kings, sailed the Nile and been to the museum to see King Tut's treasure that was once alongside his mummified body, ready for the next life. I, gleefully, pointed out to Ali that I was not the only one to believe that when you are dead, you are not dead.

My birthday arrived and Ali gave me a beautiful, gold pendant for good luck. I was wearing it round my neck when we set off to explore The Pyramids. I was absolutely fascinated as I went from tomb to tomb, almost at times, on my hands and knees and visualised how the pharaohs lived and died, centuries ago. Ali stayed out in the sweltering heat saying that he was claustrophobic or perhaps, he was just trying to get a tan.

We arrived back at the hotel early evening, feeling worn out. As we ascend in the lift with its large, gilt framed mirror, I looked at my bedraggled image with my mascara all smudged and resembling a panda. There was something wrong; I had lost my gold pendant. I became very upset as I only had it for 24 hours and now, it was gone! That was not very lucky, was it?

Ali, kindly commiserated with me and said he would get another one. 'I don't want another one, I want that one' I said, stifling back the tears. It was then that I had a brilliant idea so I asked Harry to pop into the pyramids as I must have lost it there when I was crawling about, and bring it back to me. The look on Ali, s face as I was talking to Harry, said it all but not a word passes his lips. He just raided the minibar in our room, instead. I had noticed that in times of stress, he would prop himself up with alcohol.

Well, after a sumptuous dinner, we retired for the night. The next thing I knew was Ali shaking me frantically, in the early hours of the morning. I was wondering if the hotel was on fire as I was still half asleep. As I gathered my wits and tried to understand what he was gibbering on about, I could see that he was waving my locket in his hand. So I took it from his grasp and carefully, fastened it round my neck as I thanked Harry for his very kindly deed.

Ali couldn't settle and I suspected that he was going to raid the minibar again, if there was anything left. I had no chance of going back to sleep so I patiently listened to his story. Apparently, he turned on his bedside lamp and got up in order to go to the bathroom. On his return, after spending a penny, he saw something glittering on the sheet in the centre of the bed; it was my lucky pendant. That was when he lost the plot as he knew damn well (as he put it) that when he retired to bed, it was not there. 'How could it have got there?' he said, looking rather pale. The maid had changed the bed linen when we were out so it was a mystery, indeed. He was so lathered up at this stage that I suggested he have a brandy whilst I explained what had happened. This turned out to be like talking to somebody with learning disabilities. I kept reiterating that it was 'an apport', just like his pen at the hospital.

I looked at the clock, it was 3am as I poured myself a large gin and tonic, knowing full well that Harry was, at this moment, laughing his socks off and that was why he placed the pendant in Ali's bed, rather than mine.

When we get back to work, Ali was still going on about the pendant and I was still laughing. I suppose it is really difficult for a psychiatrist to comprehend what happened. Well, as I keep repeating 'There are more things to Heaven and Earth, than logic and science, for the Lord says; my house has many mansions'.

I could not believe how the months had flown. Julie delivered a baby on the 26th November and I was thrilled to bits. She was a 6lbs 6 ounces and an absolutely beautiful baby girl. I don't remember about 'Mother Care' existing when Patsy and Julie were small but I, happily, spent a fortune there on Joely, my first grandchild.

Chapter 39

I had been to see the vet with Tara on two occasions as I knew there was something wrong but I could just not put my finger on it. They repeated, yet again, that it was her diet which was causing her weight loss. I just wished that the vet that I had used for years had not retired. 'Diet, my foot'!! so I gave them 'a piece of my mind' and took Tara to the expensive animal hospital. She was diagnosed with lung cancer which was confirmed a couple of hours later by X-ray. I had no alternative but to have her put to sleep. I cried buckets of tears but at least it was money well spent as it was diagnosed before she suffered too much.

So, now, there was only me, Woody, Honey and of course, our 'Ginger'. The lads at Elphine House reckoned that we should get another dog so it was not surprising when Ronnie came and told me that a junkie in Penny Meadow (a rough area of Ashton) was trying to sell this poor dog for a tenner as she needed 'a fix'. 'Do something, Liz' he pleaded. 'For the dog or the junkie'? I asked curiously. 'The dog' he replied as 'She is a cow'.

So I gave Ronnie a tenner and within an hour, he was back with this dog which looked a lot like Tara with black saddle and pointed ears. We named her 'Ivy' after Ronnie's' granny who had recently passed away. I was a bit dubious about the name, for I wondered if his granny would approve, but he reassured me that she would as she had loved dogs. So Ivy, it was then. I guess Harry had sent her via Ronnie, for she turned out to be a 'cracking dog'. An incident, a few months later, proved that this was so.

With thirteen under 25 yr.old residents living together, one comes to expect discord and strife; usually about the most trivial things. This time it was different as it was over a girl. My advice to staff had always been, to let them sort it out for themselves otherwise there was no closure and the animosity carries on.

The fight in the kitchen got out of hand when one of the lads grabbed a carving knife. Now whether he would have used it, Steve and I couldn't tell. The other lad was pinned against the large freezer so in we go, with arms and legs flying around and then there is an almighty screech. Ivy has got the boy wielding the knife by the arm and Steve seizes the opportunity to grab the knife just as Ivy loosens her grip on the sleeve of his sweater. Steve floors him and at this point, Woody joins into the fray and bites Steve on the leg. Well the air was blue!!! And all I can say in Woody's defence is that he was never right in the head since he stole and ate a piece of cannabis resin from Tom's bedroom. Anyway, all's well that ends well and peace returned and I was hoping that it would stay that way. As for the young lady in question, she decided that she did not fancy either of them and paired off with Tom. I can't say I blame her, for he was a tall, handsome half-caste lad with lovely blue eyes.

My Aunt Cissie used to say 'wait until you are twenty- one, Beth and your life will fly by'. 'By gum' she was right; another year had already passed by. Ali's attitude had changed since the pendant episode in Egypt. So much so that he actually encouraged these debates on reincarnation and the afterlife.

One evening, over a bottle of wine and a take-away (Indian, of course), he was listening to me jabbering on about past lives. I got to the one about the old lady who I now believed lived in Wales whereby she waited for years for her husband to return from the Indian Uprising which ended in 1858. He got up from the settee, got another bottle of wine from the kitchen and then said 'You are wrong. Liz, those uniforms were not blue but red. Trust me, I am an educated man'. I guess that was when Harry joined in as like me, he doesn't take kindly to being contradicted when he knows he is right. It was then that it hit me or rather Harry told me that Ali was the man in the blue uniform. So I said it out loud. 'Prove it' he said. So I asked Harry, 'Because of the big scar on your leg; that is what Harry tells me' I said proudly. Well, he gulped down a full glass of wine and said 'How the hell did you know that?' I didn't; Harry had just told me. My confidence was growing now so I told him 'that is why you are a Pakistani because that is where you died. You have returned now as you have unfinished business. So to do this, you need to climb the social ladder and be posh'.

Of course now it was bugging me about the colour of the uniforms as I definitely could see 'blue'. With the help of one of the librarians, we searched the historical uniforms section but it appeared that Ali was right, they were red. Apparently, only French officers wore blue. Silently, I asked Harry to help me; after all, I didn't want to be thrown out of the library. A few minutes later, the other librarian saunters up and joins in the search, as I am adamant that the British soldiers wore blue uniforms. 'I know' she said; 'I will phone my cousin as he is an authority on historical uniforms'.

Attentively, we wait and it can be really irritating when you can only hear one side of a telephone conversation. She hung up the phone and of course, Harry was right as apparently, English foot soldiers wore blue and the rest wore red. I almost jumped for joy but I restrained myself. I would most likely need to go there again and did not wish to be barred like the 'hoodies 'are. Why is it, that society is moulded on how somebody dresses? Are not the youngsters just following fashion? ; Just like I did when I was a teenager going out in the most ridiculous clothing imaginable.

Chapter 40

One day, Harry was telling me that something was wrong with one of the dogs but the problem was that I did not know which one. Anyway, I asked around for a decent vet and was told that there was a cattle vet in Uppermill named Tait. By this time, I had decided that it was Ivy as she was limping and Woody appeared fine.

Again, I had to choose my words carefully as Mr Tait was asking why I wanted her examined. I could hardly say 'For the life of me, I don't know. Harry up there told me'; so I go on about her leg. His response was that there was nothing wrong with the dog but only a pulled leg muscle which an injection of steroids would sort out. Feeling rather silly, home I take her and thought that at least he was not a rip-off merchant, like so many others.

The following Sunday afternoon I was at Elphine House when one of the lads rushed in and said 'Come and have a look at Woody, Liz'. 'Oh my God' I said as I found Woody lying on the hearth rug and literally swollen up like a balloon. So I contacted the emergency number and Mr Tait answered. I told him that I thought my dog was dying and he was very short with me saying that 'I told you there is nothing wrong with your dog'. So now I am worried and upset, consequently I forget about choosing my words and blurted out about Harry. 'What are you talking about, it is a bloody Sunday? he responded.' 'I brought the wrong dog to see you. I have two and I got my message from Harry mixed up' I said. It was then that I think he decided to humour me and said he would come from Holmfirth to the Uppermill surgery at 4 o'clock.

Actually, he was a brilliant vet as he took a long time with Woody and finally said that 'His liver has packed up'. Over the next few days he tried a number of treatments but to no avail. Apparently Woody was fairly old so I had no alternative but to have him sadly put to sleep.

I realised later when I was talking to Harry about the mix-up that I had 'jumped the gun' because Ivy was limping and I had used my logic, yet again. I made a solemn promise to throw it out the window. I guess Harry was trying to teach me a lesson, for one learns best from ones' mistakes and what was transpiring, defied understanding.

We were all missing Woody as he was such a character so I decided to get another dog from one of the animal rescue centres. I phoned around but none of them seemed to have any German Sheppard consequently, I asked Harry to find me one.

A couple of weeks later, I was up on the moors with Ivy who has many doggy friends as we often meet the 'dog fraternity' as I call them. The men and women look like their animals and were in all shapes and sizes from toy- poodles to a couple of Rottweiler. I must have looked like Ivy as she was not a pedigree dog but there again, I am also a mongrel.

Everybody had wondered what had happened to Woody and a chap asked me if I would like a lurcher which had been rescued by the R.S.P.C.A. We went for a look and needless to say, the dog came with us. He was about two years old with a lovely golden coat and looked just like a greyhound. Apparently, lurchers were originally bred by the gypsies using a greyhound and any other working dog; that is why they all look very different. Caine, as I named him, settled into our routine with ease as he was such a placid dog, spending his time on the moors chasing hares and rabbits when we were out. Thankfully, he never managed to catch them and they always seemed to outwit him. Like Honey, who sorted him out in about half an hour as he was not very brave, deciding as far as she was concerned, he would leave well enough alone.

Well, I was not best pleased with Harry although it was partly my fault as I didn't cancel my request for a German Sheppard. I should have known by now that he doesn't hurry himself and I guess there is no concept of time where he lives.

Well, about five or six days after I acquired Caine, John O' Connor returned to Elphine House, having been to the doctors to collect his medication, with a bedraggled German Sheppard attached to a piece of string. The poor thing was very thin and covered in fleas so I told John to get it out of the house before we were all covered in lice. Reluctantly, he does this but the dog just stayed outside the front door for hours whilst attempting to get in at every opportunity. Considering that people were coming and going all the time, this was easy for him. John was asking why we could not keep him and then Margo chips in and says 'Look at the state of him, Liz; he is far better with us'. Well, I couldn't argue with that so in he comes and we put him straight to the bath with John and Tom doing the necessary. I really don't know who was the wettest, them or the dog as there were pools of water all over the bathroom floor and the towels were filthy.

The residents had a meeting to decide what to name him and came up with 'Rocky'. Unfortunately, I had overlooked something as how could Ivy, Caine and Rocky Roberts as he was humorously called, all fit into my little 2C.V.6; unless one dog sat in the front passenger seat. This then led me into trouble with the police who kindly informed me that it was illegal. I knew most of the police as I had spent numerous hours in Ashton Police station extricating one or other of the residents from the cells, usually for petty crimes. I think mine and Steve's anger were more of a deterrent than the cells themselves for I could 'kick off' good style.

Ali Sayed was not impressed, saying whilst looking over his spectacles in his disapproving manner that I would end up in the cells like some of my residents and I was supposed to be a role model. Well what could I say so I replied 'you are right, Ali' this always put him in a good mood, for he loves being told that. I then, added that if he did not want me in prison, he would have to buy me a bigger car. The smug smile soon left his face as it always did when one mentioned money. Shortly afterwards, I was the proud owner of a brand new white Fox Polo with a dog grill. Ali, after all, is not 'a bad old stick'.

Chapter 41

I could not believe that a quarter of a century had passed since my friend; Harry, had commenced his journey into the other world but when I looked into the mirror, this was quite apparent. My hair was going grey and my 'bits of string' were dropping off

My other friend, Harry, I guess still just looks the same as when I first saw him all those years ago. Needless to say, I still do not know who he is or what this was all about. Nothing so far whilst writing this book has established any clue. Maybe it is me and I am a bit thick but I will continue to plod on, for something deep inside me tells me that when the time is right, all will be revealed.

One day, Harry told me that there was something wrong with Honey so I set off to the vets. At least, I could not make the same mistake as I did with the dogs as I have only one cat. So in I trot and tell Mr Tait that there is something wrong with her. I really don't think that he was best pleased to see me as I cannot, yet again, be specific but my confidence in myself and Harry had grown leaps and bounds. I just insisted that he do 'her bloods'. 'Well, it is your money you are wasting' he says and proceeds to shave a small patch of fur from her front paw. Honey was growling and struggling and it was a job to keep her still whilst he put the needle in her veins to take blood.

Within twenty four hours, he phoned me. His manner was different this time as he informs me that Honey has AIDS and will have to be put to sleep. He goes on to say that AIDS is not uncommon in cats as it is carried by rats. The moorland with its rivers and streams is a haven for most of Nature's creatures. He then says 'How did you know?' well this was the tricky part as I really had no logical explanation and answered him thus.

It is said that as one new life comes into the world, then another soul is taken. Ivy had suffered with emphysema (lung disease) for a number of years and her condition was greatly affecting her quality of life. So I made the decision to have her put to sleep, Dying, I reason is part of life and at the end of day, it comes to all of us. By the time I go and if I have not found out who Harry is, I will be up there searching for him.

Later, I eventually acquired a long-haired ginger/ white cat who seemed pregnant by the looks of her. Well, I was right and ended up with four kittens, two boys and two girls. She was an absolutely lovely mum and it was fascinating to watch her and them as they grew into mischievous, little devils that climbed up the walls and curtains, totally unafraid of Rocky and Caine.

Keith, a friend of mine, adopted two whilst I kept the others. One I called Cindy with a miss-match of shades and the runt of the litter. Her brother, a short haired, common garden, black and white tom-cat, I named Cassy; with mother being called Sparky.

I pondered on what Mr Tait said when he questioned how I knew about Honey's illness. Surely, it is preposterous that I cannot answer the question. Sadly, my mentor Lee Hadfield had passed away although I know from past experience that he would be in the same predicament; at least we could have debated this puzzle, yet again.

So I decided that I was going to form a self-help workshop for myself and buy some books as somewhere lays the answer. I was hoping that Harry would direct me to the books in question, having told him that it was the least he could do; having got me into this situation with little or no understanding of why or what I was actually doing. Time and time again, I asked him for a 'script' but no, he just laughed or apported the top of my little multi- coloured pot that I brought from Spain.

Well, I bought two books from a second-hand bookshop as the likes of W.H.Smith did not have anything in their stock that grabbed me. It was funny really how I found the shop up a back alley in Manchester where I had gone, one afternoon, to visit a friend in Manchester Royal Infirmary.

The first book that I set out to read was a great, thick, heavy, cumbersome thing which any weightlifter would be proud of. It was published in 1946 and would take me forever to read and digest. It was probably Harry's way of keeping me quiet and stop mithering him. The second which I have, so far, not attempted to read was a little, ditty thing on reincarnation. I was best pleased by the time I got up to page 29 as, there was only another 300 pages to go and I thought I had found some answers that neither Lee or Eric Bray ever came up with.

Chapter 42

The great historical figure, Plutarch (born; 47 AD.) held that the human soul had a natural faculty for divination adding that it must be exercised in favourable times and in favourable bodily states. He described the daemon (meaning a demigod and not evil) of Socrates who was gifted with precognitive perception. Socrates left no writings and his teachings and personality is preserved through the works of Plato, the most influential historian of all philosophers.

Plutarch described the daemon of Socrates as an intelligent light which resonated with Socrates because of his inner light (like attracts like). Plutarch viewed such spirits as mediators between God and Man.

One of the fathers of medicine, Galen, (born; 129 AD.) began to study philosophy but turned to medicine at the age of seventeen because of a dream his father had. He introduced many medical practises and left about twenty volumes of medical treatises, averaging one thousand pages each.

If one attempts to take an impartial philosophic stance to the evidence inquiring into the nature of 'fate'; then what use are predictions if the foretold events cannot be changed? How does free will fit into this picture or is it that we exercise an amount of free will but cannot change fate?

It seems to me that the free will part is ones' own response to fate but in order to try and understand what exactly is happening between Harry and me, then, I must use Ptolemy (110-151 AD.). His theory which is well substantiated on the basis of existing, scientific evidence and later known as Occam's razor which states that one should always use the simplest hypothesis that is consistent with the facts which I shall now list;

1. Harry can communicate with me.

2. I can communicate with him.

3. So he must be an intelligent, reasoning, humorous spirit (demigod).

4. Occasionally, I get confused i.e. got the wrong dog that was ill.

5. The information which I receive from him is, to say the least, very useful.

6. But miscommunication can happen in 'normal' conversations so I should be more attentive.

So my conclusion to the aforementioned facts is this; that Harry must just be in another place (what is above so is below). I think it says this in the Bible.

I am going to liken it to talking to Noel who spends a lot of time in Turkey (just a different place) but that costs money so Harry and I may cause British Telecom (BT) shares to take a nose dive.

Well, that wasn't difficult but it still does not answer the question of 'why' or for 'what'. Unlike when Noel and I phone one another, we state our reason, so surely; Harry is paving the way for something. I wish I knew how long he had been 'dead' or shall I say, in the other place. I, also, reason that as in the African Juju state that he must have unfinished business but what? I need to get more facts but as I haven't got any so I will have to wait. All I can liken this too, is when Noel and I are both drunk, we never get to the source.

Chapter 43

The Millennium came and went but nothing of any interest happened except that Harry appeared to have taken up permanent residence here.

Ali would be seventy in May; consequently, he would have to retire from the N.H.S. so he wanted to sell Elphine House. This was fine by me as I had worked a decade for myself and the Probation Services and to be honest, I, myself, was not getting any younger. I would be able to claim my state pension in less than two years, the thought of which really cheered me up (I don't think).

The other thing being that Harry kept putting the idea in my head of writing a book about him and me. This, as I told him, was a bit daft but I continued to ponder on the idea. After all, I, once, I had decorated my house and done all the things that one doesn't do when working such as cleaning under the beds, blitzing the large garden etc. so surely, I would be bored after retiring.

On the 18th December, 2002, our Patsy gave birth to a baby girl whom she christened Anna so now, I was a granny again.

Surprisingly, we sold the business very quickly so now, I was a free agent and spent a lot of time in London. This allowed Patsy to carry on with her career as a barrister whilst John, her partner, was working in Ireland. I decided that Anna looked like me which, frankly, did not go down too well so I just laughed it off and continued to wind them up.

Ginger, the fox, had disappeared as I was away a lot but something told me that she was dead as there was no response at all when I called her name; so that was another animal for Harry to look after for me. I am keeping count and will check when I go there.

One Thursday morning towards the end of June, 2003, I still recall, vividly, to this day. Having now retired, I had decorated, cleaned under the beds and even waxed/polished my second hand furniture. The garden, which had never received so much attention in 'donkeys' years' now had a herb garden; not that I would ever use any apart from the mint and rhubarb. So I asked my friend, Joan, who always fed my cats when I was away, if she would like some? 'Rhubarb would be nice' she replied so out we go with the dogs in tow. Sadly, I just realised that she was one of nature's fastidious creatures, for when she saw Rocky cocking his leg up on it, she threw 'a wobbler'. Despite my assertions that urine was sterile, she flatly refused to take anything from my organic garden,

Later, that same day, when I was having a good grin to myself regarding Rocky's misdemeanour, Harry suddenly came. The clarity and urgency of his instructions, quite took 'the wind out of my sails' and I was grinning no more. He insisted that I get a dog to which I replied 'Another one'; this makes no sense at all!!' He persisted, despite my arguments regarding the practicalities; what with three dogs, plus the expense, vet fees and kennels which were £15 per day. This dialogue carried on until the early hours of Friday morning when I reluctantly agreed. I recalled the time when I had popped into the off license for a packet of ciggys whilst on my way to do a demonstration at a spiritualist church. Harry told me to lock the car but I ignored him as the shop was empty and would only be a few minutes. When I arrived at my destination and took off my driving shoes, I found only a single, best shoe which had cost me £50. It then dawned on me that the kids playing outside had nicked one for a joke. I never did find that shoe.

So from the theories of one's mistakes, the best lessons are learnt. I phoned Manchester Dogs Home as Harry had told me and I inquired if they had an Alsatian or similar bitch (no extra peeing up my rhubarb and mint for me).

Well, their answer cramped my style, as they had two bitches. Saturday morning came so we set off for the dog's home with both Caine and Rocky in tow as I reckoned that they would also have to accept her into their home. We were stopped at a set of traffic lights in Harperhey and ready to turn right when suddenly, I had a vision. I saw a large, black dog's head with the most enormous pointed ears and Harry saying 'Name her Bess'. The traffic light must have changed to green as there were impatient drivers behind me, sounding their horns. I responded in the same fashion, turned right and parked up at the dog's home.

A very nice lady directed me to the pens which housed numerous, homeless animals. I only got to the second pen where I could see along with many others, a large, completely black dog with big pointed ears and a long, bushy tail. So I trotted back to the reception desk and asked the lady to get this dog so that I could introduce her to Caine and Rocky.

'Are you sure? You have not really had a proper look' she said, looking bewildered. So here we were again with the tricky bit; what do I say? If I tell the truth, she will probably report me to the R.S.P.C.A. as being quite mad and not fit to own animals. 'I dreamt about her!' I said. 'How do you know that she is a bitch?' she said, quizzing me. '20/20 vision' I piped up confidently.

When I returned from the car park with the dogs, I found her whispering in the corner with her colleagues. Now, I reckoned that with the appearance of my two, happy dogs, it would confirm, at least, my love of animals if not my sanity. Introductions went well even if Caine was trying to make babies with her so I paid my money. I was accompanied to my car by three staff which I thought was a bit odd as they were very busy at the home. 'Why three people and not one? I thought to myself as they brought Bess out in her brand new collar and lead. They insisted that I take home loads of dog food though I already explained that I did not require it; however, I became distracted when Bess got her head stuck in the dog grill so we got it sorted and home we went.

One pleasant, Sunday afternoon, we set off for our daily walkies with Bess who had been with us for a month now. We went up the hill which was almost vertical, around 'Cunnings Corner' and across a track into some fields where the terrain dramatically sloped so that the four foot stone wall, at the top of the track, was now about eight feet high. There was not a soul in sight as we headed towards the valley. The birds were singing and it felt good to be alive. Caine spotted some rabbits and disappeared. I did not worry as he was too old and slow to catch them. Rocky toddled off followed by Bess towards the stream. It was then that I spotted a flock of sheep and called Bess back as I wasn't sure how she would react to them. I did not want an angry farmer brandishing a shot gun so I put her on the lead.

Suddenly, I could see a man in his fifties about 100 yards away, walking slowly towards me. 'Can you tell me where the pub is that does a mean meal?' he shouted out. Well, I thought to myself that it must be The Rams Head. So I was just about to direct him towards the pub when, suddenly, the hairs on the back of my neck 'stood up' and something was saying 'Do not turn your back on him'. His pace quickened as he repeated the question and I thought he must be daft or something when suddenly, he started 'legging' it towards me with a menacing look. 'Oh, shit' I thought but he never got any further than the length of Bess' lead. She lunged at him and kicked off big style, frothing at the mouth as she dragged me towards him. She was now, standing up on her hind legs, totally vicious and completely out of control. Shocked and trembling, he turned on his tail and quickly fled with me being dragged in hot pursuit by Bess. He made it through the gap in the wall, jumped into his car and took off at high speed before I could get more than two digits of his registration number. God, I needed a ciggy but didn't have any with me as Bess, now, stood quietly and happily wagging her tail.

By this time, Caine and Rocky had ambled back and were totally oblivious to what had happened. I was still a bit shaken and was thanking my lucky stars that Bess was near at hand as Caine would have run a mile and Rocky, bless him, would have done his best to protect me even though he was now doddery on his back legs. I debated with myself about phoning the police but at the end of the day, what could I say. I only had two digits of the registration number and did not know the maker of the car. All I knew was that it was a bluey/green colour and that would be of no help considering I was colour- blind.

About 18 months later, I was doing a demonstration at Hadfield Spiritualist Church and was relating the story of Bess and how Harry had made me acquire her. Shortly after the service, a lady from the congregation requested to have 'a word' with me. So into the Meditation Room we went and she related her story. She told me that the police had just arrested a man in his fifties who had been targeting women on various moors around Yorkshire, for a number of years. Apparently, she had just seen it on the TV programme 'Crime Watch' and his crimes involved raping them and leaving one lady so severely injured that she almost died.

Of course, I tuned into 'Crime Watch' when I got home and it did, indeed, verify her story. Unfortunately, there was no photograph of him or details of his car but just stated that for a period of about five years, he had raped a number of women who had been walking their dogs on 'The Moors' of Yorkshire. He had been now arrested and charged.

St. Augustine (354-430 AD) fervently believed that' guardian spirits would watch over and guard us with great care and diligence in all places and at all hours, assisting and providing for our necessities with solicitudes'.

'So is it then what Fate ordains, we cannot change?' By using my free will and listening to Harry, trusting and believing in him (which is called 'Faith', it has no rhyme, reason or logic) I bought Bess and consequently, changed the outcome of my fate.

However, I was still left with the ongoing question 'Who was he and why was he looking after and protecting me? I did not follow any religious beliefs and could hardly be considered 'saintly'. If the truth be known, quite the opposite! So if my reasoning was correct, then this relationship between us must be fated for something but 'What?' Despite my constant requests for a 'script', none was forthcoming but we had moved on as he now told me, telepathically, that 'It was for me to know and you to learn'; needless to say, that statement did not go down too well with me.

Chapter 44

I felt like a little child who had a bossy teacher.' Teacher, teacher, the bells are ringing' It was then that I could see for only a second or two, a bird as black as Bess which went tweet, tweet and simply disappeared.

Could it be or was I completely mad? ; Our Mr Teasdale who sang whilst playing the piano 'Make my bed and light the light, bye, bye, blackbird'. As I sat in my rocking chair, I was completely gobsmacked. The tweet, tweet sound which I heard was not a bird outside in the garden but emanated from within the room. So Harry must have done it!

I needed a photograph of Mr Teasdale which I had not got, to see if it was the same man whose face I saw on the chimney breast and who walked across my lounge in Ivy Cottages. I was trying to put two and two together but was ending up with five. If my memory, as a small child, served me correctly, Mr Teasdale had dark hair and was a similar build to Harry. It was then that I remembered the black belt which Harry wore as did Mr Teasdale. I clearly recall wondering at the time, why he did not wear braces to hold up his trousers, just like my dad and Uncle Fred?

Despite almost a bottle of wine and umpteen ciggy later, I tossed and turned in my bed at four o' clock in the morning.

(Harry had got a lot to answer for). As my fudged up brain was going round and round, another piece of evidence came to mind. 'Elizabeth, Elizabeth' the male voice in the garden which I heard when I was pruning the rambling roses; It was, I recall, the second or third time I heard it as Muffin and I went to search for the culprit and saw only a squirrel.

There have only been two people, in my whole life, who have ever called me 'Elizabeth'. One being Harry who I saw at Butlins Holiday Camp and I originally thought him to be. This was why I called him 'Harry'; however; this was certainly not him. For one thing, this other Harry had a full head of black, wavy hair and my Harry was 52 yrs.' old and looked much older because he was going bald.

Two and two were certainly not making five; it was making four; as Mr Teasdale always insisted on calling me 'Elizabeth', instead of 'Beth' and was it not him who called my name, shortly after he died? . I was beginning to see the reason for this, for after putting up with my mother's inquisition regarding what I heard, I might well have dismissed the whole incident if he called me 'Beth'. I was adamant with my mother that it was him because of the 'Elizabeth'. He obviously meant me to remember this, so the same old question 'Who are you?' is answered (about time too, Harry!!) It is funny how the mind works, for I was now wondering what his Christian name really is. I would guess it to be something posh; just like him.

Although, my head was still in 'bits', I could sense that he was around me as I was seeking inspiration but none forthcoming. The only thing that springs to mind is the fact that most mediums have different spirits visiting them when they are giving messages. This is not the case with me as all my information comes through Harry. It is as if he is some sort of 'gatekeeper', making the rest of the dead people wait their turn.

Although I was still racking my brain as to where I could obtain a photograph to confirm if my assumption was correct; things had to go on the 'back burner' regarding Harry. You see, I was getting bored at home and applied for a part-time job with BUPA (medical group) and I was also doing every Tuesday night as an 'emergency responder' for The RED-CROSS.

The most upsetting thing was that, in the course of twelve months, I had lost both Rocky and Caine due to old age. Cassy, the tom-cat was also put to sleep due to mouth cancer. So I decided to get Bess another friend as she was missing them both, especially when I was working night duty.

One Saturday, we set off to the Manchester Dogs Home but there was no message from Harry so I guessed it was my choice to get another dog this time .In I go and it is the same lady as she recognises me from the last time. I explained the reasons for getting another dog as Bess was lonely, etc.

Although it was almost four years ago, she asked 'Is it the black one?' She went on to say that a number of people had chosen her but as soon as they attempted to put the lead on, she would attack them and had to be returned to the pen. She was within days of being 'put to sleep' when I came. Consequently, they had changed their policy so if anyone had another dog, they were required to bring it along and introduce them. The staff had reported that that she came with me and my other dogs without any problem.

Well, I could hardly tell her the real reason that Harry can put thoughts into dog's heads but I wisely decided against this. We decided on a German shepherd, about three years old and a 'dead ringer' for Rocky so we called him 'Rocky 2' and set off home.

It was a Friday evening, March 22nd, 2007 and I set off to Quaker House, Stockport to do a demonstration. I was about half way to my destination, when I sensed a male presence within the car. Now, Harry has never done this so I was a little concerned and took extra care whilst driving. After the demonstration, the church presented me with a bunch of red roses.

I got home safely and the presence had gone but just as I was putting the flowers in a vase of water, I caught the shadowy form of a male, out the corner of my eye .As my consciousness changed to being alert, he vanished.

Clairvoyance requires a certain frame of mental state. I liken it to tuning into a specific radio channel but once the frequency has changed (being alert); the reception is lost. During that weekend whilst doing household chores, I glimpsed this watery, shadow figure on a number of occasions.

Later that week, I was informed that Ali Sayed had died of a heart attack. Of course, all the pieces fell together as the roses were the exact same shade (deep red) that he would buy me after we quarrelled. He was saying 'Goodbye' whilst letting me know that he was not really dead. I guess, unlike Harry who could manifest himself from ectoplasm to become a completely solid form, so much so that one would not know the difference until he disintegrated, Ali Sayed was just a novice. I said my goodbyes and placed the exact same shade of roses on his grave, knowing that I would never see him again in this life.

Chapter 45

Being 5'2" and with very little weight behind me, I often struggled, in gale force winds, to get onto the moors as they were one of the highest points in the country. So I came up with this bright idea of keeping the dogs on the lead, hoping that their combined weight of about eleven stone would keep me grounded. Sadly, this did not work out very well as I ended up being blown around like a kite on a piece of string. The final straw being when I landed, still clutching the leads, into a very large puddle.

I decided on a different route and one day we went up the lane which, hopefully, would stop me literally being blown over when the gusts of wind came as I could hold on to the stone wall or tree. We had only walked about a hundred yards from the house (perhaps blown would be more accurate) when Bess decided to suddenly stop and refused to go any further. Rocky was tugging on the lead, eager to carry on but Bess would not budge despite my encouragement. She just plops herself down on her haunches. I was almost split in two with Rocky going one way and Bess refusing to budge. The wind was howling and the rain was 'bucketing down'. So despite the forlorn look from Rocky, home we went.

I must have been putting the key in the front door as we were back in a couple of minutes having being blown faster than my legs could carry me, when I suddenly heard an almighty crash. Thinking it was a vehicle that had hit the stone wall and gone over (not an unusual occurrence); I put the dogs in the porch and went to see what had happened. To my astonishment, I saw a huge tree, right across the lane, with its' bare branches entwined in an overhead electric cable which was sparking and sputtering in the heavy rain.

It was only after phoning the Electricity Board and then making a coffee that it dawned on me how lucky we had been. So I had to ask myself the question 'Was this purely down to Bess' instinct or was it that she was psychic, like myself, and Harry can communicate with her'. As for Rocky, bless him, he did not have a clue of the imminent danger.

Chapter 46

The winter of 2009/2010 approached and I conceded to Harry's nagging request to write a book, having been snowed in for over a week. There was hardly a soul to be seen when I was out walking the dogs who were in their element, prancing about in the snow, but not me, for the snow was so deep that it was going over my wellies. The only amusement I had was watching a man on a pair of skis with a fat spaniel trying to keep abreast of him. I was wishing that I had a pair like that so the dogs could pull me along just like a sledge.

The Red Cross ambulance was off the road as the sidestreets were so treacherous but Shaun, the driver, struggled, bless him, to pick me up and take me to Tesco's as I had run out of food and more importantly, wine and animal fodder. What funny looks we got in Tesco's car park as we piled in bag after bag into the ambulance. I had bought enough food to keep me going till Easter.

Well, we managed to get back home so I put the kettle on for a well-deserved brew and introduced Shaun to the animals. The cats, as usual, were hogging the fire which was blazing half way up the chimney as it was so cold. As he stands by the fire, warming his hands, he asks me 'Why have you called her Bess?' So I told him the story and he just started laughing saying 'Do you not realise that Bess is short for Elizabeth?' adding that he reckoned it was one of Harry's little jokes. Well, I must be daft!! ; For all those years, it never dawned on me, Perhaps he was a comedian as well as a teacher. Having said that, I could not recall him ever telling any jokes but what would I know as I was only a little child when he was alive.

Well, Harry managed to do it yet again. Not being a morning person, it is usually well past the bewitching hour when I turn off my electric blanket and perform my ablutions. I was running a bath whilst I was brushing my teeth and suddenly, the most awful feeling of fear seized me. I just had to get out of the bathroom as quickly as my little legs could carry me. As I snuggled up in bed, having not even washed my face, I tried to figure out what was so terribly wrong. 'Is it the girls?' I thought but Harry would have let me know if that was the case. As I dozed off to sleep, I started wondering if I had really lost the plot after all but it was then I remembered the incident on the motorway when I was driving to Liverpool when he made me turn back and go home.

Next morning, it was around 8am so I donned my tattered old jeans and three jumpers, dressing as usual like an onion as it was so cold. The dogs charged down the stairs, eager to get into the back garden and spend 'a penny'.

What a shock I got when I reached the bathroom and I could not believe my eyes, for I was paddling water. Part of the ceiling was hanging down with the wash basin was almost broken in two. I just could not turn off the tap which was gushing water everywhere. The cast iron bath had survived but was full of stones and insulation foam. It narrowly missed the toilet so at least I was able to spend a much needed penny; having said that, it really wouldn't have mattered where I did it as there was so much water on the surrounding floor.

I phoned my friend, Ian, who luckily was also a plumbing engineer saying 'Come quickly as I cannot even turn off the stop tap, it is too stiff'. The next half an hour or so, was spent drinking coffee and smoking ciggys whilst trying to prevent the dogs from going into the parlour (Bess loves to paddle) where water was now pouring down the walls.

I was feeling quite useless with my inability to turn off a damn tap. I then recalled that this had happened before but the situation was a matter of life and death. One of my patients had hung himself from a staircase and whilst both Sandra and I safely got him down, neither of us could turn on the oxygen cylinder thus wasting valuable time, shouting for a male nurse. Luckily, the man survived without any spinal or brain damage. This prompted me to write a ward policy to ensure that when the oxygen and other vital equipment were checked weekly, they must not be turned off too tightly. (It's a male thing).

Well, Ian finally arrived and managed to turn the water off. 'Bloody hell, you could have been killed' he says, looking very concerned. This then prompted a post-mortem as to what had happened. The conclusion was that as the deep snow had melted, it had somehow seeped into the shallow roof space, wetting the plaster board ceiling. Evidently, this caused it to collapse due to the weight of the stones that the builders (the one that put his foot through my bedroom ceiling) had left whilst replacing two four hundred year old purlins.

Of course, this caused another saga with the insurance company; so much so that I had to tell him when he came to view the damage, in no uncertain terms, that I had not climbed through the hatch and chucked down large stones in order to obtain a complete refurbishment, adding 'You are damn lucky that the cast iron bath had escaped relatively unscathed, otherwise, you would have to replace that, as well'. (They never want to pay up but good at taking your money)

Chapter 47

It was the 21st July, 2010, and I set off for a demonstration at Altrincham Spiritualist Church. Having been there many, many times, I was at a loss as to what to use for 'my philosophy'. Not being a religious person, I usually relied on my clairvoyant experiences to prove life after death. So what pops up into my head but the Minnie Mouse Ardwick Green story where the lady's voice, calling 'Beth', saved me from being injured by that wagon?

After the service, a couple of the church volunteers and myself, sat around the kitchen, eating and drinking coffee. As we were chatting away, one of them says 'I did not know you came from Ardwick. My husband went to Ardwick Municipal School!' 'So did' I responded. She then went on to talk about Mr Teasdale who had committed suicide 'Because he was a queer who liked little boys'. I nearly choked on my cheese sandwich, gulped them down and quite angrily said 'NO, no, he was, I believe, a homosexual'. I then went on to reiterate the rumour I had heard as a child, about him and others being charged with that offence and were awaiting trial. 'That is why he killed himself' I said with conviction. The other lady was quick to point out that being 'gay' was completely different and that countries such as France, did not have any laws against being homosexual, back in the 1950's.

Having known him and liking him very much, I felt so angry at her accusations; so much so that I asked her if she had a photograph of him to establish if it was the same teacher.' I will have a look' she replied.

Well, I was driving home, still feeling very angry but wondering why I felt this way... I said to myself that it was no skin off my nose what his sexual preferences were. Then, to top it all, I met a road diversion, knowing that before long, I would be completely lost. I never could, for the life of me, understand them. I headed towards Moss Side and Hulme which were familiar areas, with the intention of going up Brunswick St. and onto Higher Ardwick. At least, I knew I would find my way home from there.

Just as I pulled up at some traffic lights, I heard the familiar voice saying, telepathically; 'Clear my name'. It was then that I realised that I was not on Brunswick St. but facing the old bus depot. This was opposite Ardwick Municipal School which had been demolished long ago and the derelict land was now covered in dandelions and daisies. As the lights changed to green, I headed down Devonshire St., knowing that Harry had taken me to the very same set of traffic lights where I heard him call me 'Elizabeth, Elizabeth', shortly after he died. Out loud I said 'I know it is you now so I do not need a photograph' I then asked him 'Is the book all about this; to clear your name?' No answer from him!

'Well, what a turn–up for the books'?; for if the traffic lights had been on green, I would have sailed straight through and never noticed where I was. What to do next?—this is the burning question.

Chapter 48

I just could not believe he was a paedophile. Surely, this must have been an ugly rumour but there again; they say 'there is no smoke without fire'. My curiosity was getting the better of me so I decided to contact Noel. I was hoping he would be able to dig up some information on Mr Teasdale.

Well, I was very excited when I opened the large, manila envelope as the lady was as good as her word and had sent me an old school photograph. The young boy sat in the centre row, holding a banner displaying 'Coronation Year 1937' was now, her deceased husband. At either side of the class of boys, stood two teachers but I was very disappointed as neither of them was Mr Teasdale.

I telephoned her as she had obviously got the wrong end of the stick. Neither of them were Mr Teasdale. I also asked her if her husband had been accosted by any teacher there. 'No, no,' she said and added that it was a rumour about Mr Teasdale after he committed suicide.

The new potatoes boiled dry and my lamb chops were burned as I was talking to Noel on the phone. I had forgotten all about them on the cooker. (The dogs loved them). He told me that he had been unable to find anything on Mr Teasdale and suggested I contact 'County Records' to find a Christian name date of birth, etc.

I drove to county records at Shude Hill, intent on solving this mystery. I recalled Mr Teasdale was a no nonsense teacher who would not think twice about giving the lads a 'clip round the earhole' when they became unruly. Oddly enough, he never hit the girls.

Having spent many years working with the Probation Service and dealing with people with this type of condition, this behaviour was in complete contrast to what I would have expected. Noel who had far more expertise in this area of nursing, thoroughly agreed with me. If anything, it would have been 'the girls' who he would have tried it on with and as one of his favourites, it surely would have been me.

I often wondered why he changed my name from 'Beth' to 'Elizabeth'. It was very strange as Maggie, another girl in my class, was never called 'Margaret'. Why did he not change her name? This has always puzzled me to this day. The answer, I guess, 'is lying in the wind!'

One of my fondest memories of him was when, with great kindness and patience, he persuaded me to stand on the school rostrum, in front of the whole class to recite a poem I had learned. I guess he did this to give me some self-confidence which I needed.

Catching the Cat

The mice had met in council. They all looked haggard and worn
For the state of affairs was too terrible, to be any longer born
Not a family out of mourning, there was crepe on every hat
Something must be done and done at once, about the cat.
Then the smallest mouse in the council, arose with a solemn air
And by way of increasing his stature, he brushed up his whiskers and hair
He waited until there was silence, all along the pantry shelf
And then he said with dignity, I will catch the cat myself.

When next I hear her coming, instead of running away
I will turn and face her boldly and pretend to be at play
She will not see the danger, poor creature I suppose
For is it then, I will catch her by the nose.
The mice had faith, of course they had, all of them trusting souls
But a sort of general feeling, kept them safely in their holes.
Until sometime in the evening, when the boldest ventured out
And there he saw in the distance, the cat prance gaily about.
Now the story has a moral, short but true
When you are mice, you better think twice
Before you catch the cat

Chapter 49

At county records, I searched through two, large, tattered ledgers which went back to the late 1890's. I decided to work my way backwards; just like 'the five books in the clouds'. The dark, red ledger with the broken spine was only half full and on its last page was written, Ardwick Municipal School ceased to exist in July, 1952; it then became Ardwick Secondary Modern for Girls.

I licked my finger and started to turn back the pages. 'Glory be!' I found him.

B.B. Teasdale takes charge of school, headmaster away.

5th September, 1951; B.B. Teasdale off sick. Mrs Heap likewise, with flu.

I can remember her and so many other names. Old memories come flooding back such as, the 'Nit Nurse' visiting, searching our heads for tiny, little creatures. Derbac soap and a steel toothcomb were used in those days. I never did get head lice until I worked in A&E in Stockport Infirmary. The reason being, I think, that they prefer clean hair. As a child, I would scream the house down if my mother attempted to wash it. All in all, it got washed about a half dozen times a year.

I thumbed the pages back to the 1940's and every entry read 'B.B. Teasdale' and I did not have a clue what these initials stood for; so it was over to my friend, Noel, who would surely come up with something.

'Liz, you are supposed to be a clairvoyant, ask him what his bloody Christian name is' was his only response and he went on to add that he would need the first name to search the records. 'I tried that but it was all double Dutch to me' I said.

The most sensible suggestion was that I go to Central Library, St. Peter's Square, in Manchester. A shudder went up my spine as it was the same building where he had committed suicide.

It was as if I was taking two steps forward and three steps back as the Central Library was closed for refurbishment until 2013; but all was not lost, Elliot House on Deans gate, housed a limited number of old newspapers, etc. The other good news was that Noel (clever man) had found a website 'Friends Reunited'. He found the following;

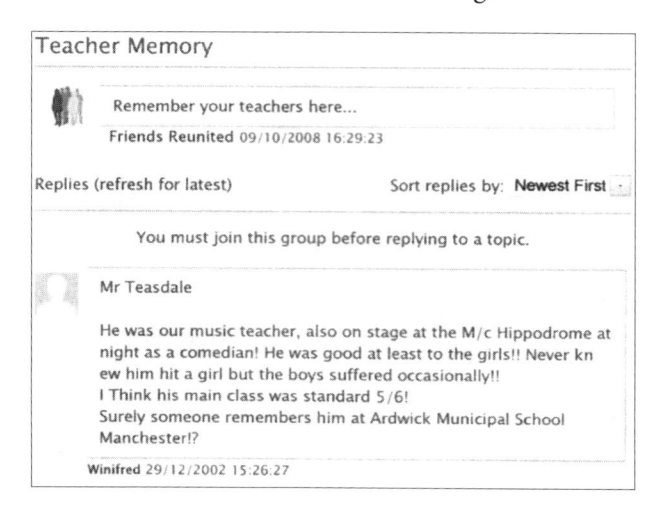

Teacher Memory

Remember your teachers here...
Friends Reunited 09/10/2008 16:29:23

Replies (refresh for latest)   Sort replies by: **Newest First**

You must join this group before replying to a topic.

Mr Teasdale

He was our music teacher, also on stage at the M/c Hippodrome at night as a comedian! He was good at least to the girls!! Never kn ew him hit a girl but the boys suffered occasionally!!
I Think his main class was standard 5/6!
Surely someone remembers him at Ardwick Municipal School Manchester!?

Winifred 29/12/2002 15:26:27

I decided to go to Elliot House where a very nice man assisted me as I gave him one my sweetest old lady smiles; the poor soul did not know what he was letting himself in for. I was hoping that he didn't know the librarian in Uppermill.

Due to a lack of space, Elliot House had no room for theatrical or historical records regarding the Manchester Hippodrome. I would have to wait until 2013 when the Library reopened where all these records were stored. I could be dead by then!

Whilst sitting in Elliot House, I was trying to think what newspaper my parents had delivered. I could remember it clanking through the metal letterbox. If Bimbo had managed to get to it first, it would be in shreds before you could say 'Jack Robinson'. Many a time, my mother could be seen piecing it together as Bimbo had gotten there first. She never went to the front page first but always went straight to the Marriage and Obituaries' column. Suddenly, that started bells ringing as I remembered her inquisition after finding his death notice in the paper.

Seeing as I was at Elliot House, I decided to follow up on this and managed to find copies of the 'Evening Chronicle' for the years,' 52,' 53.

It was quite easy really. I just put in a reel of microfilm and slowly, I wound the wooden handle

The first piece of information which I found was quite intriguing.

I noticed that it was dated December, 7th, 1953. This is not what my mother showed me. I remembered that it was a different, smaller piece of print which I kept for all those years.

> **Falls 60ft. at library**
>
> Shortly after visiting the Henry Watson music library at Manchester Central Library today an unidentified middle-aged man fell nearly 60 feet down a well between a lift shaft and a staircase when leaving the building.
>
> He was taken unconscious to Ancoats Hospital where he was found to be suffering from fractures to the skull, jaw, and thigh bones of both legs.
>
> After examining disturbed dustmarks on the lift shaft, police believe he fell from a balcony just below the entrance to the Henry Watson music library.

Although, it is the Central Library where Mr Teasdale killed himself, this poor chap was unidentified and still in hospital. I soldiered on to the Death Notices and was amazed to find the following;

The first thing that hit me was the fact that he died on a Thursday which was a school day. This was the day that I was standing at those traffic lights whilst waiting for them to turn green. It must have been the day I heard his voice. 'Elizabeth, Elizabeth'.

I also noticed that they were saying it was an accident and not

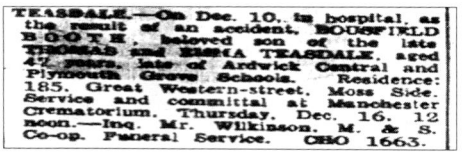

> TEASDALE.—On Dec. 10, in hospital, as the result of an accident, BOUSFIELD BOOTH, beloved son of the late THOMAS and EMMA TEASDALE, aged 47 years, late of Ardwick Central and Plymouth Grove Schools. Residence: 185, Great Western-street, Moss Side. Service and committal at Manchester Crematorium, Thursday, Dec. 16, 12 noon.—Inq. Mr. Wilkinson. M. & S. Co-op. Funeral Service. CHO 1663.

suicide. I had a good grin to myself whilst saying to Harry 'what on earth were your parents thinking of to name you Bousfield. No wonder it was double Dutch to me as I have never heard the like. I bet you got the mickey taken out of you when you were at school'.

Noel had written to Winifred requesting further information, having seen her entry on the Friends Reunited website but unfortunately, there was no response. I was very happy that her description of Mr Teasdale's character was exactly in keeping with my own impression of him.

Chapter 50

I excitedly phoned Noel to give him the good news about discovering Mr Teasdale's Christian name and armed with this information, he was able to find the following from the 'Teacher Registration Board'

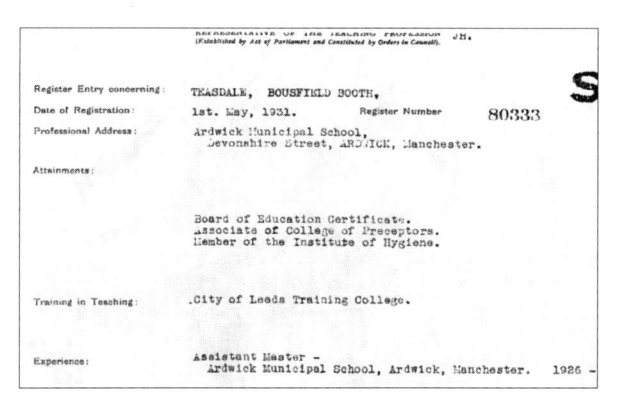

```
                         REPRESENTATIVE OF THE TEACHING PROFESSION    JH.
                        (Established by Act of Parliament and Constituted by Orders in Council).

Register Entry concerning:   TEASDALE, BOUSFIELD BOOTH,
Date of Registration:        1st. May, 1931.    Register Number    80333
Professional Address:        Ardwick Municipal School,
                                Devonshire Street, ARDWICK, Manchester.

Attainments:

                             Board of Education Certificate.
                             Associate of College of Preceptors.
                             Member of the Institute of Hygiene.


Training in Teaching:        City of Leeds Training College.


Experience:                  Assistant Master -
                                Ardwick Municipal School, Ardwick, Manchester.   1926 -
```

Noel suggested that I return to Elliot House to find out more information which I duly did.

As I entered Elliot House, I noticed it was an old Victorian building with red brick exterior and large windows which was in keeping with elegance of its high ceilings. As Dave, the nice man, set up the microfilm, he said that the building once housed the School Board offices. I didn't comment as the school board man often called 98 Higher Ardwick and my mother and him were practically on first name terms. Instead, I asked about the alcoves at the side of the spiral staircase, wondering if they once had busts or murals adorning them but he didn't know.

So I set up a copy The Manchester Evening News, 1953 and started turning the wooden handle. I got to the front page of the Monday 7th December issue and found the following;

On further investigation, I discovered on the 16th December issue, the following;

Something was bugging me so I went down the two flight of stairs, outside for a ciggy and 'a ponder'. I was hoping the nicotine would enhance my grey cells. I took the lift back up as my knee joints were feeling a lot older than me. (I guessed my bits of string were dropping off) What can one expect at my age? Not a lot!

I summoned Dave who looked mightily relieved when I asked him if there were

Man falls 60 feet

CLEANERS at Manchester Central Library to-day found a man who had fallen nearly 60 feet down a well between the lift shaft and a library staircase.

The man was identified as Bousfield Booth-Teasdale, aged about 40, of Great Western-street, Moss Side, Manchester

He is in Ancoats Hospital with skull, jaw, and thigh fractures.

Two surgeons this afternoon were at the man's bedside and he was being given blood transfustions. He was said to be "very ill."

He had only just left the Henry Watson Music Library on the second floor when the cleaners heard the thud of his fall into the basement.

Disturbed dustmarks down the lift shaft indicated he had fallen from a balcony a few steps below the entrance to the Henry Watson Library. He had music from the library in his pockets

He had fallen over a guardrail on the staircase. There is a gap of about three feet between the guardrail and the covered lift shaft.

Teacher jumped to his death after allegations

BY OUR CORRESPONDENT

FOUR days after he denied allegations of indecent behaviour made against him by two schoolboys, a music and drama teacher took his own life, it was stated at a Manchester inquest to-day.

The City Coroner, Mr. Jessel Rycroft, recorded a verdict of suicide on Bousfield Booth Teasdale, aged 47, a bachelor, of Great Western-street, Moss Side.

It was stated Teasdale fell 50ft. down a staircase well in the Henry Watson Music Library, St Peter's Square, Manchester, after he had borrowed books of Christmas carols.

The headmaster of Plymouth Grove Municipal School, Mr Charles Howarth, said Teasdale was a teacher there and everybody loved him. He was well known to producers of school plays and concerts.

On December 3, police officers came to the school and, after an interview with them, Teasdale fainted.

STRONG DENIAL

Mr. Howarth learned the interview had to do with allegations made by two boys.

Mr. Howarth said Teasdale strongly denied any such thing. When he asked Teasdale why he wanted the boys alone with him he said they were taking part in surprise items in the school concert and it would spoil the whole effect for others to see them rehearsing.

"I told him I believed him and shook hands with him," added Mr. Howarth. Teasdale was shocked and upset. He discussed the allegations quite calmly. He had a splendid reputation.

Mrs. Florence Tinsley, Teasdale's housekeeper said she considered him a thorough gentleman.

"VERY AGITATED"

P.c. James Marriott said after the boys, who were aged 10 and 12 respectively, had made complaints through their parents, he went to see Teasdale at the school.

The man became very agitated and asked: "How many boys?"

At a police station Teasdale saw a statement the boys had made and denied their allegations.

"I think a dirt mark on one of the staircase rails indicates he deliberately climbed on the rail and, when his mind was disturbed by these allegations, hurled himself down the well," said the Coroner.

Gassed wife 'complained about leak'

BY OUR CORRESPONDENT

AT the Standish, near Wigan, inquest to-day on Mrs. Evelyn Marsden, 41-year-old mother of four children, who was found dead in bed in a gas-filled bedroom at her home in Church-street, Standish, it was stated that she had complained about a leak in the house.

Thomas Marsden, who suffered from coal gas poisoning, said his wife had complained to the gas board and to a meter collector about the smell of gas.

But Mr. K. W. Dewhurst, for the North Western Gas Board, said "The board has made extensive inquiries, but has no record of the complaint."

Mrs. Edna Rawlinson, of Church-street, Standish, said Mrs. Marsden had complained to her about the gas for two years. "She was feared of it."

John Rigby, district service manager for the North Western Gas Board, said he found a fracture in a gas pipe in Mrs. Marsden's bedroom.

Verdict: Accidental death.

Man faces £96 betting charge

WHEN Dennis Clare, aged 40, asphalter, of Kingsley Crescent, Collyhurst, Manchester, was accused at Preston to-day of trying to obtain £96 by false pretences it was alleged that the names of losing horses on a betting-slip had been rubbed out and winning horses substituted.

Mr. J. D. Foy, prosecuting, alleged it was "a rather ingenious fraud." Clare was remanded on bail until Friday.

Riots: 15 guilty

Fifteen Trieste people were

any more local papers published in 1953. .He seemed to appreciate the fact that I had not 'cocked up' the machine, yet again. To date, I had managed to get the microfilm upside down and back to front.

The rest of the people there, who were doing family research or the like, seemed to be able to cope. I guessed they were industrious and intelligent. Well, me! I was just a kid from Ardwick, dressed in second hand clothes. God knows, why the posh Mr Teasdale who wore a Crombie coat and carried a long, black umbrella, took such a shine to me?

Manchester Hippodrome

Anyway, Dave suggested the Manchester Guardian, first published in 1901 (surprising what one learns) as it was a local paper in the 50's. So off he went to ferret it out whilst I sat twiddling my thumbs. I started thinking of bygone times when Ardwick Green was a hub of activity. I could still remember the men who used to sell the papers. Most of them had arms or legs missing, propped with wooden crutches, shouting 'Evening Chron.; Evening News'. Some were blind and you were trusted to place the money for the papers in a wooden tray which hung on a piece of string round their necks. Others, who were also ex-soldiers from the two World Wars, sat in wheelchairs, shaking all over. (Shell- shock). The fittest of them sold meat pies which were actually delicious. Others cleaned the leather shoes of the rich people who were going to see the variety performance at the Manchester Hippodrome.

I could even recall in the late 1940's, a man with a very long pole, lighting the gas street lamps. Most of our terraced houses had gas mantles in the kitchen and living rooms just like Aunt Cissie and Uncle Fred's house. One in those days went to bed with a candle or torch if you could afford the batteries.

Dave returned and this is what I managed to find.

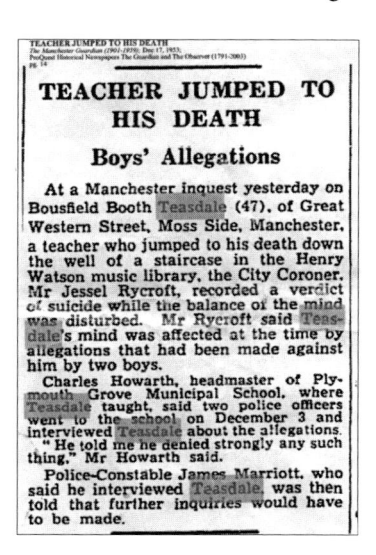

TEACHER JUMPED TO HIS DEATH

Boys' Allegations

At a Manchester inquest yesterday on Bousfield Booth Teasdale (47), of Great Western Street, Moss Side, Manchester, a teacher who jumped to his death down the well of a staircase in the Henry Watson music library, the City Coroner, Mr Jessel Rycroft, recorded a verdict of suicide while the balance of the mind was disturbed. Mr Rycroft said Teasdale's mind was affected at the time by allegations that had been made against him by two boys.

Charles Howarth, headmaster of Plymouth Grove Municipal School, where Teasdale taught, said two police officers went to the school on December 3 and interviewed Teasdale about the allegations.

"He told me he denied strongly any such thing," Mr Howarth said.

Police-Constable James Marriott, who said he interviewed Teasdale, was then told that further inquiries would have to be made.

Chapter 51

Home I went armed with my 10p photocopies and I decided to go and see Noel. After sharing a bottle of wine, I was interested to see if he was thinking the same way I did. By this time, Noel and I were half pissed and had smoked about 20 ciggys each. We came to the conclusion that Mr Teasdale did not jump. Why would anyone of a disturbed mind, choose a sheet of Christmas carol music, sign it out of the library, presumably to rehearse for the school Christmas Concert and then proceed to throw himself down the lift shaft?

Like me, Noel was a very experienced psychiatric nurse and had seen suicides in abundance. For some, it is a cry for help; others are responding to hallucinations and 'voices'. The sane people who wish to take their own lives, usually put 'their house in order', choosing their venue with great care and diligence.

To quote one example, there was a chap who owned a carpet business who had come to see Dr Sayed regarding his depression. When the story unfolded, he was in his early 40's and dying of 'AİDS'. Of course, he was depressed and with good reason as a death of this type, I would not wish on anyone. So he was not admitted to our psychiatric unit but we knew sooner or later, what he would do. Would it have been right to prolong his inevitable death by 'sectioning' him? No! A short time afterwards, he went out on the moors one night and put the exhaust hose in his van, only to be found a day or two later.

In Mr Teasdale's case, taking into consideration what the reporters had highlighted, did they also have their doubts? Why was the librarian who had booked out the sheet music, not present at the inquest? Surely, this would have been mentioned had it been requested by the coroner, after all, the housekeeper was there and she did not appear to think he was of unsound mind. If anybody goes to the library to collect sheets of music then they are looking ahead. It is extremely odd to think that one would bother to get the carol music sheets before killing oneself.

So Harry (he will always be Harry to me as I cannot cope with Bousfield) walks down to the first floor from the music library and then jumps. There must be better ways of killing yourself. Why not go to the top of the building and do it from there or just stick your head in the oven? (No North Sea Gas then)? Coal Gas Inhalation was a popular way of committing suicide and it was still a fairly common event when I worked at Stockport Infirmary. Why not throw himself into the Manchester Ship Canal which was close to where he lived or even throw oneself under a train? 'Disturbed dust marks' were reported at the scene but what does that mean? 'Jumped' or 'Pushed', of course, they would be there.

So Columbo and Miss Marple (me and Noel) decided to investigate. The burning question being, was he pushed or jumped?

My little grey cells start to come into play (it must be all the nicotine and the wine as we are on our second bottle). Columbo says that we 'should find a motive' and Miss Marple agrees, coming up with the usual suspects; money, sex, revenge or to silence someone. 'I am going to be very busy' I thought as I decided my first task would be to get the inquest details.

I wrote to the Manchester District Coroner's Office, using my very best English, to request the document. A few days late, a lady phoned me and said that they had no inquest records prior to 1959. She went on to say that this was due to a fire in the 1950's.

Noel had put a couple of messages on the Past Pupils of Plymouth Gove website, requesting information on Mr Teasdale but so far, there was no response. He did, however, notice an entry from one past pupil in relation to him.

'My years at P/Grove were from 1950/1956. The school was on three floors, infants on the ground floor, the girls on the middle floor and the boys on the top floor. The average class was 42 pupils and the teachers were strict. Our football activities were on Wednesdays; we were collected (two double decker buses) and taken to Cringle Fields, to practise football. Our canteen was just off the infants' playground in a prefab/building and close by the girls' cookery class. We also had woodwork and metal work classes; close nearby for a period of time.

I, for a period of time, was the milk monitor. My job was to get the milk to the middle floor and the top floor by way of a small hand pulled lift from the basement.

The caretaker's name was 'Pop Turner' and he was a character. The headmaster's name was Mr Howarth, a very fine gentleman; Teachers names, a Mr Kinsey Dennerly, Jordan, Greenall, Teasdale and more.

We would always start with morning assembly. I remember after we had completed our school exams each year, the results would be given out by all the class standing on their chairs and as your name was called, you would sit down until there was only one left, then we clapped.

I had happy years there and there was no bullying; on leaving at 15 yrs., I worked in Engineering which I disliked, I then moved into building locomotives and later married a beautiful wife. We had two beautiful daughters and became a manager to the licence trade for 25 yrs. But my last 12 yrs. has been caring for elderly people with many problems. I became a Christian which I enjoy sharing my faith with many.

To end my reflection of my life is to say I retired in October, this year, aged 69

Bill Singleton; December 21st 2010; 7; 19pm'

Let's hope he responds as he would have been at the school during the time of the Teasdale incident. Goodness knows rumour must have been rife. What I find to be a little odd is the fact that both he and Winifred, although eight years apart, had posted their messages in December, very close to Mr Teasdale's death.

Well, 'where there is a will, there is a way'! as they say. If they don't respond to our messages, I will just go back to the drawing board. The other thing which bothers me is the fact that there was no suicide letter. Having dealt with a number of suicides, during my nursing career, I would 'put money on it' as most people leave a note. Granted I have no statistics to prove it but the whole incident just does not feel right to me.

As the African Juju says 'Unfinished Business' so I guess it is up to me to clear his name. This man would not return from the dead if he really was a paedophile.

I had another theory that perhaps one of the boy's families had murdered him in revenge, following the accusations; but living in Ardwick and knowing 'the mind-set' of the people, I doubt that this was the case. They would have given him a 'bloody good hiding' under one of the many viaducts in Manchester, late at night when nobody was around. To do this, they would have to have followed him home from school, to where he lived. So why wait all weekend until Monday morning? (I don't think so) Then, supposedly, using the opportunity of his visit to the library where there were people about, plus the slightest noise would have attracted attention. How did they make their getaway? Most Ardwick people would not know the layout of the library and perhaps, never visited it in their entire lives; let alone, know the ends and outs of the building, in order to plan their assault. Let's not forget that hanging was the punishment for a capital offence, in those times.

When a judge put on his black cap, you knew you were about to be sentenced to hang. Albert Pierrepoint was one of England's famous executioners. From 1946, he ran the' Help the Poor Struggler' pub on Manchester Road, Hollinwood, until the mid-fifties. The last person to be hanged was Peter

Allen, on 13th August, 1964, at Walton Jail. At the same time, Allen's accomplice, Gwynne Evans, was executed at Strangeways by Robert Stewart who was born in Scotland but lived in Chatterton for many years. He had been Pierrepoint's assistant and were close friends.

Did Mr Teasdale go to the library on his own? My guess would be yes as many of the teachers at Ardwick Municipal School would arrive in the school at about 10 o'clock after assembly, taken by the headmaster, in order to commence their classes. (Bill Singleton talked about this also). It would not take him long to get his sheet of music for the school's Christmas festivities and hop on the 92 bus which stopped at the top of Plymouth Grove..

I really needed to know what time in the morning he was found by the cleaners, to see if my theory was reasonable. What would be very useful is a map of the library, entrances/exits etc. The other thing I needed to do was to contact Ancoats Hospital in order to ascertain if any records still existed, regarding his injuries.

Chapter 52

My New Year's resolution for 2011 would be to solve this mystery. I had not got off to a very good start as Ancoats Hospital, apart for its facade which is a Grade 2 listed building, no longer existed. Patient's records had long been destroyed. As I pondered on what to do next, my memories took me back to the days of my childhood, having visited the A&E Department on a number of occasions. (Split my head open and had to have stiches, to give just one example)

Off Ancoats Lane lay Mill Street, where one of my Dad's brothers had a pub called 'The Bluebell Inn'. I was a frequent visitor and Hannah, Leonard's fat wife, would give me a large brown bag, full of brightly coloured beer bottle tops. I would spend many a happy hour, sorting out the shades; much to my mother's disgust as they were very smelly which added to the fun.

The saddest memory of those happy days was when my Dad took me and Billie, Leonards and Hannah's son, to see Phyllis, my dad's niece, who was confined to an' Iron Lung'. It was a huge contraption which aided her breathing due to contracting Polio. The poor child was not much older than me and Billie and I think it was a blessing when she eventually died.

We were also frequent visitors to the Old Smithfield Market which was part of my dad's postal round. He knew everybody and I would be on my best behaviour, smiling sweetly as the store- holders would give me sixpence or even a shilling. I was given cockles, mussels and whelks also which I love to this day. Sometimes, they would give my dad a goose or turkey as a Christmas present, for he gave their letters and parcels priority.

When I got home, I would help my Dad pluck the bird and the mounds of feathers, were used to stuff pillows. I would claim the chopped off feet and tie a piece of cotton to one of the claws. I kept pulling it so that the claw would move. This I did to frighten the other kids when they were playing hopscotch or some other game. Many a time, my mother would play 'Holy Hell' as I would forget to bring the shoe polish tin home after playing hopscotch (one would kick the polish tin so that it landed in numbered squares and see who got the highest score).

My only living grandparent was my Dad's mum. She was a tiny little lady with gorgeous white hair. Oh how I envy her today as my hair has a salt and pepper appearance so I get it highlighted.

She fascinated me with her vivid, blue eyes, her fast Irish lilt and the stories she told. I remember one about my Dad's first wife Rebecca Regan who died in childbirth, leaving my half-brother Jack, twenty years my senior.

One day she got so angry with my Dad, that she clouted him across the head with a whole salmon which was obtained from Smithfield Market and knocked him unconscious.

After my mother's death, I was clearing out the rented house when I found, hidden away behind a large wardrobe, love letters and silk embroidered birthday and Christmas cards from Rebecca to my Dad; all tied with coloured ribbon. Tears came to my eyes as I read them as some of them dated back to WW1 when they were both teenagers.

Many years later, I took it upon myself to visit the tiny terraced house where my Gran had lived, just behind St Silas Church in Openshaw where my mother and father had married in 1934.

Since I had time on my hands, I drove through Ancoats towards Bradford Coalmine and on to the cemetery where Rebecca and my Irish grandfather (who I never knew) were buried. I was disappointed to find it dilapidated and closed, so I never found their graves. Aunt Bunny told me that he had died of diabetes. In those days there was no treatment as Insulin had not being discovered. The diagnosis was made by the nurse, tasting the urine for sweetness. (I would not fancy doing that)

As time travels on, I find I am much better at remembering the past than the present. I can go upstairs for something and by the time I have reached the top of the stairs, I have forgotten what I went for. Oh all the joys of getting old!

It was then that I remembered the rag-n-bone man's horse as I would get off my bicycle to give him a stroke. He had a hessian bag tied round his neck, full of oats and was munching away. Having a rest from pulling the small wooden cart, on which the rag-n-bone sat whilst travelling along the roads and streets. Shouting 'any old iron, any old iron' the doors would open along the tiny streets, and back alleys.

Housewives in their pinnys and turbans, to hide their curlers, would come out of their back yards in droves, clutching old rags, pots and pans. These were exchanged for brown or white 'donkey stones' which were used when cleaning stone steps and window-sills. As a kid, one would get two pence or two haporth for doing this task, using a bucket of cold water to wet the stones and rub them on the steps and sills. (12 pennies to a shilling in those days which is 5 pence today)

I must stop my reminiscing and get back to the task in hand, for when I was patting the horse, I recalled seeing a butcher's shop called' Teasdale' and wondering if it was a relative of my favourite teacher.

So out with the phone book and I decided to phone every Teasdale within the Greater Manchester area. Ah, so now what to say!? I needed a cover story as the truth will probably get me charged by the police for nuisance phone calls, plus an order to see a psychiatrist.

Tracing family history is quite fashionable at the moment so down that avenue I go and over the next couple of days, I phoned every Teasdale in the book. I was hoping that somebody somewhere was still alive that knew him.

No such luck, I just ended up with a hefty phone bill. The positive side being that he could have been called Smith or Jones.

Chapter 53

I lay on the settee, armed with wine and ciggys, pondering on what to do next. The spirits were all around as I can feel what is best described as a spider's web, which momentarily and spontaneously touch ones face. When it first happened, I used to think it was cat fur but since they have now both died, having lived to a ripe old age of fourteen and fifteen and a half years, I know differently. Many friends who are mediums experience the same phenomenon.

The phone was now ringing and it was Noel, better known as Columbo; for guess what he had found:

Birth Indexes									
Surname	Forename(s)	Mother's Maiden Name	Year	Sub-District	Registers At	Region	Reference		Order On-line
TEASDALE	Bousfield Booth	BOOTH	1906	Lancaster	Preston	Lancashire	LAN/108/12	Remove	

He had also got a list of phone numbers; eight in all, of Teasdale's who live in Lancaster.

The following evening, after six o'clock, having learnt from the previous phone encounters that more people are at home and besides it will be cheaper, I phoned around.

I got about half way down the list with two not answering. Having said 'my piece' about tracing my family history, one lady says 'yes, he was my uncle.' Well you could have 'knocked me down with a feather' I then realized that this is now going to be difficult for she will know I am not a relative. What an idiot I am, for not taking this scenario into consideration.

After a deep breath, a swig of the wine, I tell her the truth, adding that I do not think that he committed suicide. 'Well dear', I am glad about that' she says. She does not ask me how he did die, or any further details. She was obviously thinking that she has got a lunatic on the other end of the line and had decided to humour me but I was not going to be put off and pressed on with the following question.

Did she know much about his life and who his friends were? There was a short pause before she replied and this made me think that there may be something to hide here or perhaps she was deep in thought, trying to remember.

'Well dear, I was only a slip of a girl at the time of his death but he was a kind, lovely, well-mannered man' she finally said. She went on to say that on occasions, he took her to the theatre and Opera House. He always wanted to be on stage and had a comedy act known as 'Sid & Teasdale'. Sadly, Sid was no longer alive and she could not recall his surname.

Apparently, they used to perform in church fetes, children's parties and charity functions where he sang and played the piano.

She continued to give her family history stating that her father, Samuel, was his half-brother. The others included Joseph, a teacher and then there was Ann Margaret and another brother who was killed in WW1. John was the oldest and Richard who owned a butcher's shop in Beswick. She stopped for breath and then went on to say how angry Richard was ('jumping up and down') because Bousfield had left all his money to his housekeeper. Richard felt that it should have been his as they were quite friendly and he had done a lot of decorating at Great Western Street. He also complained that he had to pay for the funeral.

I interjected and asked her what was the housekeeper's name and if she was young and pretty? 'No, no, dear! She was quite elderly and I did not much care for her during the five years she was with him, although I cannot say why I felt this way about her. He called her 'Florrie' and her surname was 'Tinsley'. She just up and left after he died,' she said, finally taking another long breath.

I was now wondering if I had got a lead. Was Florence related to the two boys? ; But I kept it to myself as I asked which parent had remarried? 'His father, dear, after his first wife died and they just had him whom they nicknamed 'Bobby' she replied. (Well, better than Bousfield but I still preferred Harry).

It was then that I remembered the photograph so I asked her for one. 'I do not think so, dear' she said, sounding disappointed. She went on to say that she would have a look when she was feeling better, having just come out of hospital. I wished her all the best and also, for a speedy recovery and duly left my phone number.

Well, I could not sleep that night, tossing and turning. I was up and down for coffee and ciggys and wondering what was the matter with me. Round and round my head, went the conversation with Jean Teasdale. Not only was Harry posh but also appeared to have been quite rich! I decided that I needed information on Florence and her relatives as money could be a great motive for murder. It is especially clever if it is deemed to be suicide.

I must have just fallen asleep before dawn. I was awakened by the dogs barking at the postman who insisted, despite advice to the contrary, on running as fast as he could, up and down all those stone steps. Of course, this encouraged them to put their paws on the window sills and growl even more as they could sense his fear.

I would now have to' get my skates on' as I had a dental appointment at 10.30 am. 'Oh dear, I am far too old to rush about' I thought to myself. I must have eventually slept like a log through the alarm.

What I needed was a 'knocker upper'; these men, carrying their long poles, used to be up and about before the crack of dawn. They carried their lanterns whilst knocking on the bedroom windows with their wooden poles. They did this to awaken the early risers such as railway and mill workers but it is not the 1940's anymore. Thankfully, the thick fogs, known as 'pea soup', have disappeared as they were so thick that everything including trams and trains came to an immediate standstill.

We would go out with a piece of a rag or a handkerchief, if you were posh (no prizes for guessing what I had) and hold it over our nose and mouth whilst using your other arm outstretched attempting to avoid any oncoming collision from people or objects. I still recall the time when I walked home from school in dense fog and managed to injure my forehead on a pillar box. I reckon that the mucky piece of rag which I clutched, luckily managed to save my nose. First Aid treatment in those days consisted of my mother smothering a lump of 'best butter' all over my forehead. Needless to say, the butter melted, mingling with the grime from the fog so I ended up looking like one of those chimney sweep boys.

Lord Shaftsbury introduced compulsory education in 1870 but it was not until 5 years later that l children were prohibited from going up chimneys in order to clean them.

Chapter 54

Well, back to the task in hand so I discovered Florence Tinley appeared with Harry on the electoral roll for Great Western Street, Moss Side, Manchester. Further enquiries, got me no further. There were umpteen Florence Tinsleys, married and unmarried around the country. Having little if any understanding of computers, I needed someone with time on their hands as I could not keep mithering Noel who is so patient and understanding that it makes me feel a bit guilty.

Seeing as this was all Harry's doing, I guessed it was his turn to suffer so I had one of my little tantrums with him. A bit of a one-sided conversation but after all, he was the one who started all this. I even threatened 'to kill myself' on the grounds that it would make him pay attention. He would be stuck with me, wouldn't he?

About 10 days later, there was a message on my answering machine from Jean Teasdale requesting my address. Evidently, she had found a photograph of Harry, adding that it did not do him justice as it was a very old one. At least, I would be able identify if he was the same person that I had seen, twice, at Ivy Cottages.

Well, I was very chuffed and decided that I would phone her after I had made a list of questions. It was Saturday teatime and I had to be at Stretford Spiritualist Church at 7.30pm sharp to do a demonstration of my mediumship.

Stretford Christian Spiritualist Church, like many others, was a warm, friendly place to be, whether they are Spiritualist National Union or independent churches. My feeling was that people were searching for something to believe in. We would get people from many different backgrounds and age ranges that I guess were at odds with the control and dogma of the traditional places of worship.

I stepped down from the platform, having finished my demonstration of mediumship, and as always thanked Harry for his input. My greatest fear being that I commence the service, and receive no information from him. Thus looking like a right pillock standing there with nothing to say. It is not like the theatre where one learns ones lines, and follows a script.

The aim of mediumship is to prove survival, after death, by giving individual messages that are constructive and relevant to the person's life style.

I walked the length of the isle and into the parlour to join everybody for coffee and snacks. The still small voice said 'ask Steve to help you'. I had known Steve and Jonathan for many years; between them, they ran Stretford and Wythenshawe venues.

So I took a deep breath and approached Steve who is the president. In his sixties, dressed posh in a black suit, always wears a tie, and say 'Harry whom is as well-known as me, has asked me to ask you for help with my conundrum' (when in doubt, I can always blame Harry.)

It was as if he knew, what I was about to say before I said it, he is psychic I think. So without more of 'ado', arrangements were made for him to come and visit me on the following Thursday afternoon. My plan being that I would phone Jean and ask my questions, with a bit of luck, I would have the photograph, plus more relevant information.

Tuesday lunchtime came and I was just back from walking the dogs. I noticed jutting out from my wooden post box, a brown, postcard sized envelope. I was so excited, and all fingers and thumbs, as I tore it open for it is post-marked Lancaster.

There were about 30 boys, around thirteen years old, dressed in short trousers and long woollen socks. What a motley crew they looked. The tallest of them standing on the back two rows and the smaller ones, either kneeling or sitting cross legged, below the teacher, who was standing in the centre of this old black and white photograph. It was him alright, posh Mr Teasdale, adorned in his dickey- bow, whilst the lads, hardly wore a tie between them.

Ardwick Municipal, Standard Six, 1931

In the centre, at the bottom of the picture, was a placard, which read 'Ardwick Municipal, Standard Six, 1931. Although it was a very poor photograph as Jean stated. I did not need a magnifying glass this time, as it was definitely the man I saw at Ivy Cottages. The only difference being that his black hair is plastered back, not a wave in sight and he looked older than his 25 years.

I decided to phone her, as I didn't think that she went out, to thank her. So armed with my ciggys and a list of questions, added to which was the query about his hair, for it is the only thing that was different. I dialled her number whilst wondering if I dared ask her if she has any idea of what he had been up to during his life.

All sorts of theories were running through my head, one being had he ever been married as I found it a bit unusual that an attractive, educated man wasn't. I also wanted to know how old he was when he made his will and it seemed odd to me, especially leaving it to an elderly housekeeper. May be he had a life threating illness and that was why he had it drawn up in the prime of his life or was it that he was just very methodical? If he was so organised why couldn't he have he left a suicide letter?

It was then as I was listening to the dialling tone and hoping she was at home that I recalled an incident from his class. He looked extremely agitated, constantly mopping his brow with a very white handkerchief as the perspiration was literally dripping down his face. I remembered thinking to myself, as a young child, did the man who came to the classroom door, upset him?

At this point in thought, she answered the phone and I began by thanking her profusely for the photograph. I started my questions with the hair issue. 'Yes, dear, now that you say that, I recall that he did have thick, wavy hair but remember in those days, it was the fashion for men to plaster their hair with 'Brylcream' or some other product. He was always the height of fashion', she said proudly.

On the subject of his lifestyle, she became very vague, reiterating that at that time, she was 'only a slip of a girl'. She did confirm that as far as she knew, he was completely healthy. We said our 'goodbyes' and I wished her all the best.

The more I thought about things, the more mind-boggling they became. There must be a very strong bond between me and Harry. Who else comes back from the dead? I must ask Steve if he has ever heard of this. I can only assume that Harry has unfinished business which some African people believe to be the case in 'Juju' However, I have no connection with Africa or any of their customs or rituals. I had even wondered if Harry was perhaps my father but I ruled this out for a number of reasons. Firstly, I could not see Harry and my mother making 'whoopee'. As there was no unusual response or interrogation when I told her that he had insisted on calling me Elizabeth. Besides my mother had very dark hair, almost as black as Harry's and I was, what one would call a strawberry blonde. My dad, I can only remember, was bald with grey/ blue eyes. Jack, my half-brother, was fairer than myself, feature for feature. I did not resemble any of them, apart from the petite build like my mother and some of her siblings.

Sadly, Jack was born with 'a hare-lip' so it was difficult to tell if he resembled my father or Rebecca Regan, his mother. I had never seen a photo of her or come to think of it, a photograph of my dad when he was young.

So for the time being, I can only conclude that Harry and I have lived past lives together. Perhaps he was the 'Black Sultan' and I, his favourite wife, so was he a psychic and subconsciously called me 'Elizabeth'? If so, then there are other unknown powers present, for Harry, surely could not have known he was going to die or that the name changing would, decades later, become so important.

Chapter 55

Dogs were barking and the phone was ringing so back to reality whatever that may be. Reality is defined in the Oxford Dictionary as;

1. The quality of being real/resemblance to an original.
2. The real world as distinct from imagination or fantasy.
3. Something that exists or is real.

'No man is an island' and no man can be fully understood without examining him within the context of the society in which he lives.

So if I was African, then 'Harry' would be a spirit who has unfinished business and perfectly acceptable in that society; however, this is not so in England but considered insanity.

Anyway it was Noel on the other end of the phone, asking to be brought up to date. So I told him that Steve was coming and hopefully, we may have more understanding of what is actually happening.

I then go on to mention that I think Harry may have been 'The Black Sultan' in a past life and I, his beautiful, white, European, captive named 'Shams-ed-Douha' or 'Morning

Sun'. Emphasis on the word 'beautiful' and the fact that I would have had gorgeous, golden hair, hence 'morning sun'.

I ignored the roars of Noel's, riotous laughter, in the most lady- like fashion. Suddenly, the room became icy cold, just like it had been in the infirmary, all those years ago. I then began to feel most peculiar sensations running through my body and instantly said to Noel 'Harry's here'.

'What is wrong, Liz' Noel said, sounding surprised. The best description I can give is that it was as if somebody is inside the whole of my body and it is not mine any more. There are two of us sharing the same physical body.

During my S.N.U. studies/exams, I had read about spirits doing this; it is called 'Overshadowing'.

The whole incident lasted no more than 60 seconds. The room returned to its normal temperature and he was gone. So what was Harry trying to tell us?

In retrospect, this overshadowing happened when Noel was laughing, so we were now wondering if he was confirming that he was 'The Black Sultan' in his past life and me, his favourite wife. (I would not have been too chuffed about the other wives) So knowing me, I guess I would have got rid or discredited them in some way as I have always liked to be 'top dog'.

Now is Harry strongly confirming his presence, when I hit the nail on the head or when I am talking gobbledy gook'? We do not know, so I would have to ask Steve when he arrived if he had any answers. Failing that, I shall set some form of a test, by stating things that I know to be correct and see what happens.

I would have to let all possibilities in and then sift them out, one by one. Hopefully, I would then get closer to the truth.

Steve arrived an hour late, having got lost which was not surprising, considering my property does not show up on any computer system / tom- tom sat nav. I found this out, many moons ago, when there was a serious accident on the lane. The car driver apparently lost control and went over the stone wall and into the field. I spent my time (a qualified nurse) unable to assist the injured driver and passenger because the emergency services got lost and I had to stand by the phone to direct them.

I later complained to the local council who said they would amend the problem. They never did as Shaun and I had regularly checked this on the Red Cross ambulance system. God help me if I have a fire! ; For by the time they arrive, they will have spotted the flames a mile away. I repeatedly, complained to the council authorities because I could not understand how they managed to send my council tax bill, every year, when I do not exist. Again, no satisfactory answer from them! I also pointed out that the property was built around 1620, so surely they have had enough time to sort this out but as we all know, the powers that be move very slowly, Oldham council gets first prize. I have now given up on my endeavour to sort it out. The final straw being when some 'bright spark' in the council offices, informed me that he could not sort it out as I did not show up on the system. Harry give me strength and patience, not to kill anybody!

Steve made himself comfortable on the settee and thankfully, brought out a 'backy-tin' and ciggy papers from a large bag which he was carrying. 'Coffee or tea' I asked, in my most patient, reassuring voice. 'Do you like dogs?' I enquired as I noticed Bess giving him the 'evil eye'. She is good at this, being six stone and jet black, she emphasises her large white teeth by, silently, curling up her upper lip, to display them.

I did not wait for an answer because he didn't look 'a happy bunny' so I gave him the newspaper articles regarding Harry. 'It is best that you read them, in order to draw your own conclusions, without any input from me' I said whilst keeping a close eye on Bess.

This was something I learned when assessing prison inmates; are they bad or are they mad? If one goes in 'cold' without any information, there are no preconceived ideas. If one is told to assess a schizophrenic, you have a tendency to see only that. I did not wish for Steve's views to be coloured in any way.

Well, I need not to have worried. After another anxious look at Bess, there were no teeth visible, despite still giving him the evil eye. Rocky, on the other hand, was wagging his tail and trying to lick his face, He obviously, had decided that Steve was harmless.

He rolled, yet another, ciggy and I started to think that perhaps he must be of a nervous disposition. The colour had just drained from his face when Bess decided to suddenly change her position and lay down. 'That is a good sign and she thinks you are ok' I said, using my still reassuring voice. 'Could have fooled me' he said, looking very unconvinced. 'Ah well, life has its' little ups and downs; they are character building' I thought to myself.

He finally finished reading the articles and looked up.' Firstly, who goes and gets sheet music for Christmas and then, kills yourself? he said which is a good question. 'Secondly, who touches two boys up together? No self-respecting 'paedo' would leave himself wide open with a witness', he continued. This was also a good point and exactly what Noel said. 'Thirdly' he added, whilst still tentatively watching Bess, 'I think this is a set-up. Do we know if Florence Tinsley, the housekeeper, knew the two boys as you told me that she had inherited all his money? He would not be the first person to be murdered for money' he concluded.

After all those years, a very well respected teacher, suddenly, decides to seduce two boys in a school classroom, at the same time. Strange, indeed!

Over the next half an hour, I told him the story, chapter and verse. He decides to trace up Florence and, hopefully, the will, to see how much money was involved as we did not know at this point.

Steve was beginning to relax now as Bess snored her head-off and Rocky had settled down. As an after-thought, he said he would try to check out for any criminal offences adding that it should not be too hard with a name like Bousfield Booth Teasdale.

Well, I could tell that he was intrigued and well on-board now. He had never heard of somebody coming back like this before. The only explanation he could give, was that Harry and I went back a long way in our past lives. We were 'soul mates' which prompted me to tell him about 'The Black Sultan' who died an untimely death, way back in the 14th century. It looked to me like Harry was in the habit of getting himself into 'a mucky mess'. 'Like attracts Like' they say!

I went back up the steps into the kitchen, to make yet another brew. We were up to our eyeballs in nicotine and caffeine. Suddenly, I heard Steve's low screech. 'Oh, God' I thought to myself, wondering what Bess had done to him as I dashed back into the living room.

She had not done anything as Steve was just sat there, staring at the bookcase on the opposite wall. Feeling a great sense of relief that Bess had not bitten him, I asked him what the matter was. He went on to tell me that whilst sitting, frightened of getting up as Bess was now awake, he was staring at the Mensa puzzle books (he is in Mensa), behind the leaded glass doors of the bookcase, when two Mensa books on the middle shelf, started to move off on their own accord.

Well, my reassuring voice was almost worn out as I finally said 'Don't worry; it is only Harry, confirming his existence'! This voice did not portray my true feelings as Steve had gone a real funny colour, best described as a whiter shade of pale. During our conversations, Steve had told me about his failing health. Five years ago, at the tender age of 59, he had suffered a severe heart attack. He underwent a bypass operation, during which he arrested and obviously almost died. The salient point being that it were years ago since I resuscitated anybody and would obviously be, a bit 'rusty' doing it. One loses one's skills, like anything else, if they are not used. I would have to dial 999 but by the time the ambulance would have found my house, rigor mortis would have well and truly set in. Anyway thank God, all was ok. All's well that ends well!

On Steve's next visit, we dimmed the lights and burned some incense which 'would lift the vibrations', according to Steve. I did not argue, for he was the expert in these matters. Personally, I do not think that Harry cares a damn as he comes and goes, like a free spirit.

After about half an hour into my meditation, there was no sign of him and I was beginning to think that we were on a fool's errand. So I lit a ciggy and was about to make coffee, when that old, familiar feeling (overshadowing) seizes me. I told Steve that Harry was here and with that, he asks Harry a number of pre-planned questions. It was then that the pictures began to fast forward in my mind's eye.

Two men on a staircase, a black bird with its wings outstretched and a red motorbike! At that point, I became distracted by Steve, saying that he cannot look at me as I was changing, facially, into a man. Now, I could not say for sure as there was no mirror at hand. I felt incapable of standing up to look, with the tea lights flickering. The candle went out as a single, blue ball of light bobs around the room. It was similar to the spirit orbs which we had seen at Ivy Cottages but I could see a face and then Harry was gone.

During that brief period, two questions were put to Harry. 'Were you murdered and if so, who killed you'? I was not at all clear what the pictures meant but was able to describe them in great detail whilst they were still fresh in my mind. The bird in flight; was it a blackbird or crow? It could have even been a raven: I just did not know but what does come to mind is the story of Odin, a Viking God and a raven. It was summoned by the pagan warriors so that they would win the battle. So does this mean that there was violence on the library staircase?

Secondly, my description of the motor bike is, according to Steve, a Vincent bike which was definitely around in the 1950's. I doubt if I would have known this as a 10yr. old child. The two, slim men whom I felt were in their 40's, were not particularly well dressed. One was faceless but the other man's face was clear as a bell with thin, mousey, coloured hair showing at the front of the brim of the cap which was grey and his eyes were possibly brown. Steve put a photo kit picture from my description. It was like being back at the police station with one of my lads from Elphine House. I was just so thankful that he could sketch as I never could have done it. During my nurse training, the tutors told me to draw boxes as they could not distinguish a heart from a liver.

Chapter 56

We managed to trace the correct Florence Tinsley who was born in 1883 which would make her 70 yrs. old at the time of his death. I still cannot 'get my head around this' for she would surely have died before him. Why, I ask myself, did he not leave anything to his family or Jean, his niece, for instance?

According to archived records, Florence moved into Gt. Western St., as his housekeeper, in 1950, shortly after she was widowed. She left after his death in early 1954. She appears to have had a very sad life with five of her children dying before her own death in 1971. Perhaps, Harry felt pity for her but how would he know that he was going to die? One question leads to another: how could he have known that the changing of my name to Elizabeth would be significant, 60 yrs. on.

What also came to light was the fact that he moved into 185 Gt. Western St. with his mother in 1934 and she died in 1949. Consequently, Florence moved in, leaving her remaining family member in Dudley. So was there any connection with her and his mother? for if he advertised for a housekeeper, why not use the local papers?. The West Midlands was a fair distance in those days but Florence's maiden name was Bunn and his mother's was Booth, hence Bousfield Booth.

He must have left his hometown of Lancaster when he commenced teaching in 1926 so presumably; he had lodgings in the Manchester area, prior to 1934. He returned most weekends according to Jean Teasdale.

Great Western Street

Ardwick Municipal c1950

BAR 029024

CERTIFIED COPY OF AN ENTRY
Pursuant to the Births and Deaths Registration Act 1953

DEATH

Entry No. **31**

Registration district: **Dudley**	Administrative area: **County Borough of Dudley**
Sub-district: **Dudley**	

1. Date and place of death: 11th September 1971, Guest Hospital, Dudley
2. Name and surname: Florence TINSLEY
3. Sex: Female
4. Maiden surname of woman who has married: BUNN
5. Date and place of birth: 5th October 1883, Sedgley
6. Occupation and usual address: Widow of Samuel TINSLEY a Gas Engineer, 41 Avenue Road, Coseley
7. (a) Name and surname of informant: Certificate received from W. Malcolm Wright, Coroner for Dudley. Inquest held 6th October 1971
   (b) Qualification:
   (c) Usual address:
8. Cause of death:
   I a. Broncho pneumonia
   b. Fracture of the neck of the femur
   II. Ischaemic heart disease due to coronary atheroma
   Misadventure
9. I certify that the particulars given me above are true to the best of my knowledge and belief — Signature of informant
10. Date of registration: Seventh October 1971
11. Signature of registrar: B.I. Hawes, Deputy Registrar

Certified to be a true copy of an entry in a register in my custody.
S. Thomas { Deputy } *Superintendent Registrar / *Registrar
Date 24-5-20

CAUTION: THERE ARE OFFENCES RELATING TO FALSIFYING OR ALTERING A CERTIFICATE AND USING OR POSSESSING A FALSE CERTIFICATE. °CROWN COPYRIGHT

WARNING: A CERTIFICATE IS NOT EVIDENCE OF IDENTITY.

The other point being, when I heard him call out 'Elizabeth', outside Ardwick Municipal School, I still cannot remember if it was a Thursday or Friday. (Literally hours after his death) Also, for that matter, I did not know what time he died on Thursday, 10th December; it could have been the early hours of the morning or just before midnight.

So my next step was to contact Plymouth Grove School where he was teaching at the time of his death which neither my mother nor I were aware of this fact. One has to assume that he left Ardwick Municipal School due to it changing to an all-girls school in 1952. He had worked there since 1926 and throughout the War years as teachers were exempt from military service?

Unfortunately, it was the school holidays so I decided, instead, to chase the' last will and testament' up. This turned out to be £12 well spent, for what 'can't speak: can't lie'. He had left absolutely nothing to Florence Tinsley so that ruled out the possibility that she was in league with the two boys as a motive for his money. His estate of £4,972.11 shillings and 5 pence would be around the equivalent of £120.000 by today's standards. There were a number of bequests to various charities. One in particular struck me as very poignant as it was the very same dog's home from which I got Bess. Also included was the Cat's Home and the blind children's charity but nothing to family or any friends. I was left wondering why Jean Teasdale was told by Richard, the butcher from Beswick, why this was so. It seems that there was some sort of family conflict.

The will was drawn up in 1950 with all the 'İ's and the T's dotted', to the extent that he wanted to be cremated, without any fuss or mourners. It was a very plain and simple funeral service, indeed. I am me and he is he but at the age of 44 yrs., this would never have entered my head.

This then poses a question in my mind: Did he know that he would die at a youngish age or was he just, very well organised? If so, why did he not leave a suicide letter?

This is the last Will of me

DOUGLIAS BOOTH TEASDALE of 185 Great Western Street in the City of Manchester Schoolmaster

1. I REVOKE all former Wills and testamentary dispositions heretofore made by me

2. I APPOINT John Austin Naylor Solicitor of 77, King Street in the City of Manchester or the Senior partner for the time being of Messrs Atkinson Saunders & Company Solicitors 77 King Street Manchester to be the Executor and Trustee of this my Will

3. I DESIRE that my body shall be cremated at the Manchester Crematorium and that my ashes shall be scattered in the Garden of Remembrance there I DESIRE that my funeral shall be as quiet and simple as possible and with no announcements or acknowledgments in any publication whatsoever

4. IT IS MY WISH that the instructions that I shall leave to my Executor as to the disposal of my personal belongings shall be strictly complied with in all material particulars so far as it is practicable and in the interests of my estate generally

5. I DEVISE AND BEQUEATH all my real and personal estate whatsoever and wheresoever including any property over which I have a general testamentary power of appointment unto my Trustee upon trust to sell call in and convert the same into money at such time and in such manner as he shall think fit with full power to postpone the sale calling in or conversion of the whole or any part or parts of my said estate during such time as he in his uncontrolled discretion shall think proper and to hold the moneys to arise from such sale calling in and conversion as aforesaid and my ready money upon trust

(i) to pay thereout all my debts funeral and testamentary expenses and any legacies given by any Codicil hereto and the duty on any such legacy given free of duty and subject thereto

(ii) to divide the residue of such moneys equally amongst the following Societies and Institutions for the general purposes thereof respectively namely:- The Actors' Benevolent Fund   The Benevolent and Orphan Fund of the National Union of Teachers   The Crippled Childrens Help Society Manchester   The Grand Order of Lady Ratlings' "Cup of Kindness" Fund (Variety Artistes)   Henshaws Institution for the Blind   The Manchester and District Cats' Shelter   The Manchester and District Home for Lost Dogs   The Manchester and Salford Blind Aid Society   The National Institute for the Blind   The Royal Albert Institution Lancaster   The Royal Society for the Prevention of Cruelty to Animals   St.Dunstan's (The

> Organisation for Blinded Soldiers Sailors and Airmen)
> The Variety Artistes' Benevolent Fund and Institution
> Variety Artistes' Ladies' Guild and Orphanage
> (iii) I declare that the receipt of the Treasurer
> or other proper officer for the time being of the same
> respective Societies and Institutions shall be a sufficient
> discharge to my Trustee for the amount payable to the
> respective Societies and Institutions
> 6. I DECLARE that the said John Austin Naylor
> or any other Executor or Trustee of this my Will being a
> Solicitor or other person engaged in any profession shall be
> entitled to act in his professional capacity in any matters
> arising in the administration of my estate or in the execution
> of the trusts of this my Will and shall be entitled to be
> paid free of duty not only his professional charges for the
> work so done in the same manner as if he were not an
> Executor or Trustee but also to be paid his reasonable charges
> for other work done and time spent by him in the premises
> IN WITNESS whereof I have hereunto set my hand
> this Twentieth day of September One thousand
> nine hundred and fifty
>
> SIGNED by the said Bousfield Booth
> Teasdale in the joint presence
> of himself and us who at his request
> and in such joint presence have
> hereunto subscribed our names as
> witnesses   *B. B. Teasdale*

I made contact with the Law Society, in an attempt to trace a Mr Naylor of Atkinson & Saunders, 77 King St., Manchester, who was named as executor of the will. Their offices no longer existed, demolished many years ago, I guess, leaving just a paved area where they once were.

I seemed to be going 'two steps forward and three steps back', as Atkinson & Saunders till existed, dating back to the 1890's but what little hope I had, was soon extinguished as Mr Naylor, as expected, was long since deceased. They had no records dating back to the 1950's

So, I was back to the drawing board, wondering if there was a bigger picture. As far as I was concerned (though I am not an authority on the subject and neither does anyone else appear to be) it was about coming back from the dead, to seek justice. One would think that those responsible must be up there, dead also: so why can he not sort them out himself?

The only answer I can find is that reincarnation does exist and that he and I have made some sort of contract in a pre-existing life. I wish I knew what it was but there again maybe it is better that I did not know as I would obviously handle the situation differently and probably cock the whole thing up. It is said that a little knowledge is a dangerous thing!

Chapter 57

There had been no response from Friends Reunited, Plymouth Grove or Ardwick Municipal on our request for information on Mr Teasdale's death: As I said to Mandy, a friend of mine, 'another dead end'. She suggested something which turned out to be very interesting. She came up with the idea of visiting the Manchester Police Museum, to see if we could get hold of PC James Marriot's notes.

I personally could not see how this would be helpful. After all, the allegations made by boys, failed to produce any evidence so I put her idea on the back burner. A week or so later, Ann, a long-time friend from our nurse training days in Stepping Hill Hospital, contacted me and wanted to go to the police museum. She was a costume and props volunteer at the Garrick Theatre in Stockport and needed to borrow two 1920's police helmets for one of their productions. Having no idea where it was located and it was only open on Tuesdays to the public, she asked if I knew where Newton St., Manchester was. Of course, I did as when my Dad was a postman; it housed the largest sorting office within the Manchester area.

It was then that it hit me: was Harry trying to tell me something? I had never heard of the place before but in the space of two weeks, two friends had mentioned it. Maybe, I thought, I was going down the wrong road, being more interested in Bill Singleton's knowledge than PC Marriot whom I assumed was long since dead.

We set off for the museum and just as we were entering the building, I was suddenly seized with a coughing fit. It was so bad that a kindly policeman, dressed in an old fashioned uniform, produced a glass of water. Ann had hurriedly left, eager to find her helmets (some nurse she was: I could have choked to death).

I sipped my water and chatted to the nice policeman who informed me that he had now retired from the Force and worked there as a volunteer. He was obviously very proud of his position and was eager to show me around this restored old Victorian police station with its original cells, charge room and a large collection of historic items.

We were getting on 'like a house on fire' so I told him whilst browsing a collection of very long truncheons, spanning 150 years that I was doing a family history (my usual white lie: for I needed to keep my street cred.). With this, he assumed that PC Marriot must be a relative and proceeded to tell me that I could fill in a form, requesting his log books if they still existed. Off he trots and brings back the form which I duly completed.

At this stage, Ann returns looking disappointed as they will not hire the helmets. We set off to the nearest fancy dress shop, in the hope of obtaining them there.

I decided to go to Plymouth Grove School. It was Thursday, 6th October, 2011 and I was very hopeful of finding some reference to the two boys and the police visit. Surely, there must be some documentation regarding this incident.

I had decided to drive through Ardwick and up Devonshire St. through the very same traffic lights when I heard Mr Teasdale calling out 'Elizabeth', all those years ago. It was daylight and my appointment with Mr Cook, the headmaster, at 5pm so I had time to walk round the derelict area where my old school used to stand

Ardwick Municipal School-2011

Sadly, the monument which stood next to the bus depot was no longer in existence. I find this so sad and wonder what has become of it: surely, it had not been bulldozed down. In my day, people used to place poppies and cards there, in memory of all the young men who were killed in the two World Wars. Well, I guess that's progress for you!

It definitely puts things into perspective and makes me feel ashamed of myself as just then, I was worrying about a dental problem. I had a persistent nagging toothache which would not go away, despite antibiotics and local antiseptic treatment on a number of occasions. My dentist said that the front tooth would have to be extracted so I threw a 'wobbler', out of sheer vanity, and refused to let him take it out. 'I am going for a second opinion' Harry'; I said and asked him sweetly if he would make it better.

I arrived early at the school so I sat in the car for a ciggy. As I puffed away, old memories came flooding back as every Wednesday night, us Teddy Boys and Girls would jive the evening away. It was rock and roll music with such greats as Bill Hayley, Little Richard and my old time favourite, Elvis Presley. What a good time, we all had!

I was greeted by Mr Cook who directed me to a small office. The desk was strewn with dairies and ledgers, dating back to the 1880's. Of course, I ignored those and started thumbing through the ones from 1951.

I found a number of entries for Mr Teasdale:

Bousfield Booth Teasdale appointed on the 1st September, 1952

Bousfield Booth Teasdale produced a play 'The Golden West' with Class 24, at the Library Theatre, Manchester (performance went well with favourable reviews and comments from the adjudication officer of 'The Adventure Theatre Guild'.

23/7/53: Gave presentation of 'The Golden West' at the Children's Theatre.

2/11/53: Took over school in headmaster's absence.

I was astounded that there was no entry for Thursday, 3/12/53 regarding the police visiting the school. Why not? I thought to myself and did the headmaster choose to ignore it: if so, why? I looked closely again but there was no evidence of anything being erased or crossed out. There was no entry that Mr Teasdale was absent from his class on the following day so one assumes that he neither went 'off-sick' nor was suspended regarding these allegations.

The next relevant entry was for 7/12/53: Absent, received news at 1pm re: accident fell down stairway at the Central Library.

10/12/53: received news of his death.

17/12/53: Xmas Hols. : commence: school closed early half-day in respect of his death. Mr Howarth, headmaster, went to his funeral.

'Why is it, I keep meeting so many dead ends'? I ask myself as there were no Ancoats Hospital records and no inquest report; maybe because it happened so long ago! One would have thought that the headmaster, of the time, would have documented something so important regarding the boy's allegations and the police visit. Anything else of any importance appears in the school ledger.

So it was back to the 'drawing board', for I will be damned if I am not going to solve this puzzle. I owe it to Harry,' it is pay-back time'! After all, he has been my 'guardian angel' all these years. When I look at Bess who is 9 yrs. old now, I dread to think what would have happened to me when confronted by that rapist, on the moors and not to mention all the other incidents where he pre-warned me of any dangers.

Chapter 58

The following Saturday morning, I woke up, for the first time in a couple of weeks, full of the 'joys of spring'. I could not believe it as I had no more toothache and had slept soundly throughout the night but my face felt funny. I dashed to the mirror, only to see the lower half of my face, where the offending tooth was, terribly swollen. 'What to do now'? I thought to myself as I stared at my face, resembling a hamster in the mirror. The dentist was closed and it was a good job that I had no engagements, that weekend.

Suddenly, it dawned on me that Harry was at it again, sending white cells to fight the infection. Needless to say, on the next visit to the dentist, he was surly surprised to find that my tooth was completely better. Silently, I thanked Harry, thinking that there are no ends to his skills which made me more determined than ever, to find out what exactly happened to him.

I set off to the library, yet again, as I was sure that Bill Singleton must know something as this incident must have been the talk of Plymouth Grove School, at the time. Luckily, it was a different librarian who would not have heard of my incompetent computer skills. I adopted the 'sweet and helpless, old lady smile' in order to get her to help me find every Bill Singleton, over 65 yrs., throughout the country. I was determined to leave no stone unturned. With this done, I set off home and over the course of the next few days, proceeded to phone every one of them. Alas, there was no result, leaving me to wonder if he was not on the voting registrar. I supposed that he could be living abroad but that was not the impression I got from what he had written on the Friends Reunited Plymouth Grove site. It then dawned on me that the Central Library must have and accident/incident book, just like we have in the hospital wards.

Promptly, at 2pm on the following Thursday, having made an appointment, I pressed the intercom system at County Records. Up I go two flights of stairs and could not help comparing this place to the grandeur of Elliot House in Deansgate. I wondered how the staff kept so pleasant and cheerful as it would depress me, no end. The upside being that they, unlike Elliot House, had an excellent coffee machine.

It was much easier to find information now that I had dates so armed with my coffee I discover the following document:

Accident in Central Library Building - 10.40 am on 7/12/53

1. At Approximately 10.40 am on Monday 7/12/53 the body of a man, subsequently identified as Mr. Bousfield Booth Teasdale was found at the bottom of the stairwell below the Henry Watson Music Library entrance.
2. There were indications that he had fallen over the guardrail on the staircase from the balcony immediately below the Henry Watson Music Library on the second floor of the building. Enquires into the cause of the accident are being made by the police.
3. Representatives of the Town Clerk's and City Architect's departments inspected the stairwell at the instigation of the City Librarian at 4.30 pm the same day.

> 4. Mr. Teasdale had visited the Henry Watson Music Library prior to the incident.
>
> Charles Nowell
City Librarian
>
> Memm. The committee were informed that Mr. Teasdale had died of his injuries.
>
> ### 31/12/53 - **Subject – Accident in Central Library Death of Mr. Bousfield Booth Teasdale**
>
> The Town Clerk's representative attended an inquest on 16th December on the death of Mr. Bousfield Booth Teasdale. The committee will recollect that the man who was a teacher employed by the Corporation of Education Authority fell down the stairwell behind the lift shaft in the Henry Watson Music Library and subsequently died. The coroner brought in a verdict of suicide while the balance of his mind was disturbed and no criticism or comment of any sort was made with regard to the management or structure of the library.
>
> Philip B. Dingle
Town Clerk

This, unfortunately, did not tell me very much, leaving me with more questions than answers. If only I could get into the Central Library and see exactly how anyone could fall over the guardrail! The other point being that in another twelve months, after it reopens following the refurbishment, everything will have changed.

So back down the stone steps, I go, which desperately needed a shovel and broom. I returned home and decided that I needed a glass of wine, a ciggy and 'a think'. I felt Harry was around as I had a fleeting thought go through my mind: I wondered if any of the staff at Elliot House, had worked at the Central Library. If I had got this right than, surely, they could explain the layout of the stairwell and the surrounding area. It was worth a try so I phoned the nice Dave and low and behold, for once, I am in luck. There is a female staff member who may be able to help me.

Armed with my questions, I returned to Elliot House, to meet Alison whom Dave had put in the picture. We found ourselves a quiet spot behind a bookcase with its shelves full of historical information.

'Alison, is it possible in your opinion that Mr Teasdale could have perhaps fainted or tripped over the guardrail'? I asked politely as my first question. 'No way' she said, indicating the height with her right arm to be past waist level. When asked if he could have been pushed over it: 'Easy' she said, adding that one blow to the head whilst he was off guard would do the trick. She was a girl after my own heart and then it became more interesting when she produced a layout of the building and photographs. She pointed out that somebody could have waited in the toilet, next to the stairwell. 'I would imagine that it would be quiet at that time on a Monday morning and that is the only exit/entrance, down the stairs to the 1st floor' she said. Evidently, the lift only went to the 1st floor so one had to use the main staircase or lift, in order to exit the building from the Music Section of the library.

She seemed to be enjoying herself as an amateur sleuth (probably relieved the boredom) and goes on to say that the staircase from the Music Library continues down to the ground exit only. (I could not get my head around this). 'Even today, people still tend to use it as a short-cut to the street, at the side of the main entrance, It does not have an alarm and things are more stringent than in the 1950's', she went on to say.

I was thinking that she might have 'hit the nail on the head' as if I am correct then it would be easy to go quickly down those emergency stairs with not a soul in sight: then hop on a motor bike and off as Harry showed me with one's pillion passenger in tow if there were two of them.

Alison and I were becoming quite pally and friendly, so I posed the question to her that if you were going to commit suicide, would you do it there? 'Definitely not' she said adamantly: 'the top of the guardrail is very narrow and the space between that and the lift shaft is not very wide. I would go to the top of the building and outside onto the ledge (which you can still do today though it is prohibited) and jump off into the street. You would definitely be dead as it is much higher than 50-60 ft.' she went on to explain.

A debate then followed as to who would go to a library, in order to kill oneself? There are far more effective ways and besides, who would safely tuck their Christmas music sheets in their pocket before doing so? What would be the point? We also wondered why nobody appears to have asked the librarian who must have booked out the music sheets and possibly knew him as a frequent visitor. She certainly would be able to comment on his demeanour at the time, prior to killing himself, a few minutes later.

This then brings us to the fact that he lived for three days with these appalling injuries. His fractured skull could coincide to a blow to the head. The fractured femurs may have resulted from someone falling straight down as there wasn't enough room for his body to twist and turn, according to Alison. Consequently, he would have landed on his feet and his thigh bones would be pushed into his pelvis by the force of the fall. This fracturing caused the internal bleeding and serious injuries.

If I had tried to murder someone, I think I would be making an urgent visit to Ancoats Hospital, to finish the job off before he could possibly talk. One wouldn't know if he would regain consciousness and 'spill the beans'. Now to do this, even today, would be dead easy. (Excuse the pun) All one has to do is to tell the sister-in-charge that you are a close relative. On a busy Accident & Emergency unit, you would be directed to his cubicle as that is where he would likely be with blood drips, tubes and possibly oxygen at his bedside. It would not take two minutes; to place a pillow over his head and nobody would be any the wiser. In my experience, trauma units are extremely busy with lots of activity and the staff would have no reason to suspect anything as he would have been logged in as an 'accidental injuries, due to a fall.

Well, I thanked her profusely for her assistance as I picked up my handbag, feeling, for once, that I was getting somewhere.

As I type this page, I get a funny feeling from Harry. It feels a bit like one's hair standing on end but all over the body. I believe this to be 'overshadowing' which he does when I am on the right track. The only thing wrong is that he is telling me that there was only one man who sped off on the Vincent motor bike.

The Central Library, Manchester

The Music Library

Chapter 59

I was left pondering on the idea that it was possible that the two boys made up their story to discredit him because he had caught them in some wrong doing and were afraid of the consequences. I, repeatedly, asked myself 'why two boys in a school classroom?' as there is a golden rule; no witnesses to one's sins!

What Alison had said about the stairwell and the fact that an Art Library had been added, went round and round in my mind. Resident actors would perform plays for the public; after all, it was documented in the school ledgers that Harry produced a play called 'The Golden West' in that very building. It was quite feasible that he had a number of acquaintances' in the theatrical profession thus the statement at the inquest 'He was well known to producers of school plays and concerts'. So just on the off chance, I phoned 'The Cup of Kindness Charity' Artists Benevolent Fund which was one of the beneficiaries of his will, to find out if they had any information on him.

The lady who answered was very helpful saying that she would get back to me after their annual general meeting which would be held soon. This would give her the opportunity to see if any of the members remembered him. A couple of weeks later, she kindly left a message on my answering machine, stating that 'he had not come up on their radar.'

I, then, decided to have another session with Steve in an attempt to get more information before I would contact Jean Teasdale.

Within the space of ten minutes, Harry was present and Steve began to ask our pre-planned questions. The information gained was more or less the same as our previous session except for a couple of pictures which Harry showed me. The first being a large stone building with two pillars at the entrance and what appeared to be a reclining yellow stone lion on its' frontage. The other picture was of a man's arm, encased in a blue sleeve. It was adorned with three, separate, braided gold bands around the cuff. This, I interpreted as a signal of rank. The incense candle snuffed itself out or rather Harry did it as I knew he had left us.

A moment later, Rocky was prating about and wanted to spend a penny so up the steps, I went to the back door with the dog in hot pursuit. Suddenly, I was overwhelmed by the strong smell of perfume or aftershave. It was definitely not the incense as it was completely different. Steve could not smell it but there again; I was almost at the backdoor of the flat roof extension. I opened the door and the two dogs rushed out as another picture formed in my mind. I could easily identify it as the Manchester Art Gallery.

A discussion followed as to the validity of the information as I had repeatedly explained to Steve that I did not know whose thoughts I was verbalising. (Harrys' or mine). If the thoughts were spontaneous e.g. not requested (An example being of the incident with my little 2.C.V.6.) but this cannot always be achieved or acknowledged to be accurate. Usually it has to repeat itself within the next couple of days; having said that, I received accurate information which had come only once.

We could not understand the relevance of the Art Gallery so I asked Steve if there was something else there in the 1940's or 50's? He insisted that there was not so I let the matter drop. We did not fare much better on the relevance of the blue sleeve with the gold braid.

Steve repeatedly asked me as to what shade of blue I had seen but I could only answer that it was like my old, blue car. Steve sighed wearily as he remembered that I was colour-blind and this was not very helpful. He decided to look up the relevance of the gold braided sleeve cuff as I wondered if it was 'Police' or 'Air Force'.

At the next available opportunity, we wandered round the Art Gallery, looking for some clues in the paintings. There was absolutely nothing so I asked Steve if it was an art gallery during Harry's time. He frowned as he became cross with me and I could well understand it as I had kept mithering him about it.

To make amends, I treated him to lunch in their posh restaurant where all the people were 'lardy, dah'. We opted for the traditional fish and chips which turned out to be 'sautéed potatoes'. It was served with a large slice of lemon which was fine with my hake but I did notice that there was no vinegar included with the condiments on the table 'cos it was upper-class, I guess. Much to Steve's horror, I asked the waiter for some vinegar which arrived in a small bowl accompanied by a mustard spoon. (As they say; you can take the girl out of Ardwick but you cannot take Ardwick out of the girl)

It was at this rather embarrassing point for Steve when suddenly; Harry arrived laughing his socks off. It was then that I knew that Steve had been wrong so I trotted off to the Souvenir Department and requested some history on the building which she duly gave me. So Harry and I were correct and I made no bones about telling Steve this. Harry was still laughing as I stifled a chuckle.

Manchester Art Gallery

A Brief History of the Building

Royal Manchester Institution

The Royal Manchester Institution was designed by architect Charles Barry in 1824. Grade 1 listed, this Greek neo-classical style building is the only public building of its type built by Barry, who also oversaw the redesign of the Houses of Parliament in 1840. The elite of the city felt that Manchester lacked a cultural hub that could house exhibitions and lectures, providing the city with a level of culture that could match its economic and industrial success. Construction of the building began in 1825, and was completed in 1835 with the costs totaling around £30,000. The first painting to be purchased by the Institution was James Northcote's study of the black actor Ira Aldridge, 'Othello, the Moor of Venice' in 1827, which is still on display today in the Manchester Gallery. The Institution held regular art exhibitions, collected works of fine art and promoted the arts generally from the 1820s until 1882 when the building and its collections were transferred under Act of Parliament to Manchester Corporation, the forerunner to Manchester City Council. This transaction included the stipulation that the city would spend £4000 per year on art work for the following 20 years. Significant structural changes were made to the building in order to create new gallery space, however these still did not provide the space needed to house the continually growing collection.

The Manchester Athenaeum Institute

The Athenaeum building was originally constructed in 1836 as a place of education and recreation for the laboring population of Manchester Charles Dickens famously gave a lecture on October 5, 1842, praising the virtues of the Athenaeum as a 'splendid temple sacred to the education and improvement of a large class of those who, in their various useful stations, assist in the production of our wealth, and in rendering (Manchester's) name famous through the world.' Also designed by Barry, the building started out as a Gentleman's Society until serious fire damage in 1873 destroyed the original top floor of the building which included the sports hall and library Through insurance money and fund-raising the top floor was restored and extended by architects Clegg and Knowles to house a grand state-of-the-art theatre. Around the start of the Second World War the Athenaeum Institute fell into financial difficulties and had to be sold to Manchester City Council. The building was badly damaged and eventually condemned by the fire services after heavy bombing towards the end of 1940.

Growth of the Collection

Following the transferal of the building and collection to the Manchester Corporation, the gallery embarked on an exciting period of acquisitions which included Ford Madox Brown's masterpiece, 'Work.' In 1889 Manchester set out to acquire the largest painting available at that year's Royal Academy exhibition, Lord Leighton's 'Captive Andromache' (still on display today in gallery 8) and successfully outbid both Liverpool and Birmingham. The Gallery also continued to benefit from a vast number of bequests from wealthy industrial Mancunians and many of these works form the basis of the permanent collections that can still be viewed today

Now, it is not uncommon for 'spirit people' to project their own identifiable essence into the earth plane so we set off to the fragrance sections of the big stores. Having sprayed and sniffed every available aftershave from Boots chemist to Saint Anne's Square, I was reeking of the stuff at this stage. I stumbled across it (Harry again) in a very posh shop. 'What year was it first introduced? I asked politely to a shop assistant. She looked down her nose at me through her obvious false eyelashes whilst waving her hands about, flashing her red, painted acrylic fingernails and sniffed. She did this as she did not know the answer, meaning that I was unlikely to purchase it. I tried to 'best behave' so I bit my tongue, wishing that she would lose one of her false eyelashes. She should have been grateful that I only reeked of aftershave and not B.O.

I was feeling fairly positive that I had got the correct aftershave and Steve would investigate if it was, indeed, around in the 1940's and 50's. It did not take him long to discover that Dunhill cologne along with the cigarettes had been in existence since the early 1940's so I got that one right. We had no luck yet in identifying the cuff but like everything else, it would only be a matter of time before 'it comes out in the wash' as they say.

What happened next was, indeed a great surprise to me as I received a phone call from the Police Museum in Newton Street, regarding my application to see P.C James Marriot's records. Apparently, he was still alive so consequently, they did not have them. They suggested that I contact the Police Pensions Office and the request would be forwarded to him by letter. Glory be! Who would have believed it that he was still alive as he must be 'bobbing on' a bit by now.

Well, I did this the very next day using an unsealed envelope with a covering letter. Apparently, policemen make many enemies (wonder why?) and they would not send anything to him of this nature. I sent by recorded delivery just to make sure and waited anxiously for a reply.

I did realise at this stage that he must be in his eighties and that he may not be compos mentis and even if his memory is not failing. He, like Noel and me, would have seen many, many tragedies. I personally, would not have remembered names and faces five years on, let alone nearly sixty years ago. Luckily, I had the newspaper clippings and a photograph to jog his memory.

I had got a funny feeling that all was not what it seemed. My thinking may have been blinkered in respect of the fact that I wanted to identify these two boys but this may not be Harry's agenda. After all, I am in a sense Harry's puppet.

Chapter 60

One day, I was right upset when I lost my Dr Sayed's pendant. The only thing I could do was to retrace my footsteps from the back door with my eyes glued to the ground and back up onto the moorland. The dogs could not believe their luck with two walkies in one day.

I did realise that it would be like looking for a needle in a haystack. It was difficult when climbing over styles and fences, to remember exactly where I had trod. There was no luck, as expected, so we returned home without finding anything but a few used condoms and empty beer cans.

I was absolutely shattered, wishing that I had a police sniffer dog, for Rocky had trouble finding his own ball and Bess was not interested. She preferred to plod sedately by my side as she was getting old, just like me. Seven miles in the space of three hours, without coffee and ciggys, was too much at my age. The only thing left for me to do was to ask Harry to find it for me, for he would know that it was of great sentimental value to me.

The following morning I looked in every room, only to find nothing. So clutching my trowel and shovel which was usual routine, I started picking up the dog muck. Up I went the first flight of stairs and headed towards the small rose bed opposite the pond. I was thinking to myself that I might be over-feeding them as I bent down to scoop yet another lot of dirt and wishing that they would do it somewhere else. Roses only like horse manure after all. Suddenly, something catches my eye, glittering in the wintry sunlight. I picked it up minus a little gold link which must have broken.

It never ceases to astound me to this day by Harry's capabilities so I trotted happily onto the moors with the dogs in tow. I reminisced about all his achievements, for I knew full well that the pendant was not there the previous day. (Another apport)

I am grinning to myself as there is nobody around so it is ok and remembering another incident when typing this story. I put the carbon paper in the wrong way so I had a rant, blamed Harry, for I have no copy for Noel and said that he owed me 5p to photocopy it. We play these games for I know very well that he will respond and I was fully expecting to find a 5p piece, lying on the ground somewhere.

A couple of days later, I went to the CO OP supermarket and remonstrating with Harry that he had not given me the 5p. So I photocopied the page, went to the cashier, clutching a 50p piece.' I am very short of change, luv' she said and kindly uttered 'Forget it'. I wanted to burst out laughing but I did not as I didn't want a shop-full of people staring at me.

Afterwards, I was walking towards my car, unzipped my handbag to get my car keys and put the paper in, when another incident flashed through my mind. I remembered that it was many moons ago and was visiting Patsy (daughter) at her London home when the zip ended up knackered on this handbag and I was unable to fix it. So I asked Harry, yet again, because my other daughter Julie had given it to me as a present and had spent a lot of money buying it. (I know quality when I see it) and she knew I had champagne tastes and only beer money.

I guessed that Harry doesn't do handbags or goats so after my return from London, I set off to Delph village to have it repaired.' It will take a couple of weeks and we will give you a bell' he said as he handed me a receipt. I was gutted as I did not have another black bag. The very next day, the man from the shop phoned only to ask what is wrong with it. 'The zip as the teeth would not stay together' I replied. 'Come and collect it with no charge. It is not broken' he said.

Chapter 61

I decided 'to take the bull by the horns' and phone Jean Teasdale. I waited for what seemed an eternity, listening to the ring tone. I was shortly rewarded for my patience (which is very limited) when she picked up the receiver. I had planned my conversation very carefully (I call it a sandwich approach) with the good things first and last and the worst in the middle.

I asked her about her health and then referred to the will and I could tell from her response that she was genuinely dumbfounded. 'Why did Richard (the butcher) tell me that he had to pay for the funeral and had left everything to Florence' she said with dismay in her voice. Clearly, he was not telling the truth and it was then I asked her if there was any discord within the family as it was obvious that Richard wished to discredit them both. 'Oh no, dear' she responded confidently. I took a deep breath and asked her if' Bobby' was gay? 'Oh, no, no' she replied and then there was complete silence which appeared to last an eternity. Finally she said; 'You know, dear, I never knew him to have any girlfriends and of course, in those days, nobody ever spoke about such things. Well, the conversation was going fairly ok but dare I mention about the boys allegations. So 'bull by the horns again' and she quickly responded; 'That, I never did believe, for he was such a kind, gentle soul who would run down the stairs to greet us on our arrival at Great Western Street.

The conversation reverted back to his will and the amount that he had left. All she could assume was that he had accumulated it, over the years, from his teacher's salary. She added that although his father was a master builder, all his eight children were well educated before his death in 1910, at the age of 54 years. This was substantiated by the fact that not long after his father's death, Emma, his mother, moved out of the matrimonial home, after a family fall-out and moved in with her own mother. They lived modestly in a smaller rented house in the same street; no. 56 Cable Street as opposed to no. 60 which is now a pub. They lived there until 1934 and then his mother moved from Lancaster to live with Bobby at 185 Great Western Street, Manchester.

Cable Street

I was still wondering if there was any connection, family-wise with Florence but Jean was adamant that there was not and was not aware of any connections to Dudley. We both agreed that her employment as his housekeeper must have been word of mouth.

She then went on to say that her parents visited him in Ancoats Hospital and that he was in a terrible state, completely unrecognisable due to the extent of his injuries. 'The other odd thing, dear, is that although I did not attend the funeral due to work commitments, my family told me that one of the boy's mothers was at the funeral in Southern Cemetery. She was weeping profusely and obviously extremely distressed, dear' she said. 'Was it one of the boys who made the allegation? I jumped in to ask. 'Yes, yes, dear but we do not know why and I cannot for the life of me, remember her name' she replied promptly. 'Damn!! How am I going to find out about these boys' I thought to myself who surely must be still alive? I wondered what their little game was or were their allegations genuine?

The conversation ended with her telling me that his ashes were scattered in the old Remembrance Garden of Southern Cemetery.

Library Stairwell

CERTIFIED COPY OF AN ENTRY OF DEATH

GIVEN AT THE GENERAL REGISTER OFFICE

Application Number 3604680-3

REGISTRATION DISTRICT **MANCHESTER**

1953 DEATH in the Sub-district of **Manchester East Central** in the **County Borough of Manchester**

No.	1 When and where died	2 Name and surname	3 Sex	4 Age	5 Occupation	6 Cause of death	7 Signature, description and residence of informant	8 When registered	9 Signature of registrar
350	10th December, 1953 Ancoats Hospital, U.D.	Bousfield Booth TEASDALE	Male	47 years	of 185 Great Western Street, Moss Side U.D. a School Teacher	Shock and Haemorrhage- Multiple Injuries- Fell down well adjacent to lift whilst the balance of his mind was disturbed. Suicide	Certificate received from G. J. Rycroft, Coroner for Manchester. Inquest held 11th December, 1953.	Seventeenth December, 1953.	H. Wade Registrar

CERTIFIED to be a true copy of an entry in the certified copy of a Register of Deaths in the District above mentioned.

Given at the GENERAL REGISTER OFFICE, under the Seal of the said Office, the **1st** day of **November** **2011**

YD 139838

CAUTION: THERE ARE OFFENCES RELATING TO FALSIFYING OR ALTERING A CERTIFICATE AND USING OR POSSESSING A FALSE CERTIFICATE ©CROWN COPYRIGHT
WARNING: A CERTIFICATE IS NOT EVIDENCE OF IDENTITY.

Chapter 62

I made a mental note to discuss our conversation with Noel and ask him to post another message on Plymouth Grove Friends website in the hope of flushing Bill Singleton out of the woodwork.

After a lengthy debate with Noel, we both came to the conclusion that there was a strong possibility of Harry being 'Gay'. I was convinced as I could not understand from a woman's point of view why an attractive, educated man would end up unmarried, especially in that era. (The photograph does not do him justice and if it had been one of mine, it would have been straight in the dustbin before anyone could see it). He would have been 'a good catch' for any woman.

We were left pondering on the relevance of the rumour I heard as a child about the pending charges on homosexuality. I heard that he and others were due in court, however, Noel correctly pointed out that the case would continue despite his death.

Steve and I decided to go to County Records and painstakingly search through all the records for 1954. Unfortunately, they were not in alphabetical order so for over two hours we thumbed through the pages of these heavy, dusty books. I ended up with non-stop sneezing. There was absolutely nothing on Harry but there were a number of 'Powell's' (my maiden name) charged and imprisoned for a variety of offences. I hasten to add that my Dad George or half-brother Jack were not listed but there you go again, seems like criminal genes on both sides of the family.

After a sumptuous lunch of fish and chips though not the posh one this time, we set off down to Deansgate, Elliot House. Our idea was to search the Manchester newspapers which were on microfilm and find any information regarding court cases, pending or otherwise, that could be relevant. The only thing I did find, which for some reason or other caught my attention, was the suicide of Alan Turin, the famous Enigma Code-Breaker. Now to our minds, this seemed as equally unrealistic as Harry's suicide that he supposedly injected an apple with cyanide and ate half of it. This happened on the 7th June, 1954, exactly six months to the day after Harry's suicide on the 7th December, 1953.

The only thing left to do was to check if Harry had a criminal record. This, we doubted very much, for surely even in that day and age, he would not be teaching. So Steve enters the name, Bousfield Booth Teasdale, into the computer and low and behold, his name cropped up. 'Well, well, well! Who would have believed it, the little devil' I whispered to Steve. So I got out my credit card as surely this would be well worth the £30 but something was holding me back, possibly Harry. I said to Steve to put my name in and check which he duly did. It was the same response and it was only then that I recalled an incident when Dr Sayed had received a letter from the Yorkshire Bank informing him that I was bankrupt. I remember well when he came to my house, laughing his head off, for he knew full well that Elizabeth Mary Roberts had never lived in Wales, let alone owned a public house from where the bankruptcy originated. Needless to say that like Queen Victoria, I was not amused and immediately contacted my solicitor and heads rolled. Good!

It was really on a whim that I asked Steve to type in Mickey Mouse or Donald Duck and see what happens. Well, you should have seen Steve's face; it was a picture and was fully convinced that I was barking mad. He did, however, type in Mickey Mouse just to humour me and guess what? He had a criminal record too. What a con?

I later found out from Patsy, my daughter who is a barrister, that only the police have this information. So that was the end of that as I could not hack the police computer or I would end up with a criminal record.

Chapter 63

It was like the flood gates of my mind had opened up as I recalled two incidents which had long been forgotten for over a half century. The brightly, coloured pictures unearthed themselves as if it was only yesterday.

Mr Corn, a retired school teacher, lived on his own just a couple of doors from our house, 94 Higher Ardwick. On summer days, he would sit on the top, stone step with the front door ajar, reading his books. Now, my mother had warned me, in no uncertain terms, that I was never to speak to him as 'he was not a nice man'. Despite my repeated nagging of 'Why, what do you mean'; she never elaborated any further.

Being a kind of child that when told not to do something, this made me very defiant especially when to my mind, there was no rhyme or reason as to what she was saying. So instead of skipping past him on this particular, balmy day, I stopped and stared whilst he thumbed through the pages of this glorious, red and gold, leather- bound book. It was only a few minutes later before he enquiringly looked over his steel, rimmed spectacles and smiled. 'What are you reading' say I, putting out a rather grubby hand to touch his book. 'Poetry' he said with a warm smile.

I think he picked up fairly quickly that I had a fascination for books, for even as a small child, I was an avid reader such as Enid Blyton, Just William series by Richard Crompton and the like, spending many hours in the lending library. It was not long before I was spending many a happy hour in his parlour whilst browsing his wonderful books such as William Blake, Somerset Maugham etc. Of course, I never did tell my mother about my visits.

It was may be twelve months later when Mr Corn was found dead in his bedroom. All his precious books were dumped in the dustbin and put in the back entry for refuse collection. Even though they were a bit wet and soggy, I rescued what I could, bringing them home and placing them by the coal fire to dry. My mother was having none of it and after shouting at me, she binned them again. I was so sad as he was a lovely man and it was a few years later that 'he was not a nice man' simply because he was homosexual and frowned upon by my stupid mother who 'could not see past the end of her nose'

This, then, brings me to my first year at Rose Place School and my class teacher, Mr Hutton. He was a short, stocky man who must have been near retirement age. He had a mop of thick, white hair which was plastered down with Brylanteen and a hearing aid attached to a huge battery, clipped to the lapels of his jacket.

Now I was Mr Hutton's pet, just like Mr Teasdale's but that was where the resemblance ended. On a number of occasions, he tried to touch and fondle my little, sprouting breasts despite my protests. So when he called me to stay back after school, I decided I was having none of it. He touched my tiny breasts with his sweaty palms and planted a great, sloppy kiss on my mouth. Now, in those days, there was a free-standing blackboard, supported on three wooden legs. There were two at the front and one at the back with a metre long rope attached, to support it when in use. By relaxing the rope, the blackboard could be folded up and stored after the lesson was over. Now it was more luck than judgement that it was next to his desk so I dived between the three wooden legs and under the rope, in order to make my escape. I quickly straightened up to leg it out of the classroom when I caught the rope with my foot. The whole board and easel came clattering down with an almighty racket on to the flagged floor. Teachers, who had not left the premises, came running into the classroom to see what all the commotion was about.

I ran all the way home and often wondered what plausible explanation he would have come up with. Needless to say, he never tried it again, at least with me anyway.

If I had told my mother, she would not have believed me as 'the nice Mr Hutton was such a well-respected teacher'. I always say 'Never judge the book by its' cover'

Chapter 64

How time flies, the older I get, the faster it flies. 2012 and I am no nearer in solving this conundrum. Time and time again, my mind wanders back to the day in the classroom when Mr Teasdale changed my name to Elizabeth. I wondered what made him say it, was the man psychic and if so who was pulling the strings? Surely he could not have known that he was shortly to die.

There has got to be some significant reason which so far has eluded me. We still play our little games; the current one being the vet's fees, seeing that Bess is his dog, so to speak. She has ears like funnels which constantly retain grass seed and rainwater thus becoming infected frequently. I learned a long time ago that if I did not ask, I did not receive.

I remember Aunt Cissie, bless her, bought me a couple of premium bonds when they first came out. She bought the girls some when they were born, in fact it was so long ago that I had forgotten all about them. One day, a couple of months after my request to Harry, what pops through my letter box but a £50 premium bond win. This was the first win I ever had and did not know whose bond it was but I decided to keep the money as it would cover the vet's bill nicely. This, of course, could have been a coincidence but

I do not believe in them. So just to check it out and see if it is down to Harry, I asked him for 'ball money' as Rocky was forever losing them. It was £2.25 each time and it soon mounted up. Within a short space of time, I had another £25 win on the premium bonds. So Rocky has now got his own 'ball account' at the Nat. West Bank.

Other than that nothing seems to have changed much except that Harry has taken to switching off my new callowgen heater and occasionally stopping the cuckoo clock. He does this just to let me know he is around. The most important thing I have learnt is that if I ask a question, for example, 'will P.C. Marriot respond to my letter? then if the answer is 'Yes', I can feel Harry's presence encasing me. So I realise I must be on the right track although it is months since I wrote that letter. Any normal person would have given up at this stage but I know Harry would not send me on a wild goose-chase. Just to make sure, I send another letter even though the Police Pension people have assured me that they sent the first one.

The other point that is bugging me is the lack of response from Bill Singleton even though Noel has put another request on Plymouth Grove Friends website. It even crossed my mind to hire a private detective but I will discuss this with Noel as we are going to meet up, in order to up-date our book.

Eventually, I caught up with Noel and after the usual quota of red wine and ciggys, we set about the task in hand. We wondered who was 'pulling Harry's strings' from the spirit world.

As far as we were concerned, there could be no other explanation for it because I was adamant that he changed nobody else's name but mine. My school mates Maggie was still Maggie and Bill was still Bill according to him. Why not Margaret or William? We reached the conclusion that he must be psychic.

I was checking the draft of the story whilst Noel prepared the evening meal and suddenly, out of the blue, Noel shouts out from the kitchen 'He was murdered, you know'. Well, you could have knocked me down with a feather, for at that moment, I was reading the line 'was it murder, suicide or accidental death' I asked Noel how he knew this so he went on to say that the music from the Hitchcock movies had been playing over and over in his head for weeks and was driving him crazy. Suddenly, it dawned on him as he was preparing dinner that Hitchcock was famous for his murder/ suspense stories. After that, he never heard that music play in his head again. During our conversation, Noel maintained that when he was struggling to correct my terrible grammar, a sentence would pop up in his head which he believed was with the help of Harry. On a number of occasions, he heard a male voice calling out his name and after scooting around, he found nobody there; just like I did at Ivy Cottages.

It was then that a thought popped up in my head and I decided to ask Harry for help. You see Noel had suffered for years with a plantar callous on his foot which made walking extremely difficult. It was a bit like walking with a stone in your shoe and was very painful. He had seen many consultants and foot specialists over the years but to no avail. So having asked Harry for help without saying anything to Noel, I went to the loo, only to return to see him sat gazing at a flickering candle. 'I think I will put soft wax on it. The thought just came to me now' he said, looking surprised.

He still applies the wax to this day which keeps it soft and relieves the pain. It is not a permanent cure but it is superior treatment to any of the previous ones he tried. God bless Harry!

Anyway, we set back to the task in hand in solving the mystery as we had so many jigsaw pieces but could not complete the picture. We both firmly believed that the spirit world worked with us mortals in many different ways. Some of us being influenced with our knowledge whilst others like Steve, being recruited for their computer skills and analytical mind. We would not have gained so much information without his help and expertise in computer research.

We explored the idea of how many players were involved here. Surely, there would be more coming out of the woodwork whether they were aware of it or not, in order to complete our mission.

Noel, as I have said before, has the patience of a saint; unlike me who wants everything done yesterday. I decided to bow to his better judgement and do nothing about the private detective. I would just wait whilst continuing the story; Time will be our teacher.

I have read that Sir Isaac Newton (1642-1727) generally regarded as one of the greatest scientists who ever lived, was an alchemist. His deepest instincts were occult who solved a problem intuitively and dressed it up in logical proof afterwards.

Emanuel Swedenborg (1688-1772) was an individual who combined the most intense spiritualistic exploration with the most sophisticated scientific expertise. He claimed that, quite suddenly in April 1744, he was in constant touch with the world of spirits until his death 27 years later.

I do not liken myself to these great individuals but if I did, I would certainly be suffering with grandiose delusions; however, they do add authenticity to my claim as I know full well that I am only at the kindergarten stage but hopefully, as it is said 'the teacher will come when the student is ready'. I will then be able to achieve Harry's task.

Chapter 65

I knew Steve was getting fed up with the whole scenario; unlike Noel and me who I liken to two dogs with a bone.

The Central Library is still behind with its refurbishment and will not open until 2014 so that has put paid to any theatrical information I was hoping to get regarding 'Sid & Teasdale'. I really did need some discourse with Harry but none seems to be forthcoming.

Anyway, my friend Mandy, who I met at dog training classes (I was trying to stop Rocky fighting dogs that he did not like. I did know where he was coming from, as many a time I wanted to punch somebody), appeared very interested in my story, so much so that I popped down to her house which is a lovely, 18th century cottage near Dovedale Reservoir, just outside of Greenfield.

One bright, sunny afternoon, I sat in her kitchen whilst she went to get her groceries from her car as we desperately needed coffee. All of a sudden, I spotted two, yellow, spirit orbs bobbing along her fridge and washing machine. I quickly, shouted out to her but she was not in ear-shot as her car was parked at the end of the row of cottages. I sat there fascinated whist they bobbed up and down, moving across her large kitchen and onto the freezer. Just as Mandy returned carrying her shopping, they suddenly disappeared.

I did not wish to frighten her as I, myself, astounded as it was only the second time I had seen them. The first being at Ivy Cottages where we all saw a number of lighter, coloured orbs float up the wall and into my daughter's bedroom. I was wondering as I calmly told her if there was significance due to the number and shades; different spirits, I guess! Well, I need not have bothered, for she casually informs me it was probably her Dad as they were very close when he was alive. She went on to say that she had seen them on a number of occasions in times of trouble and that was why she was so interested in my story.

Well, I was 'chuffed to little mint balls', after all, the woman was psychic who would considerably add to 'the energy' in my house. Hopefully, this would give Harry a good reconstruction of 'Ivy Cottages' where my teenage daughters, plus the flowing river at the bottom of the garden, aided him to physically show himself according to the S.N.U. This, of course, I did not need as I was fully aware of who he was but it could help to prolong his visits thus receiving much, more needed information.

One Saturday night, Mandy arrived promptly at six-thirty, armed with a tape recorder. I made us a brew, dimmed the lights, lit our incense candle and started to pre-plan our questions. 'What's up with your plant, Liz'? Mandy pipes up looking puzzled. I looked over to where she was pointing and noticed it was a large Begonia, sitting on the window-sill which was tilting towards us in its ceramic pot. So out of the rocking chair, I got and straightened the plastic pot but by the time I had sat down, it only done it again. Well, we set off giggling, for as soon as I again straightened it, the same thing happened. This saga continued for about ten minutes as up and down I went, repeatedly, but I knew by this time, it was Harry. Mandy had evidently brought plenty of energy and he was acknowledging her presence; just like he did with Steve and the MENSA books. Needless to say, we let Harry have his way, leaving it lopsided.

We then asked a series of questions or rather Mandy did, starting with Alan Turin. I am not really sure why we did this but possibly because Mandy had been reading a book called 'The Code Breaker' and Alan Turin was in Manchester at the same time as Harry. It was then that I recalled a newspaper article regarding his suicide which coincided with Harry's way of getting me to go to the Police Museum. I had hardly heard of Alan Turin and for some unknown reason his name surfaced. I still had not received a response from PC Marriot but I still could not believe that Harry would send me on 'a fool's errand'.

Session 1

The session with Mandy lasted almost an hour and I have given a brief outline here in relation to the relevant points.

Mandy: were you murdered?

Liz: yes (using a tone inferring Yeah! Stupid)

Mandy: did you upset someone?

Liz: information I knew.

Mandy: where from and about what?

Liz: Described a military uniform (a blue-braided cuff) and shiny oak desk.

Mandy: Is Alan Turin involved?

Liz: yes; all to do with the war and knowledge. 'I said the wrong thing to the wrong person who I thought was a friend' I was in too deep and had to stay within the group to protect myself'

I saw a series of frames in my mind such as scissors snapping open and shut and someone to watch called Peter, a catholic and a crucifix who would come in the future. The name David was mentioned and a demolished gentlemen's club in Deansgate, number 8, a cross plus a stony house.

We held a 'post mortem' after the session which continued into the early hours. Mandy insisted that my face changed especially at the jaw line. She noticed that when I had the urge to stand up and move about, I looked very different. She concluded that was the reason why Bess staring barking at me, (in doggy terms, I was not me anymore) whilst Rocky (not having much between his ears) slept and snored throughout the entire session.

I must admit that when we played the tape recording back, some of the dialogue and speech did not appear to be mine. This then prompted me to recall something which I had completely forgotten. I remembered Joe who owned an elderly black and white collie and lived in a council flat in Dukenfield. We had met on the 'spiritualist circuit' and even though he was not a medium, he produced the most wonderful philosophy. When he would step up on the rostrum, he would completely change from a typical, down to earth, working class chap to a high powered, cultural individual. He sounded like he had been educated at Oxford or Cambridge and you had to see it to believe it.

We became close friends, so much so that he invited me to participate in in his 'rescue circle'. This had been running for a number of years and was held on a monthly basis at Doris and Ethel's house, two elderly sisters. These sessions would last a couple of hours during the evenings with the aim of contacting departed spirits through mediumship. These individuals invariably had untimely deaths and often in traumatic circumstances.

I must admit that I cannot recall even one session where we failed to contact someone. Frequently, they did not know they were dead and were often confused and frustrated that their loved ones and friends couldn't hear or see them. Some of them were very angry at their demise and I guess that I would be too if I was killed on a motorway by an articulated lorry through no fault of my own.

I probably felt the most sorry for the suicide cases as they were extremely distressed. They often brought with them the feelings and pain which led to their deaths. I, vividly remember picking up the condition of a female who was a diabetic and omitted her insulin. Now, whether this was 'a cry for help', I did not know but she was found too late. Despite our attempts to move her through the astral plane, (wherever it is, we go) we completely failed. I was left feeling dreadfully ill, despite the rest of our group who attempted to take the condition away. It lasted until the next morning.

This method of clairvoyance is known as 'clairsentient' which is to do with 'feeling' as opposed to clairaudient (hearing).

I remember once when I was doing a demonstration at Wythenshaw Forum and I got a severe pain in my right thumb. I relayed this to the audience and was promptly accepted by a young woman. I went on to give her the message and the general jist was that she was not to be so upset and worried. I must point out that I do not know whilst demonstrating, the essence of what I am saying as I believe that I am not meant to know their personal business. It would not be right to broadcast to all and sundry, for the spirits aim is to advise and help the individual whilst proving survival...

The young woman approached me afterwards and told me her story. Apparently, she was distracted by her young baby crying and her 3 yr. old daughter somehow managed to get hold of the electric carving knife, cutting off the tip of her right hand thumb. The child is now fine but she was racked with guilt about the incident. Surely, spirits message was for her to move on as accidents do happen.

It was 4 o'clock in the morning when Mandy went home (God knows what her husband must have thought). We were left wondering if the military uniform and the shiny oak desk were connected to the stony house. The names David and Peter did not mean a thing to me. The scissors meant danger as far as I was concerned. We were intrigued about the demolished club, Deansgate and the number 8. We decided to explore this further but meanwhile I had to set off to Patsy as it would be my birthday on Thursday.

I had a nice visit on my birthday with Anna presenting me with a single candle on an iced cake. İt was her idea as she could not fit all the candles so she thought one was better for my advancing years. Patsy got me a goat-skin rug which would be very useful in covering the bald patch on my living room carpet.

We visited Spitfields Market where I purchased a green-hooded jacket which I did not need at the time. My rationale for buying this expensive purchase was the fact that I had a terrible habit of losing umbrellas or they turned inside out (even if guaranteed to be wind-proof) so I fell in love with the jacket, a perfect replacement.

Chapter 66

I returned from London a few days later and was sat in the kitchen, sorting out the mail, mainly bills. I noticed the answering machine was blinking away so I pressed the button to hear my messages.

'Message for Liz Roberts from Glenise'

'We have been sorting out P.C. James Marriot's possessions and have found the letters sent by yourself. Give me a call' and she went on to give her phone number.

Well, I was all 'fingers and thumbs', praying that she was in, as I dialled the number. Luckily, she was in and I went on to explain my reason for writing those letters, using my usual 'white lie' i.e.; I was doing family research and would dearly love to speak with P.C. Marriot regarding a suicide which he dealt with in 1953. I added that I had a photograph and newspaper cuttings regarding the incident which would hopefully jog his memory.

It was then that she went on to explain to me that James was in his late eighties with failing health and poor memory. Evidently, Glenise and her husband, a retired policeman, were guardians of James as they were long-term friends, going back to the days when her deceased father and James were based at the same station, near Plymouth Grove School.

'He has just been moved from sheltered housing to a nursing home in Salford and is understandably distressed by this move' she said and went on to suggest I wait a couple of months and we would take it from there.

Well, I had no problem in waiting a couple of months, after all, this conundrum had been going on for a couple of years now. Harry would give me pieces of the jigsaw as I went along and I decided that never again, would it cross my mind that he would send me on a fool's errand. I thought I had better apologise to him, failing that I would grovel but I had not long to wait. I, suddenly, felt his presence and knew the apology was accepted.

In light of what had happened regarding P.C. Marriot, Mandy and I decided to go down to Deansgate and try to find Harry's social club, number 8. So, after window shopping, we had a nice lunch at the Italian Bistro, on Deansgate. Over coffee, she showed me a copy of the 1940's/50's street map, thus enabling us to identify what it was like in Harry's time (what a clever girl)

Firstly, we went to Elliot House where we ploughed through a huge trade directory and drew a complete blank. So we needed to do some 'leg work', luckily it was not raining, and we trundled up and down Deansgate where there was once a police station and crosses. Meanwhile, I was muttering to myself, asking Harry to let me know where we were going. There were no sign of any crosses, not even a wooden one. We were getting fed up so I had a 'tant' with Harry as we were almost back at Elliot House. Just then, I got my funny feeling which ebbed and intensified between the side and the back of Elliot House which is on Lloyd Street but there was nothing there. So round the corner we go and

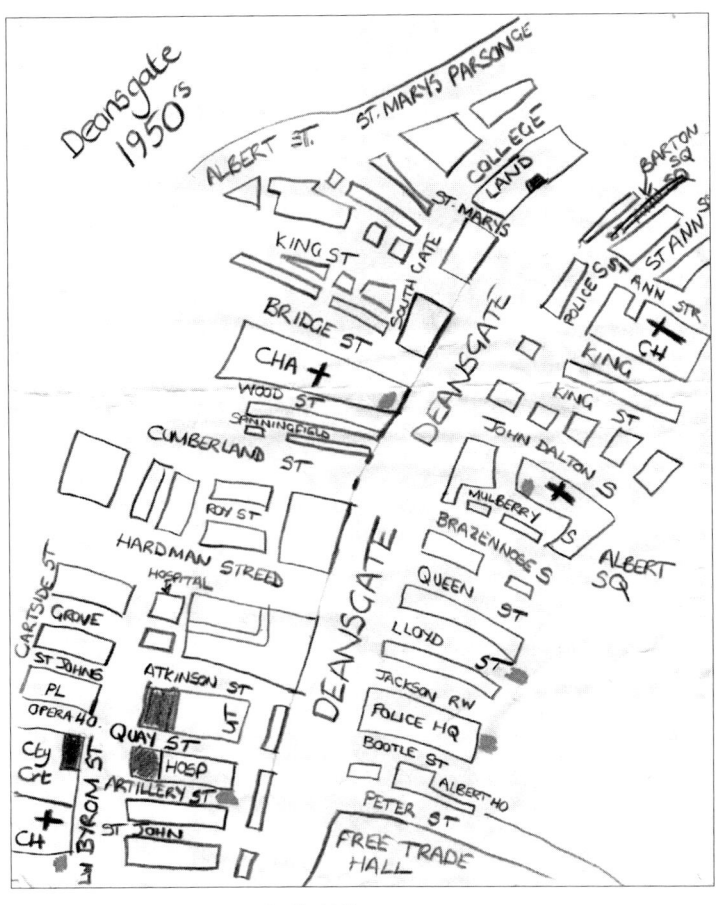

1940's/50's street map

I follow my nose into Queen Street, but this was not right so back on to Lloyd Street, stopping to have a ciggy each outside 'The Old Nag's Head' pub. As we stood there just about to give up when she says 'Liz, that pub is number 6' and there is a big empty space fenced off between it and Lloyd House and it would have been number 8.

It was now getting late and Elliot House would be closing soon, for we needed to re-examine those trade directories as we surely must have missed something. We retraced our footsteps towards the Arndale Centre when we suddenly realised that neither of us can recall exactly which NCP car park we used to park the car. She thought it was one and I thought it was another. What a pair of idiots? I even resorted to asking Harry but he had buzzed off, so in essence, we did a grand tour of the likely ones. We only found it when most of the shops had closed and people were hurrying home from work.

As we headed towards Munks Bridge in Oldham, we were still laughing our heads off. Suddenly, the traffic came to an abrupt standstill and as we crawled towards the roundabout, there were police and shards of glass all over the road. Obviously, it was a nasty accident and we both looked at each other. Was this the reason that we were delayed looking for the car? We will never know but as Mandy says 'everything happens of a reason'.

I just lit two ciggys at once for I was distracted and puzzled about Harry's gentleman's club. So next morning, I phoned the Old Nags Head pub but they did not know anything about the surrounding area, having only been the tenant for the last couple of years; but they did say that I was welcome to come to their pub and look at the old picture photographs which are hanging on the walls. Not to be put off, I rang Manchester Planning Department. I spoke to a number of individuals and after half an hour, was none the wiser. (Harry has a lot to answer for?)

The following afternoon, I put my car in the Red Cross/Fire Station building as I did not want another N.C.P. fiasco.

I then walked the couple of miles to the pub, taking a short-cut past the Queen Victoria statue. I passed where once stood Loburn College which brought back memories of my boring shorthand and typing days.

I entered the pub and noticed there were a number of framed photographs, dating back to the 1800's. Although, the pub was dark and despite the white-washed brick walls, I could still clearly see these pictures which were almost at eye level due to the low-beamed ceiling. I walked through the snug and lounge with the barman in tow as he had only got one lady customer and was obviously bored. Having viewed the pictures of horses and carts and even men in top hats, there was nothing to identify what originally existed next to it.

Having said my thanks and goodbyes, I got up and headed towards Elliot House, taking the lift to the second floor. I don't think they were best pleased as they had to drag out, yet again, the heavy ledgers. I spent an hour there but found absolutely nothing so I decided to head home. Outside, I stopped to light a ciggy but the wind was blowing a gale so I walked round the corner into Lloyd Street in an attempt to find a sheltered area. No luck there either! I was about to have one of my tantrums, for this was all Harry's fault, when I spotted a man across the street. He was just outside a café which was the only building apart from Lloyds House which is a listed building and has not changed since the 1920's. The point being that he was smoking.

I crossed over the road and asked for a light, noting he was wearing an identity badge and was probably familiar with the area. As we stood under the café awning, I noticed that it was numbers one to seven which added up to eight.

So in for a penny, in for a pound and using my sweetest of smiles, (well, he can only think I am mad) I briefly asked him if there once was a gentlemen's club located on this street. He lit another ciggy and I followed suit. 'Yes, love, you are standing on it' he said, with a smile. He went on to explain that the original entrance had been demolished, pointing to a low concrete building, adjacent to the café. 'What do you mean?' I said. 'Standing on it, love', he answered and with that, asked me to follow him.

Well, I would have followed him to Timbuktu but we only went to Queens Street where he pointed to a large doorway, displaying a sign 'Press Club'; established 1870. Apparently, this establishment runs under ground and was still used by journalists from various newspapers. Well, we are practically best friends at this stage so I briefly told him what I was about. Pointing across the road, he said 'In that area there, was the Guardian newspaper office and they used it' adding that 'I am not sure if they were 'gentlemen' but you can't get any more male than that and as for your cross; just look up there'. I was now squinting up towards the heavens and at the back of the town hall which indeed, had the shape of a cross. Well, well well! I guess Harry must have sent him but what was he doing in the Press Club?

Chapter 67

I decided to go to Hazel Grove to visit my long-term friend, Anne and this girly afternoon ended up with us reminiscing about our training days at Stepping Hill Hospital and it then led on to Harry's antics, for she always asked about him. 'Anne are you sure that you want your head done in', I responded and she eagerly nodded. So I brought her up to date, starting with the Press Club and the fact that although I had yet again visited Elliot House but still had found no connection to Harry. I had even phoned the Press Club and they kindly looked through their records which, sadly, only went back a few years due to the fact it had changed hands on a number of occasions. I also browsed through a number of photographs and old dinner menus but to no avail.

Somehow, our conversation turned to my great granny, the supposed white witch. It was then that Anne started giggling saying 'You don't look black'. What are you talking about?' I said, looking confused. 'Blackmoor, they were Africans, you know' she said with a grin. So out comes her laptop to prove her point.

'Blackmoor was the name given to North/West Africans who came over to England from places like Morocco and were engaged as servants (not slaves) by the English gentry. Apparently, it was classed as quite fashionable and a status symbol in the 1700's. They were called Blackmoor because of the colour of their skin and they were 'Moors' a black tribe of African Muslims. They, themselves, adopted English Christian names i.e. Richard meaning goodness.'

It was then that I recalled what my mother used to say when she was displeased with me which was a frequent event. 'You're a black Arab' sometimes adding that there were those black people way back in the family.

Anne then tried to bring up the Census on Sara Fleetwood, living in Hr. Ardwick but her computer 'gave up the ghost'. I was thinking she needed a new one so at the next opportunity, I would head back to Elliott House.

A few days later, I set off, taking a short-cut past where Lewis Store used to be. On the opposite side was 'the filthy picture house' as my mother used to call it, for it showed naked ladies and only dirty old men would go there according to her. Behind that, there was the Cromford Club, a well-known, night spot for 'high class crooks 'in Manchester. Many years later, it was there that I drank my first pink champagne but that is another story.

I had raided my biscuit tin in which I kept personal papers like my will and found Aunt Cissie' birth certificate dated 1890. There was a receipt for a plot of land at Southern Cemetery, all signed and sealed over a red sixpenny stamp. I wondered among other things if that stamp was worth anything. The point being, James Fleetwood and Sara Fleetwood, nee Blackmoor (my grandparents) resided at 90 Higher Ardwick which was Mrs Winter's shop in my lifetime. I do remember Cousin Kathleen showing me an old photograph of my grandmother standing outside this shop which she owned. In later years, it was sold to Mr and Mrs Winter.

At the time, I was trying to recall if it was the same woman who I used to see at the bottom of my bed as a child. I have never been sure as the photograph of her on the parlour wall was dark and faded so it was difficult to distinguish her skin colour. My grandfather, she told me, had a mass of carrot hair so that was where Patsy got it from. Apparently, he was a Mason and a 'bit of a rumun' but loved his dogs, his favourite being a red setter which got him in to lots of trouble. (Sounds familiar)

So back at Elliot House, I find the Census for 1891 where Aunt Bunny and Aunt Cissie were listed. So technically, my mother was not Welsh, having been born, I guess, in Ardwick but I am not going forward in time, I am going backwards. Maybe one day, I will get rid of my old friend, the typewriter, and buy a computer so I can do my family tree.

Having racked my brains and recalled that I was told that they all came from Bayston Hill, Shrewsbury which was part of Wales, I looked up Sara Ann Blackmoor, born 1861 and almost immediately found her. Her mother's name was not also Sara which I had previously understood. My Great granny, the witch, was named Elizabeth Blackmoor and she, like her daughter, was born in Candover Pulley Parish, Saint Julian, Bayston Hill, Shrewsbury, in 1843. (Census 1851)

I was now very puzzled, for it appeared that Elizabeth was born along with six siblings to a Margaret and Richard Blackmoor, both 34 yrs., old, in 1851. No more census details were available.

It was then that I recalled being told that my grandmother had been 'in service'. Eventually, I found her and she definitely was the same person living with a family named Price. I ploughed through the records again and came to the conclusion that Sara was born the wrong side of the blanket. (Illegitimate) This would make sense, for Elizabeth was 17-18 yrs. old at the time of giving birth; hence, they were both Blackmoors.

I am left with the fact that the story of how my grandmother heard a knock on the door and on looking out the window saw her brother in the World War I army kit. She was living in Gerald Street which was part of the 'concrete area' where the cemetery used to be. Anyway, she went downstairs to open the front door but he had disappeared. Later on, she received a telegram to say he had been killed in action. So I checked this out and they did reside at the end terraced house in Gerald Street, during WW1.

So I wondered what happened to Elizabeth. Did she marry or not? I remember that it was said that Sara's brother was much younger than her. This would make sense, for in 1914, she would have been 53 yrs. old and I do not recall any mention of any other siblings. The only other occupants of this small, two-bedroomed, rented, terraced house were Henry and a lodger named Thomas Wild, born in 1875. I wonder if she had a 'toy boy' as my Grandfather James was not on the 1911 Census, prior to WW1.

The story I was told was that he died in Ancoats Hospital of stomach cancer when my mother and Uncle Fred were very young; hence, they were both privately educated at Cheadle Hulme Boarding School, courtesy of the Masons.

Henry, I believe, was the youngest sibling who died of Tuberculosis at a young age. I still have in my possession, to this day, a Bible, dated 30th June, 1906 which Henry received as a prize from Saint Thomas' Boys School, situated alongside a cemetery opposite Ardwick Green Park.

I am intrigued by all this and one day, I will do my family tree if only to find out what happened to Elizabeth and if she really was a witch. I shall take a stab in the dark and assume she was half-caste, working on the theory that Margaret, her mother, was Welsh and Richard Blackmoor was African; making them my great, great grandparents, both born in 1814. So not only do I have Welsh and Irish blood flowing through my veins but also African/ Arab blood. I might be being too fanciful here but is this where lies the JU JU connection? For the time being, I will 'wind my daughters up' by telling them what mongrels they are and if they have any more children, they might be black. There is documented evidence explaining the 'throwback gene' whereby white parents have a black child.

Chapter 68

Towards the latter part of May 2012, I received a phone call from Glenise' husband, David. He said that James Marriot's mental state was rapidly deteriorating. He suggested that I tell my story to him and they would see if he remembered anything. After a few days, Glenise got back to me to say that James did not have a clue as to what they were talking about. She reiterated that I was welcome to visit him but this would probably not help as I was a complete stranger. We came up with the idea of something visual so without more ado, I sent the copy of the newspaper cuttings and a photograph of Harry. I thought it would be interesting to hear their thoughts since David was a retired policeman. The only information I had given was the usual 'white lie' (family tree research) and that I wished to find further knowledge of his suicide.

Within a couple got days, Glenise got back to me again but sadly, James could not recall a single thing. What she said afterwards gave me great encouragement; 'That is a set-up by those two boys and I fully understand why you had written to James'. So the only thing they could think of doing, in order to help, was to give me full access to his records in the event of his death. This she felt would not be long and they would contact me.

So as things stood, for the time being, I had come to a full stop but I could not get the vision of the pillared, stone house and the blue-braided cuffs out of my mind. I busied myself with my own demonstrations and had a house clearance to do. This involves exploring every room on the premises in order to establish where exactly the energy is strongest. After that, I discuss with the house owner what exactly the problems are. In essence, they have a haunted house and 'normal' people are not too happy about seeing apparitions or hearing the sounds of disembodied voices.

In my experience, most spirits are happy to move along and leave the occupant alone. It is essential, in my opinion, to move only the nuisance ones and leave the spirits of good intent. Thus, the home owner will not be aware of their presence unless they have psychic ability. If so, I would suggest to them to gain some understanding of this phenomenon. It is lack of understanding that causes fear and as Noel always says FEAR; is False Evidence Appearing Real.

In hindsight, I must have been having 'a Harry thought'. I had gone to the post office to pay the usual bills (there appears to be no end to them) and walked towards my car. I noticed that the library was open so I trotted in. The place was deserted and there were two very bored looking librarians who genuinely were pleased to see even me.

So off we set on the computer but found absolutely nothing that fitted the bill. It did not really surprise me as Steve had previously gone down this road. Just then, the older of the two made her escape as a customer, an elderly gentleman, clutching an armful of books, had arrived. We carried on regardless pressing the mouse but got nowhere. There was absolutely nothing to resemble what Harry had showed me. We searched the uniforms of the police, navy and the air force and essentially, anything blue but I did not have a clue what it was I was looking for.

Now, whether or not this gentleman sensed my frustration and disappointment, I do not know but he ambled over a few paces until he was stood alongside of me. 'I could not help but overhear your conversation but what are you looking for? he said politely. So I reiterated that it was three gold-braided circles on the cuff of a blue uniform. 'Where did you see it and why' he inquired further. I was getting good at this now as there was no way I could tell the truth so, as quick as a flash, I invented an old long-lost photograph of my father and his close friend who's identity I wished to discover. Well, I am a retired from the Air Force and what you are describing is the mess kit of a wing commander' he said, confidently. I was gobsmacked but it did not prevent me from asking 'what is a mess kit, luv'. He replied that a mess kit was used on V.I.P occasions and three gold braids, round the cuff plus one braid round the hat was, indeed, of a high ranking wing commander during the last war.

Well, you could have knocked me over with a feather as I thanked him profusely and left the library. I was asking myself what a school teacher was doing with a wing commander. I was beginning to think that there was more to Harry than meets the eye.

Chapter 69

The only thing that came to mind was to have another session with Harry so I let him know of my intentions. It was only a couple of hours later as I was pondering the best way forward when the phone rang. It was Mandy and as sure as 'eggs are eggs' she says 'Do you want me?' She is most definitely psychic and I went on to tell her my reasons for a further session.

Her psychic ability is obviously on the same vibration as myself and thus conducive to Harrys'. The thing that I have noticed is that vibrations are all important in spirit communication. The vibration may vary from each church or venue and if they are not of the same level as the medium, then we struggle to communicate. If the vibration is the same, it is like a walk in the park for us.

Now, this has nothing to do with one's spirituality but more to do with a personality thing. If the audience can relate to you, it is a much more fascinating experience for all concerned. In my case, I like to have a laugh and joke a lot as I am not into the sad and morbid side of death. I guess Mandy, like Noel and myself, is on Harry's vibratory level and as I always say 'like attracts like'.

So we prepared a short list of questions, relating to our previous session. This, we noted, is where Alan Turin entered the frame. Initially, this had been my idea, for I had half-watched a TV documentary on his work as a code breaker whilst reading a book. My ears pricked up when the name 'Robin' was mentioned which was a name that Harry liked to be called. Unfortunately, it was towards the end of the programme so I was left none the wiser.

Mandy read the key points of the conversation with Harry. A lot of the information was repetitive, so it is possible that some of it came from my mind and not his. Having said that, my vision of the blue, gold braided cuffs was accurate but I will have to look for the stone house which is not in the Greater Manchester area. Steve and I ploughed through every photograph of stately homes commandeered by the Armed Forces during WWII but to no avail. I am convinced that the answer lies somewhere. Why? I do not know so I am determined to find out more information on Alan Turin.

Mandy task was to follow up on 'The Swan' as we did not know what it symbolised so the only thing we could think of was 'a pub logo'. The scissors we knew symbolised trouble and/or danger and I will surely keep a lookout for 'Peter' and as for getting married, No Way! I do not want to cook, clean and wash dirty socks so what was Harry talking about? Oh! How I wished this communication was not so asunder and as for the big, fat bumble bee, we did not have a clue.

Most of my spirit communication is visionary rather than auditory. Harry gives me symbols so for example, when I am giving someone a message and see a pair of shoes; I know it means a wedding. A handbag, on the other hand, cautions the individual to be careful of their finances and so on and so forth. Like the scissors representing danger or a German shepherd dog symbolising the need for protection. However, I had never seen a bumble bee before. The only thing I could think of is that, unlike a wasp, it only stings when it is in great danger and subsequently dies.

Notes from the Harry Session No. 2

Look very closely at Alan Turin.
Many people died.
Need to go somewhere.
Look through all the paperwork.
Swan; look for the swan which just sat there on the water.
David, do not know if he is alive,
Peter, definitely alive: Be very careful. (Peter very dangerous for Liz)
Peter doesn't know yet but be very careful.
Problems with Peter.
Vision—open scissors.
Liz will meet probably Peter within 2 years. .
Peter, official position, dangerous.
Open scissors again.
Peter—showing paperwork.
Bumble bee, big, fat bumble bee.
August, probably not next month
Need to find 'PressCorp Museum
Letter A
1950
Name listed to Peter
Liz is going to have to go.
Liz will get married
Stuff still going on since the war.

Master Plan
Lizard—deception.
Rotund spectacled man
Big oak desk
He is very important

Chapter 70

Once again, Mandy came up trumps, for she had found the 'Swan'. She discovered that it was the logo of the R.A.F. Squadron 103 based at Elsham Wolds, near Lincolnshire. In order to get more information, I contacted their association and spoke to a David Fells who confirmed that this was correct until 1943. The squadron was then disbanded and renamed R.A.F. Bomber Command 576 which continued to be active during the Cold War; thus they had many bases (airfields) around the country. He also confirmed that their main uniform was grey but a Wing Commander's Mess Kit was indeed blue with three gold braids around the cuff area. The only snag was that their motto 'Noli Me Tangere' (Touch Me Not) had a black swan with its wings outstretched.

Well, that put 'the cat among the pigeons', for the swan that Harry showed me was white sitting on water. So I went on to ask if any squadrons had a white, swan logo?. 'No, but give me a minute' he replied politely. After what seemed an eternity, he was back to the phone and told me that a white swan is the logo for H.M.S. Signet ship, possibly aircraft carriers which were active during and after the War. Each was twinned with a town around England so he went on to say that it was quite possible that there was, indeed, a connection with a wing commander 'Top Brass'. They often used the same venues for meetings and briefings etc.

Of course, he then asked the question I had been dreading; 'Why do you want to know all this?. 'Family tree' I piped up, lying through my teeth, adding that as a small child, I had seen a photograph, since lost, of my father and a man who's uniform fitted the description of a wing commander. Luckily, he did not ask me about the swan which would have put me in deep water!. So I thanked him and wished him 'Goodbye'. (Street Cred. Intacta)

At the first opportunity, Mandy was at my home clutching her laptop so that we could confirm the existence of the white swan & H.M.S. Sıgnet. We found it, just like Harry had showed me.

The only conclusion we could come up with, whether right or wrong, was that Harry had led us to the air force and navy. Neither of us had any knowledge, whatsoever, of the swan logos, other than pub names. We were both now completely mystified so we would have another attempt at communicating with Harry and ask him what all this was about?

I read Alan Turin's story written by his mother, though the links are, indeed, tenuous, they are not beyond the bounds of possibility. Sir Alan Turin was the greatest code breaker (Enigma) based at Bletchley Park during the War. He was knighted by the Queen for this great work which saved many Allies' lives.

After the War, in 1948, he moved to work at Manchester University and is credited with developing the first ever computer. He was a known homosexual who frequented the 'Gay Scene' around the Deansgate area.

Now, if Harry was 'gay' which I believe is a strong possibility, then surely they would have known one another. They were both educated men who both spoke French and were interested in the 'Arts'.

I did discover that, even in those days, there were gay venues around the area of the 'Press Club' which I believe Harry frequented though the reason for this still escapes me.

Concerns over Turin's foreign contacts regarding State Secrets, posed a serious governmental problem. Apparently, his house was searched on a number of occasions and he had his passport confiscated.

In 1953, during the Cold War, he was frequently followed and a Norwegian friend who was due to visit him, never arrived and was never heard of again. One theory suggested that he was possibly a spy though his family strongly deny this. There is no doubt that during his time at Bletchley Park, he was privy to State Secrets.

On the 8th of June, 1954, Alan's housekeeper discovered him dead in bed. Evidently, death was due to potassium cyanide poisoning. According to the verdict at the inquest, the poison was self-administered while the 'balance of the mind' was disturbed. (Sounds familiar)

There was a half-eaten apple by the side of his bed as he used to eat one every night which the inquest claimed he had injected with cyanide. The point being that the apple was never tested for poison and according to his friends and neighbours, he was in the best of spirits and full of plans for the future.

There was no cyanide found in his bedroom. There were newly bought socks on his writing table along with acceptances for invitations for the near future as well as theatre tickets. He was planning to take his friends along on the week he died..

Is it me or does this sound familiar? Theatre tickets, sheet music. Hardly the actions of someone who is of 'unsound mind'. I must also add that neither he nor Harry had any financial problems.

It has also been documented that Charlie Chaplin, the famous comedian, was also suspected and investigated along with many others.

Chapter 71

Saturday night came round and Mandy arrived promptly at 6.30 pm. Before we commenced our attempts to contact Harry, I recounted an incident which happened earlier that week.

The dogs and I weaved our way through numerous, sweet-smelling pine trees which were surrounded by hawthorn bushes. There was not a soul around or at least that is what I thought. Suddenly, out of nowhere from behind a tree, a man jumped out and attempted to push me to the ground. I was nearly flat on my back when there was an almighty yell. Good old Bess sprang into action and bit him on the leg. He legged it, clean over some sheep wire fencing and was gone with Bess, frantically, trying to get through the fencing after him. I grabbed her as Rocky wanders back, wondering what all the commotion was about. To quote Mandy 'Rocky is like a baby who has been dropped on his head'.

The man, dressed in shorts and hiking gear, carrying a rucksack had crossed the field, where some horses were kept, in record time. He was quickly out of sight and then, of course, the 'penny dropped'.(I am a bit like Rocky) The point being as I said to Mandy 'he would not have seen the dogs through the shrubbery and deadly nightshade which reached up to my waist.. What I do not understand is why neither of them picked up his scent'. 'It is because he was down-wind otherwise they would have picked it up within a radius of two miles' Mandy said by way of an explanation.

She then went on to say that she still had some police connections due to her deceased grandfather who was a high ranking officer based at Longsight. So she would try to find out if any incidents of this nature had been reported. Our concerns being that I was not the only female that used this isolated area to walk their dogs. There was Deirdre, for one, with her husky. So as soon as I could, I would pass on the information to her.

It was then that it dawned on us that her grandfather would have been at Longsight/Levenshulme Police Station at the same time as P.C. Marriot and would have known about the Harry incident. What a coincidence, if you believe in them. To date, I had not had any contact from that source so he must still be alive.

It was about 8.30pm and after stocking up on more coffee and cigs, we were about to light the incense candles and ask Harry to join us. However, I guess he had already arrived as I could feel his strong presence and Mandy had gone all 'goosey'. It was then before I had time to use the crystal ball that images started to appear on the wall mirror. There was a picture of a stone statue which looked a bit like a large dog but it was not really a dog. In fact, I did not know what it really was but it stayed on the steps of the lounge for a good few seconds before disappearing. It was then that I was drawn to a picture on the opposite wall and could clearly see a sea-horse. 'I understand that image. Set your crystal ball up' Mandy said excitedly. So still feeling peculiar, I gathered my wits and gazed into the crystal ball. It was like watching a silent movie with the images rolling in from the left (past) and then to the centre (present). Suddenly, I got the most awful taste of blood in my mouth and I could hear bombs and see dead bodies everywhere. At this stage, we were both getting a bit frightened as this was serious information, if correct.

Notes from the Harry Session No. 3

Sea Cow,
Bureaux—Paperwork
Closed scissors meaning trouble
The letter 'A' and 'C'
Swans head pecking at a man in a dingy
Big dog attacking-vicious
Swans flapping, taking off
Gun-powder in the distance
Dog-like figurine
Alan/ Jack/ George
Body with no head. Lots of blood
Drummond
Firing squad
Mushroom cloud
Liz gets terrible taste of blood in her mouth
Submarine with periscope up
Secret tests of bombs
Gas masks
Near Australian Territories
Many people murdered
Want to make things right

The only thing to do was to test the ground, as they say. We started with what we knew the answers to. Mandy's sea-horse which turned out to be an amusing story.

When Mandy was a small child, she would repeatedly ask her grandfather who was a ship builder, how the sea-horse got into the glass paperweight? She could never quite understand the mechanics of it.

I popped into the kitchen, back down the steps, clutching my bottle opener which happened to have a sea-horse inside its handle. It was something that my husband's father had given to me, many moons ago. 'Identical' Mandy said with a wide grin and we both had a good laugh about it.

So far so good! The next test was the description of her father's image that I glimpsed in the mirror. She started rummaging in her large bag (that girl carries everything but the kitchen sink) saying 'I am fairly sure it was him'.

So far, Harry's information has been correct, just like the swans that we connected to the R.A.F and the Navy. 'So what is it that he is trying to tell us'? I thought to myself and wondered if he was referring to World War II or the Cold War, noting his reference to 1950.

So we donned our Miss Marple heads and looked at the clues. The letter 'C' refers to a country, the habitat of this sea creature. It appeared to be a warm place, for I could see sunshine, hills and mountains.

Mandy connected up her laptop and after half an hour, we were almost cross-eyed looking at sea creatures. We did discover that it was commonly known as 'a sea-cow' and its natural environment was the Pacific Ocean.

The word 'Drummond' grabbed my attention and I wondered if it was the name of a house, I was searching for or the name of an individual.

It was then that we noticed that the Christian names 'Jack and George' were not in our previous sessions but the name 'Peter' occurred umpteen times. This was now making me rather paranoid as it was obvious to us that he was still alive and possibly a danger. From now on, I intended to be cool with the coalman, Peter and keep Bess by my side. I had no wish to follow Harry down a lift shaft.

So, if these pieces of information made a bigger picture, then, what was going on? Where was Harry leading me? It seemed to me that we were treading on dangerous ground, for as Mandy had rightly pointed out, some images were in the centre of the crystal ball which to me denotes the present; however, nothing as yet, was appearing in the right side which would indicate the future.

Sunday morning came round and my head was 'in bits' trying to figure out what was going on. One burning question was the word 'Drummond'; Place or person? I soon got my answer because the ciggy packet just moved across the floor, just like the small, litter basket did, all those years ago at Ivy Cottages.

'It is a person' I, excitedly exclaimed to Mandy over the phone. She was not best pleased as she was half asleep so I set off to the moors with the dogs and needed to clear my head.

On my return, Steve had left a message. 'Liz, I received a message from a medium in church last night. Harry had something to do with the military' he said. This was another confirmation of the train of thought which I must follow up.

About a half an hour later, Mandy who was now fully awake, phoned and went on to say that she had found a Sir Jack Drummond which was extremely interesting. An afternoon was then set aside to see if we could connect him with Harry.

Chapter 72

Jack Drummond was an active member of the Royal Society of Chemistry, based at Burlington House in London. He received a knighthood in 1944 for his biological tests regarding nutritional problems and observing the effects of vitamins.

At the outbreak of World War II in 1939, he offered his services to the Ministry of Food where he was chief advisor on food contamination until the following year. He was then appointed Scientific Advisor, a post he held until 1946. He left to become Research Director, at Boots Pure Drug Company Ltd.

On one of his frequent visits from his abode in England, he was murdered along with his wife and eight year old daughter, Elizabeth. A younger daughter survived by hiding under the car.

Jack Drummond and his family were experienced campers and the fact that he pitched his tent at the side of a busy main road in France, close to a chemical factory, caught my attention. I asked myself why would someone go on a camping holiday to France and pitch their tent at the side of a main road, next to a factory.

On further research, I discovered the factory in question, manufactured a herbicide, known as' Agent Orange'. It was believed that Jack Drummond was mainly responsible for its creation.

Evidently, they were all shot at close range on the 5th August, 1952. The murder weapon, along with his camera, was never recovered. No other valuables were documented as missing and a 70 yr. old French farmer was convicted of their murders. The motive, according to the French authorities, was the fact that the farmer was sexually interested in Drummond's wife. This was something that his family strongly denied. Firstly, their father did not know the Drummond family and, according to his sons, he had no previous criminal history. Two years later, the farmer was pardoned and freed from prison.

So Miss Marple asks herself, yet again, what the hell is going on? Raymond Badin, a historian, uncovered evidence that Drummond was a spy. This was also stated in a book written in 1997 by William Raymond. We also dug up the fact that Drummond, a day or so before he was murdered, met up with a Catholic priest, Father Lorenzi, in a place called' Lurs'. The priest and Drummond had previously met in 1947, 1948 and 1951. Also present on the last occasion was a French Resistance fighter by the name of Paul Maillet.

I was getting more questions than answers at this stage. What was a Catholic priest doing with a Resistance fighter and more importantly, what was Drummond doing with them?

On further investigation, it turns out that Father Lorenzi was a celebrated Resistance hero who died of natural causes in 1959. It is stated that the 61 yr. old, Jack Drummond had become disenchanted with Agent Orange. This was due to the fact that the herbicide had chemical adaptations and was now lethal if inhaled or ingested by animals or humans. This was something that it was never intended for. The theory was that he and the Resistance fighters were intent on blowing up the Agent Orange factory, hence his proximity to it at the time.

So, was he a spy along with the claims that Alan Turin was also one and if so, for whom? Were these two men connected in some way? So far, the only connection I could find was the fact that they were both Fellows of The Royal Academy of Science. This Academy consisted of the most eminent scientists in the world i.e. Turin for Computer Science.

Agent Orange started out with great promise as early as the 1930s. It was a synthetic compound capable of regulating and supressing plant growth. This herbicide promised to be of great value to farmers in the eradication of weeds but its potential for military use was also appreciated. It could be used to control foliage in order to expose the enemy in dense jungle areas. It was, famously, used in Vietnam whereby many veterans died prematurely or reported debilitating illnesses. There were also claims that their children were born with serious congenital defects.

(Note: 'Agent Orange on Trial' by Peter H. Schuck. This cites tort cases (personal injury) of Vietnam Veterans against chemical companies and the United States Government.

After serious thought, I decided to contact Jean Teasdale and ask her again about Harry's lifestyle. So at the earliest opportunity and choosing my words carefully, I asked her if Harry ever went to France, for example. 'No dear, he never went anywhere like that. I think you are barking up the wrong tree' she said thoughtfully. Not to be put off, I asked if he visited anywhere in this country as he must have had some favourite places to visit. The answer was the same; he had not travelled round the country.

She asked me about the will as she could not understand why she was told that he left all his money to Florence Tinsley. She did confirm, however, that he spoke fluent French and was educated at Lancaster Grammar School and Heading College.

So I thanked her, adding that I would send her a copy of the 'Will' which pleased her. Suddenly, 'out of the blue', she said, 'He was never in the War, dear as he had 'Hammer Toes' which he told me when I spent a week with him and his mother at Great Western Street'.

This statement bugged me as it was so 'out of the blue' and as far as I was aware; people with this condition lived quite happily and were not restricted in their mobility. Besides, looking back, I never noticed any disability with Harry. In fact, quite the opposite and he could be seen going up and down the rostrum, playing the piano and not to mention his variety act. Now, if she had said 'Flat Footed', I would have accepted this, knowing fully well that these men were exempted from the Services in the War. There again, they were usually found desk jobs.

I did manage to look this up and without further ado, I discovered the following;

The only men who were exempt were the following categories:

Ministers of the Church

Ill Health

People who were still in full-time education, e.g. students
People who worked in the National interest

The age range 18 yrs. to under 41 years, were only accepted

So teachers were not exempt and I was unable to find any reference to Hammer Toes.

In this condition, usually only the second toe is affected. The head of the phalanx (joint) is subject to pressure by the toe-cap of the shoe which results in painful corns.' In adults, an operation is indicated in order that recovery may be quick and certain' according to The Essentials of Modern Surgery; First Edition; 1938

So if it was a problem, why did he not have this simple operation? I am not an expert but I do know that there were a number of serious foot conditions which affected soldiers such as Trench Foot, Gangrene etc. I guess the answer to this has been lost 'in the mists of time'.

So I have to take a mental leap here. When Harry was asked in a previous session if the two boys were a cover story to blacken his name, he replied that it was a' coincidence'. Now this word haunted me and according to the Oxford Dictionary means 'chance'.

I was of the opinion that the incident with the boys was purely to discredit him which is a strategy still in use today. So a verdict of death by suicide is usually recorded whilst the balance of the mind was disturbed, frequently follows.

Chapter 73

I enlisted the help of all my friends in an attempt to discover an island where sea cows live and identify the dog like figurine.

Meanwhile, I contacted the passport records; being very careful not to give too much information before I knew how many records they had for the 30's and 40's. This train of thought had followed me since I was informed that there were no inquest records due to a fire in the building after 1949. I remembered the stories of the Blitz and World War II and most people had managed to salvage some items.

During my hospital days, one kept important documents in large metal filing cabinets for this very reason. I find it incredible that no records survived.

The Passport Office informed me that their records were very scanty and as this seemed genuine, I gave them Harry's details. Unfortunately, they could only come up with a few Teasdales and only one Bousfield as a surname. So yet again, I was out of luck.

Meanwhile, Steve had come up with the Christmas, Easter and Marshall Islands as well as the Cocus and, Guam Islands. I never knew that there were so many atolls in the Pacific Ocean. Geography was never a strong subject of mine and in fact, I was never very eager to be educated, hence, the 'School Board man. I was always 'wagging it' and now it had come back to haunt me.

Mandy and I explored all of Steve's islands but none of them fitted exactly with Harry's information. Either the dates were wrong or there was no bombing or the use of Agent Orange. We found a number of doggie looking gargoyles/figurines on various islands but none of them fitted the picture.

All we had come up with was a 'H Bomb' named 'Orange'. Just as we were about to give up and order a curry when we spotted a logo on one of the bomber planes and could hardly believe our eyes. It was 'clear as a bell' the bumble bee was the logo on bombing planes.

We were convinced at this stage that we were on the right track (bumble bee) but where to go now? As Christmas was almost upon us, we decided to start again in the New Year. Apart from the notion I had to visit Burlington House whilst visiting Patsy and family over the holiday period, I hoped it would be open to the public. It housed the headquarters of the Royal Society which Alan Turin and Jack Drummond belonged to. It had also among other things the 'Arts' which I suspected Harry would be very interested in. My reasoning was that Turin and Drummond must have been acquainted and I needed somehow to try and tie Harry in with them. Alan Turin kept bobbing up for some reason.

I was coming to the conclusion that Harry was gay just like Turin and they could have possibly known each other. Due to their lifestyle and close proximity as Manchester University was a 'stone's throw' from Great Western Street where Harry lived. It just did not seem feasible that 'he never went anywhere' according to Jean Teasdale. I remembered posh Mr Teasdale with his long umbrella; fashionable and expensive Crombie coat and this did not fit the picture of a man who did not socialise, not forgetting the Dunhill cologne which I only smelt once. I suspect that he does not use it anymore; after all, it would be wasted on a non-physical energy form. I think he was telling me something as I said before; Uncle Fred used Vaseline on his face and my Dad, just soap and water.

Chapter 74

I was spending Christmas with Noel and the New Year with the girls. Now, I was not one for dreaming and if I did, I never remembered them but it was quite extraordinary when I had a dream about P.C. Marriot's funeral in full colour, chapter and verse.

The following morning I mentioned it to Noel whilst putting all the blame, squarely on his shoulders. After all, he was the one who forced copious amounts of wine down my throat on the previous night.

We decided to put Harry on 'the back burner' over the festive period but I guess he had other ideas. On the very next day, Noel tried to find an old film which I wished to see called 'The Corsican Brothers, staring Douglas Fairbanks Jnr; however, he was unable to do so and I ended up watching a boring documentary about a war ship sailing the North Pacific.

This made me wonder if Harry was trying to tell me something i.e. I should concentrate on the North Pacific rather than the South in order to find the island which I had seen in the crystal ball. We then checked out to see if the sea cow could also inhabit these cold waters and we were very surprised that indeed, it did. With the film truly forgotten, we looked up the Caroline Islands as they began with the 'letter C' but, unfortunately, we drew a blank.

I set off to London for 4 days as Patsy, my daughter, and her husband John were going to Germany for a long weekend. There was a 60th birthday celebration for a close friend of theirs and the plan was that I would look after Anna, my grand-daughter. She had just tuned 10 years old and I pondered just how time flies as I could not believe that a full decade had passed. I guess we spend such a short time on this mortal plain. Now when my time comes after I have finished the 'Harry Story' which at this rate of progress, I will be receiving a telegram from the Queen, I fully intend to seek him out.

So Anna and I take great delight in ignoring Patsy's orders. Sometimes, I think that Patsy forgets that she is talking to her mother and not some judge in the courtroom. If all barristers are alike, then they are a pain in the neck. All the green vegetables go out the window, along with the 'Flora' and the other rubbish. My point being that John has high cholesterol but mine is normal. So there is a lot to be said for greasy fish and chips, served in newspaper and eaten with your fingers. Who needs more washing up to do anyway?

Of course, bedtime is only when we are really tired and Anna takes great delight in watching late night TV film about serial killers. Patsy was not best pleased the last time when Anna told her friends and teacher how the police use forensic evidence; not the sort of subject usually raised at this posh, private school. My defence being that this is the dark side of the real world and one should give their children roots and then wings. I rest my case!

On the Friday morning, I set off, clutching my instructions, to find Burlington House. I got off the tube at Green Park and followed the signs for 'The Academy of Arts' whilst wondering if Harry had ever visited the place.

This large stone house, which was once an ancestral home, was very likely to be a listed building as it housed 'The Royal Society', both of which Alan Turin and Jack Drummond were members. As I walked through the stone gate house which had familiar pillars on either side along with a family crest, I wondered if this was the house that Harry showed me in the crystal ball.

I entered the courtyard, which was in the centre of this three- sided house I wondered if the military were there during the War as there were two memorials to the fallen soldiers of the two Great Wars.

There was a group of foreign tourists being led by a young, female tour guide who was ushering her group inside the building. I just had to go up and interrupt her as I recalled what my mother used to say 'You just cannot keep your tongue still'

I caught her attention and she turned as I was pointing towards one of the memorials and just about to ask her a question. Suddenly, I noticed that she was cross-eyed which made me lose my train of thought. God forgive but I wanted to laugh but I muttered something and quickly walked away. Of course, I blamed Harry immediately. One would have thought in this day and age of modern surgery that she would have them fixed so that the tourists could follow her gaze..

With this, I trotted off to the gatehouse, lit a ciggie and had another look at it. It did not feel right and did not look like Harry's house, even though, it had sandstone coloured pillars but was missing the stone lion.

It was so cold that my fingers had gone numb and wondered how freezing it must be, back home in my house. Saddleworth is one of the highest points in the country. Bess would not be a happy bunny and she never liked leaving me anyway. Rocky, on the other hand, with half a brain, spent his time barking abuse at the other dogs.

So I went inside the building to find another guide and mingled with the tourists. The only positive thing from this wasted morning was the warmth of the place and I was beginning to feel almost human again.

I spotted a tour guide and politely pushed my way to the front of the group. He peered at me through his bifocals as I asked about the military connection. Unfortunately, he did not seem to know and proceeded to ask me what exactly I was looking for? I responded with my usual spiel about a photograph of my father and a military friend outside a building. He told me that there were some photographs of old historical buildings which have just been placed in a small annex across the corridor, adding that there was no charge to view them.

I followed his directions under a massive staircase which was heaving with people. I wondered if I looked 'as poor as a church mouse' and that was the reason he sent me for a freebie. There were about a dozen black and white photos and about as many people, along the windowless, tiny room. It was divided up by a braided, red rope which was supported by two brass stands at either side.

I guessed that this would only take two minutes and I would head back to the tube. It was then that I stopped dead in my tracks and peered again at the old photo. I was gobsmacked as there was Harry's house but it was not a house, it was the frontage of the Ritz Hotel. Everything was as it should be with the windows, lions and something that looks like a coat of arms. There was one odd thing, however, I could not tell the colour of the stone pillar. This entrance was placed above an arcade and not as I had expected at ground level.

On closer inspection and after reading a short paragraph underneath the photograph, it appears that around 1933, the road and pavement were widened in order to build an arcade. This resulted in the interesting, frontage facade being placed above it. I managed to take a photo on Mandy's phone cam which I had borrowed in case I found something.

This was now making sense to me, for if Harry had showed me an arcade, I would not have been able to identify it. One arcade looks like another and I would never have thought to look above them.

Things were beginning to fall into place and I had Steve looking for a stately home which had been commandeered by the forces during the war. My reasoning being that in the crystal ball, there was a plush, carpeted stairway, gilded, framed pictures upon the walls of the interior and a baby's pram. There was also a dark, oak table which with hindsight (a wonderful thing) would be objects seen in a hotel.

My brains were working overtime and I had passed the Ritz Hotel on the way to Burlington House but did not take any notice. So I set off out the gate house and headed towards the tube station. At this stage, the freezing weather was well and truly forgotten as I needed to check the actual building.

The Ritz Hotel

Well, it was not a 'cock's stride' just across the road from Burlington House and I could imagine the likes of Alan Turin and Jack Drummond frequenting the place. As I crossed over the road, I noticed the sand-coloured, stone frontage and pillars but what had this to do with the military, I asked myself. There was nothing coming from Harry but he had definitely shown me men of high rank dressed in gold braided uniforms sat around this big, oak table.

At this stage, I had the option of exploring three avenues. Firstly, the dream about P.C. Marriott's funeral so I phoned them and learned that he had sadly died about three weeks ago in hospital following an infection at the age of 87 yrs. They had not forgotten about me but thought it best to give the Police Pension personnel time to process all the paperwork. They were very helpful and suggested that I wait another week or so due to the holiday period and then I could contact the Police Museum with their full permission. The records should be available by that time.

Well, as I later told Noel, this was the first time that I had received information from Harry in this way. I was hoping that it was not 'a one-off'!

As soon as the weather permitted, I set off for home as I never liked to leave the dogs for too long even though they were well looked after in the kennels. It was not inches of snow but feet of the stuff when I got home, even people with four-wheeled drive vehicles had difficulty getting through due to the height of the drifts.

I managed to contact Noel and told him about the Ritz Hotel episode and asked if he could find any connection to the military. An hour or so later, he was back on the phone. He sounded very impressed with my clairvoyance skills which really chuffed me, for he discovered the Ritz Hotel had a very private venue, namely the 'Maria Antoinette Suite' which was used for highly classified meetings during WWII by Winston Churchill, Charles de Gaulle and President Eisenhower along with their advisors.

Well, we were on a roll now with two out of three; one more and it would be like winning the jackpot in the Lottery; Of course, not that I ever did it as I would not know what to do with such a vast amount of money. So often, it appeared to me that it brought so much misery. There is a great difference in needing something or wanting it. I simply asked Harry if I needed anything.

I still recall the time of Bill Selby and the football pools money used to pay Patsy's bills. Harry always looked after me and it was now my turn, for one should never take more than one gives. Anyway, we had not quite got the jackpot, so to speak but only one line of it. We still could not find that island and I wondered why it was so elusive? Something hidden somewhere!

Even after reading the book 'Agent Orange on Trial', there was no reference that I could find about it being used as weaponry prior to the Vietnam War. Of course, Harry had long since left the mortal plain by then; so what was he on about? For as sure as 'eggs are eggs', I was missing something!

Chapter 75

Well, as I have previously stated, I do not believe in coincidences/ chance but a week or so later, I was having dinner with an old work colleague of mine and Noels' and catching up with all the hospital gossip. Believe me, there was plenty of it as people in the medical profession change partners as easily as the weather changes as life to us could be so transcendent.

I did my best to keep off the subject of 'Harry' as I needed a few friends left at the end of the day. Inevitably, the subject cropped up and once I started, there was no stopping me.

So here we were, sitting in this Halal restaurant with me jabbering on and on about this elusive island when suddenly, my friend stopped me in my tracks. 'I think I know which one you are talking about' he said with a grin. Well, that shut me up fairly quickly as he went on to say that in his younger days, this was his favourite subject and added that he had tons of information back home. 'Let's go' I said as I quickly grabbed my bag from the table. 'We will have a job there' he retorted. 'I mean back home, Mauritius' he went on to say.

My facial expression changed from utter delight and excitement to a despondent, woebegone stare. It lifted, however, when he went on to say that it was either Guam which was taken from the Japanese by the Americans in 1944 or the Marshall or Caroline Islands. 'The latter' I interjected, adding that it begins with the letter 'C'. He did not bat an eyelid as I guess having worked with me many moons ago, he was used to my illogical thought patterns.

So we got back home i.e. England and not Mauritius, he set the computer up on the kitchen table and decided to check out Jack Drummond first who he had never heard of and then on to Agent Orange. 'I think the one you mean is the Satawan Islands' he said as Agent Orange obviously 'rang bells' for him. 'Let me check if it was used there' he added.

Well, we never got any further as a little message popped up on his screen, basically stating that we had never used this site before and for security reasons, they were closing it down. We were both flabbergasted as my friend attempted to explain; 'They think somebody else is using it'. 'Oh, no' says me with paranoia in full swing; 'you have hit the nail on the head' but how could we confirm that Agent Orange was used in that island so we tried again and again but nothing. It was not going to give this information.

The following Tuesday, Mandy and I set off to the Police Museum as I had to request P.C. Marriot's records and Mandy had decided to seek out information on her granddad.

She would be in the driving seat, for my fear of not getting back to the dogs was a strong possibility; so with wellies on feet so that I can walk the mile or so from the main road back home.

Two heads are always better than one so we decided to try and obtain the information on the Satawan Island by a different route i.e. omitting any links to Jack Drummond and Agent Orange.

Chapter 76

As soon as I could get my car extracted from the snow, we would set about doing this. A few days later, Grains Road was passable, due mainly to the pig farmer who runs a B&B (not for pigs, I might add). As he is only about three miles from the M62, I was guessing that he had some bookings, for he had been chugging up and down the road with his little plough.

Unfortunately, if one is not quick enough to get out of the way, you could get buried in the avalanche but I had got it sussed. I waved my hand and then, 'legged' it, with the dogs in tow. He grins as I am usually the only daft person to be trudging about in all weather.

Now one would ever rightly think that the council would do this but it doesn't appear to be on their radar as the drainage grids look like tiny garden centres, flourishing with wild flowers and grass during the summer months; consequently, the rain water runs in torrents down into the village. The only benefit being that nobody can see the yellow lines, hence, we, all, park at will, fully aware that the parking attendants are not issued wellies. To see one would be as rare as seeing a policeman.

With the computer and printer at the ready, Mandy types in 'Satawan Islands'. Now, a normal person would have said it was 'more luck than judgement' but we knew better as up pops a photo of dead bodies and little, wooden boats; just like the pictures in the crystal ball. On further investigation, it appeared that the island was attacked by the Americans, aided by the British, in WWII. We pressed on and discovered it had a number of hotels and a museum.

As we viewed umpteen photos of artefacts on the museum website, we hit the jackpot, for there was the doglike creature which was, in fact, a comic figurine of a clown. It was found on the islands in the 1800's and currently is housed in a museum in New York. We printed out a picture and went back to have a look at the war photos. I was convinced that we had found the island which Harry was going on about, even though we had found no evidence that Agent Orange had ever been used there.

At first, Mandy thought that there was something amiss with her printer as she couldn't get the pictures when, suddenly, a little pop-up come up with 'technical problem'. We did, however, print out the picture of the hotel with views of the island which appeared very welcoming. So not to be out done, Mandy takes photographs using her mobile phone and sends them to her daughter at Lancaster University as she is an expert at printing them out.

We were very much intrigued, especially since I asked Anne to try and print out these war pictures but with little success, just like Mandy's attempts. So I decided to speak to Noel and guess what he finds out?

Agent Orange was used as a herbicide in 1943 by the U.S. army. It was used as a crop duster on enemy crops and also to reduce foliage. Better still, on the 17th April, 1944; the American 13th Squadron released Agent Orange on the Satawan Islands. A pilot from this squadron complained that he had been contaminated by Agent Orange whilst enclosed in his plane. The B52 bombers also released their weapons around the same date which caused untold numbers of dead and injured.

Well, we were all on board now, buzzing around whilst doing Harry's bidding. Sadly, none of us had a clue as to why we were doing it.

My Muslim friend, Eves, rightly said 'Liz, you need aims and objectives'. My futile explanation seemed to fall on stony ground when I said that only Harry had these. He got me wondering if I was completely bonkers and somehow had dreamed all of it up.

I put forward my defence by stating that; 1. How would I know anything about Drummond or Agent Orange? 2. After all, I was a babe in my mother's arms at the time of these incidents. 3. Ardwick Municipal had enough trouble trying to teach us the basic 3 R's; Reading, Riting and Rithmatic, let alone, any of this information. Eves, reluctantly, conceded to this but he was intent on getting more information on the subject.

He came up with the titles of three books, covering the subject of Agent Orange;

'Agent Orange, Book of the Dead', by Tim Donnelly.
'The Dioxin War', by Robert Allen.
'Agent Orange on Trial', by Peter H. Shuck.

I knew about the latter when I was searching for information on Jack Drummond.

As expected, these books are not on the library shelves so I, duly, placed my order. There was a 5/6 week waiting period but what did I care, for this whole conundrum had been going on for over half century.

Well, I, finally, received a standard letter from the library which stated;

No. 1   This book is not in their remit. (Whatever that means)

No. 2   this book is unobtainable at the present time.

No. 3   'Agent Orange on Trial' is available.

I read this book, cover to cover, but as previously thought, it just cited 'Tort Cases', by veterans of the Vietnam War. Evidently, they were seeking compensation from the chemical companies who produced it in the United States.

I could not see any mention, anywhere, in this book, of it being previously used prior to the Vietnam War or that anybody was aware of its' lethal consequences. There was no reference regarding the Satawan Islands or WWII.

Well, as the saying goes, 'Old sins cast long shadows'!

Chapter 77

I received just one sheet of information regarding P.C. Marriot which absolutely told me nothing. I phoned Mandy to see if she had anything relating to her granddad but no luck. So I contacted the Police Museum who informed me that they had more information in relation to P.C. Marriot but they were unable to find any trace of Mandy's granddad.

Well, the 19th March, 2013 came round and I arrived promptly at 1.30 pm to view Marriot's records, as arranged. The weather was lousy and I did not envy Mandy who was in the process of moving house to live in Chadderton. I am afraid my street cred. Was gone to pot as I arrived wearing my shabby, green wellingtons and an old, black, hooded coat which kept me warm. At my age, comfort comes before glamour, every time.

I guess the day was doomed from the start as there were no more records to view. I was not best pleased but I decided to use my sweet, old lady persona. One does not upset the police, even if they are retired volunteers, dressed in the 1940's and 50's uniforms, unless absolutely necessary.

Anyway, this chap was, definitely, bobbing on a bit and was, indeed, old enough be my 'sugar daddy'. So with this in mind, I, charmingly, insist that there must be some records somewhere as I was told this about a month ago. I noticed that he was mellowing a bit and said he would go and look in the cellar. Fortunately, he did not take his truncheon out and clout me, for all the bother.

I remember the days when as a child, one would get 'a clip round the earhole' for some misdemeanour or other and if you told your parents what 'the copper' had done, you get another clout from them, also. This is not the case in this day and age, no boundaries anymore!

About fifteen minutes later, a muffled voice could be heard from the cellar, shouting 'There is a God'. He emerged from the stairs, helmet askew, slightly breathless and sweating profusely, clutching an armful of dusty files. I spent the next couple of hours, ploughing through these files as he photocopied them for me. Bless him!

I do not know what I expected to find, regarding Harry but nothing of any great interest was found. I did, however, discover that Marriot was born in London and was a Flight Sergeant with the R.A.F. Police. He was based in Wigsley, near Nework and had enlisted in 1943. Apparently, he had received two medals during the war, for his work in France and Germany.

When I got home, I went through all these photocopies with a fine tooth comb and found nothing that would give me any clue as to why Harry had sent me to the Police Museum. The only thing that struck me was the fact that Marriot 'played by the rules', whereas Harry was a 'free spirit'. I did ask around my friends but nobody seemed to know what the RAF Police did during the War in France, let alone Germany. I would just have to consult 'the Oracle' Noel.

Chapter 78

Mandy managed to print out the photo of the Ritz Hotel from her mobile phone but, as expected, it was of extremely, low quality. It was difficult to distinguish the lions in the photo.

I phoned the Communications Office at the Ritz and using my poshest voice, asked if they had any images of the place, prior to 1933. She seemed intrigued so I gave her my usual white lie, though somewhat embellished, adding that my father was based there during WWII. I could sense that she did not know what I was talking about so feeling quite proud of myself; I went on to explain about Winston Churchill and the Marie Antoinette Suite.

She informed me that I could purchase a book from the souvenir shop which gave a history of the Ritz. She added that she would look to see if there was any image which would suit my requirements.

My next port of call was the library but I could not find the book she suggested. I did, however, get the next best thing, 'West End Front' which turned out to be a very interesting 'read'. The jist of it was as follows;

London hotels supported a number of various sub-cultures. Aristocrats, journalists, actors, criminal spies, MI5,

The Ritz Hotel

MI6 and MI9 were based at the Ritz. The 'Homosexual' subculture included members of all these groups.

As the bombs began to fall, ambivalence started to invade reports of bomb proof bolt holes in the West End. The Ritz with its comic murals of the 1st World War trenches and the 'Pink Sink' underground bar was a known venue for 'Gays' which the police turned 'a blind eye to'.

The journalists occupied the lower bar, in which two clandestine networks co-existed and one code of silence competed with another. In the decade following the War, the combination of homosexuality and espionage would prove its volatility in a flurry of defections to the Soviet Union.

None of us, including the 'Oracle' had ever heard of MI9 which along with MI5, were all based at the Ritz.

On further investigation, we discovered that MI9 was a spy network which controlled the 'French Freedom Fighters', collaborators and agents who, in fact, were all non-British allies i.e. Italians, Spanish sympathisers and informers.

It started me thinking if Harry had been somehow involved? One would need to be a certain calibre of individual to undertake any of these tasks. Michael Bentine, a well-known comedian, was attached to MI9, aiding prisoners and allies behind enemy lines. I wondered if Harry worked for England, during the long school holidays. Surely, someone who spoke fluent French would have been very useful in this subterfuge. The other option being that he somehow, inadvertently gained information of paramount importance.

The latter, I think, would have being more the case which brought me back to the Press Club in Deansgate. Was it a microcosm of the Ritz Hotel? So who did it cater for, apart from journalists and was there any evidence that Alan Turin frequented the place?

As usual, I got more questions than answers, but with all these pieces of information, I had no real answer as to what I was about. I did find it intriguing that Alan Turin, Jack Drummond and Harry had all died in unusual circumstances, within less than two years of one another. Turin and Drummond were alleged spies, along with Oliver Steel, Secretary of State for War and Trade. After the War in 1945, he became Secretary of State for the colonies. Harold Wilson, who smoked a pipe, was the Secretary for Overseas Trade. In 1950, it was claimed that MI5 had kept a file on him from 1945. Evidently, it was believed that he was a Soviet agent.

Well, it seemed that I was up to my neck 'in muck and bullets', little of which I could comprehend. On a lighter note, I received a phone call from a young lady at the Ritz Hotel. She could not find any images prior to 1933 or any coat of arms on the crest between the pillars and the lions. At that moment, I stifled a giggle, for she sent the maintenance man up on the roof to clarify that it was blank. Seeing that it was once, appeared to be a doorway, it made sense that there must have been something there once which was now obliterated? She went on to say that she could forward a photograph and requested my email address. I had to admit that I did not live in the 21st century and asked her to post.

The Rivoli Bar

It arrived after a few days with a little note attached to the photo of the Rivoli Bar which was originally the Pink Sink Bar. Oh! If only everybody was as helpful as her.

An interesting piece of information was obtained by the Oracle in his search to see if Alan Turin had frequented the Press Club in Deansgate. Apparently, Princess Margaret, along with other notables and 'Top Brass' military, went to the Press Club during the days when she was engaged to Captain Peter Townsend. Later, in the 1960's she became patron of it.

It was no great surprise that there was no mention of Alan Turin, let alone Harry as they would be 'small fish' in this big pond. Journalists had free admission and I wondered what other snippets of information could be floating around there. It, decidedly, likened itself to the homosexual subculture in the lavish surroundings of the' Pink Sink Bar', where aristocrats, journalists etc. had vagarious, underground cultures.

Chapter 79

In the light of what has surfaced, although I have to admit, it did seem to be farfetched, I decided to clue myself up as to what spies actually did.

'Between Silk and Cyanide' was an excellent read. It was a bit like a Spy CV and inspired the 'James Bond 007' films. But what was more interesting, Wing Commander Edward Yeo Thomas, a British spy codenamed 'White Rabbit' was a friend of Leo Marks, a cryptographer at Bletchley Park who worked with Alan Turin. 'White Rabbit' worked with the early French Resistance and it was said that he became a double agent. The title of this book stemmed from the fact that they used a well-remembered poem or song. The key letters were etched in the lining of their clothing and these codes were then translated at Bletchley Park. The cyanide speaks for itself. Communications sent by the French to the British, used key words or phrase sent by wireless e.g.; an empty house at Quatre Pavilions in Bordeaux to the BBC wireless network. They would then respond with innocent appearing messages which only the Resistance fighters or spies knew the true meaning. In this way, the Germans would not have a clue.

An example given was of a female spy who used the following poem

The life that I have
Is all that I have
And the life that I have is yours

The love that I have
Of the life that I have
Is yours and yours and yours

The sleep that I have
A rest that I have
Yet, death will be just a pause

For the peace of my years
In the long green grass
Will be yours and yours and yours

I vaguely recall this film which I had seen as a child; 'Carve her name with Pride' in which this particular poem was used. It was inspired by Leo Marks, the author of 'Between Silk and Cyanide' If I put two and two together', it does seem that Leo Mark's book was inspired by Wing Commander Edward Yeo Thomas.

Mandy may have an overactive imagination but she got me thinking when she asked 'Who taught you that poem 'Catching the Cat'? '. You know that I am not really sure if it was my mother or Mr Teasdale. The other odd thing is how I can recall every line, without hesitation. Other songs and poems, learnt as a child, have just left snippets in my memory, e.g.,' Bye, Bye Blackbird'. Surely, I would have remembered that as he sang it whilst playing the piano on umpteen occasions.

Well, we were off again on another search. It really was good fun, trying to find out who wrote 'Catching the Cat'. I had now been infected by her imagination and wondered if it had been used by a spy? The only thing that I was sure of was the fact it was very old and had learnt it over 60 yrs. ago.

The reference to the mice having 'Crepe on every hat' was a custom which dated back to at least the Victorian times. Folks dressed in all black for a funeral and the black crepe was used around the hats, denoting this mourning period, in respect of the dead. Alas, as expected, we drew a complete blank. I just hope that I will not take the role of 'the smallest mouse in the council'.

With that in mind, for whatever reason, we decided to have another session with Harry. So on the 15th April, 2013, we set out our stall, in order to try and get some information from him. Noel suggested that we ask very specific questions, saying that 'Surely, Harry is able to tell us if he so wished. So why doesn't he?' he went on to say. Mandy's rationale was that we would not seek all the evidence, if we knew the answers. I tended to agree with her as it would be like reading a book backwards.

So we started off, as Harry had arrived and I could feel him. I guessed he knew that we were not best pleased and totally frustrated at not getting clear answers.

Where and when did you meet Alan Turin?

Did you have sex or just friends?

Is there a photograph anywhere of you and Alan Turin or one that would help us in any way?

There was, absolutely, no response to the first two questions but then I could see a black and white photograph in which, four men were sat around what appeared to be a table. There was something placed on the table but I could not identify it, for as quick as it came, it went. It was only replaced with Harry grinning at me whilst doing an Irish jig and then, a tap dance before disappearing.

'What on earth is he playing at', I thought as I was really cross with him now. Although, I realised that he could read my mind, I verbalised my anger; adding that we were all getting frustrated and needed proper answers. Mandy piped in with her 'topenath' but it did not get us anywhere. So I asked him to alter my cuckoo clock, if we are correct in our belief regarding Turin and Jack Drummond (For we knew that they were connected to one another as Fellows of the Royal Society) and if he, himself, was connected to them and Agent Orange etc. in some way. I stipulated that if we were going in the wrong direction, could he please alter Mandy's clocks Mandy added that we did realise that this may take a few days at least.

I was remembering, with great delight, the scenarios with Harry No 2, all those years ago and the Spiritualist National Union. I chuckled when I remembered the famous 'ghost bust' at Ivy Cottage, plus the game he played at the New Year when Gladys' friend's watch got run over.

Mandy wanted to know what I was laughing about so I recounted the tale when Gladys and I were having coffee, one morning. Harry No 2 (as I called him) phoned up, bawling and shouting, saying I had done all his clocks in and was never coming to my house again because I was a witch. Well, she found the funny side of it but says out loud 'He better not bugger up any of my clocks'! I know he won't' I said as he likes you.

Low and behold! Harry is back and laughing heartily as he must be as bad as me. Suddenly, he shows me a great, big spider and it is just as well I like them and never kill them. Consequently, my house is full of cobwebs, hanging from the windows and ceilings but that is on the negative side. On the positive side, there are no flies or bluebottles as they all get eaten, saving me a small fortune in fly sprays. ….I am starting to reminisce again…… as I remembered the flies I used to swat with a newspaper as a child and would feed them to the spiders that lived in the outside lavatory. I guess he must have known this too but a spider has eight legs, therefore I now knew that eight connections were needed to form the answer.

Chapter 80

My heart missed a beat as Mandy was on the phone and I was dreading what she was about to say. I wondered if Harry had altered one of her clocks because if that was the case, we were 'down the Swanny, without a paddle'.

Oddly enough, No!, but she went on to tell me of yet another strange occurrence, for she had just received mail for a Mr & Mrs Marriot. So armed with these three letters, she went round the neighbours to ascertain when they had lived in her house.

Apparently, May Marriot died about a year ago, long after her husband and guess what? Prior to 1990, this quiet crescent, now owned by the council, was originally dwellings used by the Police Force. We concluded from this that he was a policeman and could possibly be relative of James Marriot.

Having previously, in 2011, searched the phone book in an effort to find James Marriot, I recall it was a simple task as it was an uncommon name. So out of curiosity, I counted them and there were only twenty-four listed for the whole of Manchester North East book. What are the odds of that happening?

Anyway, it was 2.30 in the afternoon and a pleasant dry day, so I decided to mow the lawns and 'potter' about the garden with the dogs in tow. I was trying to work-out if Marriot was one of the 'spider's legs'.

After mowing the lawn, I came into the kitchen for a break and a ciggy. I had set the cooker to turn off at 6.30 which would be ample time for my four legs of chicken to cook slowly. I had left them in my usual sunny spot, to defrost. I was hopping mad, for I had paid the butcher for four legs and discover there were only three. They were still in the neatly blue plastic tray, covered in Clingfilm. On closer inspection, I noticed that a corner of the Clingfilm had been carefully turned back and one of the legs had been neatly extracted. 'That was Bess, the bugger' I thought to myself and had wondered why she had been so quiet whilst I was in the garden. I thanked my lucky stars that she had only eaten one, for I wouldn't have anything for teatime. I guess that she is not so keen on raw chicken and prefers them cooked. It was a lesson learnt and that would be last time I would leave them there again. So into the oven, they went and we all set off to finish the weeding.

How time flies as I heard the cooker buzzing so we headed towards the kitchen and took the chicken from the oven. They smelled really good and I was starving so I quickly put the potatoes and veg. on the hob and went down the steps

The dogs and me in the garden

to the living room. Suddenly, I glanced over and noticed the cuckoo clock had stopped. Brilliant! I had my answer from Harry. The clock stopped at 2.15 but I knew full well, it was working perfectly at 2.30 when Mandy was on the phone. So he had not only stopped it but also turned it backwards. We had our answer so I, gleefully, phoned Mandy, knowing that we were on the right track. Marriot was definitely one of the spider's legs. We had seven more to find.

So based on what we know now, to quote Mandy; 'Who was Harry? The spider itself or surrounded by a web of deceit?

So with this in mind, Noel contacted the department dealing with 'The Freedom of Information, giving full name, place and year of birth and requesting any records of intelligence or translator personnel during WWII. They emailed back, stating that he had not given enough information and they wanted to know which area of the

İntelligence Service had he worked in. Noel responded by sending a copy of Harry's teaching certificate, explaining that we did not know but it could possibly be MI9. Yet again, he was informed that he had not given sufficient information, in order to perform a search. As Noel put it; 'If we had the information which they required, we would not be asking them with a name like Bousfield Booth Teasdale'. One would think it would not be a difficult task.

After all, the Police Pensions were good enough to search their records for James Marriot; to quote them; 'we would not do this for you if he had a name such as Roberts. Marriot is such an uncommon name and should be easy enough to locate'.

Perhaps 'Freedom of Information' should employ 'a copper'. I bet there is nobody else in their records with a name like Bousfield Booth Teasdale. So much for 'freedom of information'; just another whitewash if you ask me!

Chapter 81

I brought Noel up to date with the situation and I could tell he was a little dubious, to say the least, about mine and Mandy's conclusion. This is the logical, sensible Noel and I could fully understand his thinking, for the whole story had changed from something that, at times, was light and amusing to the other side of the coin which was more sinister and, after all, corresponded with the way he died.

It was then that the brilliant brain Noel says 'Liz, are you sure that Harry was always at Ardwick Municipal School?'. 'Yes', I replied emphatically but it did get me thinking (not an easy task). You see, I had read just one ledger and started working backwards from the closure of the school in July, 1952. After about a dozen pages, I had got fed up with reading B.B. Teasdale did this and that as I was really only looking to find out his Christian name and B.B. was of no help whatsoever.

So I contacted Dave at County Records, only to find that they were closing on the 12th September, in order to amalgamate with the Central Library which would be re-opening in the Spring of 2014. Well, that put the proverbial 'cat among the pigeons' until Dave, suddenly, says 'hang on a minute'. Low and behold, there is a God, for the school records have never been returned to storage. This was on the Tuesday and we had only until Saturday, to check it out. So on the Thursday at the agreed appointment at 2pm, Mandy and I proceeded to go through these ledgers with a fine toothcomb.

There was no mistaking it as the last entry March 1943, B.B. Teasdale; fire lecture. After that, he seemed to have disappeared of the face of the Earth, until 20th September, 1949. His name was mentioned alongside an entry which we could not decipher due to the quality of ink and the passage of time; not to mention that the handwriting resembled mine and looked like a spider had jumped in and out of an inkwell.

So where was he for six and a half years? Various theories came to mind and we wondered if he had been imprisoned as a 'conscious objector' during the War. This we would need to check out but meanwhile, we would see if we could piece something together by reading all the surrounding entries from 1939 to 1952.

At first, there was nothing of any interest, just the usual daily entries i.e. boys stole cigarettes, staff off sick and, of course, the 'Nit Nurse', God bless her, for she was, personally, determined to eradicate the little blighters of the face of the Earth as nothing seemed to deter her.

On April, 15th, 1940, air raid precautions and gas mask distribution throughout the population. Hopefully, this was the second allocation; otherwise, they were a bit behind the times as the war had started in 1939. The entries carried on with such things as the school closing due to air raid, slates off the roof due to a fallen bomb nearby, school closed because there was no coke (I do hope they were talking about fuel and not the 'snorty' stuff) and umpteen teachers with days off sick (can't say I blame them) with one described as having a nervous breakdown (whatever that means?)

We were getting a bit bored at this stage until we read an entry 'Saint Stephens School commandeered by the military. Pupils are to attend here'.

Now, County Records is very security conscious so one has to put ones belongings in a locker. Only pencils are to be used and ledgers to be placed on cushions. I got politely told off for licking my finger in order to turn over the pages as she said 'I might get germs'. She gave me a rubber finger cover, just like the ones used by the post office workers.

Everybody was sitting there, ploughing through numerous documents and the place was as quiet as the grave. That was until Mandy exclaimed in a loud voice 'bloody hell, Liz, you are in here'. I was so glad that she did it and not me as the whole room echoed with Shush! Shush!'. At least, the acoustics were good. 'Elizabeth Powell, supply teacher, just a few lines down from B.B. Teasdale entry on March, 1943. 'This is very spooky' I thought as I checked the date, September, 1943. 'You daft bugger, I had only just been born', I whispered with a grin. There was no further documentation about her that we could find so one assumes she did not stay there too long. I cannot blame her as bombs falling all over the place and double sized classes (the kids from St. Stephens). So who was she? My instinct is telling me that Harry is trying to tell me something and it has got to do with names, for this is how it all started.

Then there were entries for supply and temporary teachers and staff. 3.7.1945; Mr John Howard and Mr Lee, supply teachers and Mr Warburton and Mr Porter.

What we could not understand was why they were all coming in, in 1945. The War was almost over so why were they replacing and what for? ; As there was no mention of any teachers leaving. There again, B.B. Teasdale just vanished and it would have taken us forever to follow every single name to see if anyone else had simply vanished.

Well, it was now almost closing time the plot thickened with the following entries;

Lecturers returning from the forces at Manchester Education offices. Followed by 10.12.1945; Teachers returning from the forces Refresher Course. Mr Fisher attended. He joined the staff 3.12.45.

There was nothing of any relevance until B.B. Teasdale; 20th September, 1949. Prior to this, a temporary teacher leaves 16th September, 1949. This, we assume, is because Teasdale is back and this teacher was his replacement. I wondered if it was Elizabeth Powell.

Well, they started gathering their dusty volumes as people were leaving. I guessed we were being thrown out. So with bags removed from the lockers, pencils returned, not to mention the rubber finger thingy (Noel informed me later that they are called Rubber Thimbles. Only he could know that off the top of his head) we set off for fish and chips, plus mushy peas, with Mandy having gravy as usual. Ugh!!! Our heads were so 'fudged up' that it was five minutes later when we realised we were going in the wrong direction.

Chapter 82

So what now? Could he possibly have been working for the government in some capacity? Noel checked the listed 'Conscientious Objectors 'but found nothing. So where was he for six and a half years? We just did not have a clue!

We spent the best part of one afternoon at 'Delph Library', looking through a number of websites but we could not find any links or photographs that connected him with A. Turin or J. Drummond. The only thing we could do now was to follow the clues regarding the military and the War as Harry will not tell us. We were hoping to find something which corresponded to his absence; 1943---1949.

On January 23rd, 1941, a law was introduced that required all able bodied men and women between the ages of 16-60 years old to register their availability to become 'fire watchers' with the Civil Defence. There were exemptions for those people serving in the Forces, Police and Fire Brigade Service. The introduction of 'Fire Watchers' was a means of combating the dreaded German Incendiary Bombs which were been dropped on British cities, causing incredible damage and loss of life.

As the year drew on, 'Conscription' was extended, in an effort to build-up the armed forces in preparation for the invasion. All men, between the ages of 18-51 years old were called up for military service which reduced the work force in the factories etc.; hence, the 'Women's Land Army'.

On the 6th of June, 1944, the R.A.F. Police (James Marriot) launched 'Operation Overlord' which was the invasion to liberate France.

What intrigued me most was the fact that two weeks after the invasion, No. 6, R.A.F. Security Section, redeployed to the city of 'Caen' where they set-up temporary headquarters. They established contact with the same Catholic priest who was connected to Jack Drummond, at the time of his murder.

It would be interesting to know what section P.C. Marriot was assigned to and if there was any link? I was thinking that someone who spoke French would be a very desirable asset in some way regarding D. Day.

Did Harry leave the school in 1943, in preparation for this? If all men between the ages of 18-51 were called up for service, then I am going to bet 'a pound to a penny' that Harry must have been doing something 'hammer toe or no hammer toe'. This was bugging me and I needed to find the answer to this. Furthermore, although the war ended, the Cold War continued from 1947 till 1952 which would coincide with Harry's dates.

The very next afternoon, armed with my ciggys and a mug of coffee, I went upstairs in order to plug in my push button phone; for I knew full well that I would be almost demented by the time I have pushed this and that button. It would not be helped by having to listen to classical music. Why, oh, why! Can they not play Jazz or Rock and Roll?

My first call was to 'Army Headquarters' in London but they didn't have a clue. They suggested I make contact with the 'Historical Army Office' regarding what exemptions were made for hammer toes. I always say it is the 'luck of the draw' who one speaks to. I usually avoid Mondays and Fridays, in general, unless purchasing something as staff are facing the whole week and not in a particularly good mood. On Fridays, they are more interested in the weekend ahead. Anyway, my luck was not in as they did not know either; however, the helpful Irishman went to great lengths by asking various colleagues if they knew the answer. All to no avail until somebody suggested the 'National Archives' which was also based in London. I was losing the will to live at this stage but one last-ditch attempt and 'Glory be', I got the following information.

Firstly, it would depend on the degree of disability, even so they would be required to do a 'desk job'. However, after the conscription age was raised to 51 years old, the War Office became less picky. I then pointed out that this teacher had no mobility problems, in fact, quite the reverse, as he jumped up and down from the rostrum and agile enough to take part in amateur variety acts.

She then asked what subject he taught in school?; to which I replied 'Drama and Maths'. 'Well, don't take this as gospel but somebody with such a high standard of education, would have without doubt been working in the national interest of the government. So Harry was not just a man who to quote Jean Teasdale 'never went anywhere or did anything'. He had fooled them all!

In view of this revelation, we decided to explore avenues which related to 'Intelligence 'work. Noel discovered that a crossword puzzle was placed in a national newspaper on the 15th January, 1942, in which a prize was offered to those who completed it within 12 minutes. The real reason, in fact, was to invite these people for an interview. If they were adept at crossword puzzles or played chess, plus a background in teaching, these were highly advantageous. If one could speak a foreign language, well then, it was definitely a 'Yes'. Now we do not know if Harry liked crossword puzzles or indeed, played chess so his score for intelligence work would be two out of four. So did Harry fit the bill? We needed more evidence so Mandy set off to the library to see what she could dig-up.

In 1941, Manchester University was used for recruitment purposes and regional code breaking schools were based in all main cities around the country. Cryptoanalalysists were categorised as working for the Military and the HQ for those who were with M.I.8, was Room 47 at the Foreign Office, Whitehall, London.

In 1941, the code name for Hitler's attempted invasion was 'Operation Sea Lion'. If only it had been named 'Operation Sea Cow', we would have hit the jackpot but it was not. I definitely saw a Sea Cow in the crystal ball and not a Seal.

Apparently, M.I.8 Resistance came in to full fruition in 1943 and this was when Harry went missing from school. It was the best known of the underground armies known as the 'French Maquis' and what language was Harry fluent in, French!

I could have kissed Mandy, bless her, but I don't think she would have been best pleased, for Harry had done it again. Apparently, whilst she was scouring the library shelves for books on spying, suddenly, she was drawn away from them and to another book on the bottom shelf. From what she described to me, was exactly the same feeling I had as a child with my mother's calendar. That is how I knew it was Harry's doing, for there in black and white in the code-breakers pages, was the entry 'Those who could read sheet music were most desirable due to their ability and intelligence to unravel cryptic messages'.

We could not believe it, as what initially set the ball rolling for me, was yes, the sheet music found in his pockets. Well, I reckoned she deserved a box of her favourite chocolates, probably much better than one of my kisses so prior to my next shopping trip, I decided to play one of my 'Harry Games'. I asked him to pay for Mandy's chocolates, dark chocolate peppermint creams, after all, she was the one who came up with the sheet music clue thus convincing us all that he worked for some intelligence service.

As I drove to the shops, I was wondering how he would achieve this and recalled various scenarios i.e. my handbag zip, photocopying machine etc. Over the past few days, my eyes were peeled to the ground, looking for a pound coin, for this is what it costs at B&M.

So clutching my wire basket, full of nuts and bird seed, plus two packets of dog chews and half a dozen eggs, I joined the queue. As I went through the checkout, I was mentally complaining to Harry that it was me who paid for the chocolates.

It was always my usual habit of checking the bill before leaving as for the umpteen occasions, I have noticed that these supermarkets tend to put items on offer and then charge the original price. I have lost count of the number of times I have waited at Customer Service, in order to obtain a refund. Invariably, it is never their fault; it is always blamed on the tills. I will refrain from quoting the old saying 'Bad workmen always blame their tools'.

I must admit, I stifled a grin as I glanced over the receipt, for low and behold, not only had I not been charged for the chocolates but the dogs ended up with a free packet of chews. 'I won't bother going to Customer Service this time' I thought to myself, for after all, it will never be their fault but those tills. As I sauntered out of the shop, I wondered how Harry did it. I could never figure it out, but there again, maybe I was not meant to know.

Chapter 83

A couple of days later as I was sitting watching the late night news on TV, a strange thing happened. It came completely 'out of the blue' but I distinctly heard Harry's words in my head, saying 'Read Harry's book'. Now, I was completely befuddled, thinking 'what does it mean'? As quick as he came, he went.

Well, I sat there, on the rocking chair, trying to figure out what he was talking about. I wondered whether it was him or me but the word 'Eddouha' came to mind, for the circumstances were the same (something in the past) and then it 'hit' me; 'Harry's book'. It was the only keepsake which I had of my friend Harry who died.

So in my mind, I was going back to 1972 to my nursing days in Stepping Hill Hospital. Well, there was some consolation in this; at least I was not going back hundreds of years to Morocco and 'The Black Sultan'.

I have well over a hundred books, on varying subjects and I did not have a clue where it was. I couldn't even remember the title. Half an hour later, I was on my hands and knees, rummaging through the pile. 'Oh, boy, they need a good dusting!' I thought and suddenly, it jumped out at me. 'They Fought Alone'

As I opened the tired, yellow pages, two items dropped out. A pressed red rose which looked almost as fresh as the day he gave it to me. I was now in floods of tears as the old memories came back to haunt me; our favourite records, night clubs and secret little jokes as lovers do.

The second item was a torn off piece of the non-existent dust cover which must have been used as a page marker.

I had never read it before as I was too upset at the time. Now, Harry was an avid reader so of all the books, why this one? To my mind, this just reinforced what we were all thinking. Harry (Teasdale) was trying to tell us something, for my Harry was in the Air Force during the War so there was no connection with him.

I found the whole thing incredible as forty years on, this book supports our theory. The burning question is; was Teasdale instrumental in getting Harry to give me this book and if so (which I believe) where does it all begin?

Maurice Buckmaster

was born in Rugeley, Staffs, in 1902, and was educated at Eton. He has travelled extensively on the Continent where he has lived and worked. During the war, as Colonel Buckmaster, he was head of Special Operations Executive (French Section) and was awarded the O.B.E. Now, in

THEY FOUGHT ALONE

he tells the remarkable story of the daring exploits of British secret agents who served in occupied France and the organization that planned and co-ordinated their operations.

Early in the dark days of 1941, armed only with Winston Churchill's momentous brief to "set Europe ablaze," and his own intimate knowledge of pre-war France, Maurice Buckmaster walked into an empty room at the War Office to begin his work. Within four years he had built up the great Resistance organization in France which, in Eisenhower's words, "shortened the war in Europe by nine months."

The S.O.E. included among its agents Odette and Peter Churchill, Nancy Wake and Violette Szabo, whose heroic stories have been told elsewhere; but those of other brave men and women, who fought a desperate and lonely war from the inside, provide the dramatic highlights of this book. No less intriguing are the accounts of the intricate planning that lay behind their operations, and which could make the difference between death and survival.

Original Publishers:
ODHAMS PRESS at 18/-

IT'S THE **POPULAR** BOOK CLUB

I mean who if anybody got Teasdale to call me Elizabeth? Oddly enough, Harry also used to call me this. When the phenomenon started, I was not afraid as I always thought it was Harry; otherwise, I would not have accepted it, having completely forgotten about Mr Teasdale calling me 'Elizabeth'. I had a thousand questions to which I had no answers but what sprang to mind, Harry 1. I think;

Cometh the hour, Cometh the man
For I will find the spider in its web

Chapter 84

Mandy had found a photograph and obituary for her granddad and we were, once again, off to the Police Museum to request his records as she was adamant that they must have records somewhere. Meanwhile, I was chatting to a retired copper about my family history. Funnily enough, his name was Dave which was interesting as this was three Dave's in a row, Elliot House and County Records. I told him the bare details of how I suspected Harry was working for the government. Also, the fact that we couldn't get any information; every time we tried, we came to a brick wall.

Apparently, according to him Classified Information can only be declassified by the people who originally classified it. Given the fact that they are no longer around, it stays classified and that is how they get around the 'Freedom of Information'; in other words 'Bullshit'

Assuming Harry was a reserve, then prior to the biggest ever invasion (D Day landing, June 6th 1944) this array of people were brought in to monitor signals and take aerial photographs of what Normandy looked like. These individuals were trained in parachute jumping at Ringway Airport (now Manchester Airport)

It was then that I got a mental picture of Harry and a parachute. I immediately thought 'No way' and I laughingly responded by saying that I couldn't imagine Harry doing a parachute jump. 'Well' he said 'there are other ways of getting to France'. Evidently, a floating harbour was built named 'Mullberry' which had its own fuel pipeline called 'Pluto', Well I was chuckling at that stage and went on to explain to him that I once had a dog by the same name, a great, big multi-coloured mongrel. I was unlikely to forget this information.

Good timing as Mandy appeared, having insisted that her granddad was a policeman, filled yet another form, giving her email address yet again which I also used in an effort to get a quicker response.

ROWSTON (RONALD GEORGE) — On February 14 1999, peacefully in Hospital after a short illness, Ronnie aged 78 years. A much loved Dad of Liz, dear Father-in-Law of Pete, very dear Grandad of Nicky, Michael, Mandy and Daniel and a devoted Great-Grandad. Funeral service and committal at Stockport Crematorium on Tuesday February 23 at 2.00pm. Family flowers only please, donations in lieu for St. Agnes Church, North Reddish. All inquiries to S P Astley, Family Funeral Directors, 127 Hyde Road, Denton Tel: 0161 320 3203.

Chapter 85

The following Monday, I realised that my landline was not receiving calls and it had been making 'funny noises' when I dialled out. I contacted British Telecom (BT) who assured me that they would check the line in the next few minutes and let Joan know. (My next door neighbour)

Two hours later, I contacted BT, only to be told that Joan's phone had been engaged so they could not check the line. I could not understand as Joan said her phone had not been busy.

Day 2: I trotted up to Joan's as I still could not make outgoing calls. I was informed that my phone was the problem and made arrangements for them to visit my home on Wednesday, costing £90.

Day 3: They contacted Joan to cancel my appointment for that afternoon stating it is the overhead cable which would be repaired by Friday.

Day 4: By the Friday, the phone was still not working so I used Joan's phone to complain, only to be told that it was not the overhead cable but that my phone was the problem. They said they would come on the Monday.

So on Monday, at 5.50pm, a B.T. man arrived but he had not come to fix the phone, apparently he was here to find out where I lived. The explanation being that four different engineers had been to the wrong address but I was not best pleased, for I have lived here for well over 25 years and always received my phone bill. So back to Joan's I went and asked to speak to a supervisor. I reiterated my address and an appointment was made for the Wednesday, am.

So on the Wednesday at 8.20, an engineer arrived with what appears to be the original log sheet. At 8.40 am, with his equipment attached to the cable at the top of the stairs, he tells me that it is their junction box which is the problem. 'Luv, I will be back shortly' he says as he goes out the door. Four hours later, with the dogs dying to go 'walkies', he returns and the phone was now working. By this time, I was wondering if they were all totally incompetent and I proceeded to question him. He looked mightily uncomfortable when I pressed him on why it took so long. Evidently, he had to go to the junction box and then to the exchange to fix my phone.' This being due to bad paperwork! He said.

So, finally, we got to go 'walkies' and set off to find the junction box. I thought it was not far from the post office, about a mile from my house. So in I went to the post office and asked where the exchange was? 'It is just at the back of here, a few yards away', a helpful assistant replied. Apparently, it was unmanned and engineers had a key. I had to ask myself why had he taken over four hours just to travel over a mile and why had this repair taken eleven days?

Rightly or wrongly, I was beginning to think my phone was bugged so I decided to phone Ian, a friend who was very knowledgeable in this area. After I told him of my experiences with the computers refusing information, he suspected that 'I was on to something that was classified'.

Well, we turned the bedrooms and bathroom upside down and I had never seen so much dust in all my life. Ian managed to bang his head on the old iron bedstead and I was feeling rather silly when no bugs were to be found. Afterwards, sitting in the kitchen and feeling rather exhausted, having a brew, there was a knock on the door. Mandy appeared at the door and said 'Liz, I have been trying to phone you all week, it just rings and rings. Where have you been?' Ian pipes up 'She has been looking for phone bugs' and then tells her the tale.

Instead of laughing and calling me 'a daft, old bat', Mandy went quite pale and goes on to say that her internet system and telephone have been down for days and she had to use her mobile all the time. Ian and I just looked at each other and started wondering if I, indeed, was correct.

Ian got out his laptop to find more information on 'bugging'. Apparently, for around £300, various companies claim that they can ascertain if one's line is bugged. On further exploration, Ian discovers that there is no full proof way to confirm this, one way or the other, if it is done by the government. The only clues are that one will experience interference and a mobile phone can be warm when not in use.

Well, this whole phone scenario was taking a more sinister twist, for Mandy's dates corresponded with mine. I had overhead cables and hers were underground, so one cannot connect them together. Now, assuming we were right and this was going on, had the name Teasdale flagged something up and if so, what? Furthermore what had set them off?

Looking back, hindsight is a wonderful thing, I had left a paper trail starting with County Records and furthermore, I had connected Mandy to myself by using her email address at the Police Museum. When a number of forms had been completed, all with Teasdale and Marriot, wasn't it not odd when we think about why they said her granddad did not exist. We were now coming to the conclusion that there was a strong possibility that these three individuals were connected in some way. So Mandy decided to put more pressure on the Police Museum, in an effort to get information about her granddad. We all started to wonder what the connection was, was it that Mandy's granddad connected to James Marriot? If so, there was more than this than meets the eye. Furthermore, having informed Noel of our suspicions, the three of us decided to state quite openly that we were aware the phones were bugged and let them know what we wanted them to know. I decided to purchase an untraceable mobile phone to use when necessary, so leaving them guessing as to how much information we had. What beggars belief is why would anybody be interested in what happened almost 60 years ago. Surely all those involved must be dead. I think that Ian 'hit the nail on the head' when he said yet again, 'Liz, you have opened a can of worms'

Chapter 86

Noel phoned to say he had come across an article in the 'Guardian' newspaper which he thought we would find useful in pursuing the 'intelligence work' angle. The article itself, was very enlightening and the three of us were convinced that Harry did some sort of intelligence work between 1943-1949; possibly at Bletchley Park.

Women spies in the Second World War: "It was horrible and *wonderful*. Like a love affair"

The role of female spies is a little-known part of the war effort. Now 89, Rozanne Colchester, a code breaker and post-war MI6 agent, recalls the "strange isolation"of Bletchley, the impact of the Cambridge Three and discussing brothels with Graham Greene http://www.theguardian.com/world/2010/nov/07/women-spies-second-world-war.

Eventually, I managed to track down Rozanne Colchester and asked her if by any chance the name 'Robin' or 'Teasdale' meant anything to her? I even offered to send her his photograph.

She was a lovely lady, so helpful but unfortunately, she said 'There were about 10.000 people there during the war years and we were not allowed to communicate. Even if I saw his photograph, after all these years, I could not remember so many faces'. Her advice was to contact 'Bletchley Park', and, if necessary, pay them a visit. Evidently, there were umpteen photos and lists of names of people who worked there during the War.

So I spoke with the organiser but he could not find his name listed. He went on to tell me that unfortunately, a great number of their records had been destroyed and the ones which they had, were mainly from individuals or their relatives who claimed that they worked there.

As he was a chatty sort of chap, I decided 'to pick his brains' so I briefly gave him relevant 'Harry information' He went on to say that there was a strong possibility that Harry would have been at one of the 'Spy Schools', apparently, there were venues all around the country, namely; Special Operations Executive MI5 and MI6. His reasoning being that Bletchley was used purely as a decoding venue for information received from behind enemy lines and that Harry's profile was more fitting to the latter.

He suggested that I contact the Ministry of Defence but since I had no idea whether it was the army, navy or air force, let alone an identity number, this would prove to be a very difficult exercise. Of course, depending on what Harry did, they may withhold the information anyway.

Now this was a very 'long shot' but I would bear that in mind as a last resort, as I have a feeling that something more concrete will point me in the right direction.

Chapter 87

I was nodding off to sleep and I was feeling that I should rouse myself as otherwise; I would sleep on the settee until four o'clock in the morning. As I was brushing my teeth, St. Stephen's School popped into my head. I remember it stating in the Ardwick Municipal Ledger that all kids had moved there because it was taken over by the government/military.

The next afternoon, I was down to Delph Library, armed with a street map of the local vicinity. After all, we used 'shankey's pony' then (walking) so it couldn't be a far distance from Ardwick Municipal.

An hour later, we had found it, just off Stockport Road, on the corner of Mornington and Millton Street. The school had long since gone but the church appeared to be still standing. So what did the government use these building for and did Harry work there?

Old memories came flooding back again as Millton Street was just a cock stride from Devonshire Street which was where my first, proper boyfriend, Lawrence Stringer, used to live.

During school assembly, the headmistress, Miss McKay, of Ardwick Secondary Modern, an upgraded Ardwick

Municipal 1952, all girls 11-15 years, would make her daily announcements. One morning, Miss Mc Kay, a bespectacled, gorky woman and a paragon of the establishment, announced to the whole school that Beth Powell had been seen by a staff member with a 'Teddy Boy' and went on to say what disgraceful behaviour this was.

Well, Beth Powell knew full well that I had not been seen during school hours when 'wagging it' as 'LoL' as I called him, worked from 9am to 5pm. So from the back of the hall, I announced that it was nothing to do with her, what I did outside school hours. I can still, gleefully, see her unfortunate face to this very day. It went bright beetroot clashing with her outlandish, grey and pink, plaid two piece suit.

If one wanted to be fashionable in 1956/7, a tight, straight, knee length, black skirt would be worn with flat, 'Ballerina' shoes, acquired from C&A. The fashionable store was located in the back streets of Piccadilly and the items would cost 7 shillings and six-pence and 5 shillings, respectively.

Well, I definitely had put the 'cat among the pigeons' and was called to her office, shortly afterwards. Needless to say, I was suspended for the audacity in answering back and was sent home.

Well, nothing could have suited me better as I skipped home, grinning like a Cheshire cat. As expected, my mother was not best pleased, quickly changed into her best 'bib and tucker' and marched up to see the headmistress.

Looking back in hindsight, the powers that be should have sent Miss Mc Kay on a basic psychology course, for what, in her eyes, was designed to embarrass me. My 'street cred. 'actually soared sky high with my peers, for not only was I dating a real 'Teddy Boy' but LoL was a good looking, blond, seventeen year old, smartly clad in black, drain, pipe trousers and a long jacket with sleeked back hair and side-burns.

Sadly, after a few days, I was reinstated at the school, banned from seeing LoL which went in one ear and out the other. Shortly after that, I was packed off to Loburn College in an effort, I guess, to make a lady of me. (My mother, being another candidate for a psychology course). For the record, LoL and I were together for quite a while and I am just wondering where he is now and what is he up to?

Anyway, back to the task in hand. We had little knowing that we were going on a' fool's errand', so up to the top of Devonshire Street, turning left on to Stockport Road and past the Polish man's shop. Brawn and pies were his speciality, where my mother used to send me when she was 'flush' (had money), sadly, one Saturday morning, I joined the queue which got longer and longer until somebody decided to find a policeman. It was an easy task in those far off days; one would need a sniffer dog these days. Anyway, the copper came and broke into the shop, only to find him dead on the kitchen floor.

People in those days were much more community minded. Today, he could have lain dead for weeks.

Third right, we turned and my memory was not playing tricks. Round and round, we went but no familiar streets, let alone St Stephen's Church. Obviously, the information I got was totally outdated.

So what next? ; 'The library' said Mandy. We asked a number of individuals where the nearest library was as the one in Ardwick had disappeared, like everything else.

We eventually spotted a little old lady wheeling an empty shopping basket who directed us to Gorton. .So back we went down Devonshire Street, past where the Cenotaph used to stand and up Hyde Road, towards Gorton. I noticed that all the terraced houses and tiny shops had gone. Even 'Joys Lollies Shop' where one could buy for threepence the most delicious Vimto lollies.

Well, we found the library, housed in a modern concrete complex, and Mandy headed straight for the computers, in an effort to find the diocese of St. Stephens.

That done, we had a good mooch round Gorton Market. I bought a bacon shank whilst Mandy got a drill bit. Definitely, in character for her as she was in the process of laying flooring and putting up shelves in her new home. As for me, I just love grub.. As I drove back to my home, I was thinking what a 'kamikaze' team we were. Mandy, always the practical and creative, Noel, the intellectual one and as for me, 'well, the least said, soonest mended'

The very next morning, I tried to contact the diocese of St Stephens which was now St. Anne's Church in Royton, Canon David Sharples, only to find it non-existent so there went another lead.

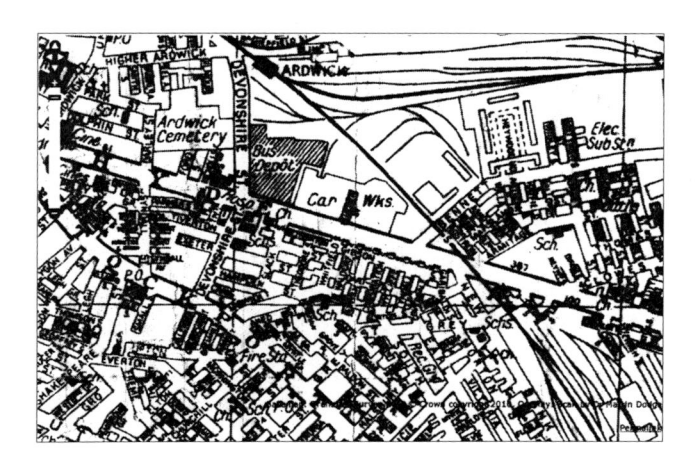

Chapter 88

On goes my 'thinking cap' as to what to do next. I suppose I could contact Manchester City Council, to see if they knew what the military used St Stephens for. But there again, umpteen venues were used during the war and I might end up chasing my own shadow.

Well, I was fresh out of ideas until a sudden flash of inspiration hit me. I wondered if 'National Insurance' held records of where people worked for at the end of the day; somebody must have paid Harry's wages for those six and a half years. He was hardly living on 'fresh air'. So, armed with coffee and ciggys, I eventually, after a number of calls, managed to establish to whom to write.

On the 30th September, I responded to a message left on my answering machine and spoke with Richard from HM, Revenue & Customs. He told me that he couldn't find any trace of a B.B. Teasdale and wondered if he went under another name. Well, my little grey cells were working overtime, at this stage but the only other alternative name I could come up with was Robin Teasdale.

At the end of the week, I received the following letter;

> **HM Revenue & Customs**
>
> MRS L ROBERTS
>
> HM Revenue & Customs
> NIC & EO
> SARS team
> BP2201
> Benton Park View
> Newcastle Upon Tyne
> NE98 1ZZ
>
> Tel 03000 560616
> Monday to Thursday 8.30am to 5pm
> Friday 8.30am to 4.30pm
> Fax 03000 560670
>
> Date 04/10/2013
> Our Ref
>
> Dear Mrs Roberts
>
> Thanks for your enquiry in respect of Bousfield Booth Teasdale.
>
> We have tried tracing a national insurance number for Mr Teasdale, using his full name and the alternative forename Robin. Unfortunately this has proved unsuccessful.
>
> Unless we can find out his exact date of birth, to allow a more precise trace for a national insurance number, we cannot provide any information.
>
> If you contact us, please quote our reference number and provide a daytime phone number
>
> Yours sincerely
>
> Richard Leitch
>
> To learn more about your rights and obligations go to hmrc.gov.uk/charter

I needed to get in touch with Steve in order to obtain Harry's birth cert. because I haven't got a clue. All I knew was that he downloads a form from his computer. The problem is that I have not heard from him in weeks. So I sent out my thoughts for him to phone me. This frequently worked (telepathy) and it did not take long, a couple of days, for Steve to ring me.

After exchanging the usual pleasantries, I was just about to ask him about the birth certificate when he suddenly piped up 'Liz, my phone is bugged'. I was stunned by his words, for like Mandy and I, Steve, too, had left a paper trail.

I asked him when he first suspected this and how he knows? 'A while ago' he said and then went on to explain the technicalities involved which went straight over my head.

So I explained what happened to mine and Mandy's phone. 'Bloody hell! What is going on?' he uttered in amazement. Oh, if only I could answer that! But I gathered my wits and explained why I needed the birth certificate. He was now very intrigued and, kindly, said he would do it, adding that he hoped he would not be shot when he presented the form at Her Majesty's post office.

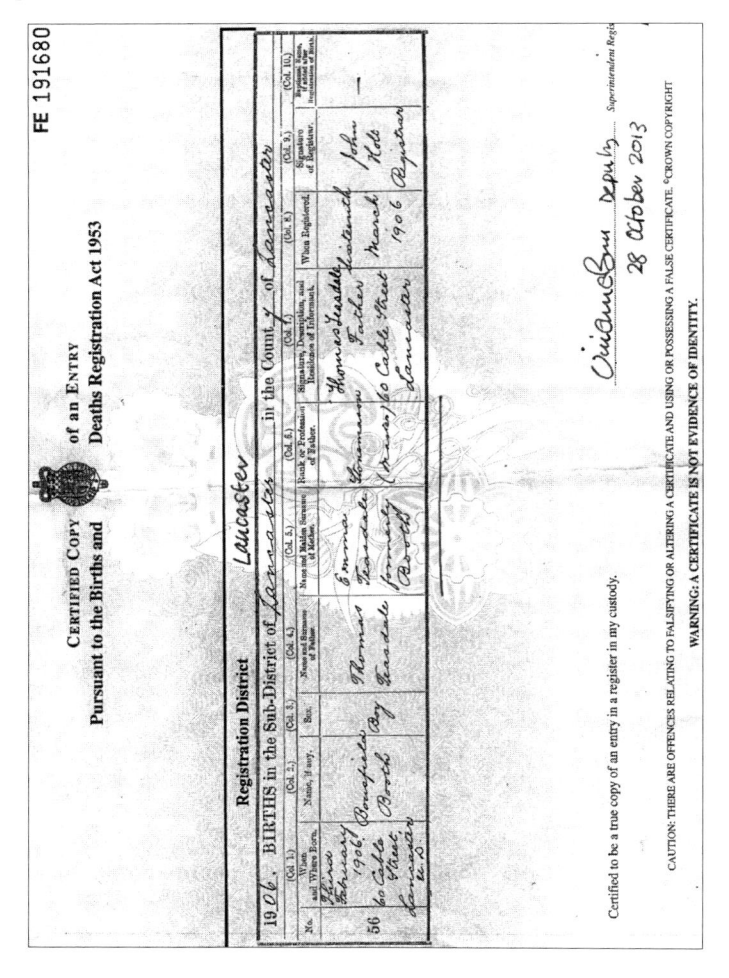

Having achieved this, I had just got time to get ready to take Rocky to the vet. On a number of occasions, his back legs had given way which only lasted a few seconds and is a very common condition in German Shepherds. The condition is untreatable but to top this, he was frequently wanting to 'spend a penny' and had been incontinent a number of times. Obviously, this was very upsetting for him, even though I never shouted at him and just mopped it up.

After a full physical examination, the vet could not find anything so the usual antibiotics and steroids were prescribed and an appointment made for two weeks' time.

I gave it ten days but there was no improvement in his condition so I arranged with the vet to have him X-rayed. Early, that Friday morning, I set off down to Mossley and the vet's surgery, knowing deep down that although he was only nine years old, he had come to the end of his days.

So I, anxiously, awaited the results and as I expected, there was a massive tumour through his bladder which could be clearly seen on X-ray. 'It is time to call it a day' said the vet, sympathetically, and without more ado, he put him to sleep.

It was a miserable weekend for I was crying and Bess was pacing up and down, all round the house, looking for him.

How does one explain to a dog that he has gone to live with Harry but I guess she already knew as in the last days of his life, she followed him everywhere and would not let him out of her sight? Now, just like me, she is miserable.

On the 4th November, I contacted Richard (Records Retrieval) giving Harry's date of birth which I had received from Steve and promised to post it to him.

About three weeks later, I had not heard from Richard so without more ado, I phoned him; only to be told (Quote;) 'I cannot give you this information because the rules have changed "to which I responded (Quote)' what! Since the 4th November, it was only three weeks ago'. I could sense he was feeling very uncomfortable and I was wondering what on earth was going on. After all, I only wanted to know where Harry worked for six and a half years. So I asked him to confirm this in writing, knowing full well that nobody can implement changes in government rules without implementing policies and procedures which have to be sanctioned by 'the powers that be' and this would take months and possibly years.

He agrees to confirm this in writing and then adds 'out of the blue' (Quote) 'If you want this information, you will have to go to the High Court and that will be very expensive'. I was feeling a bit sorry for him, at this stage as I agreed this would prove very costly. I ended the conversation with 'I think I understand' and hung up.

Well, I knew I had more chance of seeing 'a pink pig' flying past my lounge window than receiving a letter confirming his conversation. So I sat down with a coffee and a cig whilst I had a good think. I thought Noel might have some ideas and duly gave him a call and reiterated the conversation. 'What the devil is going on, Liz' he said, obviously taken aback by current events.. 'I will tell you, Liz, You have opened a can of worms here' he added. I couldn't agree more and what is so secret regarding where Harry worked during and after the war years? So with that, Noel decided to contact the Freedom of Information section, again and within a couple of days, he had their response;

Dear Mrs Roberts,

Freedom of Information Act 2000 (FOIA)

Thank you for your email dated 27 November 2013, in which you requested information on a named deceased individual, Bousfield Booth Teasdale.

HMRC Response

I have considered your request under the terms of the Freedom of Information Act 2000 (FOIA), which gives applicants the right of access to any information held by HMRC. To clarify, section 1(1) of the FOIA provides two rights to those who make requests for information. They are:-

a) the right to be informed in writing by the public authority whether or not it holds the information sought in the request; and

b) if so, the right to have that information communicated.

However, these rights are subject to a number of exemptions under the FOIA. With regard to your request, I am unable to confirm or deny whether HMRC holds the information because it is exempt from disclosure under s44(2) of the FOIA.

When another law prevents disclosure of information, it is exempt from disclosure because of section 44(1)(a) of the FOIA. Furthermore, if confirming or denying information is held would itself reveal information which is exempt under section 44(1)(a), the duty to confirm or deny information is held does not arise; section 44(2) FOIA refers.

Section 18(1) of the Commissioners for Revenue and Customs Act 2005 (CRCA) provides that Revenue and Customs officials may not disclose information which is held by HMRC in connection with a function of the Revenue and Customs. The information you are seeking, if held, would be

held in connection with our function to assess and collect tax and would identify the now deceased individual.

Section 23(1) CRCA further provides that where information falling in section 18(1) relates to a 'person' who is identified or who could be identified the exemption in section 44(1)(a) FOIA applies. 'Person' includes both living persons and legal entities (see paragraph 110 of the explanatory notes to the CRCA). HMRC's duty of confidentiality extends to all customer records, including the records of deceased customers.

Taken together, the above removes information about our customers from the right of access under FOIA. Section 44 is an absolute exemption and therefore does not require a consideration of the public interest.

Appeals Process

If you are not happy with this reply you may request a review by writing to HMRC FOI Team, Room 1C/23, 100 Parliament Street London SWIA 2BQ or email foi.review@hmrc.gsi.gov.uk. You must request a review within 2 months of the date of this letter. It would assist our review if you set out which aspects of the reply concern you and why you are dissatisfied.

> If you are not content with the outcome of an internal review, you may apply directly to the Information Commissioner for a decision. The Information Commissioner will not usually consider a case unless you have exhausted the internal review procedure provided by HMRC. He can be contacted at The Information Commissioner's Office, Wycliffe House, Water Lane, Wilmslow, Cheshire SK9 5AF.
>
> Yours sincerely
>
> Teresa Chance
>
>
> Teresa Chance | FOI Policy Adviser | Rm 1C/23 100 Parliament Street | London | SW1A 2BQ | Tel: 03000 586419

Well, we had never read such 'bullshit' in our entire lives. I needed some legal advice and guess what? I was off shortly to see Patsy and family in London as it was my granddaughter's, Anna's 10th birthday and who better to advise me but my dear, sweet daughter, Patsy, the barrister.

'What on earth are you up to mother', her first words on my arrival at her door. I could tell she was not a happy bunny because she called me 'Mother' instead of 'Mum'. 'It is my book' I responded and the look on her face said it all. I tried my best not to grin, for I realised this was the first time she had taken my writing this book seriously. To all intents and purposes, she had now donned her robe and wig and is acting for the prosecution. 'Mother, why can't you do something normal like every other 70 year old, such as knitting or other such harmless task', she said in exasperation. 'Please help the aged. What do I do with this' I said, coyly.

'Follow procedure and appeal though you will not get anywhere but it is a start. If you mean to continue with this and I can tell from your face that you will leave no stone unturned' she said, finally. 'Damn right' I said with conviction.

So having lost her case, she printed out an Appeal Form which I duly completed on my return home. I sent it recorded delivery accompanied with the copies of all the relevant documents. It was posted on the 23rd December, 2013.

Chapter 89

Bess and I set off to Manchester Dogs Home, having asked Harry to show me a picture of a male dog that doesn't cause fights like Rocky did. We had both missed him and Bess was still moping about the house.

I wasn't too impressed as the image I got from Harry of this dog's face, did little to encourage me. It's only saving grace was that it had pointed ears; consequently, I guessed it was at least, part German shepherd. Other than that, it was a mucky looking mingles of grey, brown and black.

I was hoping it was a German shepherd, for this breed, due to their intelligence, (keeping Rocky out of the equation) was easy to train. Consequently, over time, one can usually iron out any problems or issues which they may have acquired. They are a 'one man dog' or in my case, a 'one woman dog' and are very highly protective.

On my arrival, I walked to the very end of the pens. There were some lovely dogs, all gazing longingly at me, as much as to say 'Take me home with you'. It was quite heart-breaking to see and I can understand why Harry left some money to them. As for me, I have already left a percentage of what little I have, to a number of Animal Rescue Centres.

I came to the very last pen and, suddenly, I spotted him and 'Oh boy, was he scruffy! He had lumps of missing hair and I would guess he was about 6/7 years old. Yes, he was definitely a German shepherd and not to worry as it is what is inside his little soul that counts and we could all get old together.

I needed to be certain that I had the right one so out I went to have a ciggy, knowing full well that Harry would tell me when I had it right (that funny feeling) and yes, indeed, I had.

I got one of the staff to release him from the pen and asked for some background information. Apparently, he was found in a dreadful state, wandering round Oldham. His coat was so matted that they had to cut chunks of it off.

Fifty pounds and he was mine. We reached the car and he looked at Bess, wagged his tail and, yes, she liked him; so home we went.

I was going to name him 'Harry' as payback for Bess being short for Elizabeth. I could hear a chuckle from Harry. We had, definitely, got the same sense of humour; like attracts like. If I didn't know any better, I would have thought we were related.

Animal Ref		Oct2013-18548/D		
Animal Name		435		
Type of Animal		Dog		
Breed		German Shepherd Dog (Alsatian)		
Cross Breed		No		
Age/DoB		7 years 1 month		
Microchip Details		958000001392165		
Date Admitted		31/10/2013		
Notes				
Gender	Size	Colour	Coat	
Male	Medium	Black and Tan	Short	

Veterinary Details

Core Vaccination
First Treatment Date   31/10/2013
Last Treatment Date   01/12/2013
Next Due Date

Additional Vaccination
First Treatment Date
Last Treatment Date
Next Due Date

Neutering
Neutered   Unknown
Treatment Date
Due Date

Neuter Stitches Removed
Treatment Date
Due Date

Worming
Last Treatment Date
Next Due Date

Flea Treatment
Last Treatment Date
Next Due Date

Health issues prior to admission

Medication being taken on admission

Chapter 90

Having had a quiet Christmas and New Year, I found myself in a bit of a pickle on 3rd January, 2014. I was not able to stand up as my balance had gone. It was an old problem called 'Labyrinthitis' and most certainly had nothing to do with the copious amounts of alcohol consumed on New Year's Eve, I hasten to add. I literally could not stand up properly.

Knowing that my medical records had been computerised and sent to Oldham Hospital, I phoned Mandy who lives a 'stone's throw' from the A&E Department.

It was early evening by the time Mandy pushed me in on a wheelchair towards A&E, with me looking like a bag-lady. All I can say is that Mandy should stay with the R.S.P.C.A. as Healthcare would not be her forte. 'Bang, crash, wallop'; as she managed to hit every obstacle on the corridor, thus jarring my head and feeling more nauseous than ever. I thought I was going to throw up.

My luck was in as I got a brilliant Casualty doctor who spoke English so I got the full overhaul and he agreed with my diagnosis; my right ear has a temperature, confirming a virus. After collecting the appropriate medication, Mandy wheeled me out of A&E into the pouring rain. She parked the now battered wheelchair under the old Ambulance Bay and went to get her car. As I sat there, clutching my bag, I was thinking that at least everything else was normal i.e. blood pressure, bloods and heart; except my head, of course, but what's new?, I have never been normal.

I was grinning to myself as regards the pickle I was in when, suddenly, I realised that the wheel-chair had taken on a life of its own as I went sailing down the slope. Mandy had forgotten to put the brakes on. It was something like a 'Benny Hill' TV comedy with the chair picking up speed, my head spinning and not a soul in sight. It was a good job that I knew where the brakes were located as I jammed them on and came to a grinding halt. I must have covered a distance of about 100 yards and wondered if Mandy would manage to find me. After her initial panic at my sudden disappearance, she picked me up on a security camera (bright girl) as I whizzed past, looking wind swept and pale. We laughed and laughed afterwards. She should definitely stick to the care of animals who cannot complain.

I decided to stay overnight at Mandy's as the dogs were in the kennels. It was 1am and we were still laughing and I was feeling much better with a change of clothes and an Indian take-away. This soon changed when Mandy went to her computer and discovered it was being searched. 'What, at 1 o' clock in the morning' and wondered what was going on? Apparently, this had happened before on a number of occasions but she took no notice, for 'Moore' is a common surname.

We came to the conclusion, whether right or wrong, that because my name was 'flagged up' on the hospital computer system, somebody was searching for information. Over the weekend, we went through every piece of research which we had regarding Harry with a 'fine toothcomb'. We were utterly convinced that we were missing something and that, indeed, Noel was correct in saying that 'Harry was assassinated'; but why such a public venue? I reckon the reason being that he had some secret knowledge and his death was a warning to others.

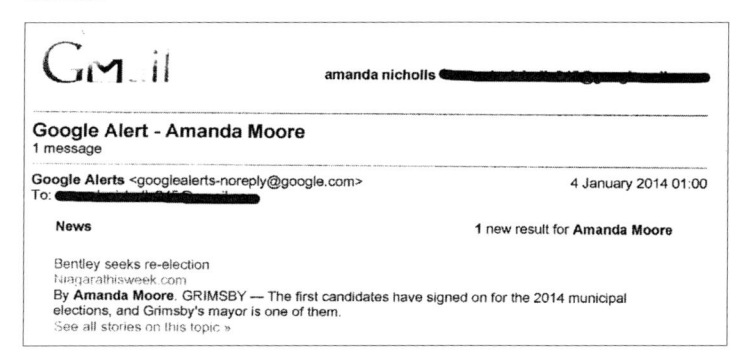

> **Gmail**
> amanda nicholls
>
> **Google Alert - Amanda Moore**
> 1 message
>
> Google Alerts <googlealerts-noreply@google.com>   4 January 2014 01:00
> To:
>
> News   1 new result for **Amanda Moore**
>
> Bentley seeks re-election
> Niagarathisweek.com
> By **Amanda Moore**. GRIMSBY — The first candidates have signed on for the 2014 municipal elections, and Grimsby's mayor is one of them.
> See all stories on this topic »

I did not like where this was going but there is safety in numbers so I ensured that Mandy and Noel had copies of this book. I also gave a letter to Patsy for safety also.

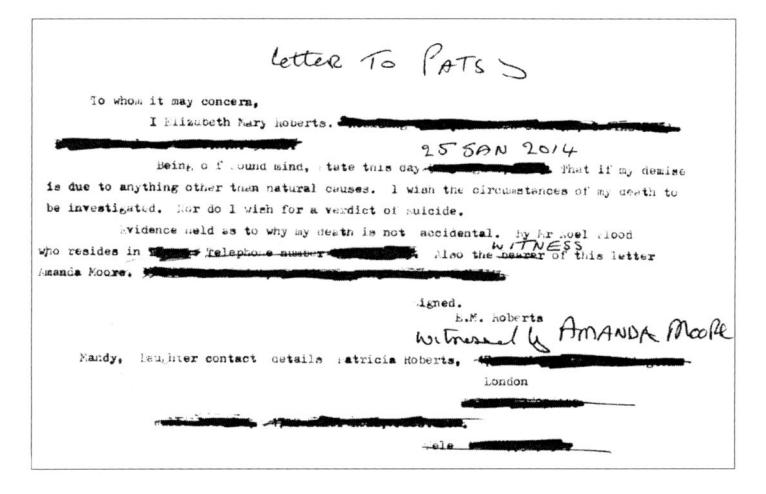

> **letter to PATSY**
>
> To whom it may concern,
>
> I Elizabeth Mary Roberts.
>
> 25 JAN 2014
>
> Being of sound mind, state this day _____ That if my demise is due to anything other than natural causes, I wish the circumstances of my death to be investigated. Nor do I wish for a verdict of suicide.
>
> Evidence held as to why my death is not accidental. By Mr Noel Wood who resides in _____ Telephone number _____ Also the *WITNESS* bearer of this letter Amanda Moore, _____
>
> Signed.
> E.M. Roberts
> Witnessed by AMANDA MOORE
>
> Mandy, daughter contact details Patricia Roberts, _____
> London

The only saving grace is that it would be preferable to end one's days down a lift shaft as opposed to ending up with 'Dementia' in an old people's home. 'OH, what a dreadful patient I would make'; hitting out at the staff with my walking stick, spitting at them and throwing all sorts of unmentionables round the place.

I believe that only the truth is sacred and I would carry on being his 'Earthly Representative'. So I started out with a fresh canvas and A.B.C. I would assume nothing, believe nobody and check everything. The Inquest details would be my first port of call, for I did not believe there was a fire.

Ann, happily, searched on her computer for any evidence that there was a fire at Manchester Inquest Office but to no avail. We discovered another person named 'Annie' from the same newspaper with Harry's Inquest details.

She had died about the same time and the same Coroner, Mr Rycroft, had carried out the inquest.

> ## Accident verdict on road death
>
> Accidental death was the verdict of a Manchester inquest jury to-day on an 80-year-old woman who was fatally injured while crossing a road with her 71-year-old sister. She was Miss Annie Prentice, of Lyme Grove, Marple, who was knocked down by a car.
>
> The coroner, Mr. Jessel Rycroft, said approaching cars were nearer than the sisters thought when they crossed the road.

O How I wish
5/9
I would be Rich!

Ann sent a covering letter to the Coroner's Office in Manchester claiming family history.

With that done, I scoffed another piece of her homemade cake which was delicious. I told her that when I ever tried to bake a cake, it either burnt or sunk in the middle. Fry-ups were my speciality and Bill would eat anything as long as it was accompanied with onions. I suppose being married to me, he didn't have much choice or otherwise, he would have starved.

At the risk of repeating myself, when I recount my many cooking calamities, the time I, mistakenly, fried daffodil bulbs instead of onions comes fairly high up on my list. The next day, poor Bill was bitterly complaining of a pain in his stomach. When I realised what I had done, I was more annoyed with myself for having to go and buy new bulbs as the onions were never going to produce the bright, yellow flowers. I never did tell Bill but was very sympathetic, telling him to change his local pub, for he must have drunk a 'bad pint of mild beer' there.

Chapter 91

I am afraid my cuckoo clock died a death and Harry wouldn't be able to play with it any longer. You would not believe how difficult it is to find an authentic one. Everything, these days, runs on batteries and why people wish to spend money buying batteries for such things, I will never understand. It doesn't take a great deal of effort to wind a clock.

I was hoping Harry would point me in the right direction in finding a replacement but failing that, I could also ask Patsy to buy one in Switzerland when they go skiing next time. I wasn't sure when that might be so, meanwhile, I would just have to wait and see which one of them succeeds.

Within the space of a week, Ann received the following communication from the Coroner's Office;

With the compliments of

Dear Ms Lawston,

Unfortunately we do not hold any inquest records prior to 1959 due to a fire at the county archives.

I am sorry we cannot assist on this occasion.

Kind regards,
Alexia O'Neill
Secretary.

NIGEL S MEADOWS
H.M. CORONER

County of Greater Manchester
(Manchester City District)

CORONER'S OFFICE
Crown Square
Manchester, M60 1PR

Telephone 0161 830 4222
Fax 0161 274 7329
Email: n.meadows@manchester.gov.uk

So, having got an answer in 'black and white', I phoned Alexia O'Neill at the Coroner's Office. When asked my business, I posed as Ann and duly requested the date of the fire. After a few moments, whilst listening to various exchanges between individuals; Surprise, Surprise! Nobody knew and Alexia O'Neill was unavailable.

Two days later, I tried again but with the same scenario, Alexia wasn't available so I requested the exact dates of available inquest records. 'None prior to January 1959' was the response. It must have been 'one hell of a fire' to destroy all those records and I wondered how many fire engines would be required?

It does not take a genius to work out that this fire must have been during the Christmas/New Year, 1958 period, in order for this to be the case and yet, there is no record of any fire in any of the newspapers and Alexia O'Neill never did return my calls.

So, it was perfectly obvious that these records were deliberately destroyed but why? Why not just state this instead of hiding behind some non-existent fire?

'Oh, what a web we weave, when first, we practice to deceive'

My next task was to try to locate these two boys who made these allegations or was this another concoction of lies? Mr Teasdale had no time to get their statements; let alone, prepare a defence. How do I know if the whole thing was not a fabrication? I recalled the time Steve had found a 'Bill Singleton', right age and area, whose mother's name was 'Seddon' but we never, did locate him. Mandy, on the other hand, had lived in West Gorton as a young child and remembered that there was a large family of 'Seddons' there.

So, off we went, knocking on doors, like a pair of gypsies and, yes, we did manage to find two families of 'Seddons' but none knew of a Bill Singleton. A couple of them did go to Plymouth Grove but later than the 1950's. One lady had an older brother who 'fitted the bill' but my hopes were soon dashed when she went on to say that he had passed away. So we went to another house and, yes, her husband had gone to Plymouth Grove, 1950's but, sadly, he died of cancer. By this time, I was beginning to wonder when my own demise would be as neither of them reached the grand age of 70.

With that, we popped our pre-written notes through a number of doors and hoped for the best.

The other thing that wasn't sitting well with me was something which Jean Teasdale had said 'One of the boy's mothers was crying at the funeral'. I don't doubt for one minute that she believed she was telling the truth but like when she said 'He left all his money to the housekeeper', I just could not see that this boy's mother would announce herself. I, certainly, wouldn't and would have kept well away for fear of retribution, even if the allegations were true.

To all intents and purposes, it could have been anybody's mother, even mine, for Jean herself, had not attended the funeral. So, it was all hearsay, just like 'Richard, the brother, had paid the costs of the funeral'. The money would have been taken out of the 'Estate' and if Richard had, indeed, 'forked it out'; he would have been reimbursed by the executors.

Mr Teasdale had everything organised such as, a simple funeral and cremation. I think he somehow, knew that his demise would not be too long. The Will was dated 1950 and he died three years later, at the age of 47.

Mr Howarth, the headmaster, believed what he said 'Wanted the boys alone with him as they were taking part in a surprise item for the school concert and the whole effect would have been spoiled for the other children, to see them rehearsing' The headmaster also stated that he had a 'splendid reputation' and I shall add that 'no paedophile would get two boys together in a school classroom'

Oh, how I wish I had the full transcript of the inquest! For the life of me, I cannot work out how 'dirt marks' on one staircase rail would indicate that he had hurled himself down the stairwell. Surely, the same could be stated if somebody hurled him down the well. I am just hoping that when the 'Central Library' re-opens, that the lift-shaft has not been altered and then, I can see for myself.

The other thing that 'springs to mind', were the parents of the boys bribed in some way? I remember well the story that Uncle Fred told me about Uncle Arthur with the roaming glass eye. (Cousin Kathleen's father)

During the 1930's, Uncle Arthur was accused of 'embezzlement' and tax evasion but he was allowed to 'clear off' to the Isle of Man, having given the police information regarding 'wanted criminals'. Uncle Fred clearly stated that, on a number of occasions, he was offered large sums of money by the 'Jew Boys' as he put it, for information regarding Arthur's whereabouts. He added that if he had accepted these bribes, he would have been a millionaire and Arthur would have been 'a goner'.

The Isle of Man at that time was not under English rule; consequently, it was a haven for the criminal fraternity. Having got immunity from prosecution, he purchased 'Bracken', a large, detached house in at least, an acre of land, plus an adjoining half acre surrounded by these huge ferns. I spent many a happy hour, observing the creatures that inhabited them and the surrounding area; something not seen in Ardwick so I guessed this was how the house acquired its' name.

Who said 'Crime doesn't pay'? For here was my Dad, Uncle Fred and Aunt Cissie living in scruffy, terraced houses in Ardwick whilst Arthur continued his lifestyle in Laxy, Isle of Man. It begs the question, how many times does the Establishment 'turn a blind eye'?

Chapter 92

There was an unexpected development when the Police Museum contacted Mandy stating they had found her father's records and that they could be viewed any Tuesday. Now, this seemed very odd as on a number of occasions, she had been told that they had no records of her grandfather. We can only guess that for some unknown reason to us, her mother had requested to see her father's police records, though there had been no mention of this.

So, seizing 'the bull by the horns', we promptly arrived at 2pm on the 28th, January, 2014. Well, you should have seen the expressions on their faces, for not unsurprisingly, they had recognised us. One cannot 'shut the stable door when the horse has bolted' but they did try, stating that the request to view the records had been made in a different surname. However, Mandy was quick off the mark stating that her mother was ill so we had come instead.

Up the wooden steps we went with one policeman in front of us and another one behind as if they were not prepared to let us out of their sight. We were definitely not welcome here.

As we sat down at the stout, pine table, another copper appeared, clutching the records. He was a chatty man and asked us what this was all about? I gave him a brief summary of the 'Harry Story'. 'I remember that story even though I did not join the Force until 1963. It was debated about until the 1980's; was he pushed or did he jump?' he said, looking interested. 'And what was the conclusion?' I asked. Immediately, one of the other officers glared at him, in an attempt to shut him up which, indeed, worked. He went

---

Form 743D

GREATER MANCHESTER POLICE

STAFF — IN CONFIDENCE

ANNUAL APPRAISAL REPORT   **UNIFORM INSPECTOR**

Surname: ROWSTON   Forenames: Ronald George
Division/Branch: 'A'   Warrant Number: 236
Date of Birth: 6.3.20   Date of Joining: 17.6.46
Date of Promotion to: Sergeant ____ Inspector: 1.10.61

PART I. TO BE COMPLETED BY THE SUB-DIVISIONAL SUPERINTENDENT.

PEN PICTURE. Please comment on his vitality and drive and on any special work done during the past year. Include any contributions to Force activities and any social work undertaken.

Management of subordinates	A
Decision making	C
Temperament	C
Administrative ability	B
Intelligence	B
Performance of day to day duty	B
Service Relationships	B
Assessment of staff	B

This officer has completed over 32 years police service, and has indicated his present intention is to retire on age limit in March 1980.

His responsibilities as deputy to the Chief Inspector at the Magistrates' Court embraces such duties as the police commitment in all the city Magistrates' Courts and Manchester Crown Court, in addition to overall supervision in the Central Detention Centre. The work brings him in to contact with Judges of the High Court, the Stipendiary Magistrate and Lay Magistrates, Barristers and Solicitors.

I cannot speak too highly of Inspector Rowston's devotion to his work and his control of Police man-power within the Court precincts, and I would wish him to continue with this work.

For many years he has been a member of the Scout movement and, until retiring from active participation, was the District Assistant Commissioner to Gorton and District Scouts. He has now been appointed Honorary Assistant Commissioner in the same district. He is a keen gardner and a member of the Gorton Horticultural Society. He actively engages himself with members of the "Inskip League", a voluntary organisation which provides transport and other assistance to the severely physically handicapped people of Gorton.

A first class officer and a credit to the police service.

Signed ____   Date: 26.10.78

PART II. TO BE COMPLETED BY THE CHIEF SUPERINTENDENT.

REMARKS. Please include impressions from an appraisal interview and comments on the Officer's objectives for the coming year.   Potential: 5

A good, loyal Inspector, who has now completed 32 years service, and continues to give excellent service.

He is not promotion conscious, and I believe is contemplating retirement.

He is not recommended for further promotion.

Signed ____   Date

silent on us. Mandy then asked a number of pre-planned questions about A.B.C. & D. Divisions as regards the areas they covered in 1953. We were both convinced that her granddad and Marriot linked in some way, for why would Harry emphasize the Police Museum and why couldn't Mandy view her granddad's records?

Afterwards, we set off to our favourite 'chippy' on Oldham Street, having decided we needed to 'brainstorm' that afternoon's information. I must admit that we did not reach any definite conclusions so we needed to look further.

Then, for some reason or other, Mandy brought up the subject of Florence Tinsley's husband, Samuel who was a Gas Engineer. She was questioning whether this occupation had anything to do with the War and what connection was there between the Tinsleys and Teasdales? There must have been one as why would Harry obtain a housekeeper from as far as Dudley, as opposed to a local 'live-in' one?

We decided to explore this amongst other things, for neither of us knew what a Gas Engineer did. I would ask my friend, Ian, who by chance, was a qualified Gas Engineer.

I phoned him, the following day and managed to get more information.

Apparently, according to Ian, a 'gas engineer' could be either a man who converts coal to gas (Gas Driver Engineer) or something completely different i.e. a 'Chemical Gas Engineer'. Evidently, the word 'chemical' would frequently be omitted due to its implications. Ian then offered to explore Tinsley's background further and the death certificate which was obtained. Unfortunately, this added further confusion as it stated 'Profession—Steelworker/Storekeeper' and not, as expected, 'Gas Engineer' which was on Florence's death certificate.

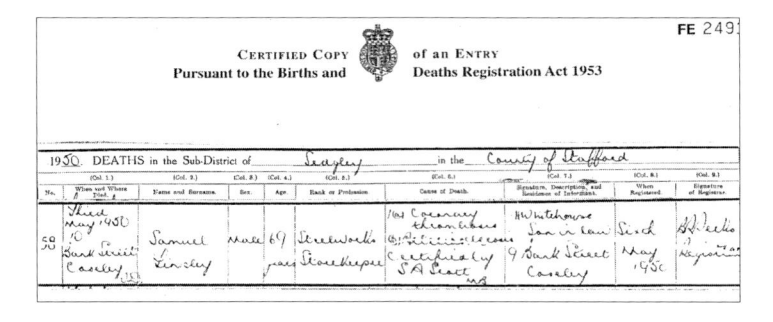

Chapter 93

Meanwhile, we were concentrating on Mandy's granddad and P.C.Marriot, for we were convinced that these two police officers and Harry were linked in some way.

We started off with the 'patches' (catchment areas) covered by each division. 'A Division' covered Manchester City Centre; 'B Division' Ancoats and Beswick; 'C Division' Gorton and Ardwick; 'D Division' Longsight, respectively. (Plymouth Grove School--Marriot's patch and 'C Division'--- Mandy's granddad) Theses patches were in close proximity to each other and remembering the information from the 'chatty policeman at the Museum', that police from one patch could be used in another, i.e. covering sickness, holidays, etc. or there was a major incident which required more 'manpower'.

What I couldn't understand was why there wasn't a policeman from 'A Division' at the inquest which was covering the Library. The solution he offered was; 'yes, it did seem a little odd as when the incident occurred, both police and ambulance would have been from 'A Division'. This I knew to be correct, for even in my nursing days at Stockport Infirmary, Police, Ambulance and Fire Departments worked in tandem.

The only explanation he could offer was that, because the boy's allegation had been made to 'D Division', that was the reason why it was handed over to Marriot. No explanation has ever been forthcoming from him or anybody else as to why the Librarian was not requested at the inquest. As I have stated before, he or she would have been a crucial witness and the best person to comment on his mental state, just minutes before plunging down the lift shaft.

Both Marriot and Mandy's granddad joined the Police Force shortly after WWII; Marriot having served in the R.A.F. Police during the war and the latter was a Royal Marine. Surely, it is conceivable that they did know each other, especially considering in those days, police stations were dotted in close proximity and open 24 hours a day. One could just walk-in, not like today, where you have a job finding one open after 5 pm, let alone, during the night.

As a child, during the 1950's, I can recall at least three police stations which were in easy walking distance from my home. As I understand it, each had 'holding cells' for drunks, vagabonds and the like. Even during the 1970's, there were a number of venues which had special nights and cheap rates for all emergency personnel. Everyone knew each other and I guess it is why so many nurses married policemen and firemen.

A week or so later, Ian was back in touch, having managed to trace Samuel Tinsley. Of all the places he could have been during the 1920's and 30's, it was Lancaster, Harry's hometown. He worked at what is now known as 'Sellafield' which was a coal, gas production facility from 1812—1949. During the period of the 1940'S –1950's, it became a British Weapons Grade Plutonium-239 production facility. In 1956, it became a nuclear power plant and also the site for British Advanced Gas-Cooked Reactor.

Having ruled out, due to his age, any connection with WWII or with Harry who from 1926, was in Manchester, we wondered if he was connected to Harry's father but he had died in 1910.

Samuel was born in 1881, married Florence in 1907 so if he was connected with chemical gases, i.e. mustard gas, it would have been during WW1. The only other conclusion that we came up with was that Harry's mother and Florence were close friends who kept in touch throughout their lives. There was only a short span between Florence becoming a widow and Harry losing his mother. This fortuitous situation would provide her with a home where household bills etc. were not an issue and Harry would have a trustworthy housekeeper.

If one accepts what Jean Teasdale said and obviously believed 'He never went anywhere, dear', and then what was his need, I ask myself, for a housekeeper? A normal person would say the reason being, to iron his shirts and cook his meals. Being a cynic, I know somehow that there is more to Bousfield Booth Teasdale than meets the eye. I continuously ask myself why did he change my name to Elizabeth and how did he know I was christened? Not everybody was and why did he come back to me? That was the question Mandy often asked 'Why me? But I could not give her or myself the answer.

Chapter 94

I did not receive any response regarding our search for the two boys, having, tactfully, announced my search for them at 'mediumship' venues. So that was 'a dead end' and I hadn't received a response from HRMC either but at least I could chase them up.

I eventually phoned them regarding my appeal and spoke to yet another 'Dave' who informed me that they had not received any correspondence dated 23.12.13. I then asked to speak to a more senior staff member and told him I had sent it by recorded delivery. Oh, dear! That 'put the cat amongst the pigeons' as his next line of defence was that Quote; 'I cannot do this as it is an internal line and it will not connect'. I was beginning to wonder if I sounded as if I had learning difficulties,for even I could have come up with a better line than that (no pun intended). I requested their fax number which was duly given or so I thought but during the next couple of days, Mandy tried three different fax machines and couldn't get through.

Well, I guess they were working under the assumption that if they ignored me long enough, I would go away. No chance as I sent off another letter, again by recorded delivery.

> N02 8·2·14
> HMRC
> FOI Team,
> Room 1C/23
> 100 Parliament St
> London
> SW1A 2BQ.
>
> Dear Sir/Madam
>   On 23/12/13 I followed HMRC
> guide lines. Lodged an appeal
> regarding a Bousquet/Booth
> Teasdale.
>   On 5·2·14 I contacted your
> good selves, spoke with
> 'Dove' who could not put
> me through to the relevant
> Department internal line!
> But advised me to
> fax my request. As to why
> I have had no acknowledge-
> -ment regarding my appeal,
> sent, redirected letters,
> Having tried three separate
> fax machines, correct fax
> number used. I have found
> you unobtainable.
> I would appreciate a
> response in the very near
> future.   Yours Sincerely
> No email address.

Well, Glory be! Theresa Chance from 'Freedom of Information' office phoned me regarding my appeal letter which they had now found. Surprise, surprise! Well she definitely lived up to her name as she was chancing her luck by fishing for information and then proceeded to explain why I could not have B.B. Teasdale's records.

I listened intently, saying hardly anything and I would bet 'a pound to a penny' that our conversation was being recorded. I pointed out to her that I did not want his employment records, just the venue. Skirting over my statement, she continued with her repertoire which had now gone on for at least ten minutes.

It was time to mention Richard's letter (Revenue & Customs) in which he stated the rules had changed. Well, she was flummoxed by this and countered by saying that she had spoken to Richard Leitch and he had got confused about their policies and procedures.

I lit another ciggy and decided to strike while the iron was hot, for it was time for me to start telling lies. 'I cannot understand why I cannot know where my dear, sweet father worked between 1943 and 1949. After all, it was almost 70 years ago so why the big secret' I said, convincingly. There was a moment's silence and I could tell that this had gone down like a lead balloon when finally she asked if I was prepared to go to the High Court. 'It will be very costly and they may not have the information anyway', she went on to say. 'Money is no problem', I responded, unfazed. (Another lie)

She, then, went to great lengths to explain that she did not make the rules and perhaps she may be able to help by seeking information from the National Archives and the Salvation Army. I let her carry on and on, trying to interject by pointing out I had already checked out the National Archives but she was suffering from selective deafness which reminded me of my dog, Pluto, who had the same affliction.

I looked at the clock and found that she had been on the phone for well over a half an hour. I did miss the cuckoo clock for it would have been well chirping away as I listened to her.

Finally, I asked her to put it all in writing, pointing out that I had not received any written confirmation from Records Retrieval (Richard) as yet. She agreed to this; quote; 'after speaking to my boss' I always think that if one has to explain oneself repeatedly, then one has lost.

Well, my old Dad, the postman, would have been most displeased for guess what popped up in my letter box, the very next day, dated 31.1.2014?

HM Revenue & Customs

MRS L ROBERTS

HM Revenue & Customs
NIC&EO
SARS Team BP2201
Benton Park View
Longbenton
Newcastle upon Tyne
NE98 1ZZ

Phone 03000 560616
Monday to Thursday 8:30 to 17:00 Friday 8:30 to 16:30

Fax 03000 560670

Web hmrc.gov.uk

Date 31 January 2014
Our ref

Dear Mrs Roberts

Bousfield Booth Teasdale (Deceased)

Thank you for your letter dated 26 September 2013 requesting an employment history in respect of Bousfield Booth Teasdale (Deceased). I am sorry for the delay in replying to you.

As you may be aware, HMRC has a duty to protect the confidentiality of the data of its customers. Under Section 18 of the Commissioners for Revenue and Customs Act 2005, we are only permitted to share information in very limited circumstances.

For enquiries about deceased account holders, we can only provide information to the legally appointed executor or personal representative of the estate. As a third party, unfortunately, you do not satisfy the HMRC conditions for us to provide you with any details of the above named.

Yours sincerely

Mrs Elaine Mulroy
SARS Team

Chapter 95

I was feeling utterly bewildered and wondered what was happening. When I claimed my 'Old Age Pension', a nice lady from the Contributions Office was having difficulty locating my ex-husband's records; quote; 'There are numerous William Roberts which one is yours'? She went on to ask if I could remember his date of birth or National Insurance number (NI number). Well, I didn't have a clue, for I couldn't remember my own NI number, let alone anybody else's. Consequently, in order to sort out my pension, there was an exchange of information on a number of occasions between her and myself. This included various places where he had been employed during our 15 years of marriage which, oddly enough, was not considered 'Classified'. So what was the difference, after all, they could not prove that I am not his illegitimate daughter who, I would believe, would have more rights to the information than to my ex-husband's employment venues.

I sat at my typewriter, lit a ciggy and asked Harry for some inspiration. A few minutes later, I could feel his presence (that funny, tingling sensation) and I, jokingly, said 'Help, Dad, I don't know where to go next'. After another ciggy, it, suddenly, hit me; if one can have an 'Operation Sea Lion', then why cannot also there be an 'Operation Sea Horse' (the humorous, little story which evolved after one of our Harry sessions on the 29th September, 2012, when Mandy, as a child, could not understand how it got into the paperweight.

A few days later, Mandy returned my call and 'in a nutshell', this is what she discovered.

'Operation Paperclip', a US government programme, was put in place after WWII whereby there was a round-up of elite German scientists and their subsequent transportation to America, in order to pursue their art of technology i.e. biological / herbicidal weaponry etc. Included in this was a top secret venue, 'Roswell' where Nazi blueprints were used. There were a number of UFO sightings reported and one on the 2nd July, 1952 which was categorically denied by the US government.

During the 'Cold War', U2 aircraft spied on the Soviet Union during and after Stalin's death in 1953. There was another incident in 1960 with a spy plane called 'Blackbird'. Now, this was a clue when I remembered Harry's song 'Bye, bye, Blackbird' we were, now, both going on an educational tour as we delved deeper.

Apparently, when 'Operation Paperclip' was up and running, there was also 'Operation Sea Horse' which was the naval part of locating and recovering top secret, German weaponry, e.g. aircraft and weapons.

So was Harry telling us that he was in either Russia or Germany between 1943 and 1949 and that we needed to explore further in order to prove this? I was not prepared to 'put pen to paper' without believing in my own research and ensuring that this was correct. At the end of the day, 'The pen is mightier than the sword' and I was beginning to understand that this was Harry's agenda; in order to reveal something that has many strings to its bow.

Having brought Mandy up-to-date, the best idea we could come up with was to ask Harry. So the following Friday night, armed with a number of pre-planned questions, we started our session using the crystal ball.

Question 1: Were you working for the Intelligence Services?

There was no response even though, we were aware of his presence in the room.

Question 2: Please show us where you were based. Almost immediately, a large, white, detached house appeared in the crystal ball, followed with a large bear and then, the front doorway of the same house. It had a large entrance with two stone pillars on either side of some steps.

Question 3: Were you a spy? Again, there was no response and he was gone.

Well, that was that and we didn't have a clue. So we consoled ourselves by opening a bottle of wine as the night was still young. We spent the next hour or so, trying to come up with a country connected to WWII that had 'bears'.

Now, I knew America had bears, for I had seen one of them in the wild whilst over there on a trip with Patsy and family. In fact, Anna and I had gone on a bear hunt, trying to follow their tracks. Eventually, Anna spotted one in the distance but it looked huge so we decided that 'retreat was better part of valour' and duly, legged it a mile or so to the ranch type house which we had rented during our stay in Pennsylvania.

Well, as you can imagine, Patsy was not best pleased and I was told off in no uncertain terms; 'Mother, you should have more sense' was her last retort. Of course, Anna was thrilled to bits with the adventure and we repeated it on a couple of occasions when Patsy and John had gone shopping. I think to this day, it is still one of our little secrets; just like our magic spells, not eating green vegetables and fish and chips out of a newspaper.

Other than America, the only others we really knew were Russia and the North Pole. So we needed to find the house but it was not in this country as Steve and I had spent hours looking at houses, commandeered during the War, prior to finding the Ritz Hotel.

It was 'out of the blue', plus a second bottle of wine, when Mandy said 'They cannot prove that he is not your father. Do you think he could have been?' 'Don't be daft. I just made it up and thought it might give me a bit more mileage with them (whoever 'them' are)! I said with a grin. 'You never were like any of your family and you disliked your mother, for she was always trying to change you to be like 'Beth' in the book 'Little Women'', Mandy added.

Well, the seed was sown, for Mandy had done this before, initially stating that she thought Harry was a spy and as things stood at the moment, she might well indeed be correct. She came up with another fascinating statement, stating that a friend of mine was once a terrorist. Well, I fell about laughing and, jokingly, said, I would ask him.

The next time I saw him, I could not resist asking him as I thought he, too, would find it amusing. My God! You should have seen the look on his face as he strongly insisted that they were called 'Freedom Fighters' back then and that I was part of the propaganda side of it. I was gobsmacked and it was never mentioned again.

Chapter 96

Of course, I could not sleep that night, for round and round in my head, Mandy's words reverberated. Geographically, Great Western St. and Higher Ardwick were only a few stops apart on the 213 trolley bus. My mother attended the Manchester School of Music, paid for by the 'Masons' (my grandfather).

She often played the piano which stood out like a sore thumb in our scruffy, terraced house. Hindsight is a wonderful thing and she probably had much more in common with Mr Teasdale than my father. She always seemed out of place which was due partly to her education at Cheadle Hulme Boarding School, for most Ardwick people were down to earth and working class. This, my mother was not and it stood out, appearing to be a bit of a snob.

What was also interesting, on reflection, was her non-response when I told her that Mr Teasdale had changed my name back to 'Elizabeth'. After all, this was the name I had been christened with and I often wondered how he knew this. In hindsight, her non-response seemed rather odd, as normally, she could have a vicious tongue.

I remember, on one occasion, when I was quite young and being rather naughty, she said 'I tried to get rid of you'.

Of course, I did not really understand what she meant but I was very upset about it and wept buckets.

In later years, for I never forgot, I confronted her about it., Eventually, the truth emerged and she admitted that she tried to abort me, adding that she glad that she hadn't succeeded.

So another seed was sown but at the time, I remembered two lines from a poem, 'The Kite'

Boys haul in their white, winged birds

But you cannot do that when you are flying words

and I promptly went next door to Auntie Cissie and Uncle Fred. Not surprisingly, I spent as much time as possible with them and they were a 'Godsend' to me.

My father never interfered in our arguments and as I got older, they became more frequent; in fact, we were always at loggerheads. I have often wondered why he never took sides so I just put it down to wanting peace and quiet. He never took any interest in my upbringing, such as going to sports or open day at school. Having said that, he was always fair with me and I much preferred him to my mother.

Even though, I knew that he did not love me like he loved 'Jack', for his face would light up whenever he visited him. This only ever occurred when my mother was out as they never got on. My rational on this was that he had really loved his first wife 'Rebecca Regan' and the love-letters which I found when I emptied the house, making it ready for the landlord to reclaim it, said it all. I wish now that I had kept them but I had burnt them, feeling that this would have been his wish.

They never, ever, slept in the same bedroom; consequently, I never had any privacy as I had to share the large, front bedroom with my mother.

Even on the rare occasions when we went for two weeks to Blackpool with Auntie Bunny, he never came with us; my mother's excuse being 'George, (not my father) had to work'. What a blatant lie, for I confirmed in later years that 'Auntie Anne', a postwoman, was his mistress and my mother was, obviously, well aware of the fact.

Suddenly, I was brought back down to Earth, I pricked up my ears as an old film had been playing in the background and I had not been paying attention. A song was been sung; 'Bye, bye blackbird, makes my bed and light the light…..' What were the odds of that happening at this precise moment? I think Mandy was right and had' hit the nail on the head'

On further reflection, she always tried to distance me from my father by saying 'don't bother your father as he is tired and will be bad tempered'; this I tended to ignore and to be fair, he was always fine with me.

One could have thought that after nine years of marriage, they would have been 'over the Moon' to have a child and I would have been 'the apple of their eye'

Not so as he did not come to the Registry Office on my wedding day and Uncle Fred gave me away. The reason my mother gave me; 'George is not well enough' which led to another terrible argument between me and her. What utter nonsense! ; granted he was not a well man but what father wouldn't go to his only daughter's wedding.

In 1960, my father retired from the Post Office and received severance pay for almost £1000, plus a small pension. There were numerous rows about this money as my mother wanted him to buy a newly built bungalow, outside of Ardwick which would cost in the region of £950. He flatly refused and the rows continued so I could not wait to get out of this unhappy environment.

When my father died in 1964, she was adamant that he had contributed to the 'Saturday Hospital Fund' which was something that was quite common in those days. If one was sick or died, a small remuneration was received.

My mother complained bitterly to me and Aunt Cissie as she had difficulty in tracing my Dad's contributions records and was very anxious to claim these benefits. It was, then, that I pointed out that she must have the £1000 from his retirement so what was her problem in finding the cash to pay for his funeral? She just glared at me and not a word past her lips as she stormed out of the room.

When she died suddenly in 1966, there was not one penny to be found. I discovered that she had sold what jewellery she had e.g. engagement ring, a lovely gold, slave bangle and various other pieces which had belonged to my grandmother. Not only that, she had sold a gold wristwatch, a ring and a necklace which Auntie Bunny had given me and which she had been keeping for me. It was at this point, having discovered that she had sold them, that I lost all interest in these 'old fashioned', although valuable items.

Bill, my husband, paid for her funeral and Aunt Cissie and Uncle Fred paid out of their own pocked for her utility bills.

Eventually, I asked Aunt Cissie what had happened to the £1000 and why she had sold all the trinkets, including the War Medals which belonged to my father and one of Uncle Arthur's. The only thing left in her jewellery box was a black, ebony crucifix which was said to be Uncle Arthur's and which I still have to this day.

Aunty Cissie would only say 'Your father gave that £1000 to Jack. He was his only son, you know' and would say no more. At that stage I thought 'Sod it' as I did not want anything belonging to her and I told Aunt Cissie to take what she wanted from the house before the 'Clearance Men' came. I was so angry that she had, effectively, sold Aunt Bunnies' trinkets which in fact, she had stolen from me and never said a word, nor ever mentioned a word about the £1000.

I was intrigued as to when Jack received it, granted, it was my Dad's decision to do whatever he wanted with the money but I always deemed him to be a fair man so why only Jack?

I remember the 'inquisition' in the parlour, with my mother saying that I could not have heard Mr Teasdale calling my name. She insisted that I had imagined it or was telling lies, for he was already dead. I stuck to my guns, for, hear him, I did and with that, she left the room and went into the kitchen.

She, then, turned to my father saying 'George, he is dead! It seemed odd at the time and even odder now, for it was as if 'George knew about this teacher'; but why would he?, for he never took much interest in me, let alone, my education. The other reason may have been Aunty Bunnies' diagnosis; 'Highly strung', in other words, a bit mad.

I can understand their thinking but if, and I am sure she did know that Mr Teasdale was my father, rather than George Powell, then that is why she always supported my mother. She continually tried to change me and maybe I was too much like him, instead of them. One could never tell my mother that children were not owned but lent.

A few nights later, I awoke with a sudden start, for somebody was giving me a loving hug. I just could not believe it so I jumped up as quick as a flash, to turn on the light (excuse the pun). There was absolutely nobody there that I could see, as the dogs were fast asleep and Bess was snoring her head off.

I was wide awake at this stage so downstairs I went, to have a ciggy and a mug of coffee whilst trying to work out if I had imagined it all or, indeed, it was Harry. I returned to bed, only to awaken with a vivid dream going round and round in my head.

I was walking along in the swirling mist. A lady suddenly appears by my side and walks with me. She was dressed in Victorian style fashion and was wearing that familiar cameo broach just as in her photograph on the parlour wall. She was the lady who would stand at the bottom of my bed as I fed 'Minnie Mouse', as a child.

I knew her to be my maternal Grandmother so I asked her if Mr Teasdale was my father. She continued to walk silently beside me as if in an old silent movie. I noticed I was also dressed in the same fashion with a number of long skirts and tiny lace-up boots.

The mist continued to swirl around as if we were weaving our way through the evening clouds. So I asked her again, adding that I must know the answer. With that, she turned and uttered 'Your mother made a big mistake, for he was a 'geek' and suddenly, she was gone.

I sat and reflected what she had said; well, yes, Mr Teasdale moved into Great Western Street in 1934, the same year my mother got married. I never did discover where he abided from 1926 until 1934 whilst teaching at Ardwick Municipal School.

The other great puzzle in the dream was the word 'geek' which I had never heard off, let alone, understand its meaning so I decided to look it up in my dusty, old dictionary. Apparently, 'geek'; from the old Scottish; meaning; to peep or look. Isn't that what a spy does?

Just then, I heard these words ringing in my ear; 'Don't be too harsh on her'.

'Harsh' is a word I would never use so I knew it was him. At the precise time that he uttered these words, I was thinking that if she wasn't dead, I would kill her myself. She was always economical with the truth but this was reprehensible, for she stole that knowledge from me.

So, if I was correct, and it was a big 'if', I would need evidence, preferably DNA.

Chapter 97

Having stewed on the idea that he could be my father, it did not seem too farfetched as I have recounted a hundred times how odd it was that he changed my name and he definitely did. Recalling what Ian Bray and Father Doyle both stated; 'You will know who he is when the time is right'

I am left wondering why it had taken him almost twenty years to make contact with me. I based this train of thought on the fact that, in 1972, I was left with a book 'They Fought Alone'. This was my only keepsake of Harry and he was the only other person who ever called me 'Elizabeth' I wondered if 'Teasdale' had manipulated this?

I do know, from my own experience, that 'Spirit' can 'put words in your mouth' without us realising it. The best example was Mandy's statement that 'your friend was a terrorist'. After that incident, I put Mandy through an inquisition, just like my mother used to do with me. Mandy had not got a clue why she had said it with her only explanation being 'it just popped into my head'. A more advanced method of 'Spirit Communication' is reflected in the incident with me and the Quaker gentleman at Stepping Hill Hospital, when he asked if he was going to die. Not only did I state the exact opposite of what I had planned to say but

I will swear on the Bible that the voice which came from my vocal cords was definitely not mine. It was a distinctly male voice. This then reinforces the fact in my mind that it would have been Teasdale who was in control of me.

On a lighter side, I then recall a hilarious incident where Harry's wicked sense of humour came into play. I was walking past two stationary cars near the golf course on a balmy, Sunday morning. I noticed a big chap in a tracksuit, stood beside his car, smoking a cigar. 'What lovely dogs you have', he said as I passed by. I stopped and thanked him as we began to pass the time of day. Suddenly, out of the blue, he uttered: 'I used to have a cat that colour'. 'Nigger Brown' says me.' Opps!!! That is not very P.C. 'I hastily added. 'It is from the French. It is a colour' he responded. Just at that moment, the other car reverses out and the driver pops his head out of the window. He was grinning like a 'Cheshire cat'. Well, he was almost the colour of Bess with gleaming white teeth, just like hers. We fell about laughing, for nowhere does one usually see an African in Saddleworth. The point being that Bess is black and I have never referred to her as 'Nigger Brown'. It was Harry's doing.

So why had he waited all those years to communicate with me?

As we pondered on this, Mandy said 'Liz, if you had been a normal child, what would you have said to your mother after being told he was dead?' Without any hesitation, my answer to my mother would have been 'He is not dead because I heard him shout out "Elizabeth" Well that would be 'a turn-up for the books' and with that, I recounted my memories of that afternoon in 1953 as Mandy had requested.

I turned my head as I had heard him call my name twice but he was not at the side-entrance of the school gates, just behind the traffic lights where we were standing. So I looked towards the front of the building which was on Devonshire Street North, only to see people scurrying about their business on that damp, wet afternoon. There was a scruffy man in a flat cap, just like my Uncle Fred wore, standing about twenty-five yards away at the kerbside. He was making no attempt to cross the road, for he was looking towards me but I thought to myself that it couldn't be him

Just then, my mother shouted for me as the traffic lights had changed and she was half way across the road. I turned from my mother's direction and looked again; the man was still standing there.

Now, when I go out shopping with one of my daughters in a large store, I, initially, make a mental note of what they are wearing i.e. colour of their coat etc., in order to easily pick them out from the crowd. As a ten year old child, I would be looking for 'posh Mr Teasdale in his Crombie coat and certainly not a man in a flat cap and scruffy jacket. He did not look the type who could sing and dance, let alone play the piano.

My mother would not have recognised anybody at even half that distance and this he would have known. She was as 'blind as a bat', even when wearing her bottle-thick lens spectacles as she was severely 'Myopic' (short-sighted). This then brought to my mind what Jean Teasdale had said; 'totally unrecognisable in Ancoats Hospital when the family visited'

So, if it was not him, who went down the lift-shaft then?

The Inquest details were reported in the 'Manchester Evening News' and the 'Evening Chronicle' on the 16th and 17th respectively. So given the benefit of the doubt that the

Inquest was held on the morning of the 16th, December and not the 15th; remembering he died on Thursday 10th, then there was little time to call any witnesses because the weekend was upon us. As I have said before, the librarian would be the one obvious, last person to see him alive.

In those days, one used a rubber stamp and an ink pad to state the return date and a little card was removed from the item borrowed, usually they were then filed away. As far as I can recall, one's surname was never documented and a library membership card was used. So how would the librarian know who borrowed the sheet music? ; One only had an identity number. For that matter, anyone could have used his card.

The other possibility being that the music sheet was never booked out at all by the Librarian, for surely, they would be able to identify their method of stamping into the little squares inside the book. For example, as an avid reader, I frequently visited the library whereby some stamped neatly in the centre of the little squares whilst others would do it anywhere and even some upside down. So I would 'bet a pound to a penny' that is why she wasn't requested to attend the Inquest. At the end of the day, anyone could have planted that sheet music in anybody's pocket.

In all the newspaper coverage, there was no mention of him being originally identified by any other method. Bousfield Booth Teasdale in his smart Crombie jacket would have carried a wallet.

During my nursing days, I have been summoned to many inquests, so much so that I would make personal notes of the incident at the time. I knew, full well, that it would be three or four months later and I possibly would have forgotten the details.

In the case of my mother's inquest in 1966, (fell downstairs and fractured her skull) it was almost five months after her death. At the time, two highly, professional policemen who were summoned by the ambulance crew after I had found her at the bottom of the stairs, did a thorough job of measuring and photographing the stairs and landing. They also took a statement from me as to how she was positioned at the bottom of the stairs and, in fact, left no stone unturned in their investigation. At one stage, I was beginning to think that they thought I had pushed her. My explanation, corroborated by Auntie Cissie, that I, indeed had seen her laying in the hall way after I got no response from knocking on the door and had to look through the letter box.

I could definitely 'smell a rat', in fact, a whole nest of them, for I was still trying to figure out why Harry had sent me to the Police Museum and what the Press Club had to do with all this. The rest was beginning to fall into place, in an odd sort of way. As the saying goes 'It is never over until the Fat Lady sings'

So I decided to phone Jean Teasdale, to see if I could jog her memory in some way. I was hoping, with a bit of luck, if she may recall something which would be relevant to me if not to her, such as 'Hammer Toes'

Well that idea soon went down the 'Swanny River' as the number was unobtainable and there was no other number listed according to Directory Enquiries for her address. So I wrote her a short letter but I was not hopeful of a reply as she never responded when I sent, at her request, a copy of the 'Will'

I still could not get away from the idea that he did not meet his death in 1953 but just prior to 1972 which would make him 66yrs. old. Jean Teasdale's words still kept ringing in my ears : 'He was unrecognisable, dear' This seemed very convenient for if the body is so mangled, relatives are asked if the person had any identifiable features such as tattoos, birth marks etc. which would confirm their identity.

Chapter 98

Having not heard 'a dicky bird' from Teresa Chance, I decided to write a letter to her.

> HMRC
> Room 1/C23
> 100 Parliament ST
> LONDON SW1A 2BQ
>
> 19 MARCH 2014
>
> Dear Mrs T Chance
>
> On the 12.2.14 we spoke at some length. Regarding a review of where my father BB Teasdale was employed between 1943-49 you stated that you would confirm in writing that this information is classified plus the gist of our conversation. I have now waited a number of weeks, and have received Nothing.
>
> As I wish to take this matter to the commissioner, I would appreciate your answer in writing
>
> Yours sincerely

I waited a couple of weeks but she still had not the good manners to respond to my letter. I, then, wrote to the 'Information Commissioners' office (I.C.O) to commence the first stage of the 'Appeals Procedure.

> The Information
> Commissioner's office
> Wycliffe House
> Water Lane
> Cheshire SK9 5AF.
>
> 7 April 2014
>
> Dear Sir,
>
> I enclose copies (7) of relevant information, which is self explanatory. Having exhausted the internal review procedure. Which is totally unsatisfactory.
>
> Due to the fact that I cannot get a written answer to my correspondence Teresa Chance phoned me to explain the reasons which made little sense! as to why I could not be informed, as to where my deceased father worked between 1943-49.
>
> Despite her promise to put the gist of our conversation in writing. This has not been forthcoming.
>
> Before I seek legal advise I would much appreciate your response.
>
> Yours Sincerely
> Liz Roberts

Well at least they had the decency to reply promptly as, at the end of the day, it is individuals like me and others who contribute by paying our taxes from which they are paid.

A few days later, I received the following;

---

ico.
Information Commissioner's Office

Upholding information rights

Wycliffe House, Water Lane, Wilmslow, Cheshire, SK9 5AF
T. 0303 123 1113 F. 01625 524510
www.ico.org.uk

Ms L Roberts

10 April 2014

Dear Ms Roberts

Thank you for contacting the Information Commissioner's Office. We confirm that we have received your correspondence.

If you have raised a new information rights concern

We aim to send you an initial response and case reference number within 30 days.

Please note that if you are concerned about the way an organisation is handling your personal information, we will not usually look into it unless you have raised the matter with them first. For more information please see our webpage 'raising a concern with an organisation' (following the 'for the public' link from our homepage), or call the number below.

If you have requested advice

We aim to respond to your request within 14 days.

If your correspondence relates to an existing case

We will add it to your case and consider it on allocation to a case officer.

Copied correspondence

Please note that we do not respond to copied correspondence.

If you have a matter you would like to discuss please call our helpline on 0303 123 1113 (local rate) or 01625 545745 if you prefer to use a national rate number.

Yours sincerely

The Information Commissioner's Office

Making a request for information held by the ICO? - For more information about the ICO's handling of requests for information please visit http://www.ico.org.uk/about_us/how_we_comply

Our newsletter - Details of how to sign up for our monthly e-newsletter can be found at http://www.ico.org.uk/tools_and_resources/e-newsletter.aspx

Twitter - Find us on Twitter at http://www.twitter.com/ICOnews

---

I phoned Mr Noel Mullarky and reiterated that I hadn't received HMRC's response regarding the outcome and this was the point of my complaint.

He reassured me that he would get them to respond as regards the outcome of their internal review. So I had to be patient to see what progress he would achieve whilst hoping that he lived up to his unfortunate namesake 'No Mullarky'. With that, I put it to bed.

ICO.
Wycliffe House, Water Lane, Wilmslow, Cheshire, SK9 5AF
T. 0303 123 1113 F. 01625 524510
www.ico.org.uk

Mrs L Roberts

14 April 2014

Case Reference Number FS50537767

Dear Mrs Roberts

Your information request to HM Revenue and Customs (HMRC)

Thank you for your correspondence of 7 April 2014 in which you complain about the above public authority's response to your information request.

From the correspondence you have provided you advise that you have exhausted HMRC's internal review procedure in relation to your request of 26 September 2013.

However, it does not appear that we have HMRC's internal review outcome which we require as evidence of this. I note that you have provided a copy of your request dated 26 September 2013, as well as HMRC's response of 29 November 2013 and your request for a review on 18 December 2013, but we do not have HMRC's review outcome.

Further, you have provided a copy of a letter from HMRC dated 31 January 2014 but this does not appear to be an outcome of an internal review and does not reference their earlier response of 29 November or the Freedom of Information Act itself.

As such in order to address your complaint please provide us with copies of the following:

- the public authority's outcome of their review

We will usually require unedited copies of e-mail correspondence. The headers and footers contain information which we often require in order to assess a complaint.

> **ico.**
> Information Commissioner's Office
>
> Once we receive the information we have requested your complaint can be addressed.
>
> If you need to discuss the matter I can be contacted on the number below.
>
> Yours sincerely,
>
> Noel Mullarkey
> Case Officer
> Information Commissioner's Office
> Tel - 01625545595

Steve got in touch to inform us that the 'Central Library' had finally re-opened and would very much like to accompany Mandy and myself. He, like us, was very much intrigued to see the 'legendary' lift shaft and I was hoping against hope that it had not been altered in any way since Harry's time.

Three heads are better than two so my plan was to role-play the actions needed to commit suicide in this way. I hoped to use Steve as Harry's stand-in for he was the nearest in height and weight to Harry though not as agile due to his age, plus his hip replacement. 'Any old port in a storm 'as they say! I had not mentioned it to him yet but hopefully he would be a 'good sport' and we would see if he could cock his good leg over the rails and throw himself down.

Bribery would be my best option with Steve, Fish and chips plus peas in his favourite restaurant should do the trick.

Chapter 99

So on the 24th April, we set-off to the 'Central Library', meeting up with Steve in the usual place, alongside 'Queen Victoria's Statue' in Piccadilly Gardens. I noticed that there weren't any trees or foliage anymore and the wild life such as squirrels and birds had also gone. They were obviously unable to survive in the concrete complex though there was a fountain surrounded by modern benches.

These gardens were placed on the site of the old 'Manchester Royal Infirmary', way back in the 1800's and it was said to have also housed a number of pauper's graves.

I had decided 'to kill two birds with the one stone' and inform Steve who was limping badly that we had requested the Ardwick Municipal Ledgers. We would try and ascertain who Elizabeth Powell was as it seemed very odd that her name was just above B.B. Teasdale. However, Steve was more interested in the lift shaft and was eager to see if it was in its' original state.

My brainwave that I could persuade him to try and climb over the guard rail had 'gone to pot'. By the way he was walking, we were more likely to have to hire a wheelchair; ah, well! 'The best-laid plans of mice and men often go awry'

The exterior of the building was still in its original state but looked really well, having been sandblasted. So in we trotted and could not believe our eyes, for their in the forum was a huge picture of the lift shaft with the word 'Leave' scrawled across it.

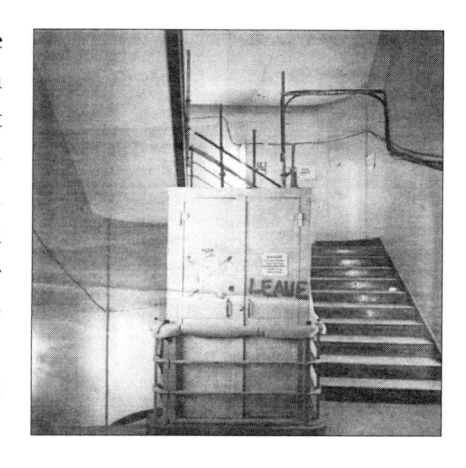

'Bloody hell'; Steve pipes up. 'Do you think Harry has written that word on it?' Mandy started cracking up in hysterical laughter and I was going 'to wet myself' if I didn't stop giggling; meanwhile, everyone was staring at us.

But the best was yet to come as we walked towards the reception area, 'low and behold' there was yet another smaller version of the same picture on the wall. My first task was to locate 'the loo' so off I went, leaving those two still falling about laughing.

The interior was totally unrecognisable, for gone was the central staircase with its' carved, wooden hand-rail with new furnishings and carpets leading up to the First Floor. The place had entirely lost all its character and I was disappointed with the new look. As I climbed the modern staircase and gazed around, I wondered if it was the same architect who designed 'Piccadilly Gardens'. The place seemed so cold and clinical.

On my return, Mandy had found the page with 'Elizabeth Powell' and a few pages further on, it appears she had got married so 'Powell' being her maiden name. The only person I could recall, as a small child, was my Aunt Lizzie (Elizabeth), one of my father's sisters who I believe, married twice but I did not know her husband's surnames, let alone if she was a teacher or not. What we found quite interesting was the fact we were given three ledgers, instead of the usual two, though incomplete, it did throw some light on bygone times of teaching and did, in fact, mention Mr Teasdale, as the Music Teacher who appeared to be a kind and generous person.

> at nearby Centres. In addition a group of senior girls attend the Horsfall Museum for talks on local history and art, while a group of boys go to Parr's Wood Gardening Centre. Visits are made to numerous places of interest and talks are given in School by outside lecturers on geographical subjects.
>
> The work in English in the Senior forms shows a wide variation. Written expression is not, on the boys' side, distinguished either in content or form; on the girls' side however some of the work is original and interesting and corrections are made in a helpful way. The presentation in both cases is satisfactory. With the juniors little opportunity is given for independent writing but many of the children are beginning to write at length on carefully prepared themes. Reading throughout the School is receiving careful attention but there are several cases of backward readers for whom suitable books are not available; The girls in the top Senior class read fluently

and intelligently. The top juniors are making good use of the local public library but this interest in books is not sustained generally among the older children; only a limited number of books is available in the class libraries although these are supplemented by books brought from the children's homes. A serious weakness is the lack of opportunity provided for the children to make an acquaintance with their heritage of English literature.

Drama is taken throughout the school by a teacher who makes this, and Music, his special interest; in some cases percussion instruments & music are used very considerably in connection with mime. The work in drama gives consistent training in play production and has led to a high standard of performance; the work is directed with great enthusiasm. Attention could be given to some of the wider uses of drama, in giving the children more opportunity for expressing their own dramatic ideas informally, and in connection with other subjects.

Music is shared between two members of staff. In the junior classes a pleasant and fairly good variety of songs is learned and a conscientious effort is made with sight-reading; the senior girls sing quite well and the boys have memorised a fairly extensive repertoire of songs. The Master responsible for the music has purchased a great deal of sheet music & the percussion instruments at his own expense. He takes community singing with the whole school once a week, for half an hour, with commendable success. By this means the children have become acquainted with a suitable range of national & folksongs

History is taken throughout the senior classes by one Master; in the first three years the work is centred round events or people; notes are dictated by the teacher; a few illustrative history models have been made. In the leavers' classes opportunity has been given for some independent work on topics arranged on a terminal plan. In the junior

Sadly, we could not find any records regarding the' Manchester Hippodrome' or his children's play 'Golden West'. I was hoping against hope to find a descent photograph of him.

We traced Harry's footsteps to the Music Room and down the modern staircase to the now cordoned-off lift and staircase which he would have used. I noted that the guard rail around the lift was about two and a half feet in circumference thus making it impossible for anyone to jump or be thrown down it. The only way was for Harry to have either lowered himself or be dropped in a vertical position. We then proceeded down to the basement where he was supposedly found.

I could not get my head around this, for the more I thought about it, the more impossible it seemed. Firstly, why did he not land on top of the lift? Granted, the space was so narrow, his body would be unable to twist and turn during the decent; unless the lift was already on the second floor and then he would free-fall.

So, in my head, I went through the motions of planning to murder him. Firstly, how do I make sure the lift is at the top so that once I have lowered him down the side of the shaft, he then freefalls. The only thing that came to mind was to place an 'Out of Order' sign in the basement and then on the first floor or leave the cage door open. This surely would have been far too risky as people would have to use the stairs which would not be a good idea to encourage witnesses.

If, indeed, he did commit suicide which is equally unbelievable, why did he go and choose his music sheet and then, wait for the lift to be stationary on the second floor. He had never walked down to the first floor as initially thought.

Now, even if the lift was already stationary on the second floor so he then has to squeeze between two and a half feet gap and lower himself down. There was no guarantee that somebody was not going to use it. So, how on Earth did he end up in the basement?

Even if the same scenario happened on the first floor, then the same result would apply. He would have surely landed in the lift space and not the stairwell.

So if I take the front page headline which appeared on the 'Manchester Evening News', Monday, 7th December, 1953; 'A man had fallen nearly 60 ft. down a well between a Lift Shaft and Library Staircase' out of the equation and just accept the nearly 60 ft. for he did hurl himself down the well as the coroner had stated, then, no matter whether from the first or second floor, both are much more than 60 ft. to the basement.

I suspect that he actually went over the staircase handrail which was about 4 ft. high and landed on the first floor but I could not figure out how the dirt marks on the staircase rail indicated that he had deliberately climbed over when his mind was disturbed.

So, if Mr Jessel Rycroft, the City Coroner, was correct, then B.B. Teasdale got washed and dressed and quite possibly had some breakfast, set off to the library to choose his sheet music, must have spoken with the librarian and then decided to climb on the bannister rail, jumping down 50 or 60 ft. to his death.

Why would he go to the trouble of getting a tram or a bus to the library when he could have easily hurled himself out of his bedroom window at Great Western Street? He would have more chance of killing himself that way than hurling himself down a flight of stairs.

It was really on a whim as we left the library and were walking past the 'Art Gallery' towards our favourite chippy in Oldham Street that we decided to go in as Steve's leg was troubling him and we needed to sit down. As we walked into the building, we could not believe our eyes as there was another large photograph of the, now, infamous lift shaft hanging on the wall. We were falling about laughing again as this was three of them and we were beginning to think that Harry was trying to tell us something.

Steve and I sat down whilst Mandy, knowing the story of how Harry had led us there, decided to go on a walkabout. I had explained to her that it was just like the Police Museum and the Press Club which did not seem to lead us anywhere; At least Burlington House and the Ritz cemented connections to WWII, Drummond and Turin.

A few minutes later, back she came with a triumphant, facial expression as she clutched a pamphlet. 'Read this' she said, shoving it towards us and we did.

It confirmed that there was, indeed, a Gentlemen's Club and theatre during Harry's days but best of all 'During the war years, part of the building was acquired by the 'Ministry of Food' We all looked at each other, for who was in charge of the 'Ministry of Food but Jack Drummond so he must have spent at least some of his time during the war in Manchester. This could, indeed, link him with Harry, for we knew full well that Drummond and Turin were most likely acquainted and if Harry belonged to either the 'Gentleman's Club' or the 'Theatrical Society' which was highly likely, then that is why he led us here.

We needed more information so we ambled over to the reception desk, only to find that the Curator, Ruth Shrigley who had worked there for umpteen years knew the history of the building, was on two weeks leave. I obtained a phone number and would contact her on her return.

Well, this had been an interesting afternoon and what a good laugh we all had. It was almost 6pm and we were sitting in the chippy when Mandy came up with one of her 'out of the blue' statements whilst staring at the photo of the lift shaft. 'Does Harry mean for us to 'Leave It' as we have got it all wrong' she said, looking deep in thought.

This was a fair point and another reason to reinvestigate this and try to find out why they decided to take photographs and enlarge them into pictures which had been placed in at least two venues.

'With the best will in the world', one would have thought that something of more interest would have been more appropriate such as the ground floor with its' lovely staircase and surrounding features, in the olden days.

Obituary

SIR JACK DRUMMOND

JACK CECIL DRUMMOND was born in 1891. He was educated at King's College School and East London College, taking his degree in 1913. After acting as Research Assistant at King's College, London, and serving for a short time in the Government Laboratory, he went to the Cancer Hospital Research Institute, where in 1918 he became Director of Biochemical Research. In the following year he was appointed Reader in Chemical Physiology at University College, London, and was made the first Professor of Biochemistry in 1922. At that time such Chairs were few, and Drummond concentrated on the mode of action of vitamins and other food essentials. His school of research workers specialised on a variety of nutritional problems and became well-known in this field. Biological tests were essential for observing the effects of vitamins, and the writer remembers the occasion when the late H. E. Armstrong greeted Drummond with the query, "Well, Drummond, when are you going to give up ratting and do some chemistry?"

Various papers in *The Analyst* show the interest that Drummond took in the early chemical tests developed for determining vitamins and the researches he made to separate the minor constituents of the unsaponifiable matter of oils with which vitamins are associated. In this connection he was one of the first to use chromatographic techniques; his batteries of adsorption columns were impressive for their size and the amounts of material dealt with.

Although working on the newer knowledge of nutrition, he was convinced that man had developed a natural aptitude or instinct for selecting food that would provide the necessary adjuncts. His researches into the food habits of the past were collected in "The Englishman's Food," published in 1939 in collaboration with Miss Wilbraham, whom he married in 1940.

At the outbreak of war in 1939 he offered his services to the Ministry of Food and was Chief Adviser on Food Contamination until the following year, when he was appointed Scientific Adviser, a post which he held until 1946. He was concerned with feeding a people at a time of shortage, when there were great restrictions on the availability and choice of imports. The problem of emergency feeding after raids was a specially difficult one. Throughout he always insisted that special attention must be paid to the diets of children, adolescents, expectant and nursing mothers, the sick, and heavy industrial workers. His work was rewarded by a knighthood in 1944, and in the same year he was elected a Fellow of the Royal Society. He resigned his post with the Ministry of Food in 1946 to become Director of Research to Boots Pure Drug Co., Ltd.

Between 1914 and 1948 Drummond published about 200 scientific communications either alone or jointly. About one-third appeared in *The Biochemical Journal*, the remainder being widely dispersed; ten appeared in *The Analyst* and about double that number in the *Journal of the Society of Chemical Industry*. They include references to almost all the then known vitamins and his contributions to nutritional science are noteworthy.

Drummond served on the Council of the Society, on the Council of the Institute of Chemistry, for which he acted as examiner for six years, and was Chairman of the London Section of the Institute while the writer was Secretary. He was a member of the Interdepartmental Committee on Food Standards from its formation in 1942. In 1947 this Committee was reconstituted as the Minister's Food Standards Committee and Sir Jack retained his seat on the Committee until other commitments compelled him to resign in 1950.

Drummond was always a young man, always a good companion and always ready to be of assistance to others. The tragic news of his death and that of his wife and daughter came as a great shock.

J. R. NICHOLLS

Chapter 100

Over the next few days, I made a number of attempts to contact Mr Mullarky but to no avail. In desperation, I contacted the 'Helpline' who informed me that 'he is usually in his office'. I had already left three messages on his answer-phone during the week so I devised a little plan whereby I would withhold my number and guess what? 'Low and behold', he answered his phone. Of course, he came up with two excuses i.e. 'I have been on holiday', 'I was just about to phone you', 'Oh, that's nice. Where did you go? I responded politely. He was a bit flummoxed by this and eventually added 'I did not go anywhere'. Isn't it funny that the 'Helpline' did not know he was away?

Knowing full well that I was about as popular as the 'Plague' and not giving a 'damn' at this stage, I repeated yet again that he had the relevant paperwork and had not received, as promised, an H.M.R.C. response to my internal review. I went on to say that I would appreciate it very soon.

I received the following letter and a copy dated the 17th April from H.M.R.C. and enclosed was a letter from Noel Mullarky dated 23rd May.

ico.

Information Commissioner's Office

Upholding information rights

Wycliffe House, Water Lane, Wilmslow, Cheshire, SK9 5AF
T. 0303 123 1113 F. 01625 524510
www.ico.org.uk

Mrs L Roberts

23 May 2014

Case Reference Number FS50537767

Dear Mrs Roberts

Your information request to HM Revenue and Customs (HMRC)

Thank you for your recent telephone call on 20 May 2014 in which we discussed your complaint about the above public authority's response to your information request.

As advised, after liaising with HMRC about your complaint they informed me that they had issued a response to your internal review on 17 April 2014. I enclose a copy for your reference.

As discussed if you are dissatisfied with the outcome of HMRC's review you may raise a complaint with our office giving reasons for this.

If you need to contact us about any aspect of your complaint please contact our Helpline on 0303 123 1113, being sure to quote the reference number at the top of this letter. You may also find some useful information on our website at www.ico.org.uk.

Yours sincerely,

Noel Mullarkey
Case Officer
Information Commissioner's Office
Tel - 01625545595

HM Revenue & Customs

Central Policy

FOI & DPA AdviceTeam
1C/23
100 Parliament Street
London
SW1A 2BQ

Mrs E Roberts

Phone 03000 586938

Fax 03000 586902

www.hmrc.gov.uk

Date 17 April 2014
Our ref
Your ref

e-mail aidan.callan@hmrc.gsi.gov.uk

Dear Mrs Roberts

I am writing with reference to your letters dated 18 December 2013, 6 February 2014 and 8 February 2014. I must apologise for the fact that the first two of these letters were not acknowledged. I have also been provided with a copy of your most recent letter dated 19 March 2014, addressed to Mrs Chance.

I understand, and your latest letter confirms, that Mrs Chance telephoned you on 12 February 2014, following receipt of your letter dated 8 February 2014. She explained HMRC's position regarding your request and she understood that her explanation satisfactorily addressed the concerns raised in your internal review request letter dated 18 December 2013. She advised you that you would receive a written response to your internal review request and that is why I am writing to you now. I note that your latest letter indicates that you wish to take this matter further by way of a complaint to the Information Commissioner's Office (ICO), as you are entitled to do.

I will first address the FOI position, as this is what the ICO would need to look at if you were to make a complaint about HMRC's compliance with the FOIA. I will then go on to address the position regarding your separate correspondence with HMRC's Records Retrieval Service which is not a matter for the ICO.

Your Request

In an email dated 27 November 2013, you made the following information request:

Requesting information on; Bousfield Booth Teasdale, D.O.B 3RD February, 1906 @60 Cable Street. Lancaster. Died on 10th December 1953

Information is available in large print, audio and Braille formats.
Text Relay service prefix number – 18001

Director: Marie-Claire Uhart

FOI 3051 14 E Rob.

In conversation with Mrs Chance and with reference to your separate correspondence with HMRC's Records Retrieval Service, you confirmed that the particular information you were seeking was details of the employment record for this person for the period 1943 and 1949.

HMRC Response

On 29 November 2013, Mrs Chance provided HMRC's response to you. She explained that she was unable to confirm or deny whether HMRC held the information you were seeking, because to do so would breach HMRC's statutory duty of confidentiality. As such, HMRC was able to rely on the exemption at s44(2) of the FOIA.

Internal Review

In her conversation with you on 12 February 2014, Mrs Chance explained that HMRC's statutory duty of confidentiality means that we cannot disclose information about named taxpayers, even when they are deceased, except in certain specific circumstances. The statutory provisions explicitly state that these circumstances are not relevant to any consideration of a request for disclosure under the FOIA. Mrs Chance confirmed that her response to you on 29 November 2013 set out HMRC's consistent position regarding disclosure of information about a deceased person under the FOIA. I am satisfied that this is correct. Mrs Chance advised you that the FOI position has not changed and you accepted this.

For completeness, I have added an appendix to my review letter, which sets out the statutory provisions which apply to your FOI request. Although customer information is excluded from the FOIA regime, HMRC may disclose on a discretionary basis if one of the conditions set out in section 18(2) or (3) of the Commissioners for Revenue and Customs Act 2005 (CRCA) applies. These conditions do not affect the interaction between sections 18(1) and 23(1) CRCA so the disclosure is not made under the FOIA. The absolute prohibition against disclosure contained in section 18(1) is the only relevant provision in this regard. An amendment to the CRCA was introduced in 2009 to make this explicit (See s19(4) of the Borders, Citizenship and Immigration Act 2009).

Discretionary disclosure outside of the FOIA

I will now go on to address the position regarding your separate correspondence with HMRC's Records Retrieval Service which is not a matter for the ICO. Any dissatisfaction with HMRC's exercise of its discretion should be taken forward as part of HMRC's complaints process and the ICO has no jurisdiction over these matters.

With your letter dated 18 December 2013, you enclosed copies of correspondence exchanged with HMRC's Records Retrieval Service and made reference to the phone contact you had had with that team. Mrs Chance explained to you that she only became aware of these communications when she received your letter on 30 December 2013. She told you that she had spoken with Richard Leitch about your enquiry. She established that the Newcastle team had clarified the rules around disclosing information about deceased customers. That team is able to disclose information where it is necessary to resolve any outstanding tax matters in respect of the deceased person or in relation to pension / benefits entitlements of relatives or dependants of the deceased.

Your letter of 26 September 2013 made it clear that your enquiry was for the purposes of completing your family history and you specifically asked for details of the employment record for this person during 1943 and 1949. As such, the purpose of your enquiry would not meet the requirements of the clarified rules. You told Mrs Chance that you had finally received a letter from the Newcastle team, explaining the changes to the handling process following clarification of the rules.

She advised that, outside of the FOIA, HMRC is able to disclose information if a Court order, binding on the Crown, is obtained by an applicant. However, to be helpful, she confirmed that HMRC was unlikely to hold employment details in respect of an individual who died in the 1950s. Personal tax records are generally only retained for 6 years. HMRC holds national insurance contribution records which show the complete history of an individual's contributions as this is used to determine the individual's entitlement to a state pension and other state benefits. However, any pre-1975 records held by HMRC would only show the value of the national insurance contributions and would not include any employment details.

Mrs Chance further advised you that there might be information accessible from The National Archives on teachers' employment history. I have copied below a link to The National Archives website and also to the Findmypast website and I have enclosed screenprints from these sites. You will see that there is a record for a Bousfield Booth Teasdale on the Findmypast website but it is necessary to register / pay to access the particular record. You may wish to access this for yourself to see if it contains the information you are seeking.

http://www.nationalarchives.gov.uk/records/looking-for-person/teacher-or-pupil.htm
http://search.findmypast.co.uk/search-united-kingdom-records/teachers-registration-council-registers-1914-1948#./teachers-registration-council-registers-1914-1948?&_suid=139774381767408064631707776766

Conclusion

I am satisfied that Mrs Chance's response to your information request was in accordance with our obligations under the FOIA. It is extremely unlikely that HMRC would hold the employment information of an individual who died in the 1950s but HMRC would, in the circumstances, be unable to disclose such information to you without a suitable Court Order. To be helpful, we have suggested alternative sources of the information you are seeking.

Appeal Process

As previously advised, if you are not content with the handling of your request under the FOIA, you may apply directly to the Information Commissioner, who can be contacted at:

The Information Commissioner's Office
Wycliffe House
Water Lane
Wilmslow
Cheshire
SK9 5AF

Yours sincerely

Aidan Callan

Appendix

Legislation relevant to disclosures under FOIA

Freedom of Information Act 2000

http://www.opsi.gov.uk/acts/acts2000/ukpga_20000036_en_1

44 Prohibitions on disclosure

(1) Information is exempt information if its disclosure (otherwise than under this Act) by the public authority holding it—
(a) is prohibited by or under any enactment,
(b) is incompatible with any Community obligation, or
(c) would constitute or be punishable as a contempt of court.
(2) The duty to confirm or deny does not arise if the confirmation or denial that would have to be given to comply with section 1(1)(a) would (apart from this Act) fall within any of paragraphs (a) to (c) of subsection (1).

Commissioners for Revenue and Customs Act 2005

http://www.opsi.gov.uk/acts/acts2005/ukpga_20050011_en_1

18 Confidentiality
(1) Revenue and Customs officials may not disclose information which is held by the Revenue and Customs in connection with a function of the Revenue and Customs.

23 Freedom of Information
(1) Revenue and customs information relating to a person, the disclosure of which is prohibited by section 18(1), is exempt information by virtue of section 44(1)(a) of the Freedom of Information Act 2000 (c. 36) (prohibitions on disclosure) if its disclosure—
(a) would specify the identity of the person to whom the information relates, or
(b) would enable the identity of such a person to be deduced.
(2) Except as specified in subsection (1), information the disclosure of which is prohibited by section 18(1) is not exempt information for the purposes of section 44(1)(a) of the Freedom of Information Act 2000.
(3) In subsection (1) "revenue and customs information relating to a person" has the same meaning as in section 19.

Explanatory Note to s19 CRCA

http://www.legislation.gov.uk/ukpga/2005/11/notes/division/1/13/2/20

110.Subsection (1) makes it an offence for any person to contravene the non-disclosure provisions of section 18(1), or of section 20(9), in relation to "revenue and customs information relating to a person" whose identity is revealed by the disclosure. The term "person" includes both natural and legal persons, and, for example, the tax affairs of a limited company are also protected by the provisions of the subsection.

Borders, Citizenship and Immigration Act 2009

http://www.opsi.gov.uk/acts/acts2009/pdf/ukpga_20090011_en.pdf

19 Application of statutory provisions

(4) In section 23 of the Commissioners for Revenue and Customs Act 2005 (c. 11) (freedom of information), after subsection (1) insert—
"(1A) Subsections (2) and (3) of section 18 are to be disregarded in determining for the purposes of subsection (1) of this section whether the disclosure of revenue and customs information relating to a person

is prohibited by subsection (1) of that section."

Legislation relevant to disclosures outside of FOIA

Commissioners for Revenue and Customs Act 2005

http://www.opsi.gov.uk/acts/acts2005/ukpga_20050011_en_1

18 Confidentiality
(1) Revenue and Customs officials may not disclose information which is held by the Revenue and Customs in connection with a function of the Revenue and Customs.
(2) But subsection (1) does not apply to a disclosure—
(a) which—
(i) is made for the purposes of a function of the Revenue and Customs, and
(ii) does not contravene any restriction imposed by the Commissioners,
(b) which is made in accordance with section 20 or 21,
(c) which is made for the purposes of civil proceedings (whether or not within the United Kingdom) relating to a matter in respect of which the Revenue and Customs have functions,
(d) which is made for the purposes of a criminal investigation or criminal proceedings (whether or not within the United Kingdom) relating to a matter in respect of which the Revenue and Customs have functions,
(e) which is made in pursuance of an order of a court,
(f) which is made to Her Majesty's Inspectors of Constabulary, the Scottish inspectors or the Northern Ireland inspectors for the purpose of an inspection by virtue of section 27,
(g) which is made to the Independent Police Complaints Commission, or a person acting on its behalf, for the purpose of the exercise of a function by virtue of section 28, or
(h) which is made with the consent of each person to whom the information relates.
(3) Subsection (1) is subject to any other enactment permitting disclosure.

Results for Teacher's Registration Council Registers 1914-1948

Your search criteria

Bousfield Booth
First name

Teasdale
Last name

New search

1 result

Order by Relevance

First Name	Last Name	Country	Collections from	Where	Category	Record collection
Bousfield Booth	Teasdale	England & Wales	Great Britain	England & Wales	Education & work	Occupations

1

Well, having read all this 'bullshit' plus a helpful teaching certificate which I already had, I came to the conclusion that they think I am utterly stupid, maybe so! As I was pondering all of this, Richard's (Records Retrieval) words were ringing in my ears; 'If you wish to know where he worked, you will have to go to the 'High Court'

I decided to seek a second unbiased opinion, for I had many unanswered questions. What started out as a documentation of my psychic experiences has turned out to be something beyond belief; for who is he and what is the real Teasdale and why had all this come about? I hadn't a clue but all I knew for sure was that Harry is the real Teasdale. He changed my name to 'Elizabeth' way back in those far off days when I was a child and I heard him call me after he was dead.

So I phone my solicitor, Mr Musgrave's secretary to make an appointment for a consultation. 'Booth Inc. & Knowles' offices were based near Denton Market so I set off early in order to browse around and hopefully find some bargains. Alas, when I arrived, the market had disappeared only to be replaced with a fountain. It was just like the one in Piccadilly Gardens and I wondered what this obsession was with these concrete fountains. Let's face it, one cannot say they are the most attractive piece of architecture around and even my dogs would not drink out of this one.

With almost an hour to spare, I mooched around the now non-existent stalls and shops. 'Apple Sands', known for its cooked meats and pies, was now boarded up. The butchers was now an 'Amusement Arcade' with the 'Wool Shop' and the 'Milliners' turned into to 'Charity Shops' I guess people did not wear hats anymore and even the 'Post Office' had disappeared. So with well over a half an hour to spare, I spent the time browsing in the soft furnishings which was the only familiar shop left and even that lacked any quality items. So much for the 'Recession' sending small businesses to 'the dogs', I thought to myself.

It was almost 3 o' clock so I made my way to see Mr Musgrave whom I had known for a number of years. Up the stairs to his office I went, to find that it had not changed at all. He was a mild-mannered, kindly man who always welcomed me with a warm handshake. We reminisced a little and I asked him how his hobby of 'bird watching' was progressing, having clarified initially that he meant the 'feathered 'variety.

Without further ado, I plonked the relevant papers on his desk, briefly explaining that I wanted an objective opinion and without any information from me. I only informed him that I was doing my family history and believed this man to be my father.

After digesting all the correspondence, he placed it back on his large, oak desk whilst peering at me over his spectacles. 'What on Earth are you up to?' he said with a perplexed expression. 'All of this is complete poppycock if they have not got the information you requested. Why write all this and it must have taken them many hours to put it together?' he went on to say.

I, then, produced the cuttings from the newspapers regarding the manner of his death. At no time did I mention 'Harry' for obvious reasons. 'Tell me' he said: 'Is the man who left the school in 1943, the same person who returned in 1949?' Well this had never entered my head and I said so, going on to explain that I was in his class at school (1950/51) and had a photograph of him taken in June, 1931 which was the same person.

'Well if this is the case, then he has to have been behind 'the Iron Curtain'. An agent or a double agent' he went on to say. The time lapse off over sixty years leads me to think that he must have been connected to someone very interesting.

'Take, for example, the memoirs of Queen Victoria which are not to be released for 200 years due to her indiscretions and lovers. Who cares what she got up to?' I said. 'Not I' he replied, looking amused. This was always the way of the 'Establishment' and the great lengths they would take to ensure that nobody who would know the truth was alive.

'The only way you are going to find out is to consult a solicitor who specializes in 'Freedom of Information' and who could find their way around all this 'Poppycock' as I have not got the expertize for doing this', he said. 'There is another way and that is to hire a good, private detective but there again, I do not know anyone of this calibre. Either way, it will prove very costly', he added.

I, then, told him that I thought my phone was 'bugged'. 'I am not surprised' he replied, pointing to Noel's email to Patsy.

As we said our 'goodbyes', he gave me a warm handshake, stating that he was intrigued and that I must let him know the outcome of my investigation.

Well that was £50 well spent, for it reassured me that I was on the right track. I made a mental note to Harry, to find the appropriate person regarding 'Freedom of Information' so he had better come up with some cash, adding that I was not made of money. Granted, he always came up with the funds for Bess' mobility injections if not a premium bond win. Something always turned up, like a Tax Rebate etc.

I then wondered how long she would last as she was well turned 12 years old which was a very good age for a dog of her size and breed. The average life-span was 9 to 10 years as the bigger the dog, the shorter the life. Take 'Bimbo', for example, which I had as a child for he was just turned 15 years and very deaf when he had to be put to sleep.

Bless her, for I will be 'in bits' and miss her terribly when she goes to live with Harry. When my time comes to join him, my first task will be to ascertain that all my animals are in good spirits, even down to 'Ginger', the fox. If not, he will be in 'Big Trouble'.

Chapter 101

The next morning, I contacted the 'Law Society' and requested a list of solicitors who specialised in 'Freedom of Information', in the Greater Manchester area. Surprisingly, there was only one, a 'Slater & Gordon' whom I, immediately, contacted and spoke with a helpful lady, named 'Elizabeth' I gave a brief summary of my requirements and after a short chat about having the same name, she informed me that there was nobody available at the moment but that she was sure that they could help. She assured me that someone would get back to me within 24 hours.

Three days later, I phoned again and was told by a receptionist that they were no longer dealing with 'Freedom of Information' cases. I insisted on speaking to someone more senior and as you can imagine, this went down like 'a lead balloon' but I persisted and I would stay on the line until my request was granted. After a lot of back and forth mutterings between various individuals which I could not fully make out, another female came on the phone and informed me that the person specialising in these types of cases had left their company. I pointed out that they were listed in the current information from the 'Law Society', only to be told; 'They are out of date with their information.'

That evening, I phoned Patsy who checked Slater & Gordon's website and they were, indeed, specialists in these cases. Having, initially, not given much weight to my claim that my phone was bugged and suggested I was paranoid, she now changed her tune and stated that I was either correct or that the name 'Teasdale' was flagged up.

'You could come here and make an appointment in person to consult somebody else; however, there again, if the 'Powers that Be' have not got your attention by a bugged phone, the same thing will happen. Your name or 'Teasdale' will flag up again and you could be on an expensive road to nothing' she said, after careful assessment of the situation.

I was now utterly convinced of B.B. Teasdale's link to Alan Turin, for when I went to the library on the off chance of finding the meaning of the 'braided cuffs', Harry sent in that retired Air Force man who said that they signified a 'Wing Commander'

So was Wing Commander Edward Yeo Thomas, the British spy with the code name 'White Rabbit', the one that Harry was alluding to?; and if so, his friend, Leo Marks, a cryptographer who also worked at Bletchley Park along with Alan Turin and Jack Drummond must also be linked, in my opinion, with what was going on.

I must also remember that Turin and Drummond were said to be spies so my next port of call would be the 'Manchester City Art Gallery', to see what I could dig-up on Jack Drummond. My guess was that Harry was a member of the 'Gentlemen's Club' or the 'Theatrical Group' which were all in the same building. I was still unclear where the 'Press Club' came into the equation, other than the fact that it appeared to be another 'Pink Sink', the bar at the Ritz Hotel.

Chapter 102

We set off to the 'Manchester City Art Gallery' as we had an appointment with Ruth Shrigley, the Curator, who had promised to extract as much information as she could find on the 'Ministry of Food', the 'Gentlemen's Club' and the 'Theatrical Club' from the archives, down in the basement. Needless to say, our prime concern was to confirm if we could tie Jack Drummond and Harry together. We also wanted to see if Alan Turin, along with Harry, were members of the 'Gentlemen's Club'

As we drove towards Manchester City Centre, through Collyhurst (A62), old memories came flooding back of the good old times and Terry Mc Donagh. As I was prattling on to Mandy about him, suddenly, just for a second, a man's oblong ring, agate in colour with a small snake entwined around a stick, appeared before my face. This was in a similar fashion as when Bess' face appeared to me.

The next moment, we were talking together; me about the ring whilst Mandy was asking if Harry wore anything around his neck. We could not believe that, in essence, we were both thinking the same. As we explored the possibility of whether Mandy was mind-reading me or, in fact, Harry had just given us a clue i.e. some kind of insignia that he wore around his neck or on his finger, was immaterial.

The only emblem of a snake entwined around a staff which I know, not a crude stick which this definitely was, is the one on my nurse's badge; a symbol of 'Medicine' As far as we were aware, Harry had no links to this so Mandy thought it was possibly something to do with the 'Masons'. Her grandad Rowston (the policeman) had been a 'Mason' for as long as she could remember.

'Oh, Shit! 'Mandy screamed as I went down a one-way street but the wrong way. I had not been concentrating on my driving so with horns blaring and irate drivers shaking their fists, I took a quick look to see if a policeman was around and seeing the coast was clear, I duly did a U-turn. With Many still uttering obscenities at me, I, thankfully, parked whilst telling her that it was all Harry's fault for distracting me.

As we walked towards the 'Gallery', I recalled a family story about my Grandad Fleetwood who was also in the 'Masons' It was said that he was into 'Magic' but having no understanding of what they were talking about at the time. I now believe they meant the 'Occult' (hidden)

At some point, we would have to try and ascertain if the Masons were into this, in some cases, and if Harry was a member. I did not really know as it was a gut feeling but Harry, like myself, would have been very interested in such matters. In my mind's eye, I could still see the ring as his fingers fly across the piano keys whilst singing 'Bye, Bye, Blackbird'

Having been introduced to Ruth Shrigley, we, dutifully followed her down the steep steps into the basement. She seemed a very nice person and was very interested as to why we were there; So much so that I told her about the mysterious circumstances in which my father died, adding that I believed his death could be linked to Alan Turin and Jack Drummond, both of whom, we believed, were acquainted and also died in dubious circumstances

Having ushered us to a large, Formica table, she duly returned carrying an armful of ledgers which we divided up. Whilst Mandy began ploughing through the 'Ministry of Food' section, I commenced with the 'Gentleman's Club'.

Low and behold, what do I find but a lecture given in 1939 by a J. Dudley Johnson entitled 'Canyons of the Golden West'. This surely was Harry telling us that he was a member of this club and this was where he got the title for his school play 'Golden West'

I caught Ruth's attention and asked her if there was a members list? Sadly the answer was 'No, there would not be'. She went on to say that this Gentleman's Club was a special interest society with a newsroom frequented by journalists. Also, it had a language class and chess club but most importantly, it was used as a 'Tactics Room' during the War. Apparently, it had various telephone lines and intercom systems which were connected through old tunnels which ran under the City Centre, linking various venues and newsrooms.

I wondered if these tunnels linked to the 'Press Club' which was underground. If this was so, then this could also have been a tactics venue and that was why Harry had led us here, just as he did the 'Pink Sink' bar in the 'Ritz Hotel'

The next moment, my mind flashed back to a game we played as children, often at birthday parties and especially if it was cold and wet outside. It went as follows; small pieces of paper with clues written on them were hidden around the house. The brightest child who found them and followed the clues, ended up with the 'Treasure', usually sweets which was a great treat in those far off days when 'Ration Books' still existed (one exchanged ones allocated coupons for chocolate, fruit etc.). I recall the time my mother sent me to the greengrocers to exchange coupons for three bananas (one each) our fortnightly ration which I,hastily ate on my way home. Needless to say I was never sent again.

So, OK, Harry, having educated me on uncovering happenings that I never knew existed during the War years, I will begin your 'paper chase' but leave the spelling and punctuation to Noel, for I am hopeless at them.

I wasn't even sure what 'Tactics 'meant so I looked it up. Tactics; the art of planning or manoeuvring forces in a battle (Distinct from strategic) '. Planning or planned skilfully.

In 1939, the 'Gentleman's Club' negotiated with Manchester City Council to sell the building due to financial difficulties (they couldn't pay the Rates'. They retained the lease and were still there in 1940. From that point, the evidence of their existence becomes a little sketchy, for in August, 1941; some of the building was used as fire watchers dormitories as well as an evacuation point for 'Central Government' personnel, as opposed to 'Local Government' people. I wondered where these lesser mortals went. So who were the privileged ones who were allocated down in bunkers as opposed to tunnels?

Also, in that year, 'Home Guard' volunteers (Dads Army) had the top floor for training purposes. The 'Central Food Committee' (Jack Drummond) Ministry of Food was on the ground floor but in June 1945, the Ministry of Food rented the whole building for two years from the Council.

According to Ruth, the 'Gentleman's Club' lectures carried on during part of the War years. 'I do not know where they moved to or if they were disbanded, for the Ministry of Food stayed on in the building until 1952 when food rationing ceased' she said with a huge frown across her intelligent face.

Having ascertained that Jack Drummond must have, at least, spent time in Manchester, if not been allocated there on a permanent basis it is highly likely that his and Harry's paths crossed during the War years.

The 'Central Government' people, the ones who had priority evacuation were based in the Town Hall. So based on one's hunches, I asked Ruth if she had any plans that illustrated these tunnels and where they led to. So off she trots, only to return after a few moments with a pile of dusty, tatty plans. Sadly, we could not discover where they led to in the end. Now, bearing in mind that the Town Hall is within a 'stone's throw' of this building, as is the 'Press Club', I wondered if the elite Town Hall individuals and the Gentlemen's Club Tactics room people were also considered the 'chosen few' and granted the same privileges. Surely when the bombs were dropping, they were hardly going to walk out into the street or stay in the building whilst Dads Army took the brunt of the raids.

Regarding the 'Theatrical Group', there was nothing to show who the members were but Ruth did confirm that they were there during the War; saying that we could contact a 'Sue Maher' whom she believed may be able to help us as she was in possession of old photographs and programmes.

Chapter 103

It had taken until the 11th June to make contact with Noel Mullarkey regarding his letter of the 23rd May. Despite leaving two messages informing him that I was very unhappy with H.M.R.C. response to my request of the 17th April, I wished to take this matter further. I received no response.

His excuse this time was a little more original than the last one. 'I have been on holiday and you were assigned a different case worker. This is the reason for the delay in responding to your messages' he said.

He was giving me 'the run around' and I informed him in no uncertain manner. 'What is the name of my new case worker as nobody has informed me of this' I said with some degree of scepticism in my tone. I could hear him fiddling on his computer in an effort to find the name of the person who was allocated to my case but 'guess what? Surprise, surprise, 'It is not on my computer', he said in an exasperated voice.

I reiterated that I wished to take the matter further and that I would put it in writing. 'No need to write, I will deal with this' he said. 'Immediately' says I and hung up. Well, I must have 'put the shits up him' for the following day, I received this letter.

ico.
Information Commissioner's Office

Upholding information rights

Wycliffe House, Water Lane, Wilmslow, Cheshire, SK9 5AF
T. 0303 123 1113 F. 01625 524510
www.ico.org.uk

Mrs L Roberts

11 June 2014

Case Reference Number FS50537767

Dear Mrs Roberts

Your information request to HM Revenue and Customs

Thank you for your telephone call received on 11 June 2014 in which you make a complaint about the above public authority's handling of your request for information.

Your case has now been allocated to a sector specific team who deal with cases that require more detailed consideration and will be allocated to a case officer as soon as possible who will contact you to explain how your complaint will be progressed.

If you wish to send any further documentation while the case is awaiting allocation, please quote the reference number at the top of this letter. This will ensure that the information is added directly to your case. Please be aware that this is an automated process. The information will not be read by a member of our staff until your case is allocated to an officer.

If you have any specific concerns before your case is allocated to an officer, please contact our helpline on 0303 123 1113, or 01625 545745 if you would prefer not to call an '03' number, being sure to quote the reference number at the top of this letter.

Yours sincerely

Sent on behalf of
Alex Ganotis
Group Manager
Information Commissioner's Office

Chapter 104

I went for an early walk with the dogs as Mandy was collecting me at 11am. She had never been to 'Bury Market' and I had been promising her for ages to show her around it.

We were just coming down 'Cunnings Corner' and onto the lane when, suddenly, Bess' back legs buckled from under her. 'Oh, Harry, what am I going to do"; I thought to myself as she was almost six stone in weight and there was nobody around to help me. Even if there was, there was no way she would let them near her. After what seemed an eternity, she managed to struggle up with my help whilst Harry was waiting patiently as I guessed he understood. German shepherds reportedly have an I.Q., in general, of about 60 ; (much brighter than some humans I know).

Luckily, it was only about 100 yards or so and we eventually got up the steps and into the house. I needed Mr Mc Connell and not one of his underlings as he knew her full history. Unfortunately, it was Saturday morning and I would be very lucky if he was even at the surgery, let alone come to the house.

I phoned the receptionist and yes, he was due to be there shortly for an emergency and she asked to bring her down.

I was thinking how the hell do I get her back down the steps and into the car?; but as I looked at my watch, I knew Mandy was on her way.

By the time, Mandy and I got her into the car, I just knew her time was up. The only consolation was that she was almost twelve and a half years old and she had good 'innings'; as they say, no one lasts for ever and she had been with me for 11 years.

So I stayed by her side while she faded away, telling her she was going to Harry. God knows, he will have few friends when she arrives, for she was a witch and she was to tell Harry from me that she was never 'nigger- brown' but black.

I also thanked Harry for his help as we had to cancel Bury Market on a number of occasions so Mandy was at hand and also the vet. Knowing that 'Spirit' cannot change things, 'what will be, will be' but at least he made the whole situation less traumatic. For as Mandy put it. 'You could have been miles from home and unable to contact me. Luckily, I was only around the corner as we were going to the market'.

It will take a while but when I recover from this, time heals all things as they say, I will ask Harry to find me another 'Bess', for she and 'Muffin' will always have a special place in my heart. Meanwhile, Harry and I will soldier on as he is a lovely, softy dog and he is missing her already but he understands and we will have a good cry together.

Chapter 105

I went to the 'Wythenshaw Forum' to demonstrate my mediumship, knowing that Steve would be there so I had decided to ask his help in ploughing through all the phone books in order to trace 'Trevor Powell', Jack's son.

We arrived early and headed up the staircase to the vast library and for the next half hour or so, we wrote down every 'T. Powell'. Surprisingly, there were not many, maybe two dozen or so.

At the next opportunity, I set about phoning them, one by one. After about an hour, I found him. Although the conversation, at first, was a little confusing as I initially asked if his father was called 'Jack' and if he had a 'Hare Lip'. No! Was the answer to the first question, going on to say he was called 'George' and yes', he had a 'Hare Lip'. I asked if he had a sister called 'Hillary' and if his mother was named 'Edith'? To which he replied 'Yes but my Dad did not have a half-sister'. 'Well, he did or at least I think he did' I said, going on to briefly explain that I believed his grandad was not my father.

We then continued the conversation, comparing memories etc. Firstly, he vaguely remembered being told that his grandad had been a postman and had been married twice but reiterated that he never knew about me. The only other memory he had was when he was a small child and visited a terraced house where there was a little, old lady but was told that it was not his 'Granny'. 'No, she wasn't', I replied and went on to tell him that his real grandmother, (his first wife) was called 'Rebecca Regan' who I was told had died in childbirth. 'Bloody' Hell, I always thought I was of Welsh descent, not Irish' he said, sounding amazed.

Sadly but not surprisingly, Jack, his father, had died in his eighties and was buried in Australia. His sister, Hillary, was also deceased, dying in her early fifties of 'Cancer' but, Edith; his mother was still alive and now aged ninety-two. My hopes rose up as I said 'maybe she could throw some light onto this'; for we both agreed that it was odd that he never knew I existed.

Unfortunately, Edith, was living in a nursing home in Australia but Trevor phones her every Sunday and would definitely ask her about me, adding that she was very deaf but fully 'Compos Mentis' (Latin for 'sane')

I then carried on telling him that when his grandad had died in 1964, I tried to make contact with his father, against my mother's wishes, and managed to trace him and his address through a firm named 'Tootal' where he was once employed. Although Jack never came to his father's funeral which I thought was rather odd, Edith however, did, adding that she would remember me. She thanked me for letting them know and apologised for Jack's absence due to illness. Of course, both Edith and I knew that this was a lie and for whatever reason, he did not wish to see my mother. Equally, she would not want to see him either for reasons which evaded me. Hopefully, Trevor would do some digging on my behalf as he seemed totally intrigued by our conversation.

Well, I did not have to wait long as Trevor, being as good as his word, made contact the following week, having talked to Edith, his mother. Her response, he said, was that she didn't know a thing, adding that Jack was in the army in WWII and she lived with her family in Longsight. He felt that she was holding something back and would have another try the following week. I reassured him that I or anybody else would not be upset in any way, for all concerned were dead.

We then went on to have a lengthy conversation about his/mine family. The only scant information I could give him, was that his Grandmother, Rebecca Regan, was buried in Clayton Cemetery, near the old coal mine and gas works. His great Granny, I added, came from Connemara well known for its ponies and an old film 'The Quiet Man' starring John Wayne who was famous for his 'westerns' in the old days. I also added that I had visited Connemara in the West of Ireland which was so quaint with its thatched cottages, dotted around the rolling countryside.

I then volunteered to send him a couple of old photographs, one of his father, Jack and one of his grandad, George, with me and my mother. 'George', it was said, in his younger days, had a resemblance to 'John Wayne'

He could still not get used to me calling his dad, Jack' but when he asked his mother, she explained that since they were both called 'George', his dad was nicknamed 'Jack' to avoid confusion so that cleared that query up.

We were getting on like 'a house on fire' so I mentioned the £1000 which Aunt Cissie had said his dad received. As the story unfolded, it all began to make sense. Trevor was born in 1947 and they went to Australia in the early 1950's when Hilary was just a baby. Returning in the late 50's, they lived in a number of council houses, living from 'hand-to-mouth' His mother, along with his father' both worked, with Jack having two jobs at one time, a paper and window cleaning round to make ends meet.

Then, 'out of the blue' as he put it, they bought a posh semi-detached house in Cheadle. He was absolutely sure of the date, 1960/61, oddly enough that was the year I got married and after we had done our sums, this tallied with my Dad's retirement money. So Aunt Cissie was right after all.

Trevor said that he never knew where the money had come from and had never been told but he would ask his Mum when they next spoke. He agreed that it was odd that his Dad got all the money and even odder that he never knew I existed. 'Something amiss here', he thought and would definitely do his best to find out.

Jack and Edith returned to Australia, after he and Hilary had been married a few years. He added that he had himself been married twice but had no children. He mentioned that he was a 'diabetic' like his father and I added that so was his grandad and his father before him, I was told.

'Diabetes' we thought, definitely ran in families, for I recalled that my Dad's brothers Joe and Leonard who kept the 'Blue Bell Inn' in Ancoats (the one with the smelly bottle tops which I loved and my mother detested) were also diabetics.

There was another brother named 'Harry', I added who went to prison for what? I do not know as I only saw him a couple of times but remembered he had two boys who never kept in touch. There was also a sister named 'Phillis' who, sadly, had the girl in the 'Iron Lung' due to contracting 'Polio'

Trevor's next phone call was even more intriguing. He had asked his mother where the money for the house came from with her responding that she did not know anything about it. 'What utter rubbish, she was always very secretive but this takes the biscuit' he added. 'I did try, Liz, reassuring her that there would be no come backs and I even told her that it was utter nonsense to think that no one comes home with £1000 and buys a house without their spouse knowing about it' he said, sounding exasperated. 'One would want to know as it is human nature or did she think he had robbed a bank?' he added. 'She must have known where the money came from so why not tell me?' he said, sounding disappointed.

The only reason we could think of was the fact that if she admitted that the money came from my Dad, then this would lead to more difficult questions; e.g. Why just Jack who was married then and not his daughter?

'On balance, Liz, I think you are right' he said, summing up the situation. He added that her reaction to these questions was as if she knew but did not want to get involved. 'Knowing my mother, I would have expected her to have expressed some surprise, at least about your parentage' he said and added the fact that I was never mentioned supports this theory.

He, then, very kindly agreed to take a DNA test so further arrangements were made for me to contact him when I had acquired the necessary information.

Chapter 106

I must admit that I did not have a clue as to how to acquire a legitimate DNA for both of us so I contacted the receptionist at my General Practitioner's surgery. Unfortunately, she didn't know either so the only option was to make an appointment which would be a week later at the earliest. It was a good job that I was not dying, granted it was quite a few years since I had seen my G.P. and had not even realised that they had changed their venue.

Gone were the days when one could visit the surgery and wait one's turn to see the doctor. Prior to and after the 'National Health Service N.H.S', Dr Ford, our G.P. who resided in a little stone house adjacent to the Methodist Church at Ardwick Green, would make up his own medications from numerous, coloured, glass bottles of different shapes and sizes which lined the walls of his dispensary.

If one required a home visit, he would promptly arrive, alight from an old Bentley car, driven by his wife, clutching his doctor's bag. Dr Ford had a glass eye, just like Uncle Arthur; however, it did not roam about as much in its socket. Consequently, I did not stare at him in the same manner.

My mother always said that it was 'unseemly for a woman to drive' and for that matter to go into a public house to purchase a 'gill of ale' (quarter of a pint) which one carried home in a little, brown jug covered with a cloth.

Promptly, at 2pm the following Monday, I arrived in this nice, young doctors surgery and announced 'I am not ill'. He raised his eyebrows at my unusual request and said 'I haven't got a clue but it won't take me long to find out'. After about five minutes, he returned, armed with the relevant information with a broad smile on his face. 'You have made my day. No moans or groans, just a healthy person with an odd request' he said, looking amused.

I contacted the 'D.N.A. Team' only to be told that Trevor and I were too distant due to Jack and I having different mothers. Of course, the same would apply to Teasdale siblings (different mothers). It would have been a costly exercise (£500) but well worth it in my eyes.

So other than popping over to Australia and digging Jack up out of his grave, I was left with no evidence other than circumstantial.

Well, if I could not dig up Jack, I decided to have a 'dig' at the I.C.O. and remind them of my existence.

Well, well! They certainly put their skates on, having realised that I was not going away; I received the following letter ten days later.

ico.
Information Commissioner's Office

Upholding information rights

Wycliffe House, Water Lane, Wilmslow, Cheshire, SK9 5AF
T. 0303 123 1113 F. 01625 524510
www.ico.org.uk

Mrs L Roberts

28 July 2014

Case reference number FS50537767

Dear Mrs Roberts

Freedom of Information Act 2000 (FOIA)
HM Revenue and Customs (HMRC)

Further to our letter of 11 June 2014, I write to inform you that your case has now been allocated to me to investigate. This letter will explain how I intend to do this. It will also provide you with contact details so that you can get in touch with me if you need to.

What happens now

Where possible the Information Commissioner prefers complaints to be resolved informally and we ask both parties to be open to compromise. With this in mind, I will write to HMRC and ask it to revisit your request. It may wish to reverse or amend its position. If it does, it will contact you again directly about this.

In any event, it must provide us with its full and final arguments in support of its position. Once I receive its arguments, I will consider its reply before either contacting you to discuss the matter further or preparing a decision notice. Further information is available on the Information Commissioner's website:
http://www.ico.org.uk/complaints/~/media/documents/library/Freedom_of_Information/Practical_application/how_we_deal_with_complaints_guidance_for_complainants.ashx

ico.
Information Commissioner's Office

The scope of the investigation

I understand your complaint is about a request for information that you made to HMRC on 26 September 2013. You asked to be provided with the following information under the FOIA:

Details of the employment record for Bousfield Booth Teasdale (D.O.B 3rd February 1906, died 10th December 1953), for the period from 1943 to 1949.

HMRC informed you on 29 November 2013 that it could not confirm or deny whether it held the information you requested on the basis of the exemption at section 44(2) FOIA.

I understand you requested an internal review on 18 December 2013. You disagreed that confirming or denying whether the requested information was held would lead to the identification of the deceased individual because you already had prior knowledge of his identity.

On 17 April 2014 HMRC wrote to you with details of the outcome of the review. The original decision not to rely on section 44(2) was upheld.

The scope of my investigation therefore will be to determine:

- Whether HMRC was entitled to refuse to confirm or deny whether it held the information you requested above on the basis of the exemption at section 44(2).

Please contact me within the next 10 working days, that is, by **8 August 2014** if there are matters other than these that you believe should be addressed. This will help avoid any unnecessary delay in investigating your complaint. If I do not hear from you by this date, my investigation will focus only upon the matters identified above.

It would be helpful at this stage to explain how the *neither confirm nor deny* (NCND) exemptions in the FOIA work.

Section 1(1) of the FOIA provides two rights to applicants. They are:

a) The right to be informed in writing by the public authority whether or not it holds the information requested, and

b) If so, the right to have that information communicated.

Both these rights are subject to exemptions.

> # ico.
> #### Information Commissioner's Office
>
> The NCND exemptions may be used by public authorities to deny the right granted in section 1(1)(a) – ie the right to be informed whether or not information requested is held. Section 44(2) is one of a number of NCND exemptions in the FOIA.
>
> Please note that a public authority relying on NCND is basically refusing to disclose (under the terms of the FOIA) whether or not it holds requested information. Therefore, the focus of my investigation will not be to determine whether the information requested should have been disclosed to you. Rather, it will be to determine whether HMRC was <u>entitled to refuse to confirm or deny whether it held the information</u>. You will appreciate that both are two separate things.
>
> If you have any queries at any time you are welcome to write to me at the address at the top of this letter or alternatively to casework@ico.gsi.gov.uk (please ensure that you quote the above case reference).
>
> Yours sincerely
>
> Terna Waya
> Senior Case Officer
> 01625 545366

I wrote an immediate response, for yet again, I was not asking for B.B.Teasdale's employment records; just the venue.

I.C.O

31 July 2014

CASE NO FS50037767.

Dear Terna Wga,

Thank you for your letter 28.7.14. May I draw your attention Page 2 Para 2. Details of employment records B.B Teasdale.

If you refer to the copy of my last letter 26 Sept 2013. To records retreval. you will note that I did <u>not</u> request details of my fathers employment records.

I requested to know where he worked between 1943-49.

I strongly object to the I.C.O. "putting words in my mouth", and hope you will take this matter up.

Yours sincerely

Chapter 107

As I sat in the old rocking chair, clutching a ciggy and a glass of red wine, I pondered at where 'Harry's Book' was leading me. Not in a thousand years would I or for that matter Noel had any inkling of what had transpired.

The information I had gathered over the last few years was mind boggling, for I had to read many books and spoken to numerous people. During my research on WWII, spies and symbols such as 'The Swan', not to mention 'Agent Orange' which I never knew existed, were intriguing to say the least. I also learnt though not to anyone's surprise that 'The Powers that be' are surrounded by chicanery.

The untimely and mysterious deaths of Jack Drummond, Alan Turin and Harry still cast long shadows but as it is said 'what is done in the dark, comes out in the light' Perhaps it is the 'teacher' in Harry, for I have been on an 'educational tour' that has left me with more questions than answers.

Although, there were times when I had 'done my own head in' and everybody else's, thus sending them to an early grave. In retrospect, that would not have served any purpose as we would all have to contend with Harry. ('Send me to an early grave' was one of my mother's famous sayings as she glared at me)

So there was nothing else to do but 'soldier on', trying to tie up all loose ends. As to the 'why' and 'what' this was all about, was, indeed, 'The Million Dollar Question'

So far I had not found any meaning to the snake ring that Harry wore, other than that it is used in the medical field. I was sure that there must be another meaning which would require more research.

At the very least, Harry kept my brain functioning in my old age. Lord above! I would be no use to him if I suffered from 'Dementia' though I frequently felt he was driving me that way. Round and round in my head, the questions would pop up; is he my father or is he not? Did he go down the lift shaft? If not, who did and why? Questions, questions, questions!

For the time being, a simpler task would be to connect with 'Sue Maher' who according to Ruth Shrigley from the Art Gallery, has in her possession photographs and programmes of plays performed in that building, prior to WWII. I needed to see if Harry was in any of its productions.

So on a more light-hearted note, I made contact with Sue Maher regarding the' Theatrical Group', having given the usual explanation as to why we wanted this information. With that done, a date was set for us to visit her. In the meantime, she would seek out all the old photographs and programmes to see if the name 'Teasdale' came up in any of them.

The following week, we set off towards 'Moss Side' although through the passage of time, all the old familiar haunts had gone. Apart from the odd, old, church buildings and 'Ardwick Green Park' everything had changed. Where once stood 'Shorrocks Irish Club' on Brunswick Street, surrounded by umpteen, tiny shops including the horse meat shop which most people in Ardwick ate due to the low cost, had now totally disappeared. Of course, beef and pork in those days were far over budget and we never could afford chickens, unless my father managed to acquire a fowl from 'Smithfield Market'.

I am sure Mandy was bored senseless at this stage with all my reminiscence of 'Barbara Ravenscroft, Monica O'Neil' and myself with the good times we had at Shorrocks Club when we were in our early teens.

There were no more familiar places except 'Alexandra Park' where we parked the car and walked the short distance to Sue Maher's house. It was a large, Victorian house surrounded by a low, bricked wall which would have once had wrought iron railings; something that most garden houses had prior to WWII. I believe they were confiscated by the government and used in the manufacture of bombs and such like. Her garden still retained the 'Laurel' bushes which was something I hadn't seen in years, along with the iron railings, everybody had them in those times. I fully expected to see an old, fashioned, rambling rose which was equally common in those days. I managed to see one by peeping through some bracken. Eventually we walked up to the front door and rang the bell.

We entered the parlour where umpteen old photographs and mementos of those bygone years were strewn over various pieces of antique furniture. There were also five cats of various colours and sizes, to which we were introduced as they happily purred whilst brushing against our legs.

She explained that she could not find any reference to 'Teasdale' or 'Sid & Teasdale' adding that though she was an actress herself, he was way before her time. Evidently, she had never married and was born in this great house. She, now, rented out a number of rooms to theatrical people who were performing at local venues, such as 'The Palace Theatre' and the 'Opera House' in productions of 'Evita' and such like.

It was a good job that I had the foresight to bring my magnifying glass as the photos were so 'yellow' with age, it was almost impossible to distinguish any of the actor's features.

Although our visit proved fruitless, Sue did say that her collection was incomplete and if anything came up, she would phone me. Even so, we thoroughly enjoyed ourselves listening to her chatting away about the theatrical way of life. We had nearly eaten her 'out of house and home 'after scoffing loads of biscuits and sandwiches, not to mention the numerous cups of coffee.

I can now understand why Harry wanted to be on stage as Jean Teasdale had once said. According to Shakespeare; 'All the world's a stage; and all the men and women merely players'. This left me with 'a million dollar question'; what was Harry's role?

/ HISTORY

BBC Local | Manchester | Things to do | **People & Places** | TV & Radio |

15:08 GMT, Tuesday, 20 April 2010 16:08 UK

The oldest Am-Dram in the world

Manchester has an artistic claim to fame to sit alongside its industrial and scientific accolades as home to the world's oldest amateur dramatics ensemble.

The Manchester Athenæum Dramatic Society (MADS) first gathered in May 1847 as the Dramatic and Literary Reading Society.

They were based, as their current name alludes to, at the Manchester Athenæum Institute, a gentlemen's club dedicated to the pursuit of knowledge.

Now part of the Manchester Art Gallery, the Athenæum opened in 1836 and hosted a wealth of scientific, artistic and cultural societies and events in its Victorian heyday.

MADS president, Sue Maher, says the club started in Manchester as a result of a similar one being opened in London.

"The local businessmen thought that it would be very good to have one in Manchester that catered for the office men and warehouse staff.

"The mechanics had their institute, where they could go and do courses, [access a] free library and get the papers, so they set one up for the brown and white collar workers."

Plays without acting

The Dramatic and Literary Reading Society developed 11 years later and were originally based in the Athenæum's Lecture and Concert Hall and Theatre, a room which now hosts the Gallery of Craft and Design.

In those early years, the Society boasted some superstar names of the day as guests, with readings from writer Charles Dickens and future prime minister Benjamin Disraeli amongst others.

Sue says the members began by "reading plays to very small audiences, but then a little down the line, people wanted to act."

Their first public performance was a simple reading in front of an audience in 1857 - the actors read from large books and did no acting.

Chapter 108

So on that theme, I decided to try and find out about the symbolism of his 'Snake Ring', commencing with the 'East Lancs. Lodge' on Bridge St., Manchester, a familiar building, for I once had a Saturday job in a café on that very street.

I cast my mind back to the days of Gladys and Ken (Ivy Cottages) and my many invites to the 'Lady's Evening' etc. as Ken was the 'Grand Master of the Peace Lodge' in 1983, I still have a tankard commemorating this event, hanging amongst other mementoes on my kitchen beams. Many of the lodges, I attended along with Gladys, had symbols on the outer and inner walls. Of course, at that point in time, they meant nothing to me but now I recognise them as occult symbols.

I made contact with a 'Mike Dowling' giving the usual explanations and after a few days, he phoned me with some information. Apparently, to his surprise, there were five 'Teasdales' listed in the 'Freemasons' within my time frame.

Unfortunately, there was no 'B.B Teasdale' and all were born between 1878-1917. He did suggest that they may be relatives; however, having checked all Harry's sibling's Christian names, there was no match. I did go on to tell him that 'Teasdale' hailed from Lancaster but their records did not cover this area, Greater Manchester only. He felt quite sure due to the tender age of Harry when he left Lancaster in 1926 (20 yrs. old) that he would not have participated in the 'Masons' there.

> **[2] The Staff of Asclepius** (Æsclepius, Asklepios)
> [Personification of Medical or healing Art and its ideals]
>
> Professional and patient centred organisations (such as the NZMA, in fact most medical Associations around the world including the World Health Organization) use the "correct" and traditional symbol of medicine, the staff of **Asclepius** with a single serpent encircling a staff, classically a rough-hewn knotty tree limb.
> **Asclepius** (an ancient greek physician deified as the god of medicine) is traditionally depicted as a bearded man wearing a robe that leaves his chest uncovered and holding a staff with his sacred single serpent coiled around it, (example right) symbolizing renewal of youth as the serpent casts off its skin. The single serpent staff also appears on a Sumerian vase of c. 2000 B.C. representing the healing god Ningishita, the prototype of the Greek Asklepios. However, there is a more practical origin postulated which makes sense [See

The 'Snake Ring' could, apparently, be a symbol for 'an inner sanctum', adding that as a general rule, these rings were 'swivel rings'; only the symbolism to be displayed when required, like the 'handshake'

My next stop was at Mandy's house, to see if 'Wikipedia' could throw some light on the symbolism of the snake entwined on the stick. Whilst Mandy was making the coffee, I settled myself in the lounge and browsed through a couple of 'Dan Brown's' novels which she had borrowed from her friend, Helen.

My attention was caught by a quotation written in italics;
'In the beginning was the Word and the Word was with God'

I then started muttering to myself 'and the word was God. The same was in the beginning with God'. Meanwhile,

Mandy returned armed with coffee and ashtrays which she nearly dropped. 'What!' she said with her mouth open.' I never knew you read the Bible, Liz' as I carried on 'the same in the beginning with God'. We both looked at each other 'gob smacked'. 'No, I have never read the Bible 'I replied as I reamed off some more 'the light shines in the darkness, and the darkness comprehended it not'. What was more, I knew it was a quote from St. John which nearly sent Mandy scrambling for the 'smelling salts'.

Well, the snake went on the 'back burner' as we looked up the 'Gospel of St. John' in the Bible.

'In the beginning was the Word and the Word was with God. The same was in the beginning with God. All things were made through him, and without him was not anything made that was made. In him was life and the life was the light of men. The light shines in the darkness, and the darkness comprehended it not'

Well, we didn't have a clue what was happening. All I knew was that these words were not mine as I have never had any interest in the 'Bible' or for that matter, anything religious. The only thing I did whilst Mandy was brewing up was to browse through Dan Brown's book; 'The Lost Symbol' The title, in itself, we felt was rather odd as that was exactly what we were about 'The Snake Symbol'. So why had I quoted almost word for word, these verses without any knowledge?

I was inspired to pick up a pen and the other Dan Brown book 'Inferno' and shut my eyes. I, then, opened a page and stabbed it with the pen (I am sure Helen would not be best pleased). Guess what? I marked Chapter 56; 'Seek and ye shall find'

The only conjecture we could come up with was this; 'Good is fighting Evil' Oh, if only Stephen Doyle, the catholic priest from Ashton Hospital was around. He would have been able to throw some light on it. (Excuse the pun)

Over an hour later we were back to the task in hand and determined not to get side-tracked. On my travels I have seen a couple of snake rings in Pawn Shops and I have gone in on the pretext of buying one. Both rings had been dated around 1910 but that was as much as I could find out.

At this stage, we were both 'losing the will to live' because the snake and stick merged into antiquity and there were a number of biblical references in the Book of Numbers (No21;5_9)

Example:

5. And the people spoke against God and against Moses wherefore have ye brought us up out of Egypt to die in the wilderness. For there is no bread, neither is there any water and our soul loathed this light bread.

6. And the Lord sent fiery serpents among the people and they bit the people and much people of Israel died.

7. Therefore, the people came to Moses and said 'We have sinned, for we have spoken against the Lord and against thee. Pray unto the Lord and he taketh away the serpents from us' and Moses prayed for the people.

8. And the Lord said unto Moses, 'Make thee a fiery serpent and set it upon a pole; and it shall come to

> pass that every one that is bitten when he looketh upon it, shall live'

9. And Moses made a serpent of brass and put it upon a pole and it came to pass; that if a serpent had bitten any man when he beheld the serpent of brass, he lived.

'The Pre-Dynastic Period' demonstrated the earliest known representation of a single serpent entwined around a pole (in this case, a papyrus reed).

These two symbols are also linked to magic and the occult e.g.; Hermes, the Greek God of Trade & Commerce.

'The Rod of Asclepius' takes its name from a particular type of non-venomous snake which freely crawled around the floor where the sick and injured slept; hence its connection to medicine and the Greek God 'Asclepiou', associated with healing and medicinal arts in Greek mythology.

These two symbols, whether combined or separate, are used in numerous countries and religions throughout the World; e.g.: the Roman equivalent of 'Hermes' is 'Mercury'

Encyclopaedia Britannica explains that the staff represents the one carried by 'Hermes' as a symbol of peace. Basically it was a badge of 'Diplomatic Immunity' for the heralds, ambassadors and his staff. I wonder if that is how 'employees' were named as 'staff'. 'Rod of Asclepius originally meant 'Power of Ambassador'

So Harry was still a teacher at heart, for I was on yet another educational tour. What with 'Agent Orange' and the 'War', not to mention 'Drummond' and 'Turin', plus the notorious lift shaft. However, I was still not entirely satisfied with this explanation. Poor student, I may be, but this symbol might be significant in some way, otherwise, why would he have shown it to me.

I looked up the exact meaning of the word 'Ambassador' in the 'Oxford Dictionary'. 1. A diplomat sent by one country as a permanent representative or on a special mission to another. 2. an official messenger.

Chapter 109

So off I set to Delph Library for further exploration on Harry's snake.

After about an hour, the only information we could come up with, was the usual medical symbols. These, I am sure, were not the answer, plus the fact that a circled snake represents eternal love. As I returned to my car, I thought of all the time and effort, Noel and I, had put into this book. This would not have been possible if we both had not retired. This then begged the question, 'Did Harry wait for almost twenty years or as Mandy had suggested that he only died in the early 70's, thus making contact with me shortly after his demise?

I drove up to 'Uppermill' knowing that somewhere in one of those little backstreets was a second-hand bookshop that had survived 'donkey's years'. This small area was now covered with traffic yellow lines so it was no wonder that these shops had nearly all disappeared. I, like most drivers, avoid these parking problems as they are too expensive especially when the wardens are forever on the lookout to get you, ending up with a fine of £30. I paid exactly that once when my back wheel was just touching a white line in a side-street. Luckily, Noel taught me how to overcome this problem. 'Simply ask Harry for a 'Parking Angel', he said with a grin and believe it or not, it never fails.

As I walked up the steep, narrow, cobbled road, hoping it still was in existence, my thoughts turned again to the possibility that if it was not Harry that went down the lift shaft, in order, for whatever reason, to change his identity. If this was the case, then that was the reason he insisted I visit the 'Police Museum'; thus putting P.C. Marriot and higher powers in cahoots. But who then went down the lift shaft and how was it achieved? I decided not to go down that road until I had some evidence.

Damn it! I was now ambling past a row of quaint cottages covered in variegated ivy so I retraced my footsteps, for the only thing I could see in the distance was a line of trees. So I must have gone too far whilst contemplating Mandy's theory.

Luckily, I found it and had to duck my head as I entered this tiny shop with its old-fashioned bell above the door. Tingaling, Tingaling! As I inhaled the smell of the old books and dust, I fully expected to see a little wizened, old man but to my surprise, a very modern, middle-aged lady, clad in blue jeans and a red sweater emerged from the back of this pokey, little shop. There were wooden shelves from floor to ceiling, stacked with books of all shapes and sizes. Some were so dilapidated with broken spines and tattered, leather covers that they looked as if they would collapse into a heap on the floor.

As I gazed around and to my great surprise, everything was clearly marked into numerous sections i.e. 'History' and yes. 'Occult' etc. so I pounced at the same moment she was asking 'Can I help you'. 'Snakes' I said. Well, you should have seen the look on her face so I gathered my wits and explained further.

About a half an hour later, the little, old-fashioned bell, above the tiny, wooden door went 'tingaling' again as I made my triumphant exit, clutching a book by 'Philip Gardineer' titled 'Secret Society', one of which was the 'Serpent Cult'

Well, that was yet another one of Harry's educational tours but I was left disappointed as it did not give me the required information.

The 'Serpent Cult' is represented by a snake around a sword. This being symbolic of a fighting tool and has been with man for more than 4,000 years. It was also a symbol of wisdom and energy. Having read the entire book, cover to cover, none of the Secret Societies (Freemasons, Templars, Illuminati, and Nazis etc.) had the symbol that I was seeking.

The only snippet of interest that I read was that the snake around the sword was linked to the 'Templars'. They were very much associated with 'Robin Hood' and these tales also matched the format of 'King Arthur' ('In the tales of Robin Hood' written by Henry Gilbert (1912); there is a mention of a pig-like serpent)

This, of course, made me think why Harry had chosen the nickname 'Robin'?

Etymologically 'Robin' comes from the 'Norman; Robert' a form of the Germanic 'Hrodebert' and it originally meant 'famous or bright'. 'Robin Hood' is therefore 'Bright Robin'

This then brought me back to him being an ambassador.

Chapter 110

Harry must be having a right old barking session as I heard the postman; Oh, I wished he would not run away! It makes Harry think that he has chased him away again, perhaps. Anyway, it was good exercise up and down those stone steps.

I waited until he drove away and opened the front door to find a large, brown envelope sticking out of the post-box. So I tore it open, only to discover that the I.C.O. had turned down my request to reveal any information regarding Harry's work-place on the basis of Section 44 (2).

---

ico.
Information Commissioner's Office

Upholding information rights

Wycliffe House, Water Lane, Wilmslow, Cheshire, SK9 5AF
T. 0303 123 1113 F. 01625 524510
www.ico.org.uk

Liz Roberts

11 September 2014

Dear Ms Roberts

Freedom of Information Act 2000 (FOIA)
HM Revenue & Customs – FS50537767

Please find enclosed a decision notice relating to your complaint about a request for information that you submitted to HM Revenue & Customs.

Your complaint has been considered by the Commissioner and the decision notice sets out the reasons for the decision. If you disagree with the decision notice, you have the right to appeal to the First-tier Tribunal (Information Rights).

The Commissioner will publish this decision on the ICO website, but will remove all names and addresses of complainants. If the public authority also chooses to reproduce this decision notice, then the Commissioner expects similar steps to be taken.

I hope the above information is helpful.

Yours sincerely

Terna Waya
Senior Case Officer

Reference: FS50537767

Freedom of Information Act 2000 (FOIA)

Decision notice

Date: 11 September 2014

Public Authority: HM Revenue and Customs
Address: 100 Parliament Street
London
SW1A 2BQ

Complainant: Liz Roberts
Address:

Decision (including any steps ordered)

1. The complainant requested information relating to the employment records of a named person. The public authority neither confirmed nor denied whether it held the information requested on the basis of section 44(2) FOIA.

2. The Commissioner's decision is that the public authority was entitled to neither confirm nor deny whether it held the information requested on the basis of section 44(2).

3. No steps are required.

Request and response

4. Although the request was properly made under FOIA on 27 November 2013, the complainant had originally written to the public authority on 26 September 2013 in the following terms:

   '.....I am completing my family history and would like to know the following work record of a close relative. [Named Person] BORN 1906 in LANCASTER DIED 10TH December 1953 Age 47 [sic]. A qualified Teacher

   he taught from 1926 at ARDwick municipal School.......until its closure in July 1952 [sic]. But from 1943 until 1949 there is a gap of six years.

   His address from 1934 until his death. [Address redacted] st moss side m/c....'

5. The request above was made directly to the public authority's Records Retrieval Service which deals with requests for employment histories on a business as usual basis. This resulted in a number of exchanges between the complainant and the Records Retrieval team.

6. On 27 November 2013 the complainant made the following request through the public authority's *FOI Online Portal* which is dedicated to requests for information under FOIA:

   'Requesting information on; [Named Person], D.O.B 3RD February, 1906 @ [Address redacted] Lancaster. Died on 10th December 1953.'

7. The public authority responded on 29 November 2013. It refused to confirm or deny whether it held any information within the scope of the request on the basis of the exemption at section 44(2) FOIA.

8. On 18 December 2013 the complainant requested an internal review of the public authority's decision above. She queried the authority's response in view of her previous exchanges with the Records Retrieval team.[1] She also disagreed that confirming or denying whether the information requested was held by the authority would lead to the identification of [Named Person] because, in her own words; '....I have prior knowledge of the identity of [Named Person] and in fact identified that individual to HMRC rather than HMRC identifying him to me.'

9. Following an internal review the public authority wrote to the complainant on 17 April 2014.[2] It clarified the position in relation to her exchanges with the Records Retrieval team and upheld the original decision in relation to the exemption at section 44(2) FOIA.

---

[1] The Commissioner cannot go into details of the exchanges between the complainant and the Records Retrieval team as to do otherwise would defeat the purpose of the exemption at section 44(2).

[2] The lengthy delay in issuing the internal review was due to the confusion that arose as result of the complainant's correspondence with both the FOI team and the Records Retrieval Service team during the relevant period.

Reference: FS50537767

10. The Commissioner should mention at this stage that any responses provided by the Records Retrieval Service team to the complainant in connection with the request of 26 September 2013 is outside the remit of his jurisdiction under section 50 FOIA because those responses would not have been issued to the complainant under the terms of FOIA. The Records Retrieval team would have taken the identity of the complainant into account before responding. The FOIA is however applicant blind and the subsequent responses issued by the public authority to the complainant under FOIA clearly reflect that fact. Therefore, the Commissioner did not take into account any of the responses issued to the complainant by the Records Retrieval Service team during the course of his investigation because they do not constitute FOIA responses. To be clear, the Commissioner has only referred to the request of 26 September 2013 in order to provide some context to the subsequent request of 27 November 2013 and to his findings further below.

Scope of the case

11. The complainant contacted the Commissioner on 7 April 2014[3] to complain about the way her request for information had been handled.

12. During the course of the investigation, she informed the Commissioner that she did not request *details of* [Named Person]'s *employment records from 1943 to 1949*. Rather, she wanted to know where [Named Person] *worked from 1943 to 1949*.

13. The scope of the Commissioner's investigation therefore, was to determine whether the public authority was entitled to rely on section 44(2) to neither confirm nor deny whether it held any information about *where* [Named Person] *worked from 1943 to 1949*.

Reasons for decision

Section 44(2)(a)

14. Section 1(1) FOIA provides two rights to applicants. They are:

---

[3] This was initially to complain about the fact the authority had yet to complete its internal review. After the review had been completed, she asked the Commissioner for a decision on the application of section 44(2) by the authority.

Reference: FS50537767

a) The right to be informed in writing by the public authority whether or not it holds the information requested by the applicant, and

b) If so, the right to have that information communicated.

15. Both these rights are subject to exemptions in FOIA.

16. The right in section 1(1)(a) is commonly referred to as a public authority's "duty to confirm or deny" whether it holds information.

17. Section 44 of FOIA (prohibitions on disclosure) states:

'(1) Information is exempt information if its disclosure (otherwise than under this Act) by the public authority holding it-

(a)   is prohibited by or under any enactment,

(b)   is incompatible with any EU obligation, or

(c)   would be punishable as a contempt of court.

(2) The duty to confirm or deny does not arise if the confirmation or denial that would have to be given to comply with section 1(1)(a) would (apart from this Act) fall within any of paragraphs (a) to (c) of subsection (1).

18. As can be seen from the above, a public authority is, by virtue of the provisions in section 44(2), excluded from confirming or denying whether it holds information requested by an applicant if to do otherwise (ie to issue a confirmation or denial) is prohibited by or under any enactment, is incompatible with any EU obligation, or would be punishable as a contempt of court.

19. The exemptions at section 44 are absolute. This means that they are not subject to a public interest test. Once it is determined that any of the exemptions is engaged, a public authority is not required to consider whether there is a public interest in confirming or denying whether it holds the information requested or in disclosing the information held (in the case of section 44(1)(a)).

20. The public authority submitted that to confirm or deny whether it holds the information requested by the applicant would itself reveal information considered exempt from disclosure on the basis of section 44(1)(a). It explained that sections 18(1) and 23(1) of the Commissioners for Revenue and Customs Act 2005 (CRCA) prohibit the authority from disclosing any information held in connection with a function of HM Revenue and Customs under FOIA.

Reference: FS50537767

Commissioner's findings

21. Section 18(1) CRCA states:

    'Revenue and Customs officials may not disclose information which is held by the Revenue and Customs in connection with a function of the Revenue and Customs.'

22. The Commissioner is satisfied that the requested information if held, would be held by the public authority in connection with its functions. The places where [Named Person] was employed from 1943 to 1949 (which would form part of his employment records) if held by the public authority, would be held in connection with its function to assess and collect tax.

23. Although there are exceptions to section 18(1) contained in sections 18(2) and (3) CRCA, section 23 CRCA was amended by section 19(4) of the Borders, Citizenship and Immigration Act 2009 to make clear that sections 18(2) and (3) are to be disregarded when considering disclosure of revenue and customs information relating to a person under FOIA.

24. Notwithstanding the above, section 23(1) CRCA states:

    'Revenue and customs information relating to a person, the disclosure of which is prohibited by section 18(1), is exempt information by virtue of section 44(1)(a) of the Freedom of Information Act 2000…..if its disclosure

    (a) would specify the identity of the person to whom the information relates, or

    (b) would enable the identity of such a person to be deduced.

    (2)Except as specified in subsection (1), information the disclosure of which is prohibited by section 18(1) is not exempt information for the purposes of section 44(1)(a) of the Freedom of Information Act 2000.'

25. Therefore, information prohibited from disclosure by virtue of section 18(1) CRCA (in this case, on the basis that if held, it would be held by the authority in connection with its functions) is exempt information by virtue of section 44(1)(a) FOIA only if its disclosure would identify a 'person'.

26. It is clear that confirming or denying whether the information requested by the complainant is held by the public authority would identify [Named Person]. The request clearly mentions [Named Person] and his residential addresses in the relevant period.

27. The Commissioner finds that confirming or denying whether the information requested is held by the public authority would reveal information which if held by the authority, would be held in connection with its functions to assess and collect tax. He also finds that confirming or denying whether the information requested is held would reveal the identity of [Named Person].

Reference: FS50537767

Right of appeal

30. Either party has the right to appeal against this decision notice to the First-tier Tribunal (Information Rights). Information about the appeals process may be obtained from:

    First-tier Tribunal (Information Rights)
    GRC & GRP Tribunals,
    PO Box 9300,
    LEICESTER,
    LE1 8DJ

    Tel: 0300 1234504
    Fax: 0870 739 5836
    Email: GRC@hmcts.gsi.gov.uk
    Website: www.justice.gov.uk/tribunals/general-regulatory-chamber

31. If you wish to appeal against a decision notice, you can obtain information on how to appeal along with the relevant forms from the Information Tribunal website.

32. Any Notice of Appeal should be served on the Tribunal within 28 (calendar) days of the date on which this decision notice is sent.

Signed ....

Alexander Ganotis
Group Manager
Information Commissioner's Office
Wycliffe House
Water Lane
Wilmslow
Cheshire
SK9 5AF

As luck would have it, I would be going to Patsy's on the next Thursday and would ask her to appeal to the First-Tier Tribunal for me. The other thing which came to mind was to ask John to try and find a picture of the four-pillared, white house which if Harry was really an ambassador, it must be either in Russia or France. Being at war with Germany, the British Embassy must surely have been vacated if we had one prior to the War.

I decided to check with John to see if he could come up with any other ideas. I know he will humour me, due to the fact that he believes I am slightly mad.

I settled back home after my four day, successful trip to London which I really enjoyed as it was great to see them all. I was, especially, delighted to see my granddaughter, Anna, who was growing up to be quite a young lady.

Patsy had processed my appeal which I had posted 'recorded delivery' and as for the 'White House', I was really quite chuffed with John. He had followed my description of the house and low and behold, he found a picture that fitted exactly my description, 'The British Embassy, Moscow' during the war years. Needless to say, John's face looked 'a picture' (excuse the pun) when he said 'What a good memory you have, Liz, to be able to describe it so well from an old photograph'. 'I have never physically seen it before, Got it from Harry in Spirit', I replied and that was that.

The British Embassy, Moscow

Now, I had no way of knowing if I was on a 'wild goose chase' or not so another session with Harry was required. Now, I could foresee a problem, being that I had so much information in my head that it was going to be difficult to separate his thoughts and pictures from my own; i.e. If I ask him if I am correct about the 'White House'?, I may automatically think that he said 'Yes' because that was what I thought.

So, with his help, I would have to try and devise a plan so that he could give me the answers without interference from me. I had already ruled out using a foreign language as I have enough problems spelling in English, my foreign language spelling skills would be atrocious if anyone could understand them in the first place so on with my 'thinking cap'.

Chapter 111

So Mandy arrived a week later and we settled ourselves comfortably before the session. I sat in the rocking chair with Mandy opposite me. Having lit a couple of candles, we commenced our communication with Harry. The only problem was that we still did not have a clue what to ask him to do, in order to get the answers independently, ensuring they were not coming from my mind. So, again, we repeated 'Give us answers that we cannot understand but can interpret/ translate later.

The first picture to appear in my mind's eye was of a small aircraft flying over murky waters with a man who appeared to be taking aerial photographs. This entire scene was in black and white so it was in the past.

My mind went blank and then as if out of nowhere, I could see the letter 'M' which repeated itself on the stone steps; just as the 'dog-like image' did which turned out to be a laughing clown, found on the Satawan Islands.

A minute later, I saw letters firstly on the wall and then in the old pictures on the wall. They were coming so fast that I could hardly keep up with them. I just kept saying them out loud as Mandy, feverishly, wrote them down. I could see the letter 'D' again and again, then 'C' and so forth. My mind suddenly went blank so I knew Harry had gone.

Well, we stared and stared at what Mandy had written down and we were still clueless until it dawned on us that they were 'Roman Numerals'. We had two 'Ls' and a 'V' and the problem was that apart from the letters 'I' and 'V' which we knew as five and one,, we had no idea what the others meant. The only conclusion we came up with was that Harry was giving us a date.

Well, well, well! Bloody hell!, of course, something we could not understand but could interpret later. We fell about laughing about how clever he really was.

Well, the librarians in Delph would be in for a treat. I would certainly make their day when no historical or spy novels were needed on my next trip there; just a book on 'Roman Numerals' which will give me the key to the placement order of the letters.

Not long afterwards, I duly went to the library and you should have seen their faces as I entered the building. Only one of the ladies managed a forced, half smile whilst the other lady scurried off to the back room, muttering something. It was a good job that I was 'thick skinned' so I smiled sweetly whilst repeating my request.

Now, these librarians were all elderly volunteers, otherwise the library would have closed many months ago due to the 'Council' cutbacks. So if it was not for their goodwill, I would be forced to either travel to Uppermill or Oldham. As it is, I can walk the mile or so to down to the village thus no parking problems.

The sweet smile stayed transfixed on my face as Harry stood at the side of me and obviously, I could not acknowledge his presence, after all, they thought I was barking mad already; no need to make it worse. Of course, this was not the first time that Harry had done this, purely for his own amusement. He knew how difficult I find it to keep a straight face and not fall about laughing. My strategy was to ignore him whilst the librarian consulted the computer, in a brave effort to comply with my request.

Meanwhile, I was browsing the book shelves in the hope that something would 'jump out' at me but I was having no luck so I wandered back to where she was sitting at the computer. There on her computer screen was a list of Roman Numerals staring at me. 'Can you print them out for me' I asked, politely.

I was thinking to myself how smoothly this was all going when suddenly, the printer went 'haywire' and for the life of her, she couldn't get it to work. She had now a much stressed expression on her bespectacled face and I could read her thoughts: 'God, I am never going to get rid of this old bat now'. With that, I stifled a grin and proceeded to ask Harry to fix the printer. But too late, he had gone as I had ignored him and after about ten minutes, neither of them could get it to print. My only option was to copy them down, M—1000, D—500, C—100, L—50, V—5, I—1, X—10. But how the devil was I going to work out in what order they went. I didn't have a clue other than there were two examples at the bottom of the sheet; No. 39 in Roman Numerals was XXX1X AND No. 91 was XC1. I set off home in the vain hope that I could work them out for myself.

Now this proved to be an absolute nightmare as after umpteen hours, I had definitely lost the will to live. No matter how I tried, I could not get two separate dates of four digits each, using all the letters which Mandy had written down. Unless I was suffering from some sort of 'learning disability', my reasoning was that there were too many letters for just one date.

My only option now, was to ask Harry how to plus and minus them. Oh! How I wished we had been taught all this at school as it would have been far more advantageous than 'cookery' and 'italic writing'. Having said that, I spent half my time 'wagging it' off school and would not have taken much notice anyway.

I could now sense that Harry had responded to my request and with that in mind and a 'wing & a prayer', I came up with the following; MDC11L—-The year of our Lord, 1648; MDCDL1V—1954.

The '1954' I was not sure about because where was I to place the 1, before or after the 'V'. Subtracting 1V = adding it by placing it in front of the 'V' makes it 1956.

I knew Mandy, Helen and I were dog training the next day so it would have to wait. Patience not being one of my strongest attributes and God knows, I may not have many of them but I didn't have to wait too long for them to get into their computers and ascertain what world events happened on those dates.

Well, one could have knocked us 'down with a feather' as we just could not believe our eyes. Having asked for World Events, this is what they came up with; (Both 1648 and 1954 are important dates in this article)

I will never really know if I had translated the Roman Numerals correctly but as they say; 'the proof of the pudding is in the eating'

Seventeen Moments in Soviet History

1954: The Gift of Crimea
The Gift of Crimea

Party Central Committee, USSR Council of Ministers and Presidium of USSR Supreme Soviet, On the 300th Anniversary of Ukraine's Reunification with Russia. December 9, 1953

Original Source: Pravda and Izvestiia, 9 December 1953, p. 1.

The Communist Party Central Committee, the USSR Council of Ministers and the Presidium of the USSR Supreme Soviet have adopted a decree calling for widespread observance of the 300th anniversary of the Ukraine's reunification with Russia, which falls in January, 1954, as an outstanding historical event, a great national holiday of the Ukrainian and Russian peoples and of all peoples of the Soviet Union.

The decree states that this remarkable event was the consummation of the Ukrainian people's many centuries of struggle against foreign enslavers to reunify with the Russian people in a single Russian state.

The Ukrainian people, who have sprung from a single root of the ancient Russian people, are bound with the Russian people by unity of origin, geographical proximity and a common historical development and have constantly struggled for unification with the fraternal Russian people. For a long time the Ukraine was under the yoke of foreign bondage and suffered terrible ruin and devastation from the aggressive attacks of nomadic hordes of the Turko-Tatar Khans and the oppression of the Polish szlachta. The Ukrainian people, threatened with annihilation, struggled constantly against the oppression of foreign enslavers.

In the 1648-1654 war of liberation the Ukrainian people, under the leadership of Bogdan Khmelnitskii, eminent statesman and military leader, fought heroically to free the Ukraine from the yoke of the Polish szlachta and reunite their country with Russia. Bogdan Khmelnitskii reflected the Ukrainian people's desire for close union with the Russian people and led the course of the formation of Ukrainian statehood with a correct understanding of its tasks and perspectives, seeing in unification with the Great Russian people the salvation of the Ukrainians. Therein lies his contribution to history.

The oppressed peasantry, fighting to liberate the Ukraine from foreign enslavement and opposing the social yoke of the feudal serf owners, became the main and decisive force in the war of liberation. The Ukrainian people's struggle against the Polish szlachta found wide response and sympathy among the Polish peasantry, who suffered from the yoke of the Polish feudal lords. The constant help and support of the Russian state and the Russian masses in particular promoted the broad scope of the people's movement in the war of liberation and to its outstanding successes.

The Pereiaslavl Council's decision Jan. 8 (18), 1654, to reunify the Ukraine with Russia, was a mighty expression of the will of the freedom-loving Ukrainian people and a manifestation of their age-old desires and hopes and marked a turning point in their life and was the consummation of this nationwide struggle.

The Ukrainian people, who have forever linked their fate with their blood brothers, the fraternal Russian people, whom they have always considered their reliable champions and allies, saved and preserved themselves as a nation by this decision.

The reunification of the Ukraine with Russia, despite the fact that the Tsar and landowners then ruled Russia, had increasing importance in the further political, economic and cultural development of the Ukrainian and Russian peoples. Despite the reactionary policy of Tsarism, the Russian and Ukrainian feudal lords and the bourgeoisie, the unification of the two great Slavic peoples drew together the peoples of Russia and the Ukraine, who chose the only correct path in the common struggle against all foreign enemies, against common oppressors, against serf owners and the bourgeoisie, against Tsarism and capitalist slavery.

Despite the reactionary Tsarist policy of brutal national and colonial oppression, the best sons of the Russian people recognized the right of the Ukraine to national independence and, together with advanced representatives of the Ukrainian people, fought against the shameful policy of inciting the Russian peoples against each other, a policy pursued by the Russian and Ukrainian landowners and the bourgeoisie and their myrmidons, the great-power chauvinists and Ukrainian nationalists.

The consanguineous bond and indissoluble friendship between the two great fraternal peoples developed and grew stronger on the basis of common struggle against oppressors and foreign invaders, who encroached on Russian and Ukrainian lands. The great achievements of this friendship clearly and convincingly expose the anti-popular nature of bourgeois nationalist distortions

> in evaluating the historical importance of the Ukraine's reunification with Russia and show clearly the futility of all attempts by the bourgeois nationalists to undermine and violate the indissoluble union of the Ukrainian, Russian and other peoples of the Soviet Union.
>
> The appearance on the historical arena of the Russian proletariat, the most revolutionary in the world, and the Communist Party, its militant vanguard, had decisive importance in the further development of the Russian, Ukrainian and all other peoples of Russia.
>
> Under the leadership of the Communist Party, the peoples of Russia, having accomplished the great October socialist revolution, liberated themselves from the chains of capitalist slavery and opened up the path to socialism for the peoples. The Ukrainian peoples were the first to follow the Russian people along the path to socialism and they finally realized their age-old dream: establishing their own national Ukrainian state and beginning a new and truly glorious epoch of their history.
>
> The fraternal union and friendship between the Russian and Ukrainian peoples grew stronger and was tempered in the great October socialist revolution, in the fire of the Civil War against internal counterrevolution and foreign military intervention, in the course of social construction and in the historical battles of the great patriotic war against the German fascist invaders.
>
> As a result of the world-wide historic victories of the peoples of the Soviet Union and thanks to the realization of the Leninist-Stalinist national policy, the Ukrainian people achieved their national rebirth, reuniting all Ukrainian lands into a single Ukraine Soviet socialist state.
>
> Having achieved tremendous successes in economic and cultural construction, the Russian and Ukrainian people, together with all our country's fraternal peoples, are now advancing along the path to communism under the leadership of the Communist Party.
>
> The inviolable and eternal friendship of the Ukrainian and Russian peoples and of all peoples of the Soviet Union is a guarantee of national independence and freedom and of the flowering of the Ukrainian people's national culture and prosperity, as well as of other peoples of the Soviet Union.
>
> The decree of the Party Central Committee, USSR Council of Ministers and Presidium of the USSR Supreme Soviet requires that local Party and Soviet organizations extensively observe this notable historic event–the 300th anniversary of the Ukraine's reunification with Russia–as a great national holiday and organize lectures, reports and talks devoted to this important event in the history of our fatherland and to further strengthening friendship among the peoples of the Soviet Union.
>
> Source: Current Digest of the Soviet Press. Vol. V, No. 49 (1954), p. 10

Harry had taken me right back to Russia. What are the odds of that happening? The British Embassy in Moscow; the statement of Mr Musgrave (solicitor); 'he was behind the Iron Curtain'. So what were Teasdale's political affiliations?

We wondered if we could find any further information regarding the Crimea during 2014 but nothing came up

I do know that I see 'conspiracies'' everywhere, for I have a vivid imagination but if one looks at the top of the page 'Party Central Committee', the date is different and I don't understand why December 9th, 1953?. Harry went down the lift shaft on the 7th December, 1953 and died on the 10th. What are the odds on that? Hopefully, Noel will be able to throw some light on the subject.

I was beginning to view the poem 'Catching the Cat' in a completely different light. Firstly, why do I recall it so well?; Because Mr Teasdale had me recite it and still for the life of me, I cannot remember where I learned to memorise it so well and who taught it to me.

On reflection, it must have been Teasdale, for as a young child, I would have hardly told him what I wanted to recite and, for that matter, it was not a poem a 7 or 8 yr. old would choose.

If I dissect the words to mean something, then Teasdale is represented by the 'Cat' and the 'mice' sat around the pantry shelf would be the 'Powers that be' sat around a large oak desk.

There is an old saying which my mother and many of her generation would use to insult men who did not fight in WWII; 'He is a mouse, not a man' or another common one; 'Is he a man or a mouse?'

So if the mice didn't kill the cat (the word 'If' being a very big word) then who went down the lift shaft. If that was the case, then Teasdale was very much alive when he shouted 'Elizabeth, Elizabeth' whilst I stood at the traffic lights with my mother. But why would he do that? Because he was my father, wanting a last glimpse of me before he went wherever. He knew full well the changing of my name from 'Beth' to 'Elizabeth' would be something that would always stick in my mind. Just like the poem had done.

As I was placing the carbon paper between two fresh sheets of A4, I was mentally mulling over the three dates which had cropped up i.e. 1648, 1954 and 1956. The latter I assumed was incorrect due to the fact that 1954 belonged with 1648. So, now I was unsure but the next time I am speaking to Noel, my walking encyclopaedia, I would definitely ask him about 'World Events, 1956'.

Chapter 112

I eventually caught up with the oracle, Noel, and yes, the year 1956 was a very eventful year. Of course, this was the year that 'The Oracle' was born; (he did stress that this was probably the most important event of that year) but the rest, in comparison, was no less significant. In March 20th, 1956, Russia ran 'Nuclear Tests' as did America. The West also tested the first airborne, hydrogen bomb (missile). Britain, Russia and the US were also flexing their muscles.

I was not going to assume anything which I had promised myself but I did wonder where all this was leading. Russia seemed to crop up, time and time again. If I reflected back to the symbol of the snake ring as being an ambassador then surely Harry was behind the Iron Curtain. All these dates took me in the same direction.

I checked out Harry's inquest details again, thinking that a time lapse of only six days could be significant for a cover-up. It appeared, as far as I could tell, to be normal procedure. It makes me wonder why, in this day and age with all our modern technology, it takes so much longer. So I must congratulate them on their efficiency.

It became obvious from the scant information I could find during the same period of time as Harry's inquest that eye witnesses were routinely called as you can see from the following extracts from the 'Manchester Evening News; December 31st, 1953

So I rest my case. Why did this not apply in Harry's inquest?. The time frame was the same and both these cases occurred over the Christmas period, not just at 'weekend'. 'The plot thickens' as they say.

I started turning back the pages of my mind to the original story which I believed was that Harry had killed himself due to being charged along with other individuals for the crime of 'Homosexuality'

Mate died in rescue bid

ONE of two men who lost their lives at a West Cumberland quarry on Monday died trying to save his workmate it was stated at to-day's inquest at Cockermouth.

The inquest was on John Simpson, aged 56, a lime burner and Ernest Lomas, aged 33, a mill hand, who tried to save Simpson.

Simpson, it was explained, climbed down a ladder into the kiln to recover a shovel. A workmate went down to help him, but was forced back by fumes.

Then Lomas and a friend tried to save Simpson, but the friend was forced to climb out of the kiln and he blacked out. Lomas was unable to get out.

Recording a verdict of accidental death, the jury said that Lomas gave his life for his fellow-worker.

Drama of "hello" boy's father: "I offer body to science"

MR ARTHUR ANDERTON, father of eight-year-old David Anderton, the Worsley "Hello" boy whose body was found in a brook after a four day search, said at the Wakefield inquest to-day that he wished the body to be bequeathed to medical science for research

After agreeing David's mental faculties had never developed properly, he said. "We feel he was sent to the world for some purpose - perhaps to further the cause of backward children.

"There does not seem to be a lot done for them," he continued. "and we feel that if the body is taken for research it may help children at present handicapped or even those unborn."

"FOUND DROWNED"

Doctor Charles Arthur St. Hill, Home Office pathologist, said the body had been in the water for three or four days and was unfitted for scientific examination.

The Manchester County Coroner, Mr F G Ralphs, recorded a verdict that the boy, who lived in Partington-street Worsley, was found drowned

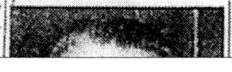

He said it was "simply a case of a child eluding the vigilance of his guardians—in this case devoted parents—and straying from home."

Water had an attraction for children.

Mr. Anderton said all David could say "in his little fashion" was "Hello". He never cried even when he bumped himself.

He did not get into mischief or danger. He liked to go to the boxroom and look through the window. Everyone knew him and said "hello".

WANTED FREEDOM.

About 18 months ago he strayed from the garden, but his mother ran after him. Two men caught him.

On another occasion, Christmas Day 1952, he tried to get away again. He was caught.

He always had an urge to leave the house. He wanted to be free. Special locks had been put on the doors.

On Christmas Day, Mr. Anderton continued, David spent a normal day. After tea a neighbour came across to say she had seen the front door open. David was missing.

David Pritchard, of Wordsworth-street, Little Hulton, said that he was searching for the boy when he found him lying across the stream.

Mr Anderton, at the end of the inquest, said he and his wife were grateful to the many people who had helped in the search.

The coroner thanked him for his public spirited and unselfish research offer. He issued a burial order.

3 Britons

Both Steve and I had searched court records for any evidence of this and found absolutely nothing. I started wondering if the time frame was incorrect i.e. 1943 as opposed to 1953. Could he have been in prison from March, 1943 until September, 1949? I did not hold much hope with this theory, for surely, he would not have been allowed back into the teaching profession. So I searched the 'Manchester Evening News' and the 'Chronicle' for any such charges or court cases of that nature from 1942 to 1944 and drew a complete blank.

I was now beginning to think that these rumours i.e. homosexual, paedophilia and even his suicide might be fictional. Mark Twain stated 'Lies get around the world before Truth gets its trousers on'

World Events of 1956

- Egypt takes control of the Suez Canal.
- Morocco gains independence from Spain and France.
- There is an unsuccessful uprising of Polish workers against the communist rulers.
- 2nd Arab Israeli war is fought.
- Soviets crush anti-Communist uprisings in Hungary.
- Hollywood inundates the Western world with an endless string of "B" movies.
- French minister Pierre Mendès-France resigns due to his government's policy on Algeria.
- The US tests fully serviceable Hydrogen bomb over the Bikini Atoll in the Pacific, with the equivalent force of 10 million tons of TNT.

- Elvis Presley first makes a splash in the US.
- The first practical videotape machines are introduced.
- Great Britain abolishes death penalty.
- The hard-disk drive is invented by IBM. It contained 50, 24-inch disks. Its total storage capacity was 5MBytes.
- The European singer Dalida has her first big hit with "Bambino". She goes on to become one of the biggest selling recording artists in history.

With the Russian theory firmly lodged in my mind, I contacted Noel for his assistance. Leaving no stone unturned, he researched the 'Special Operations Executive' (S.O.E.) for some official secrets have currently been released regarding WWII. He found that there were a number of S.O.E. individuals whose names had been listed but no B.B. Teasdale.

The list was not complete and for whatever reason, a quantity of information was still sat in the archives gathering dust and these probably would never be released. Well, if I was looking for transparency, I suspect I just might have to wait for the 'Pink Flying Pig.'

One example of information, not disclosed after WWII and in the 'Cold War' was that of English, 1950's, Soviet Union spy, Cedric Belfrage who was never charged with treason. This was due to the fact that it would have been a complete embarrassment for the government of the time, to apprehend him so he got away with it. Of course, the government were perfectly aware he was spying and one wonders where their priorities lay and how many British deaths he was responsible for.

The other little snippet of information that I stumbled upon was the existence of the 'British Expeditionary Force' which I believe was connected to 'M.I.7.' Noel also explored this but found it only to be active abroad from 1938/39 to 1940 thus ruling Harry out as he was still teaching at Ardwick Municipal School until 1943

This was like looking for 'a needle in a haystack'. Where the devil was he between the years, 1943 to 49?

Chapter 113

I then received the following letter regarding my appeal and I was very interested to see how they would respond;

HM Courts & Tribunals Service

First-tier Tribunal
General Regulatory Chamber
PO Box 9300
Leicester
LE1 8DJ

Website: www.justice.gov.uk/tribunals
Telephone: 0300 123 4504
Fax: 0116 249 4253
Email: grc@hmcts.gsi.gov.uk

Ms E Roberts

Our Ref: EA.2014.0253

15th October 2014

Dear Parties,

Re: EA.2014.0253 Elizabeth Roberts v Information Commissioner

Appeal received

The Tribunal received an appeal from Elizabeth Roberts on 13th October 2014.
The appeal was late and has been accepted by the Registrar.
A copy of the appeal papers is attached/enclosed.

Respondent to respond to appeal

The next stage is for the respondent to respond to the appeal[1]. This response is to be served within 28 days of the date on which the respondent receives the appeal – assuming receipt today that would make it due by 12th November 2014.

Would the appellant please wait until receipt of the response before sending any additional documents to the Tribunal office.

Hearing to be fixed

The appellant has asked that this matter is dealt with at a hearing. Please would parties let the Tribunal know by 29th October 2014 their availability for the period from 26 January 2015 to 16th March 2015.

When letting the Tribunal know about their availability would parties please also let the Tribunal and other party (or parties) know if they intend to call any witnesses at the hearing

Bundles

I enclose a copy of the Good Practice Guide about bundles. Parties are asked to think at this stage about what documents are relevant to the issues and how they can best be presented to the Tribunal. At a later stage, the Tribunal will write to parties to ask whether agreement has been reached about who will prepare the necessary bundles and the date on which they will be provided.

---

[1] Per *Rule 23* of the *Tribunal Procedure (First-tier Tribunal) (General Regulatory Chamber) Rules 2009*

Other matters

When writing to the Tribunal each party should send a copy of their correspondence to the other party (or parties).

The Tribunal office seeks to deal with cases in a way which avoids unnecessary formality.

However, if you believe that a formal direction from the Tribunal's Registrar will assist to progress your case, please request a direction in writing, explaining why you believe the direction will assist.

Should you require any further information, contact the tribunal or you may like to look at our website http://www.justice.gov.uk/tribunals/information-rights.

This decision was made by the Registrar, a party may apply in writing within 14 days for the decision to be considered afresh by a Judge.

Yours sincerely

Aisha Iqbal

(On behalf of Yvonne Lowe)

Hearing Bundles – Good Practice Guide 2014

"FOIA" means the Freedom of Information Act 2000

"EIR means the Environmental Information Regulations 2004

The overriding objective

The overriding objective of the Tribunal is that cases are dealt with fairly and justly.

<u>Dealing with a case fairly and justly includes</u>: *avoiding unnecessary formality and doing what is possible to enable a party to participate fully in the proceedings.*

> *The parties will work together to ensure that all relevant documents are before the Tribunal[1].*

<u>Dealing with a case fairly and justly includes</u>: *dealing with cases proportionately.*

> *The parties will only seek the assistance of the Tribunal by way of requesting directions if matters are unable to be agreed and/or a party is causing a case to become disproportionate because of the irrelevance of documentation that they seek to include in the bundle.*

Bundles in Information Rights Cases

1. It is always important that the Tribunal understands each party's arguments in an appeal. To enable this to happen, it is helpful for the Tribunal to have a bundle of papers provided in advance of a hearing.

2. For a bundle to help the Tribunal to focus on relevant issues, it is important that parties consider carefully what needs to be in the bundle.

Who should prepare the bundle?

3. Usually, the ICO (the Information Commissioner being the first Respondent in every appeal) will agree to prepare the bundle where the Appellant is an unrepresented litigant in person.

4. It may be that when the appellant is a public authority, a commercial entity or legally represented that they will agree to prepare the bundle instead of the ICO.

   What should be in the bundle?

5. The bundle will usually include a copy of:

   5.1. the disputed Decision Notice

   5.2. the Notice of Appeal

   5.3. the Respondent's Response (and any Response by Additional Parties)

---

[1] The ICO is of course aware of their duty to put before the Tribunal all relevant evidence regardless of whether it is favourable to their own case or not – CIS/0473/2007 paras 36-37, a decision of Judge Jacobs, when a Social Security Commissioner

- 5.4. the Appellant's Reply/Replies (and any Reply submitted by Additional Parties)
- 5.5. copies of all orders and directions made by the Tribunal including any requests for directions made by any party to the proceedings
- 5.6. the document requesting the information, the Public Authority's response (i.e. s.17 letter) and any document from the applicant requesting an internal review of the decision and the Public Authority's response to that request
- 5.7. any other necessary and relevant documents
- 5.8. all witness statements to be relied on

6. If a document to be included in the bundle is illegible a typed copy, to be provided by the party relying on that document, will be included in the bundle next to it, suitably cross-referenced.

7. The bundle will be kept as relevant and compact as possible.

8. The bundle will contain an index with a description of each document and the page number.

9. The documents will be in the bundles filed chronologically in the sequence listed above.

10. The bundle will be paginated and bound[2]. Each bundle will be clearly marked with the case name and appeal reference.

11. If the documents are unable to be contained in a single binder or file, a core bundle will be prepared containing the core documents essential to the proceedings, with references to the supplementary documents in the other bundles.

12. The party preparing the bundle will supply the other party/parties with 1 copy each of the prepared bundle. 4 copies will be supplied to the Tribunal.

13. Any documents (such as the requested information that is the subject of the appeal) that have been ordered to be disclosed to the Tribunal but not to one or more of the parties (see the *Practice Note – Closed Material in Information Rights Cases* dated May 2012) must be included in a separate bundle clearly marked "Closed Bundle". This bundle will also contain any closed witness statement(s) which concern the confidential information. The document(s), witness statement(s), skeletons and bundle must be clearly marked: **"Not to be disclosed to [name of relevant party] or to the public"**. This information will not be disclosed to any person except with the consent of the party who provided the information. The closed bundle will usually be prepared by the public authority if it is a party to the appeal. In other cases the ICO will prepare the closed bundle.

---

[2] Due to the risk of ring binders getting damaged in the post, the Tribunal does not require the party preparing the bundles to place them in ring binders prior to posting. If the bundles are not placed in a ring binder or lever arch file, the party should use treasury tags (or similar) to keep the bundles in order

> 14. The party preparing the closed bundle will supply the Tribunal with 4 copies.
>
> *Bundles sent with ICO's Response*
>
> 15. In the following cases, the ICO will usually send bundles to the Tribunal and the Appellant with their Response[3]:
>   15.1. When they have found that the information is not held by the public authority (*s.1 FOIA, Reg.3 EIR*).
>   15.2. The issue is vexatious request (*s.14 FOIA*).
>   15.3. The issue is cost of compliance exceeding the appropriate limit (*s.12 FOIA*).
>   15.4. The issue is the request is manifestly unreasonable (*Reg. 12(4)(b) EIR*).
>   15.5. When the ICO is likely to have nothing to add to the papers they already possess in connection with the case.
>
> *Bundles not sent with ICO's Response*
>
> 16. If it is an Oral Hearing, the bundles will usually be sent to the Tribunal and parties no later than 6 weeks in advance of the hearing date[4].
>
> 17. If it is a Paper Hearing, the bundles will usually be sent to the Tribunal and parties no later than 4 weeks after the last Reply is due.
>
> *Bundles of Authorities*
>
> 18. If the ICO refers to a decision which is binding upon the FTT (i.e. that of the Upper Tribunal or a Court of Higher Authority, they will provide a copy of that authority to the Tribunal and the other party/parties.

Well, the postman was back again, I never knew I was so popular and Harry was having a right, old, barking session. I guess he was feeling lonely though Mandy and I had been looking to find another 'Bess'. We looked at various rescue centres i.e. 'Dog Trust', 'R.S.P.C.A.' etc. but had not seen what I wanted.

HM Courts & Tribunals Service

First-tier Tribunal
General Regulatory Chamber
PO Box 9300
Leicester
LE1 8DJ

Website: www.justice.gov.uk/tribunals
Telephone: 0300 12345 04
Fax: 0870 739 5836
Email: grc@hmcts.gsi.gov.uk

Ms E Roberts

EA/2014/0253

10th November 2014

Dear Ms Roberts

The Tribunal has received a copy of the commissioner response and you too should have received a copy. You may if you wish, submit a written reply to it, to the Tribunal and send a copy to the commissioner within 14 days of the date that the commissioner sent the response to you.

After 14 days, I shall place the case papers before the Tribunal registrar, for any case management that might be necessary.

Yours sincerely,

Yvonne Lowe

Clerk to the Tribunal

0116 249 4143

IN THE MATTER OF AN APPEAL TO THE FIRST TIER TRIBUNAL (INFORMATION RIGHTS)
UNDER SECTION 57 OF THE FREEDOM OF INFORMATION ACT 2000

EA/2014/0253

BETWEEN:-

ELIZABETH ROBERTS   Appellant

-And-

THE INFORMATION COMMISSIONER

Respondent

RESPONSE
BY THE INFORMATION COMMISSIONER

Introduction

1. This Response is served by the Information Commissioner ('The Commissioner') in accordance with Rule 23 of the Tribunal Procedure (First Tier Tribunal) (General Regulatory Chamber) Rules 2009 in reply to an appeal against the Commissioner's Decision Notice FS50537767. The appeal is brought under section 57 of the Freedom of Information Act 2000 ("the Act").

2. The Commissioner intends to oppose this appeal. The grounds upon which he relies are set out below.

Legislative Framework

3. Under section 1(1) of The Act a person who has made a request to a 'public authority' for information is, subject to other provisions of the Act: (a) entitled to be informed in writing whether it holds the information requested (section 1(1) (a)) and (b) if it does, to have that information communicated to him (section 1(1) (b)).

4. The duty to provide the requested information imposed under section 1(1) (b) will not arise where the information is itself exempted under provisions contained in Part II of the Act. The exemptions provided for under Part II fall into two classes: absolute exemptions and qualified exemptions. Where the information is subject to a qualified exemption, it will only be exempted from disclosure if, in all the circumstances of the case, the public interest in maintaining the exemption outweighs the public interest in disclosing the information (this is the public interest test – see section 2(2) of the Act).

5. Section 44 of the Act provides (in so far as it is relevant to this appeal):-

   '(1) Information is exempt information if its disclosure (otherwise than under this Act) by the public authority holding it –

   (a) Is prohibited by or under any enactment ...'

(2) *The duty to confirm or deny does not arise if the confirmation or denial would have to be given to comply with section 1(1)(a) would (apart from this Act) fall within any of the paragraphs (a) to (c) of subsection (1)'.*

6. The relevant 'enactment' under section 44 for the purposes of this appeal is the Commissioners for Revenue and Customs Act 2005 ('CRCA'). Section 18(1) CRCA states:-

'*Revenue and Customs officials may not disclose information which is held by the Revenue and Customs in connection with a function of the Revenue and Customs'.* NO FUNCTION?

7. Section 23(1) CRCA states:-

'*Revenue and customs information relating to a person, the disclosure of which is prohibited by section 18(1), is exempt information by virtue of section 44(1)(a) of the Freedom of Information Act 2000... if its disclosure*

(a) Would specify the identity of the person to whom the information relates, or

(b) Would enable the identity of such a person to be deduced.

(2) Except as specified in subsection (1), information, the disclosure of which is prohibited by section 18(1), is not exempt information for the purposes of section 44(1)(a) FOIA of the Freedom of Information Act 2000'.

Section 4

Request by Complainant

8. On 27 November 2013, the Appellant made the following request to HM Revenue and Customs ('HMRC') through the HMRC's FOI Online Portal:-

   '*Requesting information on; Bousfield Booth Teasdale, D.O.B. 3RD February 1906 @ Cable Street, Lancaster. Died on 10th December 1953* '[1]

9. HMRC responded by refusing to confirm or deny whether it held any information within the scope of the request on the basis of the exemption at section 44(2) of the Act.

The Commissioner's Decision

10. The Commissioner served a Decision Notice dated 11 September 2014 in relation to this matter on in accordance with s. 50 of the Act. The Commissioner concluded that the HMRC was entitled to neither confirm or deny whether it held the information requested on the basis of section 44(2) of the Act.

The Commissioner's response to the Grounds of Appeal

11. Generally, the Commissioner relies on the Decision Notice as setting out his findings and the reasons for those findings. The Commissioner nevertheless

---

[1] The Appellant had made an earlier request on 26 September 2013 for this person's work record though this was made directly to the public authority's Records Retrieval Service.

makes the following observations in respect of the Appellant's grounds of appeal:-

Article 8 ECHR

7. The Appellant firstly argues that, as she believed that the person who is the subject of her request is her father, "the information requested will assist in confirmation of that and also to trace other family members. The refusal of the information sought is therefore a breach of my right to family life" (Article 8 European Convention on Human Rights as adopted by Human Rights Act 1998).

8. The Commissioner does not dispute that FOIA must be interpreted and applied so as to give effect to Convention rights. However, a breach of Article 8 in its terms and effect necessitates the taking of a step which constitutes a prima facie interference with an individual's Article 8 rights, in particular, whether the resultant impact of the breach could be said to attain the necessary "level of seriousness". Article 8 also entails the need to show that such interference is not in accordance with the law or that such interference is unjustified and/or disproportionate in the interests of national security, public safety or the other major eventualities listed in Article 8(2).

9. The Commissioner finds it impossible to see how the refusal by the HMRC or more importantly, the Commissioner's decision would or could entail such an

interference with an Article 8 right. Moreover, though she may be the Appellant in this appeal, the Appellant is not a victim of an alleged unlawful act and would appear not to be a person capable of presenting a claim for interference under section 7(1) of the Human Rights Act 1998.

10. Further, the Commissioner would submit that whether or not the refusal of the HMRC is a breach of Article 8 is not an issue which falls within the jurisdiction of this Tribunal regarding this appeal. The Tribunal's jurisdiction is limited to section 58 of the Act, namely to consider whether the decision notice is brought in accordance with the law. The Commissioner would contend that the decision of the Commissioner relating to whether the HMRC has complied with the Act does not breach the Appellant's Article 8 rights.

Interpretation of Section 23(1) CRCA

11. The Appellant argues that the Commissioner erred in his interpretation of section 23(1) CRCA in 3 ways:-

    i) The Commissioner should have concluded that the section relates only to the current function of the HMRC;

    ii) If the identity of the person in question is already known to the requester, disclosure would not therefore "specify the identity of the person".

    iii) The section does not relate to deceased persons

Section 23(1) CRCA relates only to the current function of the HMRC

12. The Commissioner in his decision notice was satisfied that the requested information, if held would be held by the public authority in connection with its functions. The Commissioner maintains that the places where the relevant person was employed from 1943 to 1949 (which would form part of his employment records) if held by the public authority, would be held in connection with its function to assess and collect tax.

13. The Appellant argues that, given that the information requested relates to records almost 70 years old and "*cannot relate to the current function of the HMRC*", the records, if held were only "*held for historical purposes*" and that the HMRC "*has not and could not have collected or assessed tax in respect of this person*".

14. Section 18(1) CRCA refers to "*information which is held by the Revenue and Customs in connection with **a function** of the Revenue*" (emphasis added).

15. The Commissioner would submit that there is nothing in the wording of the section to suggest that it is restricted to the "current function" of the HMRC as suggested by the Appellant.

16. The Commissioner accordingly remains satisfied that the requested information, if held, would be held by the HMRC in connection with its function to assess and collect tax.

> If the identity of the person in question is already known to the requester, disclosure would not therefore "specify the identity of the person".

17. The Appellant argues that the Commissioner erred in his interpretation of section 23(1) CRCA 2005 given that "*the information requested will not lead to the identification of the person; I already know the identity*".

18. The fact that the Appellant may already know the identity of the person to whom the information request relates is not relevant. Disclosure of information under the Act is disclosure to the public as a whole and not just to the requester of the information. Therefore, it is the public as a whole who would be able to identify the person if, in response to the request, the HMRC were to confirm or deny whether the information requested is held. As stated before, the request clearly mentions the person and his residential addresses in the relevant period.

The section does not relate to deceased persons

19. The Appellant further argues that the Commissioner erred in his interpretation of section 23(1) given that the section only refers to a "person" and not a deceased person.

20. The Commissioner would again submit that, on the wording of the section, there is nothing to suggest that the reference to a "person" could not include persons

who are deceased if its disclosure would "specify the identity of the person to whom the information relates".

21. The Commissioner maintains that he was correct to conclude that confirming or denying whether the information requested by the Appellant is held by the HMRC would identify the person to whom the information requested relates, given that the request clearly mentions the person and his residential addresses in the relevant period. The Commissioner would submit that a response to the request is inextricably linked to the wording of the request.

22. In light of the above, the Commissioner would submit that the HMRC were entitled to rely upon section 44(2) of the Act as confirmation or denial that the information was held would be prohibited by the CRCA.

Conclusion

23. In light of the above, the Commissioner invites the Tribunal to dismiss the Appeal.

Mode of hearing

24. The Appellant has requested a decision after a hearing. The Commissioner considers that it would be appropriate for the Tribunal to decide the matter on

the papers. In the event that the Tribunal list this matter for an oral hearing, the Commissioner will be content to rely upon his written submissions.

DATED this 7th day of November 2014

Name and address of Respondent / Address for service:-

Richard Bailey
Information Commissioner's Office
Wycliffe House
Water Lane
Wilmslow
Cheshire
SK9 5AF
Email: richard.bailey@ico.org.uk

IN THE FIRST-TIER TRIBUNAL (INFORMATION RIGHTS)   EA/2014/0253

BETWEEN:

ELIZABETH ROBERTS

Appellant

-and-

THE INFORMATION COMMISSIONER

Respondent

APPLICATION TO BE JOINED AS A PARTY
AND
FOR STRIKE-OUT

---

1. This is an application for Her Majesty's Revenue and Customs (HMRC) to be joined as a party to this appeal under Rule 9(3) of The Tribunal Procedure (First-Tier Tribunal) (General Regulatory Chamber) Rules 2009 (the Rules).

2. HMRC is the public authority to whom the request which is the subject of this appeal was made and it is important that HMRC has an opportunity to make representations in support of neither confirming nor denying that the information which is the subject of the appeal is held.

3. If successfully joined to this appeal, this is also an application for a strike-out of this appeal under Rule 8(3)(c) of the Rules on the ground that there is no reasonable prospect of the Appellant's case succeeding.

4. The law is clear that information held by HMRC for the purposes of its functions, disclosure of which would identify the person to whom it relates, is exempt from disclosure under the Freedom of Information Act 2000 (FOIA) by virtue of sections 18(1) and 23(1) of the Commissioners for Revenue and Customs Act 2005 (CRCA) and section 44(1)(a) FOIA. Where that is the case, the duty to confirm or deny does not arise by virtue of section 44(2) FOIA. There is no question that confirming or denying whether the information requested is held would identify the person named in the request. The Appellant has no reasonable prospect of successfully arguing that it would not, and, in light of the cost in time and the parties' resources of proceeding to a hearing, HMRC requests a strike-out.

5. Although not relevant to the arguments on the application of section 44(2) FOIA, it may assist the Tribunal to be aware of published guidance on HMRC's website about employment history records, available at: http://www.hmrc.gov.uk/industrial-compensation/index.htm#1. The relevant extract from the guidance states: "*Please note that employment history records are only available for each tax year from 1961-62 up to and including*

> the last full tax year. For years 1948-49 to April 1961 HMRC only hold National Insurance details." This means that these records show the value of the National Insurance Contributions only and do not include any employment details.
>
> 6 November 2014
>
> **The General Counsel and Solicitor to HM Revenue & Customs**
>
> HMRC Solicitor's Office
> Room 1/45
> 100 Parliament Street
> London
> SW1A 2BQ
> (Ref: Juliette Seddon Tel: 03000 586 201)

Well, I had definitely stirred a 'hornets' nest' as they were quick enough to respond now that solicitors and courts were involved. They probably thought I was just a 'nobody' and a nuisance but what goes around, comes around and I was not accepting their request for a strike out. Little did they know that I had a daughter who was barrister and I could play them at their own game so I got on the phone to Patsy who sends the following appeal on my behalf;

3 About the decision notice

The decision notice reference number: FS 50537767

Name and address of the regulator issuing the decision notice

Name: ALEXANDER GANOTIS

Address: GROUP MANAGER
INFORMATION COMMISSIONERS OFFICE
WYCLIFFE HOUSE, WATER LANE, WILMSLOW

Postcode: CHESHIRE SK9 5AF

Date on the decision notice you are appealing against: 11/9/14

Date you received the decision notice you are appealing against: 15/9/14

You must attach a copy of the decision notice with this form
Please tick the box to show that it is attached: ☑

4 Time limit for making an appeal/application

An appellant is required to lodge an appeal with the tribunal **usually** within 28 days of the decision notice being sent to them (see explanatory notes). The tribunal may accept a notice of appeal outside this time limit under certain circumstances.

For the tribunal to do this, you should request an extension of time and provide reasons why it is late. The tribunal will then consider whether to grant you the extra time you have asked for.

Please tick this box if you would like the tribunal to consider an out of time appeal. ☐

Please give reasons what you would like the tribunal to take into account when considering whether to accept your out of time appeal.

5 Grounds of appeal

Please give your grounds of appeal.

Your grounds should explain why you think the decision notice you have been given is wrong. You may find it helpful to refer to the individual paragraphs you disagree with and explain why you disagree with them. If required, please use an extra sheet of paper.

I believe the named person to be my father; the information requested will assist in confirmation of that + also to trace other family members. The refusal of the information sought is therefore a breach of my right to family life (Article 8 European Convention on Human Rights as adopted by Human Rights Act 1998

I maintain that the information requested will not lead to identification of the person; I already know the identity + therefore the ICO has wrongly misinterpreted S23(1) CRCA 2005

Moreover the information requested relates to records almost 70 years old + cannot relate to the current function of HMRC. I do not believe HMRC existed 70 years ago; nor did it exist at the time of the person's death. Thus records in HMRC's possession now do not relate to HMRC collecting + assessing tax in respect of that now deceased person. The records if held can only be held + were only held for historical purposes; HMRC has not + could not have collected or assessed tax in respect of this person.

S23(1) CRCA does not specify "a deceased person" only a person + again S23(1) CRCA has been wrongly misinterpreted

6. Outcome of appeal

Please tell us what outcome you are seeking from your appeal

CONFIRMATION AS TO WHETHER THE REQUESTED INFORMATION IS HELD BY HMRC + IF SO THE INFORMATION NAMELY THE PLACE OF EMPLOYMENT OF THE IDENTIFIED PERSON BETWEEN 1943 + 1949.

7. Type of hearing and venue

The tribunal makes its decision after reading all the papers in a case. Please indicate by ticking the appropriate box whether you wish your case to be considered on the papers only or after a hearing where parties can put their arguments in person. Please see the explanatory notes before making your selection.

☐ Paper decision ☒ Decision after a hearing

The tribunal will decide where any hearing takes place but will usually take into account the preference of the parties.

If you would like the hearing to be in a particular town or city please state it here. (The tribunal will endeavour to meet this request. However, HM Courts & Tribunals Service do have limited facilities and so this may not always be possible.)

MANCHESTER OR OLDHAM.

Parties will be informed in writing by post or email as soon as the hearing date has been set.

Supporting document

Please list any documents that you wish the tribunal to consider in support of your appeal. You may use an extra sheet of paper if required.

Please attach the documents and tick the box to indicate that they have been attached. ☐

ALL OF THE DOCUMENTS ARE WITH ICO. IF REQUIRED I CAN PROVIDE COPIES.

About your requirements

Please state if you, your representative or any witnesses have a disability or other special needs that you need to bring to the attention of the tribunal in order to help at your hearing. Please also state if an interpreter is required and, if so, please state the language needed.

Declaration

Signature of person appealing or their representative	*(signed)*
Date	5/10/14

Please refer to the contact details for the individual General Regulatory Chamber jurisdictions at www.justice.gov.uk/tribunals

We can help if you need information in a different format (e.g. Braille, large print). We can also provide this form in Welsh if required. If you need any of these services please contact the tribunal.

HM Courts & Tribunals Service

First-tier Tribunal
General Regulatory Chamber
PO Box 9300
Leicester
LE1 8DJ

Website: www.justice.gov.uk/tribunals
Telephone: 0300 12345 04
Fax: 0870 739 5836
Email: grc@hmcts.gsi.gov.uk

Mrs E Roberts

EA/2014/0253

12th November 2014

Dear Mrs Roberts

Please find enclosed a Case management note from the registrar, in addition the application from HM Revenue & Customers as it states in the Case management notes

I have not sent all documents as you should already have them.

The progression of the case is set out in the case management note.

Yours sincerely,

Yvonne Lowe

Clerk to the Tribunal

0116 249 4143

FIRST-TIER TRIBUNAL – GENERAL REGULATORY CHAMBER
Information Rights

Tribunal Reference:	EA.2014.0253
Appellant:	Elizabeth Roberts
Respondent:	The Information Commissioner
Second Respondent:	Her Majesty's Revenue and Customs
Registrar:	R Worth

Case Management Note

1. Her Majesty's Revenue and Customs is made a party to this appeal as the Second Respondent.

2. Tribunal staff should send a copy of the documents in the case so far to Her Majesty's Revenue and Customs.

3. Her Majesty's Revenue and Customs' document titled "Application to be joined as a party and for strike-out" will be accepted as their response in this appeal.

4. The Tribunal staff will send a copy of the "Application to be joined as a party and for strike-out".

5. Would Ms Roberts please by **3 December 2014** provide to the Tribunal and parties any reply and representations in relation to:

    (a) The Information Commissioner's response

    (b) Her Majesty's Revenue and Customs' response

    (c) Her Majesty's Revenue and Customs' application for the case to be struck out – that is why she says that she believes her case should go ahead and how it might succeed

6. In light of the application for the case to be struck out, a hearing date will not yet be arranged.

This decision was made by the Tribunal's Registrar. A party is entitled to apply in writing within 14 days of the date of this document for this decision to be considered afresh by a Judge.

R Worth

Registrar, dated **12 November 2014**

IN THE FIRST TIER TRIBUNAL (INFORMATION RIGHTS)　　　　EA/2014/0253

BETWEEN

ELIZABETH ROBERTS

Appellant

-and-

THE INFORMATION COMMISSIONER

Respondent

-and-

HMRC

Second Respondent

APPELLANT'S RESPONSE TO BOTH THE HMRC'S APPLICATION TO BE JOINED AS A PARTY AND FOR STRIKE OUT AND THE RESPONSE BY THE INFORMATION COMMISSIONER

---

1. I continue to rely on my previous grounds of appeal and continue to seek a hearing date for the Appeal. I do not accept that there is no reasonable prospect of success in my Appeal.

STRIKE OUT

2. I do not accept that confirming or denying the information requested is held would lead to identification of the person as I am already aware of the identity of the person.

3. Moreover I do not accept that the costs in time or the parties resources adds any weight to the application to strike out; the Information Commissioner does not

1

intend to appear at any hearing; similarly it is a matter of choice for HMRC to attend or make any further written representations as they wish. I would wish to attend the hearing. The costs of such a hearing for the other parties is therefore de minimis and this matter is of the utmost importance to me. There is no prejudice to any party if an oral hearing causes some delay.

4. Moreover for the reasons referred to below I do not accept that the information requested is exempt information and thus the HMRC argument that provision of the information sought will inevitably lead to identification of the person is both irrelevant and misguided. Since that argument forms the basis of the HMRC's strike out application, then the strike out application should fail

INFORMATION COMMISSIONER'S RESPONSE

5. I continue to argue the decision of the Information Commissioner is a breach of my Article 8 rights and rely on my original appeal grounds. The interference is neither justified or proportionate since I seek only limited information to establish my putative father's whereabouts in the period requested and none of the eventualities in Article 8(2) are relevant or apply to the information sought.

6. I remain of the opinion that the Commissioner has erred in his interpretation of s18 & s23(1) CRCA. In order for the information requested to be "exempt information", the information sought must be held by HMRC in relation to one of its functions. There can be no function of the HMRC which requires information dating back to 1943. Thus it is plain that that the information sought must relate to a current function and there is nothing in the wording of the section which includes past functions. Further HMRC was only established in 2005 and it cannot in 2005 or today

2

have any function which relates to the retention of the information sought since, when the information was provided in 1943-1949, HMRC did not exist. At best it has the information for historical purposes only. HMRC should specifically identify the function for which it says it has (as HMRC) the information sought. That function cannot be the assessment and collection of taxes from someone who has been dead for about 60 years prior to the inception of HMRC.

7. I remain of the opinion that the Commissioner has further erred in his interpretation of s18 & s23(1) CRCA in that that section does not include "deceased persons". I submit that that the ordinary use of the words "person" should be considered when defining that word and ordinary use of the word does not include a deceased person. A deceased person has no protection in law as a person; they cannot be defamed or be the subject of slander nor can they bring any action against the state regarding data protection. Given that breaches of personal data protection is the mischief at which s1 of Freedom of Information Act is aimed at preventing, it must follow that the protection is to be afforded to a living person and not a deceased person. if the section meant to include a deceased person it would have specifically stated so.

8. I am of the view that all the points I raise in this Response and my original grounds of Appeal involve both substantive points of fact and law which need to be fully considered and argued at an oral hearing and that there are very real prospects of success in terms of my appeal.

9. I therefore ask for an oral hearing in order to do so.

Elizabeth Roberts   17 November 2014

I received the following letter, dated 3rd December from the 'HM Courts & Tribunals Service' regarding a letter of the 25th November, 'HM Revenue & Customs' and since they had been roped in and are now the second respondent, I was truly happy to have the lot of them 'jumping up and down'.

HM Courts & Tribunals Service

First-tier Tribunal
General Regulatory Chamber
PO Box 9300
Leicester
LE1 8DJ

Website: www.justice.gov.uk/tribunals
Telephone: 0300 12345 04
Fax: 0870 739 5836
Email: grc@hmcts.gsi.gov.uk

Mrs E Roberts

EA/2014/0253

3rd December 2014

Dear Mrs Roberts,

Her Majesty's Revenue and Customs' letter dated 25 November 2014 will be added to the documents in the appeal as an additional response to the appeal.

Ms Roberts has had sight of the document, although her reply was received at about the same time as the letter was received. If Ms Roberts' wishes to add anything to her reply she may do so by 17 December 2014. After that date, the documents will be sent to the Chamber President so he can consider the application to strike out.

Yours faithfully,

Mrs R Worth

Registrar, General Regulatory Chamber

HM Revenue & Customs

HMRC Solicitor's Office

Room 1/45
100 Parliament Street
London
SW1A 2BQ

Clerk to the First-tier Tribunal (Information Rights)
GRC & GRP Tribunals
PO Box 9300
Arnhem House
31 Waterloo Way
Leicester
LE1 8DJ
GRC@hmcts.gsi.gov.uk

Tel   03000 586 201

Email juliette.seddon@hmrc.gsi.gov.uk

Sent by email and post

Date	25 November 2014
Our Ref	SLR284130
Your Ref	EA/2014/0253

www.hmrc.gov.uk

Dear Sir / Madam

Appeal of Roberts, reference EA/2014/0253: Amended response of Second Respondent

You notified HMRC on 12 November 2014 that we had been made a party to this appeal as Second Respondent and that our application to be joined and for strike-out (dated 6 November 2014) would be accepted as our response in this appeal.

Having only been joined on 12 November 2014, HMRC only had sight of the Appellant's grounds of appeal and the Respondent's response on that date. If we had seen those documents at the time of drafting the application referred to above and known that it would be treated as our response in this appeal, we would have addressed the following point. We would therefore like to add the following to our response.

Interpretation of section 23(1) CRCA

The Appellant argues that section 23(1) CRCA only applies to information held by HMRC for its current functions and that the information requested, if held, cannot be held for a current function of HMRC.

The Second Respondent submits that it does not matter that HMRC did not exist at the time this information would have been collected or when the person who is the subject of the request died. Section 5 CRCA provides that all of the functions formerly held by the Inland Revenue and HM Customs and Excise are now held by HMRC. Schedule 1 to the CRCA

Information is available in large print, audio tape and Braille formats.
Type Talk service prefix number – 18001

> lists the functions of the former Inland Revenue, which include national insurance contributions.
>
> The Second Respondent agrees with paragraph 15 of the Response of the Information Commissioner where it says that there is nothing in the wording of section 18(1) CRCA to suggest that it is restricted to current functions of HMRC. Even if it were, because the National Insurance Contributions of an individual may determine the pension and benefit entitlements of their surviving spouse and dependants, it is necessary for HMRC's functions to retain records after an individual dies. More generally, in order to maintain the integrity of the National Insurance system and to reduce the risk of fraud or identity theft, records are not deleted from the system immediately after an individual dies. This information, if held, would therefore be held for a current function of HMRC, namely the broader collection and management function described in section 5(1)(a) CRCA.
>
> Yours faithfully,
>
> **Juliette Seddon**
>
> CC by email:
> Respondent (Richard Bailey, Information Commissioner's Office)
> CC by post:
> Appellant (Elizabeth Roberts)

I sent an extra request to Harry;' please, please, do not let the tribunal strike it out'. I wanted my day in court, not for one minute believing that it would get me the information I required. If ordered to confirm or deny, they will surely say they haven't any records.

I thought back to what Mr Musgrave had said about Harry being behind the 'Iron Curtain', also adding that if they had not got the information requested, why not just state this which was a very good point.

I had so much paper work from them that it could easily form a book in itself. How could this be?, as from my eyes this was a perfectly simple question i.e. where did B.B. Teasdale work between 1943/ 49?

I was left with the question; 'what was Harry up to? I am sure he could have given me this information by himself. The only answer I could come up with was the fact that Harry had unfinished business (African Juju, I believe). Not only that but the more I thought about the lift shaft in Manchester Library, the more I wondered.

So Mandy and I decided we were going to explore it again, later in the New Year, for I was convinced that I was not seeing the full picture.

Chapter 114

Having contacted umpteen animal shelters, one would not believe it would be so difficult to find a suitable 'bitch'. Finally, Mandy and I decided to play a 'Harry Game'. We would ask him to show us, on an individual basis, a picture of the dog to get

Now, one German shepherd looks very much the same as another, with the same face and body with a black saddle so we required, as we said to Harry, some distinguishable features. About a week went by when Mandy phoned. 'Harry had shown me a picture of your dog and I have written it all down' she said excitedly. 'Me too' I replied. The salient point being that in both cases, this dog had an unusual black face.

This then, gave Mandy the task of scouring the websites for this particular dog, knowing full well that if we were correct, it would be a bitch.

As sure as 'Eggs is eggs', there she was on a Dogs Trust website. This six year old bitch had been with them for two years and they had been unable to re-house her. This was due to the fact that' she had bitten them' and each placement ended in failure thus she was returned and languished there.

I made contact with them and apparently, they were looking for a female owner with experience with this breed who already had a male German shepherd in situ. Harry, the dog, would fit the bill. They also required a country place with lots of space and no children or men. Se we set off all the way to Shresbury to view this vicious dog.

I could not fault the 'Dogs Trust' with their spacious grounds and one could easily see that these dogs were well cared for. Their golden rule was to 'never put a healthy dog down'. Each dog had its own case worker and we were introduced to 'Jane' who gave us a full history of 'Ruby'. She had been originally housed in a pen in Ireland and according to Jane; they were rescuing as many as twenty five dogs some weeks from that country. The reason being due to the recession which had hit Ireland very badly, people could not afford to keep their pets.

Finally, we were introduced to Ruby who was muzzled and on a leash. She spent about an hour walking around whilst gradually extending the leash and then allowed her to sniff us. According to Jane, things had gone exceedingly well as she had not attempted to attack either myself or Mandy.

With that, another meeting was arranged so that she could be introduced to Harry and see how they got on. She was a lovely bitch and I had no concerns regarding Harry who was well adjusted and the opposite to Ruby who had never been socialised. The vast majority of dogs are put to sleep because of their behaviour. I feel this is so sad for it is not the animals fault but down to us humans. Give me animals any day!

A time and date was arranged for the following Sunday so Mandy and I had planned to make a day of it as Shresbury was where my grandmother and her mother, Elizabeth, the witch, were born. We managed to find 'Bayston Hill' but ran out of time before finding the 'Parish of St. Julian' (I promised myself that one day, I will explore this and see exactly where my roots were)

Things went very well and Harry liked her so much that he made numerous attempts to make babies but she saw him off. Good for her!

I must admit that I do, at times, regret calling him 'Harry' as it becomes so confusing when I am referring to 'Harry' in spirit or the dog. If we were correct and the phones were, indeed, bugged then I bet their heads must be done in. Good!

The following week, Jane brought Ruby to my house so off comes the muzzle and the only aggressive behaviour was directed towards Harry who insisted on repeated attempts to mount her.

As Jane and I went through the paperwork, I was even more impressed with the Dogs Trust as they allowed up to three hundred pounds vet fees for any ongoing condition. Ruby , at some point, had torn a muscle in her rear leg.

Well, it was a nightmare as she was not house-trained and totally unsociable as expected. At least she had not tried to attack or bite me. In fact, I was falling in love with her for she her black face reminded me of Bess and she had claimed the exact same spot to lie down near the fire. Harry, at this stage, had given up trying to make babies and they were getting on fine. She was an early Christmas present from Harry.

One day, I was upstairs making the bed when I heard an almighty racket. I dashed down stairs, only to find Ruby running around with my half-defrosted turkey which I had left on the window sill without a second thought. The next ten minutes were spent chasing her round the house with Harry closely bringing up the rear. I eventually pounced on it but was left with one leg hanging off whilst the pair for them were gorging themselves on the giblets, plastic bag and all.

Well, there was only one thing for it. I scooped it up, gave it a good rinse in the sink and wrapped a few rashers of bacon round it to keep it together. I popped it in the oven and 'Mums the word' it was enjoyed by all on Christmas Day.

I did wish that I had seen that coming but nowadays, needless to say, I have to defrost everything in a cupboard. However, she is very intelligent and learned very quickly how to open it and I have lost count the number of times I have come home , only to find bird nuts and half-eaten dog food etc. all over the floor in the kitchen,

Ruby

Everything now goes in tins, obtained from Mandy but Ruby is determined not to be outdone. To give her 'her due', she does share her ill-gotten spoils with Harry. When I leave the house now, I have to jam a chair against the fridge door but she still hasn't given up; the sod!

Chapter 115

Today, I received the 'decision notice' from the H.M.R.C. and as the copper stated regarding James Marriot's notes; 'There is a God'

What was even more intriguing was that the 'Chamber President' was named 'Peter Lane' who was also a judge. So I referred back to 'Harry's Session' 2&3, to find them all almost 'spot on', apart from his description which I needed to confirm.

So 'in two shakes of a lamb's tail', I phoned Patsy and gave her the good news and also thanked her for all her help and expertise, without it, I could not have succeeded.

I needed to know what Judge Lane looked like so without more 'ado', Patsy looked him up as I waited patiently at the end of the phone. Meanwhile, Harry had showed up with a picture of a judge's wig whilst I was lighting a ciggy.

Patsy came back on the line and apparently there was no photo but he was aged 61 which fitted and I guess most people wore spectacles even if it was only for reading. I then asked Patsy if different types of judges wear different style wigs and proceeded to describe what Harry had just shown me.

'It has long blobs on it' I said, hoping she might have some idea. 'Mother', she said, sounding exasperated (she was not best pleased, I could tell) 'With the best will in the world, I do not understand your description. 'The House of Lords wear different wigs as do many other judges', adding that I should drag myself into the 21st Century and buy an iPad.

I did not think for one minute that Judge Lane was a danger to me but he may well have knowledge or association with where this danger was coming from which Harry had warned about. I needed to find this wig in order to ascertain which department of the legal system Harry was referring to. If, indeed, Judge Lane's wig fitted my description, then Harry was just confirming his previous warning. I needed to know.

I think Patsy must have been feeling a little guilty about her lack of patience with her dear, old, sweet, gentle mother, for a few days later, I received the following from her along with pictures of different wigs.

PETER LANE

Peter Richard Lane, aged 61, will be known as Judge Lane. He was admitted as a Solicitor in 1985. He was appointed as a fee-paid Immigration Adjudicator in 1996 and as a salaried Immigration Adjudicator in 2001. He was appointed as a Senior Immigration Judge in 2003 (becoming Judge of the Upper Tribunal, Immigration and Asylum Chamber in 2010) and became a member of the Special Immigration Appeals Commission in 2005.

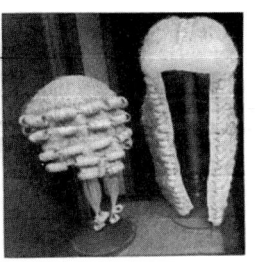

'Low and behold', the wig accompanying the information on Judge Lane fitted my description but as yet, for the life of me, I could not figure out where the danger lies.

FIRST-TIER TRIBUNAL
GENERAL REGULATORY CHAMBER
Information Rights

Tribunal Reference:	EA/2014/0253
Appellant:	Elizabeth Roberts
Respondent:	The Information Commissioner
Second Respondent:	Her Majesty's Revenue and Customs
Judge:	Peter Lane

DECISION NOTICE

1. On 12 November 2014, the Registrar issued a Case Management Note, inviting a written response from the appellant in relation to (inter alia) the second respondent's application for the appeal to be struck out under rule 8(3)(c) of the Tribunal Procedure (First-tier Tribunal) (General Regulatory Chamber) Rules 200, as having no reasonable prospect of succeeding. The appellant responded in writing on 17 November 2014.

2. The strike-out application turns in part on what is the correct interpretation of the expression "person" in section 23(1) of the Commissioners for Revenue and Customs Act 2005. The second respondent appears to take the view of the first respondent; namely, that the ordinary meaning of "person" in this legislation includes deceased persons. At paragraph 7 of her response, the appellant contends (by reference to the Freedom of Information legislation) that the expression must, in this context, be limited to living persons.

3. I am not satisfied that the second respondent has demonstrated, on the basis of the materials currently before the Tribunal, that its interpretation is unarguably correct.

4. Likewise, I am not persuaded that it can be concluded at this stage that there is no arguable merit in the appellant's argument that the information sought is not held in relation to one of the second respondent's functions, given that it dates back to 1943 (paragraph 6 of the response).

5. Acting pursuant to the overriding objective, in all the circumstances I decline to strike out the appellant's case. This is in no way to be taken as any endorsement of the appellant's case; merely that, as matters stand, it would not be in the interests of justice to decide these issues against the appellant.

Decision Notice Continued	Tribunal Reference Number:	EA/2014/0253
Appellant:	Elizabeth Roberts	
Date of decision:	28 January 2015	

6. The appeal will, accordingly, proceed to a hearing (as requested by the appellant).

Peter Lane

Chamber President

Dated 28 January 2015

I contacted Yvonne Lowe regarding her letter dated 3rd February and requested the 31st March for the 'Tribunal Hearing' refusing to go to London as H.M.R.C. had wished, on the grounds of the weather conditions where I lived, plus the cost. After all I was an old age pensioner and would find it difficult to pay £21 per day for the dogs in kennels.

The true reason was that I thought the H.M.R.C. were being as difficult as possible so let them do the necessary travelling. So Manchester it is.

HM Courts & Tribunals Service

First-tier Tribunal
General Regulatory Chamber
PO Box 9300
Leicester
LE1 8DJ

Website: www.justice.gov.uk/tribunals
Telephone: 0300 12345 04
Fax: 0870 739 5836
Email: grc@hmcts.gsi.gov.uk

Mrs E Roberts

Appeal No EA/2014/0253

Date 3rd February 2015

Dear Mrs Roberts

The HM Revenue & Customers has come back to me over sitting dates they can do, can You please have a look and see if one is alright for you

March 31st, 14th, 17th, 23rd, & 24th April 2015

The information commissioner has said they are not attending your hearing, so it just you two, to decide on a date

Yours Sincerely,

Yvonne Lowe
General Regulatory Chamber
0116 249 4143

Chapter 116

I began to wonder if there was any evidence to support what Ruth Shrigley (Art Gallery) had stated i.e. that there were communication tunnels under it. If so, could they possibly lead to the 'Press Club' which was also underground?

As yet, I had not tied in or had not understood why Harry had led me there or for that matter to the 'Police Museum'. So I obtained a map of 'Manchester Underground' and yes, after scrutinising it with my magnifying glass, the tunnels did appear to correlate. So was the tactics room in the 'Gentleman's Club' passing and receiving information to and from the journalists in the 'Press Club'

Map showing the Art Gallery, Mosley St. & The Press Club, Queen St.

I required more information so after a little research by Mandy, I wrote to 'Dr Martin Dodge' who was an authority on the subject.

> DR MARTIN DODGE
> Senior Lecturer
> Arthur Lewis Building, 1.051
> School Environment
> Education Development
> M/C University m.13 9PL
>
> 10.2.15
>
> Dear Dr Dodge,
> I am researching my family history. Consequently this has led me to the Manchester underground tunnels.
> These I believe were used during the Cold War.
> As an expert on such matters please could you clarify if these tunnels were used in conjunction with the air raid shelters?
> The reason I ask, is that I cannot ascertain when exactly they were constructed.
> As a small child living in Ardwick I have memories of a Tunnel in Downing Street, Ardwick being used WWII and the Cold War. For safety and communication purposes from venue to venue.
> Dr Anticipation.
> Yours Sincerely

I received a reply on the 18th February, 2015.

> **MANCHESTER 1824**
>
> The University of Manchester
>
> Department of Geography
> Arthur Lewis Building
> The University of Manchester
> Oxford Road
> Manchester
> M13 9PL
>
> +44(0)161 275 3622
> m.dodge@manchester.ac.uk
> 18th February 2015
>
> Dear Mr L. Roberts
>
> Thankyou for your recent letter regarding underground Manchester, Second World War air raid shelters and cold war tunnels.
>
> In reference to your questions:
>
> 1. The underground telephone exchange (known by code name 'Guardian') in the city centre has a cable tunnel running out to entrance shaft on Russell Street, Ardwick. This was built in the mid 1950s for the GPO and was completed in 1958. It had no role as a civilian air raid shelter and was not equipped as such. It was purely to protect telecommunication equipment and cables, and only ever occupied by authorised GPO engineering staff.
>
> 2. I am sure there was an air raid shelter in Ardwick area during the Second World War. I do not have details to hand but the enclosed copy of the Map of public air raid shelters shows several dots in the right area. The local studies and archives in Manchester Central Reference Library will have more information on air raid shelters. It might also be worth a visit to the GM Police Museum and they hold some information relating to air raid protection.
>
> I also enclose a copy of an article I have co-written on the Guardian underground exchange that might be of interest. There are two local history books published by Keith Warrender that give some more details on various tunnels and underground spaces beneath parts of Manchester and these could be worth consulting if you've not done so already.
>
> Yours sincerely
>
> *martin dodge*
>
> Dr Martin Dodge
> Senior Lecturer in Geography
> Email: M.Dodge@Manchester.ac.uk

He included an article which he had written, giving reams of information but this information did not categorically confirm or deny if there was a communication system prior to 1943, as far as I could see.

However, it did confirm from the red dots (Shelters) that there was no shelter at the Town Hall, thus their elite exclusively used the 'Art Gallery' during the air-raids whilst the lesser folk were not permitted.

CITY OF MANCHESTER CENTRAL AREA

So as Dr Dodge recommended, I set-off to the library and just to give them a treat with a normal request, I ordered 'Keith Warrender's' book ; 'Manchester Underground' which cost me 60 pence. A couple of weeks later, I received it.

It proved to be a fascinating read but I will try to not get too carried away and stick to the task in hand. So the question was 'Did tunnels exist and were they used for communication purposes during WWII?

A letter to 'Manchester City News,' 1882;

In my boyhood, I found on my rambles, a canal tunnel with a tow path for horses. I found that it passed through and came out near the 'Black Horse Hotel', Airport Town (where now stands Central Station, off Lower Mossley Street)

I have been speaking to an old waterman who had gone with boats under this tunnel for years before Central Station was thought of. The Central Station end was boarded up and the remaining part of the tunnel continued in commercial operation with the building of the 'Great Western Railway' warehouse in Deansgate which was large enough for a single –decker bus.

Two branch tunnels were built in 1900, off the main tunnel. This continued until 1922 when work ceased and the canal tunnel was officially closed for commercial traffic in 1936.

The tunnel came into different use during WWII when it was drained and became a shelter during the 'Manchester Blitz'. Although most of the tunnels were used as public shelters, however, a section was reserved for the wool spinners 'Copley & Sons' of Lower Mossley Street. I wondered why this company was so privileged as their part of the shelter/tunnel was equipped with electric lights, power plugs and radio with an emergency store of food.

I remember 'Lewis Department Store' on Market Street well but has long since gone, where Aunt Bunny (she having the money) my mother and I would go shopping. I would frequently ask my mother why all the ladies were standing under the arches of this store?

Now, at the tender age of 11/12, I knew well that they were prostitutes, drumming-up business but it just gave me great pleasure to see their embarrassed expressions and their fumbled responses to my persistent questioning. It was great fun as I continued to mither them in order to hear their ridiculous answers. My favourite one being 'These ladies are lost and they are asking these gentlemen for directions'. Oh, what a wicked kid, I was!

In the 1900's, 'Lewis' presented the first ever concerts which lasted about half an hour, 'Penny Concerts' were a training ground for many artists. The sub-basement had penny slot machines, distorted mirrors and 'Edison's Phonograph' (record player).

There was another basement attraction called 'The Venetian Scene', where the public were taken on gondolas under the 'Bridge of Sighs' using a replica of a small section of the Grand Canal, to see the sights of Venice. This cost one penny and ended up near the foot of a stone staircase which led to the dismal reality of the street at the back of the store.

The Bridge of Sighs (Built in the 1600's-links Doge's Palace with the prison. Takes its name from the sighs of the prisoners as they made their way across the bridge to meet the State Inquisitors)

Excavations in 1993, revealed a huge WWII bunker under Victoria Station equipped with emergency communication which came into use in December, 1940. This cavern was manned by 36 people.

Tunnels also led towards and into Deansgate to where the 'Press Club' was on the corner of Lloyd Street and Queen Street.

The evidence speaks for itself. Ruth Shrigley was indeed correct with her information. I reached the conclusion that both the Press Club and the Gentleman's Club were, undoubtedly, a hub of communication with the Tactics Room in the Art Gallery, during WWII.

Chapter 117

A quote from Benjamin Franklin kept popping into my head;

"For the want of a nail the shoe was lost,
For the want of a shoe the horse was lost,
For the want of a horse the rider was lost,
For the want of a rider the battle was lost,
For the want of a battle the kingdom was lost,
And all for the want of a horseshoe-nail."
– Benjamin Franklin

So we returned to Manchester Library to have another look at the lift shaft and ask if there was any possibility of gaining access to the prohibited area. The other reason being that I recalled that the 'Ardwick Hippodrome' was once named the 'Ardwick Empire' many years ago. I wondered if Harry did, in fact, perform his variety act at the Manchester Hippodrome which I suspected was near Manchester City Centre. So to try and make sure if there was any truth in these rumours, Mandy and I would also check this out.

The Manchester Hippodrome was demolished in 1935, so it was unlikely to be the one. However, Harry commenced his teaching position in 1926 so just to be on the safe side, we ploughed through what programmes were available but drew a complete blank.

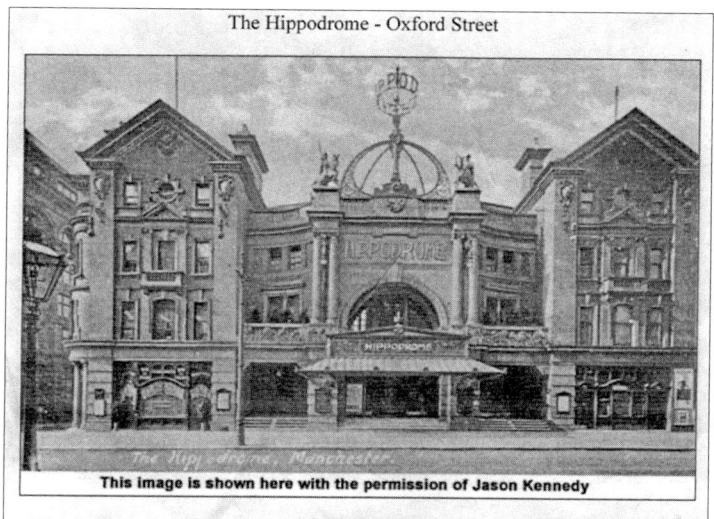

The Hippodrome - Oxford Street

This image is shown here with the permission of Jason Kennedy

The Hippodrome sat on the west side of Oxford Street across from the monumental St. James Building. It was designed by the famous theatre designers Frank Matcham who was responsible for many theatres throughout the country, including the Buxton Opera House, the Everyman Theatre in Cheltenham and the Ardwick Empire. Matcham also had a hand in refurbishing the Manchester Palace of Varieties across Oxford Street, later known as the Palace Theatre.

In 1935, the Hippodrome was demolished to make way for the construction of the art deco Gaumont Cinema, seen on the left of the image below. It took only 6 months to erect the Gaumont on the site.

Its demolition not only made way for the building of the Gaumont but also sparked a refurbishing of Matcham's Ardwick Empire and its renaming as the Manchester Hippodrome.

Our next step was to ask at Reception what we needed to do in order to view the entire lift shaft. After a couple of internal phone calls, we were advised to put our request in writing.

Unfortunately, Alison, who was extremely helpful and had given me the layout of the building when I visited Elliot House, was unavailable.

> David Green
> Central Library
> ST Peters Square
> m/c m25 5PD
>
> 3 March 2015
>
> Dear Mr Green,
> I have been researching my family history. Sadly in Dec 1953 my father was in an incident on the stairwell within the library. Having spoken with a member of your staff. It is suggest I contact your good self.
> In order to gain permission to access the original details of the staircase + lift shaft which is now a "staff only" area.
> I am sure you will understand how much I wish to ascertain how exactly my father B.B Teasdale fell to his death.
>
> Yours sincerely

I received the following letter from H.M.R.C. informing me that they had now put yet another solicitor to conduct the case.

I often think that their letters from 'solicitors' are designed to intimidate people. They are fully aware that the ordinary individual cannot afford vast legal fees; hence, they would drop their case. They would be left feeling that they would not stand 'a cat in hells' of achieving their goal. Well, I could not 'give a damn' for them.

HM Revenue & Customs

Solicitor's Office

Hey Garners Cottage

Room 1/45
1st Floor
100 Parliament Street
London
SW1A 2BQ

Tel   03000 558 689

Sent by post only

Email sarah.stephanou@hmrc.gsi.gov.uk

Date	5 March 2015
Our Ref	SLR 284130
Your Ref	EA/2014/0253

www.hmrc.gov.uk

DX   146765 LONDON
(Bush House)

Dear Ms Roberts,

Appeal of Roberts, reference EA/2014/0253: change of lawyer at HMRC

I am writing to inform you that I have taken over conduct of this case from Ms Juliette Seddon on behalf of HMRC. Please refer to my contact details above.

Yours sincerely,

Sarah Stephanou

I was fervently hoping that David Green would respond favourably to my letter but I didn't need to worry as he phoned me shortly afterwards. His response was very positive and would be quite happy to show me around the restricted area, adding that if he was in the same position as myself then he would have done the exact the same thing.

We met David a couple of days later in the foyer of the library. My luck was in as he was the same 'David' who had helped me out with the micro films at Elliot House and had introduced me to Alison, now retired.

Bless him! He had definitely done his homework and handed me the following which he had dug up, prior to our visit.

> **TEACHER JUMPED TO HIS DEATH**
>
> **Boys' Allegations**
>
> At a Manchester inquest yesterday on Bousfield Booth Teasdale (47), of Great Western Street, Moss Side, Manchester, a teacher who jumped to his death down the well of a staircase in the Henry Watson music library, the City Coroner, Mr Jessel Rycroft, recorded a verdict of suicide while the balance of the mind was disturbed. Mr Rycroft said Teasdale's mind was affected at the time by allegations that had been made against him by two boys.
>
> Charles Howarth, headmaster of Plymouth Grove Municipal School, where Teasdale taught, said two police officers went to the school on December 3 and interviewed Teasdale about the allegations.
>
> "He told me he denied strongly any such thing," Mr Howarth said.
>
> Police-Constable James Marriott, who said he interviewed Teasdale, was then told that further inquiries would have to be made.

He had also studied internal plans as to where the Music Library was situated in 1953, for apparently, it had been moved on several occasions.

So for all intents and purposes, we had all been surveying the wrong parts of the stairwell. With that, we commenced our little journey through the prohibited areas towards the stairwell, still on the second floor, where Mr Teasdale had jumped to his death.

At the side of it was a storage cupboard which would have been just big enough for someone to hide in, according to Dave. A skeleton key was used in those days and would have been very easy for someone to obtain.

When Mandy and I looked at the well of the staircase and the barrier, we found that there was no possible way that anybody could have thrown themselves down the original staircase. Yes, one could climb over the barrier but then there was no place to go. The space between that and the lift shaft was just over a foot wide, making it impossible to slither down, let alone jump from the second floor. Now, even taking into consideration that Mr Teasdale was slim and agile, even I, myself, could not have done it. (I am eight and a half stone, 5'2 inches tall and side on measurement including boobs which sadly are a 36 'C', would have got stuck 10 inches side on with clothing)

December, 1953 was in the middle of winter and we knew that Teasdale had sheet music in his jacket pockets and presumably wearing an overcoat. There was no doubt about it; he would most definitely have got stuck. The only way he could have got down to the basement would be to either push him in an upright position or head first position.

This then confirmed 100 % our suspicions and we could see that David also agreed with this conclusion. We also confirmed with him that the librarian would have stamped the sheet music, even in those days and with it, a return date two weeks later. So the same old question; why wasn't she summoned to the inquest, being the last person to have seen him alive?

David was so kind and helpful so I thanked him from the bottom of my heart. He also agreed to look into the archives for the play 'Golden West' and let us know the outcome.

I was intrigued and amused so I asked him what had happened to the ugly pictures of the original lift shaft which had now disappeared. 'Haven't a clue', he said with a grin.

We, now, could prove for certain that Teasdale did not commit suicide so somebody must have shoved him with great effort down the lift shaft. This would have been a difficult operation for one man unless the victim was already unconscious.

If one unpicks the whole scenario, then there must have been at least two persons involved. One on the lookout and one hiding in the storage cupboard as according to Dave, most people would have used the lift that exited on that floor and only used the staircase if in a hurry.

Of course, this begs the question; how on earth they know he would not use the lift? I think this is a damn good question, confirming in my mind that the whole incident was in some way staged.

Chapter 118

> 13th March 2015
>
> Dear Liz,
>
> I'm writing to let you know that unfortunately we've been unable to locate the venue where your father worked on children's theatre productions of 'Golden West' and 'Little Nut Tree' some time around 1953.
>
> The Manchester Youth Theatre, that I mentioned was for some time based here at the Library Theatre, but was not established until the 1960s. There was a famous children's theatre operating in Manchester after the war until the late 1950s call 'Stretford Children's Theatre'. However, we have a book about the history of this theatre which lists all the productions, and the two you mentioned to me are not included.
>
> We have searched the index of our theatre collection (one of Central Library's special collections) and also the archives index but there's no children's theatre references for this time. I have also searched the Manchester Evening News index in case there was a report of either production, without any success.
>
> It would be my assumption that the productions were based in schools – with some schools likely to have a full theatre set-up, as there is today for example at Sheena Simon College in the city centre, and at Chorlton High School (the Blue Box Theatre). However, we don't have records for school productions like this.
>
> I'm very sorry that I've not been able to find anything for you.
>
> Yours sincerely,
>
> David Green
> Central Library Customer Service Manager

Oh well! Yet another disappointment, another dead end and it was not for the want of trying. The play 'Little Nut Tree' was an after-thought on my part so I contacted David as I knew this play had been performed in a theatre. I had a part as a bearded Spanish nobleman but for the life

> DAVID GREEN
> CITY LIBRARY
> TOWN HALL ext
> m/c.   16·3·15
>
> Dear David
>
> Thank you so much, for your time and effort
> my father I believe had a variety act 'Sid + Teasdale' Although it was an elderly lady who told me his act was performed at the Ardwick Hippodrome. Which was previously the Ardwick Empire, Ardwick Green.
> I wonder if you have any programmes etc. for this Theatre from 1926-1953. That we could search
> Much appreciation
> Kind regards
> Les Roberts

of me, I couldn't remember if it was prior to 1953. It also could also have been the time when I returned to Ardwick Secondary Modern in 1954 at the age of eleven thus Mr Teasdale would not have been there.

I do clearly remember my mother and Aunt Cissie sitting in the centre of the stalls as most parents came to see their 'off-spring' perform. Another clear memory was of a female teacher whose name I cannot recall, constantly telling me not to move my face. Every time I grimaced, my long beard went askew and ended up somewhere around my ear.

The foul smelling glue did not adhere perfectly to my skin and I got really pissed off with her 'Child, don't move your face'. 'How am I supposed to speak my lines without moving my face? I retorted with a smug smile. With that, she stomped off to supervise a more amenable kid and that was the end of that. She did not have the decency to apologise for her stupid remarks but she got her answer as my beard continued to take on a life of its own.

Chapter 119

If only I could turn back the hands of time, going back 40 or 50 years when people of Teasdale's generation were still alive and kicking.

I had definitely been on an educational tour and it still continued but, unfortunately, the reason still escaped me. Time and time again, I asked Harry 'where are you taking me and what is the destination?' I travel on, so to speak, down all the roads he leads me, knowing full well that I was going somewhere or to something; but what?

Granted, my entire understanding of what I thought I knew about Teasdale had gone completely to pot. Was he homosexual? as I first believed but I think not now. In my eyes, the circumstantial evidence of him being my father holds more water than the latter. I asked myself was this the reason for his return? Was this his unfinished business? But my instincts kept telling me that there was more to B.B. Teasdale alive or dead than meets the eye.

As I typed this, old memories came flooding back. I remembered the little, brown bear that I had for donkey's years, originally named by me 'Teddy' but who gave it to me? It was not Father Christmas but then I remembered, it was an old lady who made such a fuss of me when my mother and I went to visit her. It was she who gave it to me but I never saw her again. I do recall the terraced house and the fact that she had a photograph of me. I can only guess that my mother must have given it to her.

With that, I set-off round the house in search of the replica which I found when my mother had died, along with Aunt Bunnies' snapshots. The odd thing was that I, distinctly, recalled it being taken, even though I was very young. The photographer and my mother had me sit on a stool but I would not stay there as I was afraid of falling off it. I finally stayed only when my mother placed her hand at the back of me for support.

I was now asking myself why this was so vivid in my memory; was it just an old memory or something Harry was bringing back? If so, why?

Later in the afternoon I found it and yes, I was sat on a stool but no mother's hand. I suppose it was blanked out in order not to spoil the photo.

This then begs the question why did she take me to a professional photographer and spend money which I guess she could ill afford? The answer could be that she just wanted a nice photo of her only child but I threw that reasoning out in the rubbish bin. It was never enlarged or displayed around the house as it had been put away and only retrieved after her death.

Stamp dated on the back -25th July, 1945. I was 2 yrs. old

There was no other explanation that I could think of, other than the old lady who had given me the 'teddy', had requested it but why? And why did my mother comply?

The house was posh with a fancy-tiled fireplace, a vast contrast to the iron-grate hob and oven that my mother used for cooking. There was a very little, neat, front garden which I noticed on the way out.

I suspect that Harry had rekindled this memory to show that this old lady was indeed his mother and had earlier requested a photo of her only grandchild, which took pride of place in her sitting room. Great Western Street, after all, was only a bus ride from 98 Higher Ardwick.

Mr Teasdale as you can see, was not a paedophile and the allegations regarding the two boys must have been trumped up charges, in order that he could either disappear or was murdered; but why?

Chapter 120

Well, 'D Day' was nearly upon us so I spent the next few days ploughing through the Tribunal's paperwork, in order that I ask the relevant questions and state my case clearly.

Of course, the phone started ringing which was another distraction. So up I got to answer it and surprise, surprise, it was Teresa Chance from H.M.R.C. She asked if I had received her letter and would I be cancelling the tribunal, 'in order, not to waste the judge's time', she added in an admonishing tone. Bloody cheek! I thought to myself and proceeded to tell her that I had not received any letter. 'What has that to do with anything at this late stage?' I added, sounding annoyed.

In fact, I was so angry, I just told her that I no longer wished to converse with her and put down the receiver.

So I returned to the task at hand, lit a ciggy and just as I was settling back into the paperwork, low and behold, the phone went again. It was her again, uttering something or other but I just put the phone back down. I had not a clue which letter she was referring to, as the postman had not left any message regarding a recorded delivery mail and I would assume they would have sent it by this means.

Having been 'round the block' so many times, I began to wonder if the letter ever existed. Of course, this was one of the oldest tricks in the book. 'You do not need to go to court because of this letter' a more gullible person would then cancel and the letter would never arrive.

Now as regards her statement 'wasting the judge's time', this was crap. It was the H.M.R.C. who didn't want to go to court, with total disregard for the amount of time and effort everybody had spent.

Well by Friday afternoon, I had received no less than three phone calls from various members of the H.M.R.C. team, requesting to speak to Mrs Roberts. I simply said she was unavailable. At 4pm on the Friday afternoon, a solicitor made a last ditch attempt with 'Where is Mrs Roberts, it is imperative I speak to her at once?'

I have always considered myself to be a little creative so I invented a story. 'Mrs Roberts has gone on a weekend ramble and does not possess a mobile phone' I said by way of explanation. 'Where is she staying at over the weekend so that I can make contact?', she demanded with increasing frustration. 'Haven't a clue but she will be back very late on Monday night, if that helps' I replied whilst hearing deep sighs over the phone. Well that put paid to that as the hearing was Tuesday afternoon.

**HM Courts &
Tribunals Service**

First-tier Tribunal
General Regulatory Chamber
PO Box 9300
Leicester
LE1 8DJ

Website: www.justice.gov.uk/tribunals
Telephone: 0300 12345 04
Fax: 0870 739 5836
Email: grc@hmcts.gsi.gov.uk

Mrs E Roberts

Our Reference: EA/2014/0253

Your Reference:

Date 4th March 2015

Notice of Hearing

Dear Parties,

I can now confirm that the half day oral hearing for the above case will be taking place on Tuesday 31st March 2015.staring at 2.00pm, at IAC 1st Floor Piccadilly Exchange, Piccadilly Plaza, Mosley Street, Manchester, M 1 4AH

Please provide the names and roles of those attending the hearing by 12pm, Friday 20th March 2015.

I enclosed a map for reference

Yours Sincerely,

Yvonne Lowe
Clerk to the Tribunal
General Regulatory Chamber
0116 249 4143

Chapter 121

Having parked Mandy's car a short distance away, we braved the driving rain whilst fighting with our inside-out umbrellas. We eventually got to Piccadilly Plaza, opposite what used to be Piccadilly Gardens, looking like drowned rats.

As we reached the 1st floor, we were immediately met by a H.M.R.C. solicitor who handed me the following letter;

HM Revenue & Customs

Central Policy

Information Policy and Disclosure
1C/23
100 Parliament Street
London
SW1A 2BQ

Mrs E Roberts

Phone 03000 586419

Fax 03000 586902

www.hmrc.gov.uk

Date 12 March 2015
Our ref FOI 3051/13
Your ref EA/2014/0253

e-mail teresa.chance@hmrc.gsi.gov.uk

Dear Mrs Roberts

FIRST-TIER TRIBUNAL (INFORMATION RIGHTS) EA/2014/0253

I am writing with reference to your information request and appeal to the First-Tier Tribunal (Information Rights), scheduled for hearing on 31 March 2015.

HMRC's position under the Freedom of Information Act 2000 (FOIA) has not changed and I am satisfied that our reliance on s.44(2) FOIA to refuse your request was and is correct.

> However, HMRC has looked again at the possibility of making a discretionary disclosure to you under the provisions of s.18(2) of the Commissioners for Revenue and Customs Act 2005 (CRCA), and has decided in this instance to exercise its discretion to do so.
>
> You will recall that, in the internal review response, Mr Callan explained that consideration of disclosure under the provisions of the CRCA is entirely distinct from our obligations under FOIA. Therefore, the exercise of our discretion under CRCA is without prejudice to our position under FOIA and in the appeal, which remain unchanged.
>
> Accordingly, HMRC can confirm that it does not hold any information within the scope of your request as, due to the passage of time, any records that might have been held for this individual would have been disposed of in 2004. HMRC is keen to avoid taking up the Tribunal's time in this case, where we have established that no records have been retained by HMRC.
>
> N07
>
> I am sorry that this will be a disappointing response, but I hope that this will bring this matter to a conclusion. If, as a result of this disclosure, you decide that you no longer wish to pursue the FOIA appeal, you will need to confirm this to the Tribunal. Given that the hearing date is only a few weeks away, we would appreciate if you could let us know by telephone what your intentions are regarding the appeal.
>
> You can contact me on 03000 586419 during office hours.
>
> Yours sincerely
>
> T.S.Chance
>
> Teresa Chance

As expected he was trying to pre-empt the situation but I was determined to have 'my day in court' and told him so. 'If this information was true, why not say so in the first place' I said, adding that this would have saved tax payer's money, time and effort for all concerned. He turned on his heels, disappearing down the corridor without saying a word.

We got a coffee for ourselves from the vending machine and noticed around a half dozen people hanging round waiting. From the snippets of conversation we overheard, they seemed to be asylum seekers who were appealing against deportation.

Promptly, at 2 o'clock, we were directed toward the same corridor that the H.M.R.C. solicitor had gone and entered a room at the end. There were three rows of plastic chairs facing a large oak desk, just as Harry had described, now all I needed was to see 'Peter'

We all stood up including the H.M.R.C. Legal team as well as the I.C.O. female solicitor as an usher opened a door behind the oak desk. We all sat down when the three middle aged/ elderly men had settled themselves. There were two lay persons on either side of the Q.C. who put on his spectacles whilst arranging folders etc.

I promised never to doubt Harry again, for when I took a closer look at this pleasant looking, rotund, bespectacled Queens Council, he fitted exactly with Harry's description. However, I did notice the name 'Brian Kennedy' on his badge and not 'Peter'

Well, it never entered my head that Harry could be referring to two separate individuals belonging to the 'Establishment'

As the case opened, a copy of the letter which had been handed to me earlier was handed to the panel. There were raised eyebrows as it was not in their 'bundle' with the legal team explaining that it was a late decision (please note dated 12th March) having just been photocopied at this late stage. (Because they had expected me to cancel)

I interjected and asked him if I should address him as 'Judge'? 'No' he replied with a pleasant smile. I proceeded to tell him that I had never received this letter and since their legal team had stated that it was sent by recorded delivery, I now wished to see the signature on the receipt of such sensitive information.

Well that put, as I expected, 'the Cat among the Pidgeon's' as a short adjournment was called, meanwhile two solicitors were scrambling out of the room, in order to track down a copy of the signature which, of course, didn't exist.

Returning empty handed, it was blatantly obvious they had been caught out in a lie. I asked the panel to look into this matter, adding that I was deeply saddened that this information should have gotten into the hands of strangers.

They were definitely leaning towards my side now and said that they were sorry that there was no information available to guide me in my most understandable request and they would most certainly be looking into the matter of the 'letter'

The panel were being most helpful by making various suggestions as to how I might find further information but unfortunately I had been down that road many times before. However, they did suggest that perhaps I could do a' Family Tree' and maybe some member might have some information.

IN THE FIRST-TIER TRIBUNAL
GENERAL REGULATORY CHAMBER
(INFORMATION RIGHTS)

Appeal No: EA/2014/0253

BETWEEN

ELIZABETH ROBERTS

Appellant

and

INFORMATION COMMISSIONER

Respondent

and

HMRC

Second Respondent

Tribunal

Brian Kennedy QC
Paul Taylor
David Sivers

Hearing: 31 March 2015.
Location: Piccadilly Exchange, Mosley Street, Manchester.
Decision: Appeal Refused.

Subject Matter: The Freedom of Information Act 2000 ("FOIA") and reliance by the Second named Respondent ("the Public Authority") on Section 44 (2) to neither confirm or deny whether the requested information was held.

Introduction:

1. This decision relates to an appeal brought under section 57 of FOIA. The appeal is against the decision of the the First Named Respondent, the Information Commissioner ("the Commissioner") contained in a Decision Notice ("the DN") dated 11 September 2014 (reference FS50537767) which is a matter of public record.

2. An oral hearing took place on 31 March 2015 where the Appellant appeared as a Litigant in Person, the Commissioner relied on his DN and his written Response, dated 7 November 2014, to the Grounds of Appeal from the Appellant dated 5 October 2014 and the Public Authority was represented by Robin Hopkins of counsel.

Background:

3. The Appellant wrote to the Public Authority on 26 September 2013. The request, made in the following terms was made directly to the Records Retrieval Service which deals with requests for employment histories on a business as usual basis: "I am completing my family history and would like to know the following work record of a close relative. This person, born 1906 in Lancaster died 10 December 1953 Age 47. A qualified teacher he taught from 1926 at Ardwick municipal school —- until its closure in July 1952. But from 1943 until 1949 there is a gap of six years. His address from 1934 until his death was (redacted) etc.". This resulted in a number of exchanges between the Appellant and the Records Retrieval Team.

4. On 27 November the appellant made the following request by way of a FOIA request; *"Requesting information on;* [Named Person redacted], *d.o..b. 3 February, 1906 at* [Address redacted] *Lancaster. Died 10 December 1953."*

5. The public authority responded on 29 November 2013. It refused to confirm or deny whether it held any information within the scope of the request on the basis of the exemption at section 44(2) FOIA. This decision was challenged by the Appellant who requested and internal review on 18 December 2013. She queried the public authority's response in view of her previous exchanges with the Records Retrieval team and also disagreed that confirming or denying whether the requested information was held by the public authority would lead to the identification of [Named person] because in her own words; *"I have prior knowledge of the identity of* [Named person] *and in fact identified that individual to HMRC hater than HMRC identifying him to me."*

6. Following an internal review the public authority wrote to the Appellant on 17 April 2014. It clarified and distinguished the position in relation to her exchanges with the Records Retrieval team as opposed to the FOIA request and upheld the original decision in relation to the exemption at section 44 (2) FOIA. The Commissioner has at all material times distinguished the request of 26 September 2013 from the request under FOIA of 27 November 2013.

Scope of the Case:

7. The Appellant contacted the Commissioner on 7 April 2014 by way of complaint against the Public Authority's handling of her request for information. She informed the Commissioner that she did not request details of [Named Person]'s employment records from 1943 to 1949. Rather she wanted to know where [Named Person] worked from 1943 to 1949. The scope of the Commissioner's investigation therefore, was to determine whether the public authority was entitled to rely on section 44(2) to neither confirm nor deny whether it held any information about where [Named Person] worked from 1943 to 1949.

Legislative framework:

8. Under section 1(1) of the FOIA, a person who has made a request to a public authority for information is, subject to other provisions within the FOIA: (a) entitled to be informed in writing whether it holds the information requested and (b) if it does, to have that information communicated to him. This duty to provide the requested information will not arise where the information is itself exempted under provisions contained in Part II of the FOIA.

9. In this case the Respondents argue that the exemption relied upon is an absolute exemption under section 44 of the FOIA which (in so far as it is relevant to this appeal) provides:

   "(1) Information is exempt information if its disclosure (otherwise than under this Act) by the public authority holding it - (a) is prohibited by or under any enactment —" & (2) The duty to confirm or deny does not arise if the confirmation or denial would have to be given to comply with section 1(1)(a) would (apart from this Act) fall within any of the paragraphs (a) to (c) of subsection (1).

10. The relevant "enactment" under section 44 for the purposes of this appeal is the Commissioners for Revenue and Customs Act 2005 ("CCRCA") at Section 18(1) CRCA which states: *"Revenue and Customs officials may not disclose information which is held by the Revenue and Customs in connection with a function of the Revenue and Customs."*

11. Section 23(1) CRCA states: *"Revenue and customs information relating to a person, the disclosure of which is prohibited by section 18(1), is exempt information by virtue of section 44(1)(a) of the FOIA — if its disclosure:*

    (a) Would specify the identity of the person to whom the information relates, or
    (b) Would enable the identity of such a person to be deducted.

The Decision Notice:

12. The Commissioner found that the exemptions at section 44 are absolute. He further considered the factual matrix pertinent to this request and found that confirming or denying whether the requested information is held by the public authority would reveal information which if held by the authority, would be held in connection with its functions to assess and collect tax. The Commissioner further found that confirming or denying whether the requested information is held, would reveal the identity of [Named Person].

13. The Commissioner clearly indicated in his reasoning that the reason for the appellant making the request is irrelevant and requests under FOIA are considered motive blind. The public authority, he explained has to provide a response which is not just for the benefit of the Appellant, but also for the benefit of the public at large.

The Grounds of Appeal:

14. The Appellant argues that the requested information will assist her in tracing family members and their personal history and the refusal to disclose any such information, if it exists is a breach of her Article 8 right under the ECHR Act 1998. While the Commissioner recognises Article 8 rights, he argues that the Appellant is not the victim, and in any event the interference is justified under statute and is not disproportionate.

15. The Appellant argues further that the Commissioner erred in his interpretation of section 23(1) CRCA in three ways: (a) in that the Commissioner should have concluded that the section relates only to the current function of the HMRC, (b) the identity is already known to the Appellant therefore disclosure would not "specify the identity of the person" and (c) the section does not relate to deceased persons.

16. The Commissioner was satisfied that the information, if held, on places where the relevant person was employed would be information held by the public authority in connection with its function to assess and collect tax. The Commissioner found that there is nothing in the wording of the section to suggest that it is restricted to the "current function" of the HMRC as suggested by the Appellant. The Commissioner determined that the fact that the identity of the Named Person was known to the Appellant is not relevant. Disclosure under the FOIA would, through the name and or address and or work details, if held permit identification of the named person to the public. Finally, and again, the Commissioner found that there is nothing in the wording of the relevant section to suggest that the reference to a person could not include persons who are deceased if disclosure would *"specify the identity of the person to whom the information relates"*. This again the Commissioner found includes information such as the place of work or home address of the Named Person all of which could inform members of the public of the identity of the named person.

REASONS

17. The Tribunal accept and adopt the reasoning as set out by the Commissioner in the DN and in his Response to the Grounds of Appeal as referred to above. At the hearing, the Appellant recognised the weight to be given to the Commissioners reasoning but simply sought assistance in finding information on the lost years of a much loved relative. It is fair to say that the Tribunal observed and the Appellant acknowledged that the Public Authority went beyond the bounds of their duty to assist the Appellant in this matter both prior to the hearing and at the oral hearing herein. The Tribunal also suggested a number of ways in which the Appellant might find more information on the lost years of the loved relative. However the Tribunal explained the particular difficulties for her appeal in relation to the exemption raised and relied upon under section 44(2) of the FOIA in this case and in the reasoning provided by the Commissioner in support of the DN, the subject matter of the appeal.

18. If there were any doubt about the veracity and soundness of the reasoning given by the Commissioner in his DN and in his Response to the Grounds of Appeal, the Tribunal, and apparently the Appellant were left in no doubt about the reasoning in the comprehensive and cogent submissions at the oral hearing by Mr. Hopkins on behalf of the Public Authority. It is often very difficult for those coming to FOIA for the first time to appreciate it covers information which satisfies public interests rather than matters of private interest. To compound this, when one corresponds with a public authority in connection with a request this may seem to be done, and was at the early stage of this request, in private. However, at the point of disclosure or refusal this is a matter of public record (save for the requestor's

personal details). In other words, when a public authority considers a request it must ask itself whether the information can be disclosed to the world at large, rather than just to the requestor. Section 1(1) of FOIA says *"Any person making a request for information - - -";* - consequently it cannot disclose to one person and not another.

19. In this case, under FOIA, the appellant requested information about a deceased loved relative. Her formal request followed a period whereby the public authority were, understandably, doing their best to assist her with her inquiries outside the FOIA. However at the point when the request was presented under FOIA, the public authority had no choice but to respond as they did given that any information, if found, would have been to the world at large. In particular this meant, they had to take account of the provisions under the Commissioners for Revenue and Customs Act 2005, and specifically sections 18(1) and 23(1). These provisions form a statutory bar against disclosure which is why the public authority properly claimed exemption under section 44(2) of FOIA. The Tribunal wish to acknowledge the kind consideration given to the appellant by the public authority, the HMRC and their team, in the way they handled the appellants sensitive request up to and including the oral hearing. This Tribunal has every sympathy with the appellant and wishes her success in tracing any records that she so deeply and understandably desires to find.

20. Further to the submissions on behalf of the public authority, this Tribunal find section 44(2) is an absolute exemption and the public interest test to be applied to qualified exemptions does not arise.

21. We find that for the public authority to confirm or deny whether it holds the requested information would itself reveal information, if it existed, that would be considered exempt from disclosure on the basis of section 44(1)(a).

22. We find by virtue of the fact that sections 18(1) and 23(1) of the CRCA which effectively prohibit the public authority from disclosing any information held in connection with a function of HMRC under the FOIA, the public authority in the circumstances of this case were correct to rely on the exemption under section 44(2).

23. We repeat, accept and adopt the reasoning of the Commissioner as set out in paragraphs 22 to 27 of the DN as supported by the detailed submissions by counsel on behalf of the Pubic Authority. For the avoidance of doubt we accept the interpretation of "function" is wide and can and does include information relating to a workplace or employment details pertaining to a person living or deceased. We accept that there is no reason why information should no longer be exempt because of the death of an individual who might be identified from that information.

24. For the above reasons we refuse the appeal herein.

Brian Kennedy QC   **8th April 2015.**

I was truly disheartened and wondered if I would ever find out where Harry had been between 1943-1949.

As always with Harry, it was a double-edged sword; Rotund, bespectacled man of importance and repeated the name 'Peter'. This information was correct but not in the way I envisioned it.

Maybe I was being too logical in my thinking and should, as they say, 'listen to a different drummer'

Chapter 122

I received a letter from Dave at the Manchester Library so we decided to pay a visit.

MANCHESTER CITY COUNCIL

Liz Roberts

Growth and Neighbourhoods

Telephone: +44 (0)161 2341331
d.green1@manchester.gov.uk

City Library, Town Hall Extension
Manchester M60 8LA

2nd April 2015

Dear Liz,

thanks for your recent letter with further information about your father's variety act and the years he appeared in Manchester theatres.

I think there are several sources of information that might be interesting and useful for you to check. Mainly this would be from our special 'Theatre Collection'.

There is a very comprehensive history of Manchester theatres in a book by Terry Wyke and Nigel Rudyard called 'Manchester Theatres'. We have a copy to borrow – you would need to register for a library card. In this book there is a full listing of the library's special theatre collection and I noticed a couple of entries that might be worth you investigating:

- TH792.094273 MA43
  Programmes (1904-1961 incomplete) 2 vols.
  Includes programmes from the Hippodrome Theatre on Oxford Road and the New Hippodrome in Ardwick which became the Ardwick Empire
- Collections of newspaper cuttings and scrapbooks which cover the dates you're looking for.

To view these items in the Central Library searchroom you would need to make an advance request. There are details of how to do this on our web pages and the enclosed. You would need to complete an online booking form and give at least 24 hours notice.
See:
http://www.manchester.gov.uk/info/200062/libraries/6336/see_archives_rare_books_and_special_collections%20

> If you could establish the dates of your father's shows you could then view local newspapers in the library (on microfilm) from the time.
>
> I hope this helps to get you started. The staff in the Archives+ area of the library on the ground floor would be able to help you too.
>
> Yours sincerely,
>
> *David Green*
>
> David Green
> Central Library Customer Service Manager

We wanted to plough through every available programme from 1926 to 1953. Most of the artists were before my time, like Max Wall and Tommy Trinder who were well-known comedians in my parent's era. But, alas, no B.B. Teasdale ever appeared at the Ardwick Hippodrome.

Mandy had also explored the Q.C. Brian Kennedy's idea of the family tree but it only seemed to take us backwards. Joely, my granddaughter had also put a message regarding Teasdale on the Ardwick website but drew a blank.

My last hope was Steve so we met up one evening when I was visiting Stretford Church to demonstrate my mediumship. He asked how Harry's Story was progressing so I gave him a brief up-date. 'Funnily enough, I have just started a Genealogy Course' he said and went on to say he would also do a one name study which might produce something. He did however, say that it may take some time but my hopes were raised and we shall see. But to no avail.

We both agreed that nothing with Harry pans out as every rumour or statement is incorrect i.e. the 'Will', his suicide and not forgetting Jean's 'Hammer Toe' story 'that is why he wasn't in the War, dear'

I think the time has come to throw logic out the window and listen to a different drummer, as I said before. By this I mean trust my own instincts.

Chapter 123

I have, like most folks, 'odds and sods' which have been in my kitchen for more years than I care to remember. Aunt Cissie's half pint silver plated milk jug which sits on the pantry shelf alongside a wooden egg timer almost as tall which cost one and sixpence in old money (seven and a half pence today).

When I was first married, I literally couldn't boil an egg. Obviously no significant improvement as it is still in use today. I am partial to the old boiled egg.

A lovely, sunny morning, early June 2015, I was sitting in the living room along with the dogs whist gathering my wits with my first cup of coffee and ciggy, when we heard a loud thud. The dogs started barking like crazy as I dashed into the kitchen to investigate, only to find that the egg timer had leapt off the shelf and hurled itself almost the length of the kitchen floor.

I just knew this was Harry's doing, for if it had just actually fallen off the shelf, it would have landed on the freezer underneath.

So this was the answer to my question, the timing had to be right; just like a properly boiled egg.

Hopefully, he was appreciative of my ability to clear his name, the time at Altrincham Spiritualist Church when I was so angry, not knowing why, that he had been called a 'paedophile'

I was left in no doubt that these allegations were a smoke screen but why?

Chapter 124

Autumn was turning back into winter and there had not been any developments regarding Harry, So I was either wrong about the egg timer or the time just wasn't right.

On Wednesday, 4th November, having put the wrong digit of my car registration into the 'pay as you park' machine in Ashton Town Centre, (I blamed Harry for my lack of concentration) I had to put another quid to correct it; otherwise those parking attendants would put a ticket under my window wiper and fine me £30.

Afterwards, I trotted towards Stamford Street for my yearly eye test which one gets free but there was little consolation in that you didn't get the spectacles free. Anyway, that is of no consequence, for I rarely changed them and only used them when driving. Last year, however, a new pair cost me £100 as when getting out of the car to go into the butchers, they fell off my lap into the road and got run over.

There was no doubt that this was a result of my own stupidity so I couldn't blame Harry. It was then that I realised that I had walked passed the opticians for more than a block so I hurriedly retraced my steps. I suddenly saw through a quaint little shop window, a second-hand cuckoo clock. The shop was called 'Bargain Cave' which I never knew existed, having never walked past the opticians before.

With the eye test completed, I returned to the shop, paid £45 and the cuckoo clock was mine. Thank you, Harry

Chapter 125

So where to go from here other than follow my 'distant drummer', so with this in mind, I sat back, lit a ciggy and decided to look at the entire case again.

The Allegations;
'Whether the two boy's allegations were true or false'

I find it incredulous that their parents ever went to the police station to give statements in the first place. For one, who would believe two working-class families against a highly respected middle-class teacher?

Common sense would surely have prevailed that they would not be believed and they would have dealt with it in 'Ardwick Fashion'. Things of that nature would be swept under the carpet and never mentioned.

Mr Teasdale was known to be stricter with 'boys' and a more likely scenario is that this story had been concocted by the two boys as 'an act of revenge'.

You must remember that Mr Teasdale had a long career in the teaching profession He was highly respected and had never been accused of this crime before.

B.B. Teasdale would have known that nobody would have believed them. The case would never get past C.P.S. (Crown

Prosecution) and if it did, it would only to be thrown out by a judge at a later date..

So later in his life, he supposedly discovers this aspect of his personality and acts it out, not with one boy but two at the same time.

I will leave it up to you!

The Suicide;

So how come this extremely upset and distraught teacher (according to the Inquest) of unsound mind, managed to continue teaching in the school, the very next day?

He spent the whole weekend without incident, getting up and dressed Monday morning to go to the library for sheet music.

Having put the sheet music safely away in his pocket, he then proceeds to go out the door and throw himself down the lift shaft.

Whatever happened that day remains a mystery but it certainly was not 'suicide?'

The Will;

Probate; the net amount left in his estate was £4,900 which was a vast amount of money in those days.

The average salary in those days was £2-£3 per week. An experienced, qualified teacher's salary would obviously have been higher.

According to Jean Teasdale, when his mother came to live with him in 1934, she was 'as poor as a church mouse'; having previously moved into her mother's house following the death of her husband.

So how come she left £2,704 on her death in 1949, from her son during his absence 1943-49?

So how did B.B. Teasdale manage to acquire such a large sum? I found no evidence to support a second income from the Ardwick Hippodrome etc.

A Crombie overcoat, fine leather shoes and not forgetting the Dunhill aftershave are the trappings of a wealthy man.

So, again I was faced with another mystery. Perhaps the period when he was missing and unaccounted for, would shed some light

Missing Years;

This was probably the most intriguing aspect of the entire story.

According to Jean's hammer toe story, this was the reason that he was not accepted into the Armed Forces so he must have undergone a full army medical examination to be refused entry.

You can just imagine the scene with Mr Teasdale, a highly educated man who spoke fluent French sitting in front of a senior officer and being told that the Services don't want you because of your 'toe'.

Military Intelligence was desperate for people who could speak French or German at that time. They were used for espionage, decoding and in other clandestine areas of the Secret Service. I certainly don't think that having a 'hammer toe' was part of their exclusion criteria.

This, I believe was the most likely scenario. You have to remember that his job was kept open for him and he returned after 6 or so years to this position.

When I tried to find various records for that time period, I was met with great resistance from the Establishment. It was almost like he had never existed.

Even today, families of loved ones who worked in the Special Forces and had fallen in Iraq have the same problem. They are met by 'a brick wall' when attempting to find out what happened to their loved ones.

Conclusion;

So was Mr Teasdale a 'spy' who later died under very mysterious circumstances in the Central Library in Manchester, leaving a vast sum of, unaccounted for, money?

James Bond is portrayed in films as dapper, highly intelligent, multilingual and wealthy; not unlike B.B. Teasdale.

Chapter 126

Having set the clock up in the same place on the wall as the other one, I just could not believe my ears. It cuckoos' on the half hour but cuckoos' and chimes intermittently on the hour. So if it is 3 o'clock, I hear three cuckoos' plus three chimes. Definitely, a 'Harry Clock'

Noel phoned and was excited to receive a message left on 'Friends Reunited' about Ardwick Municipal.

I just received this message from Friendsreunited.com

Mr Teasdale

I was at Ardwick Muni from 1947 until it closed in 1953 when I went to Ross place. The infants school had Miss Amos and then Mrs Goulden as headteachers. We moved to the big school after standard one (Miss Waugh, later Mrs Hollows . I went in Miss Higgin's class (later Mrs Jessop). Mr Bradshaw was the head, Mr Hillier had just retired.. The music was shared by Mr Teasdale and Mrs Quinn.Mr Teasdale also did drama . I remember him showing us how to apply theatrical make up.My own favourite teacher was Mr Frith who started me off in science. I learnt about Mr Teasdale's suicide from Mr Garnham at Ross Place in 1954. Some years later Mr Bradshaw helped me get into teaching when he was head of Wheler Sec. School in Openshaw. In all I have some good memories of growing up in Ardwick. We lived in Old Elm Street opposite the Apollo cinema. Best Wishes Tom Handforth.
From tom Handforth 25 November 2015 21:36

My Response

Dear Tom,

Delighted to hear from you and you brought back so many memories of my time at Ardwick Municipal, thank you.

I would to love to meet up for a coffee if you have time and go over old times.

I have attached my address and phone number below.

I really look forward to hearing from you again,

Best wishes and kind regards,

Liz

To our untimate dismay, we heard nothing back and then after a few weeks, the site was closed down.

So my typewriter is definitely 'giving up the ghost' now and so am I, for I haven't got a clue where to go now.

Something tells me that I am right in my thinking that Harry is not going to leave me yet. His unfinished business is not finished and he has something up his sleeve.

'After all, a broken clock is right twice a day.'

Time will tell

Acknowledgements

Sincere gratitude is due to Steve Newby, Mandy Moore and Ian Johnstone for their invaluable help and support on the long journey in compiling this book.

There are so many more people who assisted me along the way and I would just like to say;

I couldn't have done it without you. Thank you

I should also mention Noel Flood, 'The Oracle' who is probably, as we speak, languishing in some secure psychiatric facility with 'Post Traumatic Stress Disorder' following the completion of this book.

Bless him but I think I did 'his head in'.

Please note the poem 'Catching the Cat' by A. Mouse is a children's story.

Can you help solve this mystery?

If you have any information please email
noel_flood@yahoo.com